Praise for *A Lady, First*

"This breezy read is filled with humorous, behind-the-scenes stories. . . . Baldrige shows us what it's like to be hostess to the world."
—*Rocky Mountain News*

"Lively."   —*The Washington Post*

"This is a book that will both entertain and enlighten you."
—*Nashville Tennessean*

"[Baldrige's] descriptive details and breezy style offer an inside view of the people and places that played a vital part in the second half of the twentieth century."
—*The Indianapolis Star*

"An engaging glimpse into the world of a gutsy, hardworking woman who has led an extraordinary life."
—*The Cleveland Plain Dealer*

"A vivacious memoir . . . vibrant and delightful . . . a humanizing look at the rich and famous of the past six decades above all."
—*Kirkus Reviews*

"Letitia Baldrige has us in on the fun of her extravagantly glamorous career, as aide, administrator, companion, chargé d'affaires."
—William F. Buckley, Jr.

"A fascinating life of Letitia Baldrige, who writes with candor and grace of the people she has met and worked with, of course Jackie Kennedy amongst them. A charming story of a charmed life."
—Bill Blass

Letitia Baldrige, author of nineteen books, fourteen on manners and entertaining, received her B.A. from Vassar College and did graduate work in psychology at the L'Université de Genève in Switzerland. She served in the American embassies in Paris and Rome for eight years, and was the first woman executive at Tiffany & Company. During the Kennedy administration she served as Chief of Staff in the White House for Jacqueline Kennedy. She has run her own company, Letitia Baldrige Enterprises, since 1964, which is currently involved in management training. She is a director of several nonprofit institutions and a pioneer woman director on several corporate boards. She is a professional lecturer and the editor of *Executive Advantage*, a monthly newsletter on business behavior. Visit Letitia Baldrige's Web site at www.letitia.com.

A Lady, First

MY LIFE IN THE
KENNEDY WHITE HOUSE
AND THE
AMERICAN EMBASSIES
OF
PARIS AND ROME

Letitia Baldrige

PENGUIN BOOKS

PENGUIN BOOKS

Published by the Penguin Group

Penguin Putnam Inc., 375 Hudson Street,
New York, New York 10014, U.S.A.
Penguin Books Ltd, 80 Strand, London WC2R 0RL, England
Penguin Books Australia Ltd, 250 Camberwell Road,
Camberwell, Victoria 3124, Australia
Penguin Books Canada Ltd, 10 Alcorn Avenue,
Toronto, Ontario, Canada M4V 3B2
Penguin Books India (P) Ltd, 11 Community Centre,
Panchsheel Park, New Delhi – 110 017, India
Penguin Books (N.Z.) Ltd, Cnr Rosedale and Airborne Roads,
Albany, Auckland, New Zealand
Penguin Books (South Africa) (Pty) Ltd, 24 Sturdee Avenue,
Rosebank, Johannesburg 2196, South Africa

Penguin Books Ltd, Registered Offices:
Harmondsworth, Middlesex, England

First published in the United States of America by Viking Penguin,
a member of Penguin Putnam Inc. 2001
Published in Penguin Books 2002

3 5 7 9 10 8 6 4 2

THE LIBRARY OF CONGRESS HAS CATALOGED
THE HARDCOVER EDITION AS FOLLOWS:
Baldrige, Letitia.
A lady, first : my life in the Kennedy White House and
the American embassies of Paris and Rome / Letitia Baldrige.
p.   cm.
ISBN 0-670-89453-2 (hc.)
ISBN 0 14 20.0159 7 (pbk.)
1. Baldrige, Letitia.   2. Social secretaries—Washington (D.C.)—Biography.
3. Businesswomen—United States—Biography.   4. Kennedy, John F. (John Fitzgerald),
1917–1963. 5. Onassis, Jacqueline Kennedy, 1929–1994.   I. Title.
CT275.B316 A3   2001
973.922'092—dc21
[B]   2001026544

Printed in the United States of America
Set in Bembo
Designed by Lorelle Graffeo

To my long-suffering husband, Bob,
and our wonderful kids, Clare and Malcolm, and
to their superb spouses, Jim and Carey, and their
respective super-charmers of children:
Luke, Lila, and Liam, and Alice and Mac.
Oh yes, and to any future little
charmers to come.

ACKNOWLEDGMENTS

I am grateful to Jane von Mehren, my brave-hearted editor—oh, am I ever grateful to her! She had the courage to publish this story of my life, devoid as it is of salable components, like gore and sleazy sex. And I am unremittingly grateful to Jennifer Ehmann, who shouldered the editorial work on my tale. It was enough work to sink a ship, but she stayed courageously afloat. I am grateful to Miranda Ottewell and Katherine Griggs, the copyeditor and production editor, respectively, who wrestled me back to the world of reality. The proofreader, Jo Jane Pitt, has to be a hero, too. (I know *I* couldn't have done it!)

And, of course, my brilliant agent, Loretta Barrett, who knew exactly where to head—to Viking Penguin—once the manuscript was in her hands. It was genius thinking!

A tremendous wave of thanks flows to Helen Brown and Dede Dunn, executive assistants, who accomplished miracles in keeping me afloat and my histrionics hidden from everyone except my husband and our dogs. I am grateful to computer consultant Derrick Ford as well, who received my SOS messages morning, noon, and night. Many times I would have thrown the computer out the window had he not saved me from doing it (and killing someone passing on the street below).

A friend of mine accused me of throwing French and Italian words around "as though I were sprinkling grated Parmesan on top of rigatoni." I only hope that my Viking colleagues had a little bit of the enormous fun I had in remembering these delicious times, with or without the sprinkling of Parmesan cheese.

Contents

INTRODUCTION

There is something exhilarating, and obviously very egotistical about writing the story of your life. When you look back upon it in its entirety at the age of seventy-five, as I am doing now, there is frankly a lot to look back upon—a giant truckload, in fact. If you choose to go through it and give it a cursory inspection, you'll discover that my load is devoid of the traditional stuff that makes a best-seller—rape, murder, child molestation, incest, drugs, suicide, and the like. Mine was a very scandal-free, normal kind of family. In fact, we all loved one another—imagine that.

Mine is the story of someone who never had a lot of money, yet lived around people with great amounts of it, which is almost like having it oneself. In fact, it's better. You don't have to come up with the taxes, or worry about people loving you for anything other than yourself. If you wipe the stardust out of your eyes and are able to observe and learn from what is going on around you, you are twice blessed, and if you find yourself in close proximity to people who are making history, so close that you feel you're holding one of the spoons that's stirring the pot, then you are more than thrice blessed. If, in addition, you can manage to see something funny in whatever happens in life, you are one of the luckiest creatures on earth, and boy, have I been lucky.

If you need money for investment, I can't help you. I've never had any. But if you need stories about the good and great times—the glittering, glamorous, historic times—then do come to me.

My first job was in Paris, at what was then the most powerful embassy in the world. My bosses were the David Bruces, one of the most charismatic, gifted couples in diplomatic history. The time was at the height of the Cold War, just at the conclusion of World War II, when gun smoke still hung in the air, and when Europe was still suffering but beginning to peek out from under the blankets, hoping, praying, that life could begin anew, and that things would be happy and bright once again. It was a time when you could notice the lack of food and heat, the misery of many people, and you could hold your head and moan, "How terrible!" Or you could notice all the construction and restorations, the new businesses being launched, the opera singers practicing their arias, the designers finding inspiration at their drafting boards, and people smiling once again just to be breathing air that was free. The chestnut trees on the avenue des Champs-Élysées have never bloomed so brightly as they did in the springs of 1947 and 1948. It was renaissance time—big time.

Then there was Rome and another plum embassy job. Who gets to have Paris and Rome as the first job sites on the résumé? Who is lucky enough to have Clare Boothe Luce, the first woman ambassador from the United States to a major foreign country, as her boss, and Henry R. Luce, her publisher husband, as boss number two at the residence of the American embassy? And with people such as the president of the United States, William Faulkner, Eleanor Roosevelt, and Joe DiMaggio going through the swinging doors of this house all the time?

Then there was 1600 Pennsylvania Avenue. I don't care what your politics are, I would wager that if you asked any American woman which administration would she have most liked to work for as social secretary, she would pick Jacqueline Kennedy's White House as the place to be. John F. Kennedy's inauguration in January 1961 was over forty years ago, but I was there, with a spoon stirring in the pot.

Fortune kept smiling in my direction. I was one of the first women business owners, one of the first female corporate directors, and, oh yes, a bride at the age of thirty-seven and a mother at thirty-nine and again at forty-one—which was considered obscenely old in those days to be entering the delivery room.

I have the same husband, and have now published nineteen books. I fully intend to set minirecords in the future. I write about and lecture on people's manners, civility, formal protocol, and just plain knowing "how to have someone come over for dinner." For several decades I have been a guest and watched heads of state invite people to come over for dinner to their palaces. The key to success in these great stately functions is, of course, to put a little heart into it. That's what makes it work.

I am thrilled and feel vindicated when someone who has read my books has learned how to be a good host in his backyard or in the local hotel's banquet room. So, although my life has changed course in recent years, I still have much yet to see, enjoy, write, and laugh about.

Mom and Dad, I guess I owe you a thing or two or three.

School Days

*M*ost people look upon Miami Beach as a place where you go to get old and play golf, or as a place to go when you're young, to partake of "what's hot" at the South Beach nightspots. It was actually my birthplace, in 1926, in St. Francis Hospital. I was baptized in a properly posh spot—Star Island No. 2—replete with mansions, none of which belonged to the Baldriges. My father, Malcolm, a young lawyer from Omaha, Nebraska, at the time, had taken my mother and their two boys, four-year-old Mac and two-year-old Bob, to Miami Beach to make a quick killing in Florida real estate, which had begun to boom. My parents must have looked upon the experience as a sort of how-to-become-a-millionaire gamble, which unfortunately they lost. Shortly after I was born, the real estate along Collins Avenue in Miami Beach turned sour. At least I have one souvenir of this Florida experience: a birth certificate printed on pale pink parchment, with gold lettering, announcing "Your Treasure is Registered," a document that would cause me great embarrassment every time I entered a new school and had to present it.

In 1928 my parents packed us all up and took us back to Omaha, from whence they had come. My father returned to the practice of law in his strict father's office, smarting under the I-told-you-so attitude of his gruff parent. Mother, Regina ("Jean"), was the beautiful titian-haired daughter of one of the town's most respected horse-and-buggy doctors, James Connell. She and my father, a Yale football star, captain of the wrestling team, and a World War I hero, had married a couple of years after he had returned from France.

People who were born around the Great Depression of the 1930s, which began with the crash of the stock market in 1929, remember that period as a great leveler of society, a time that drove families together with iron ties and that made you appreciate your blessings more than ever before or ever after. I didn't understand or remember the economic theory and sociological results of that era. I just remember having young parents, two grandmothers whose lifetimes extended far beyond those of their husbands, and two brothers who were to make my life absolutely miserable, even though they were the best thing that ever could have happened to me.

Our grandfathers died before I was born, but we lived in Grandpa Baldrige's big old house in Omaha. Both grandmothers, as was the custom in those days, came to live with us, at separate periods, of course. World War II would have started early if they had shared the big house with us simultaneously. There was a real respect for grandparents in those days. They were considered special and wise, and were paid honor by the younger generations. They were instrumental in the installation of values in their grandchildren. Manners, too. At dinner they would make mental notes about everything from "Bobby was particularly noisy with his soup tonight" to "Malcolm and Letitia had an unacceptable fight over the last piece of cake, carried on under the table." There would be a private conversation with each child later about these transgressions, parents not included.

I remember every detail of that house at 124 South Thirty-ninth Street, it was so big and utterly fascinating. There was a large stained-glass window on the landing of the carved wood stairway, which culminated in a two-foot-tall bronze statue of a nude Winged Mercury. This statue was much scrutinized and disrespected. My brothers would adorn him with their neckties, sometimes a stocking cap or baseball cap over his curly head, and often a bandage taped with adhesive on his private parts.

My father, an only child, marveled at the wonderful calm and serenity that surrounded my mother, who had grown up in a family of boys and therefore knew what all the noise was about. My memories of my mother are clear, luminous, spiritual. She ran a perfect household, was always at the front door when my father came home, and spent every hospital stay of her three accident-prone kids by sleeping on a cot by our beds until we could go home again. She was a beautiful woman with shiny auburn hair and perfect skin. She welcomed all of her children's friends, fed them, soda-ed them, dispensed advice on their love life, and made them clean up any mess they made in the kitchen. Growing up, I heard so many times the reaction of our friends, "Gee, your Mom's great!"

There is no argument there.

My relationships with my brothers were always paramount in my life. We were combative in our younger years, but mutually supportive in our later ones. My earliest memory is also the first in a long line of encounters between my brothers and me. One day when I was two years old, they undid the safety gate at the top of the long stairway and pushed me down it as I sat on my kiddie cart. It was a head-over-heels action—perhaps Mac and Bob had wanted to see how well their little sister could bounce. My mother was certain that I had been killed, although she was together enough to call the pediatrician instead of the funeral home. Dr. Brown heard my screams over the telephone and asked, "Is that hollering coming from your daughter?" When told it was, he instructed my mother to bring me down to his office at once, but not to worry. I was "obviously fine and was possessed of an extremely strong pair of lungs." So it was that my first memory was also my first experience in practicing survival among my brothers, who explained their actions as an attempt to toughen up their sissy, overprotected sister.

The main drawback to our house in Omaha was that I had to share a bathroom with Mac and Bob. They were always leaving dirty things like sneakers and sweat socks on the floor of this room without locks. When girls came over to play with me, my brothers would burst in on us without so much as a knock on the door. A younger sister has no delusions about the opposite sex. She learns how to handle herself and to give as good as she gets. It's the kind of expertise that is very helpful later in life in the working world.

As contentious as my relationship was with my brothers, my relationship with my father was loving. I could always count on a kind word and a straight answer from him. None of my friends were as close to their fathers. From a very young age I was aware that one of the tools used by "Big Mac," as my father was called, to make people happy was his ease of speaking, in public or in private conversation, and on any subject. I was his biggest littlest fan. I loved how he interacted with people—with everyone. I noticed how he had become intimate friends with the policemen in the neighborhood, the haughty art museum curator who lived around the corner, the butcher, and the mayor of the city of Omaha. As Mother explained it, "Your father knows how to talk to people." This attribute became especially valuable when he later became a congressman. He never said no to anyone, whether he was asked to submit legislation to raise the subsidy for museums, or support raising the retirement fund for police and firemen, or help a young boy who wasn't making good grades get into Andover, or labor to keep the Chicago stockyards from swallowing the Omaha stockyards.

It wasn't only that he knew how to talk to people, but that he made the time to do it. He was an artful storyteller, and whether he encountered an old man, a little child, or a young couple, he gave them his undivided attention and promised to help. He never talked about it or bragged about it. He just did it. His children did not have to be told to admire their father. We just did.

When my father ran for Congress, I was the only one in the family who wanted to accompany him on his campaign swings to western Nebraska in the old maroon Pontiac, hoping to pick up some votes. The candidate made a policy of giving a political speech only if there were more than four people sitting outside the grocery store on a town's main street. They were mostly men, smoking, leaning back on their wooden chairs, passing the time of day together. But they were voters, and my father was determined to reach them—ten-minute speeches, many handshakes. I did not understand the message my father was relaying over and over, but it was fun to see this part of the state that was so different from our big, sophisticated city of Omaha.

We would often be invited to lunch in a farmer's kitchen, served at a big round table that was usually covered with a printed oilcloth with a special scent. The women always looked tired, but also proud of their food, which took them all morning to prepare. There would be fried chicken, steaming mashed potatoes dotted with blobs of melting butter, platters of wholesome breads, and separate serving bowls of whatever vegetables happened to be available. Pies, too, hot delicious fruit pies. My father explained to me afterward that our host family would do without to serve us such a special meal. Many of them lived a humble life, some without indoor plumbing. I was amazed to see they used outhouses instead of bathrooms. Eventually other farmers would join the table to ask my father questions about what those overbred, elitist, patent-leather-pumped politicians in Washington were going to do about the drought-stricken bread basket of America. Because of the presence of the congressman's little daughter, they edited out the cuss words. I didn't understand what they were saying, but I certainly understood the emotions involved.

By far the most important piece of furniture in the house in Omaha was the heavy oval mahogany dinner table. It must have weighed a ton. The ersatz Queen Anne chairs were constantly occupied at mealtime with family, adult friends, and child friends. Millie never knew how many would be coming for dinner. If Mac, Bob, or I were late for meals, woe be unto us, because certain small punishments would head in our direction. We had to come to the table with hands washed, hair combed, and clean clothes. The boys had to wear sweaters or jackets, with their shirttails tucked in. If there was no guest for dinner, I could get away with not having to change from my drab brown convent uniform. Millie, the cook-housekeeper who was with us for many years, cooked mountains of food and washed vast piles of laundry without a word of complaint, and kept us from stealing our favorite food from her kitchen. She worked six days a week, twelve hours a day, for a salary of about $15 weekly. She loved her job, was cheerful, and lorded it over her friends because she worked for the well-known Baldrige family. It was the Great Depression; she and her daughter Clarice were part of our family, and we were part of hers.

The dinner table was the training lab where our manners were observed and corrected. ("Malcolm, put down your knife! You do not use it to clean the corn out of your teeth!" "Tish, stop slurping your soup. I don't want to hear one sound out of you from now until the last spoonful of soup is gone!") Each meal was an active class in grammar and civility. "Thank you, Millie, for the fried chicken," "Please pass the peas, darling little sister Tish" (always said with a sneer). If the behavior instructions were not followed, there would be no more dinner for that recalcitrant child. From the child's point of view, it was much easier and more pleasant all around to obey. We had to eat everything served to us on our plates, which was common in those days. I hated beets, but a violent dislike of something was no reason for not eating it. I ate my beets.

When the Baldrige kids lapsed into heated arguments at the table, raucous teasing, and occasional biffing of one another, a deep voice would suddenly ring out with the solemnity of a Moses presenting the Commandments. My father would command, *"Table silence!"* All noise would immediately stop. The head of the house would lay his wristwatch down on the table for exactly ten minutes, during which time only he and Mother could speak. We were not allowed to say one word. It was torture. We suddenly had so many things we wanted to say.

The dinner table was where each child reported on what he or she had done that day. If we stumbled over our words, our parents immediately picked up on it and asked how things were going in that department. All our problems and hang-ups were vocalized in the middle of the meat loaf and peas and dealt with, right then and there. No sibling was allowed to make fun of anyone else. We were taught to give support when it was needed. When I reported, for example, that a girl at school that day had made fun of me for being so tall, a brother would suddenly rise to my defense and say, "She's not on the basketball team like you, is she? She's probably really jealous. Next time she pulls something like that, tell her to go stretch herself a foot or two, and then maybe she'll make an athletic team." We'd all laugh, and I would be over it. The dinner table was definitely the problem-solving area for the family. When Bob complained that his softball team didn't have enough money to get equipment needed for the opening spring game in Elmwood Park, Mother would ask just why the boys weren't out earning the money themselves on weekends—mowing lawns in summer, raking leaves in the fall, shoveling snow and bringing in wood in the winter for the neighbors. Maybe my brothers would not jump to embrace our parents' suggestions, but it got their own brains going as to how they were going to solve the problem. Crafty parents.

Sunday lunch, although it meant an agonizingly long time spent at table, also meant great food, particularly in summer, when the fresh peach ice cream always resulted in fistfights over "who gets to lick the ice cream paddle" in the hand-turned freezer. The most regular guest at our Sunday lunch table was my father's Baptist minister. We would go to Mass Sunday morning, while my father would go later to the service at his church, returning in time for lunch with the minister, who was handsomely dressed in a dark gray formal suit, with striped trousers, like an usher in a wedding. Small and slight, he looked minute next to the big bear who was our father. He greatly enjoyed Millie's food, and even more his weekly treat from my father: a pint of bourbon with branch water, finished within a two-hour time frame. My father would then "escort" him home in his car and see him safely to his bedroom, where the pastor surely slipped away swiftly into the loveliest of Sabbath slumbers.

When I was less than four years old, my life was suddenly changed by the death of "Nana" Connell, my mother's mother, who was living with us at the time. It was my first contact with death, and I remember praying on my knees by the side of the bed, next to my mother, for an endlessly long time until "she breathed her last," as the nurse in attendance described it. Mother drew the picture in my mind of two angels bearing her aloft to heaven. It was clear, uncontested, very pleasant. Nana lay in an open casket for viewing for two days downstairs, as was customary in the Catholic Church at the time. (I have not gazed into a casket since.) The children in the neighborhood were fascinated, I remember. They came in and out giggling and being shushed by the grown-ups who arrived to offer condolences to my mother and her Connell relations. No light ever seemed to penetrate the room, with its dark blue velvet walls where Nana lay in state, except when someone sat reading in the Morris chair, with a nearby bronze lamp casting a small amount of light through a jewel-encrusted metal shade.

Nana wore a pale gray silk dress, ghostlike, with a fresh rose at the V-shaped neckline. I was sure that it would stay fresh all the way to heaven, and of course she was wearing her pearl necklace. I never saw her without that. Maybe they wouldn't let her into heaven without it.

The Blue Room loomed large in my mind because it was also the repository of my parents' rare collection of large brown leather volumes on World War I, hidden away in bookshelves, behind metal mesh doors. The Baldrige children were forbidden access to these books, so of course we looked at every page, some bearing photographs of horribly burned, gassed soldiers in

France. The books were there because they had been given to my mother by the U.S. Army medical corps. My mother's cousin, Dr. Karl Albert Connell (named for Queen Victoria's consort, Prince Albert, which lent him a special cachet), had invented the gas mask, a remarkable innovation that saved many lives in World War I, but not in time to prevent the loss of thousands of earlier gas attack victims.

Our other grandmother, "Bawa," who actually owned our big old house, came to live with us shortly after Nana's death. I had been named for her, and she had been named for Letizia Bonaparte, Napoleon's mother. (Bawa explained to me how the first Letitia in her family line was named for Napoleon's mother, as were thousands of other baby girls born in western Europe in the early nineteenth century. The mothers must have been hoping to raise their own Napoleons.) She was really Letitia Blanche Coffey Baldrige, but since Bawa was the only sound my oldest brother could make of the combination of the "Grandmother" and "Baldrige" names, "Bawa" was it. She was the closest thing Omaha had to a dowager duchess, I suppose— even if she did scandalize Omaha society by leaving her husband and young son for a two-year fling in an apartment in Paris on the avenue Foch in the early 1900s. Years later, when I was in my early twenties and living in Paris, I often used to drive down the avenue Foch to the Arc de Triomphe, looking at the magnificent apartment buildings lining both sides of the wide boulevard, trying to guess which building housed my grandmother's apartment, and also wondering about what went on there. The rumor was that she had a French lover, and my cousin Keating Coffey heard from his parents that Omaha people talked a lot about it, just as they did about the cigarettes she came home puffing. Ladies did not smoke in those days in the Midwest, only nonladies did. My grandfather Howard Malcolm Baldrige was, from all reports, exceedingly dull, and I remember that one of Bawa's friends made a remark to me at an age when I couldn't quite comprehend it. She said, "If I had been married to a man like your grandfather, I would have sought a lover, too."

Bawa came back from that Parisian experience with trunkfuls of fabulous dresses, hats, boas, and boxes of exotic-looking cigarette holders, which she put away in the attic of our house. By the time I was four, my friends and I were hounding her to be able to dress up in her Parisian creations. I would steal a cigarette from her cache and stick it into one of those ebony, rhinestone-studded works of art. With a feeling of misguided sophistication, I would stand in front of a mirror with my teeth clenched on the holder, sucking on it and pretending to smoke. When I wrapped around my forehead one of Bawa's silvery embroidered headbands, which she wore with her evening dresses, and waved the cigarette holder at my reflection, I felt that nothing more glamorous had ever been seen in the world at large. Unfortunately, the inhalation of stale nicotine fumes from the holder made me slightly nauseous every time. (Bawa was to pay for that smoking habit later in life with terrible emphysema, which eventually killed her.)

Bawa would show me countless times, simply because I asked her to, her photo album filled with postcards, menus from her sojourn in France, place cards, and invitations to the parties she attended. "Ah," she would say, turning to look out the window longingly, dreaming of her experiences in Paris, "comme je me suis bien amusée!" Her stories were all equally wonderful: she described everything from listening to the rhythm of the clip-clops of the horses and carriages taking their elegant passengers to lunch in the Bois de Boulogne, to dining on oysters while seated on a crimson velvet banquette at Maxim's (when she showed me drawings of the plates of oysters, I couldn't imagine eating "those things"). Listening to her was like being in a cinema, watching an ever-changing, fascinating film that portrayed only beautiful, chic people. I copied her little French phrases, using the words "Oh, ça c'est tellement chic!" without having any idea what they meant, but I loved the sound of the French words. Someday, I would learn them, too. She told me I would, but I knew it before she told me. "You must travel, Letitia," she said many times. "You must see everything, not just Omaha." She needed to tell me that only once.

Bawa returned to Paris in World War I to serve for a short time with the American Red Cross, again a gutsy action for a woman of her era. I adored her. She was a free spirit, a rebel, one strong woman. "Leadership is in your genes, don't forget it," she wrote me once. "Remember, you must work at it. Nothing permanent comes without work. Just go do it." When I would inevitably ask the same question, "What is it that's supposed to be in our genes?" she always gave the same puzzling answer, "Leadership. I expected it of your father, and I expect it of the three of you children. Don't ask what it means. Just do it. Take charge. You're strong enough."

If there was one place in the house that I adored and in which I felt completely safe, it was my bedroom, with its never-changed pale peach wallpaper festooned with gold stars, and its pale blue ceiling. (In the 1930s, once wallpaper was put up, it stayed up.) Nana's old maple bedroom furniture had been painted white for me. It was very ordinary, but to my eyes, with its fake bronze gilt drawer pulls, it looked like the furniture in the Palais de Versailles that Bawa had shown me on her postcards. The bedroom door didn't lock, but it slammed beautifully as a sign to my brothers that they could not enter. At nap time I would remove the contents of the bureau, drawer by drawer, laying all of the "merchandise" out on the bed. Then I would play a double role—that of salesperson and customer. I sold my ribbons, underwear, socks, and barrettes over and over to Mrs. Imaginary Customer. I even had a little toy cash register with nickels and pennies to handle the sales.

Sitting on the top shelf of my white bookcase was a lovely statuette of the Virgin Mary, dressed in pale blue and white. During the month of May ("Mary's Month," as the nuns called it) I made an altar and placed white votive candles in glass cups in front of her statue. I picked fresh lilacs and lily of the valley from our front yard. Empty jelly jars made fine vases. At night, before going to sleep, I would turn off all the lights after lighting the votive candles. I would kneel, say a few prayers, and watch the El Greco–elongated shadows of the Madonna on the wall. The flickering candlelight made lacy patterns on the ceiling through the flowers and leaves. It was very magical. It made me feel pious and spiritual—at least for a half hour every night during the month of May. The Blessed Virgin Mary became my good friend during those early years of my life, a friendship that would remain forever.

My brothers, aware of this devotion, kept telling their friends that their sister was going to enter a nunnery, ha, ha, but I denied it vehemently. Nuns were not allowed to hit their brothers back, so it was not to be a vocation for me.

My battles with my brothers continued, even after the incident of Mac and Bob pushing me down the stairway on my kiddie cart. The Redhead, alias Bob, succeeded in knocking me out cold and giving me a concussion one Christmas afternoon when he was trying out his much-adored new baseball bat with vigorous swings in the living room. For years to come he swore it was not intentional, but I felt it was. Those two were always seeking revenge on their "adorable little sister," who was "her Daddy's pet."

At the age of five I had had enough of this sibling persecution. I sought escape from my brothers in a most creative way. A glass transom over my door admitted a cheerful light from an electric wall sconce just outside. I was afraid of the dark, a fact of which my brothers were happily aware, and at night the light from the hall through the transom was my protection, my security. One night when my parents were in Washington for the winter session of Congress, my brothers waited until Reggie, our Irish nursemaid, had gone to bed in the back of the house. They drew up chairs to the closed door of my bedroom, reaching as high as the transom when they stretched on their toes. They turned off the hall light, shrieked ghastly ghost noises, and waved flashlights in eerie patterns through the transom. The ceiling came alive with fast-moving, dancing, shadowy figures.

I almost died of fright. Something horrible was happening. Then, after some heart-pounding moments of cringing under the covers, the cold truth suddenly took over my senses, and it quickly turned to rage. It was my brothers who had done this. Without another thought, I got dressed in my school clothes and packed my favorite doll inside her little suitcase, which I had received from Santa. I slipped out of the house with the doll suitcase in one hand and a streetcar token in the other. I knew exactly what I was doing. I was taking action, deciding my fate, making things better. It was about ten at night, and Farnam Street was brightly lit, so I wasn't scared. A streetcar came by almost immediately. The conductor opened the door and looked at me, surprised and worried. "What are you doing, little girl? Where's your mommy and daddy?"

"I'm going to Union Station," the conductor reported that I had answered. "I'm going to find my mommy and daddy." Coincidentally I had also escaped those two beasts of brothers back in the house.

"But where are your mommy and daddy?"

"In Washington. My daddy's in Congress. They have meetings all the time. I know how to get on a train."

He must have been panic-stricken by now. A congressman's daughter!

He had to get help from the only place he knew—at the end of the line, his last stop, Union Station. He sat me up front and kept a running stream of conversation going, not wanting me to be as frightened as he probably was.

Once we reached the end of the line, conductors in black suits and visored hats, trainmen, policemen, and passengers suddenly surrounded me. I was given hot chocolate and a cookie, my doll and her wardrobe in her suitcase were admired by everyone, a frantic Reggie was called, and when a police car sped me back to Thirty-ninth Street, Reggie was standing on the curb in her nightgown and bathrobe, her face an abstract painting of pink-and-white blotches. I remember how hard she was shaking, and I suddenly felt sorry that I was the cause of it. She kept moaning through her tears, "What will Mr. and Mrs. Baldrige think of me? Mother of God, how could I have let this happen?"

She immediately put me to bed, with the hall light and even a table lamp on, and I heard her on the telephone talking in a high-pitched, emotional voice to my parents in Washington. The next morning my mother boarded the train back to Omaha, and after that, she never left us alone again when Congress was in session. I don't know what punishment was meted out to my brothers, because it was Top Secret. All I know was that "they really got it." I was proud that I had almost pulled off a great coup—getting to Washington by myself—and that everyone, absolutely everyone, told my brothers how naughty they had been. I exulted in the extra attention I was now receiving, which my brothers informed me later was the most irritating of my many irritating qualities.

Eventually it became time for me to enter school. A really fine public school—Columbian School—was twelve blocks away from us, and my brothers went there until high school. I went for my first two years, but I longed to go to "The Convent," Duchesne, a gloomy dark red stone building where the "Mesdames du Sacré Coeur" taught grade school through high school, and four years of college beyond. The Mesdames were an international top-of-the-line teaching order of nuns, who considered themselves to be on an intellectual level with the Jesuit priests. *Mamma mia,* but they were strict! We marched in neat ranks to classes, moving to the clicking signal of the nun in front who carried a kind of castanet—meant not for dancing, but for giving orders. As a group we had to curtsy to any visitor we passed, as well as to all of the senior nuns. If we passed Reverend Mother, we began to look like a bunch of Texas debutantes, almost bowing down to the floor.

The Sacred Heart convents all over the world were dedicated to learning, but also to the principles of order and discipline. It was like boot camp in many ways, and it was exactly what I needed. The students were under control at all times. We wore dismal reform-school-style brown uniforms—a straight skirt, matching brown bolero jacket, and a tan blouse with a big Peter Pan collar. The color was drained from our faces. No one could wear makeup anyway. As student bodies go, I'd say we looked really unhealthy. We loved our dress uniforms—the same thing as the brown ones, but all in white. The nuns kept saying on those special occasions and holidays that called for white uniforms, "You all look like innocent angels. It's too bad you're not!"

I spent a week in confinement, imprisoned in an empty little classroom with my books and assignments because of having committed a terrible crime: I had bitten a classmate on the arm. During this period of incarceration, my lunch was brought to me on a tray, and I passed the days with my books, notebooks, and assignments in silence. For me, it was agony. The incident was over a new party dress my parents had bought for me for a congé at school, a special event in which there were no classes, and the day was spent in having fun and playing games for prizes. My new dress meant a great deal to me, partly for my own vanity's sake, but partly because of the financial sacrifice involved. My enemy in class, a girl named Sally, was always jealous and taunted me, but on this day she really went too far, tearing the wide pink satin sash right off the back of the dress. My inner voice commanded me, "Grab the offending arm responsible for the dirty deed and bite it." Every nun in the convent hastened to give me a sermon on this dastardly deed. More than one nun said that she couldn't believe that a "child of the Sacred Heart" would do anything like it. My parents were aghast, and my brothers told me, each in turn, that I was a real jerk to have bitten her instead of slugging her. I have never bitten anyone since.

Hinky Hamilton and I, the tallest girls in the school by far, were logically put on the basketball team. As I watch the outstanding professional women basketball players in competition today, I remember how different our approach was. The killer instinct in sports was against the spirit of love that Sacred Heart girls were meant to represent. The nun referee was constantly blowing her whistle at me and suggesting that I let everyone else on the team have the ball and shoot the baskets.

Every Monday morning we had "primes," at which we were given grades for our comportment of the preceding week. The entire school convened in a cavernous study hall. The student leaders in good behavior wore their colored sashes on the diagonal, like diplomats in full dress, the green, pink, or blue ribbons representing their age groups. Reverend Mother and the other nuns, with very serious expressions, sat on a raised platform as each student's name was called. The girl would then go up, receive her card from Reverend Mother, and return to her seat. The card had a drawing of the Sacred Heart, crowned with thorns, plus a French phrase: *très bien, bien,* or *indifférent. Très bien* meant you were a goody-goody, *bien* meant you were slipping a little, and *indifférent* meant you were hopeless in your comportment (or on your way to hell, however you wished to express it). If you were *Très bien,* you got a ribbon to wear for one week, diplomat-style. Every week I did something wrong—chewing gum in study hall, or getting out of line while marching in ranks, or whispering in class. During Lent no one could talk during lunch. A nun read sacred scriptures to us. It was a given at this time that when Letitia Baldrige's name was read out, there would be an *Indifférent* following it. (One night, thirty years later, I was the banquet speaker for a big reunion of Sacred Heart alumnae at the Ambassador Hotel in Chicago and finally received a *Très bien* card—only this one was a fourteen-karat-gold replica of the card for my charm bracelet!)

I don't remember the stock market crash, but I do remember that the 1930s were really tough in Nebraska. The depression hit the Midwest hard; the main livelihoods of farming and ranching, upon which all other businesses depended, had been clobbered by relentless droughts, blizzards, and dust storms. The cattle died, the corn was stunted, and there was even a plague of locusts. Our parents managed to give us support and a feeling of security in spite of the bad times. I heard them voicing their worries long into the night because their bedroom was adjacent to mine, connected through a mutual closet.

My father had been born with a gold spoon in his mouth; my mother, the child of a hardworking family doctor, with a silver spoon; yet during the Great Depression they became part of the upper middle class that had to make do with tin spoons. I remember one conversation in particular when Mother cried unusually hard. I heard her say, "We can't afford the Duchesne tuition anymore. Tish will have to return to public school." In June I bid my class a heartbroken good-bye. Then, miraculously, I found myself returning to the convent in September. Twenty years later I learned why. Paul Gallagher, a wealthy food manufacturer in Omaha, whose daughter Anne was my best friend, had offered to pay my annual tuition bills, but only anonymously. Not even my parents had known. I will never stop being grateful to him, and only wish he had still been around when I found out.

Small things hurt during the depression years. Mother was heroic about all the sacrifices she had to make, except for one thing: her hats. In those days, a lady did not go out of her house without a hat. It was a symbol of her class, education, and taste. The ladies who came to visit Mother at home kept their hats on in the house. When Mother was elected president of the Omaha Junior League, I learned a bit of hat etiquette. All of the members who came to meetings at our house kept their hats on, but she, as the hostess, was meant to be hatless. I loved those league meetings. I sat there as the proverbial fly on the wall, loving the conclusion of the business part, when they would drink cups of tea and eat dainty sandwiches of watercress and mayonnaise or creamed cheese and olive or egg salad, all on crustless white bread. Then they would gather around our piano and sing songs of a light classical variety ("Who Is Sylvia? What Is She?" or perhaps "Stardust"). My brothers and I found their singing hysterically funny because they all sang regardless of whether they could stay in tune.

My mother went for three years without buying a new hat. The house went unpainted. The family had to resign from the country club, which meant no more golf or tennis for my father, or swimming in the pool for the Baldrige kids. My father had to give up his membership in the Omaha Club, an eating club for businessmen down on Dodge Street, which had been helpful to him in his law practice. The farmers could no longer pay him in currency, so they paid him in produce, chickens, and eggs.

Dad had one rich widow client who had lost millions in the stock market crash, but once paid my father's legal fees bill with an opera-length strand of large, magnificent oriental pearls—natural pearls, in other words, as opposed to today's cultured pearls, which are not an accident of nature. "I'm going to put these away in one of my drawers to save for you," Mother said. "These are too pretentious for me to wear in these hard times, and you are too young to know how beautiful these are, and how rare." About once a year she let me put on the necklace when I was playing dress-up with Bawa's French designer dresses.

There was always concern for friends and neighbors in those days. If our parents heard someone was ill, Mother went into immediate action like a one-woman 911 emergency team. She would make soup, run errands, change the sick person's linens, and leave quarts of freshly squeezed orange juice in the icebox. The Baldrige kids were assigned little chores to help out a sick neighbor, too, such as running to Green's drugstore for some medicine, walking the dog, or feeding the cats.

Mother, seeing the jobseekers grow thinner and more forlorn each month, took action to help as best she could. She organized her own soup kitchen for the men in the area who were jobless and destitute. Every morning she called on the women in each house in the vicinity to collect scraps of food left over from their family meals. Women or their children would bring them to our kitchen every day. She kept pots of hot water going on the stove day and night, huge pots once used for boiling men's shirts but now filled with meat and fowl bones, leftover vegetables, potatoes, remnants of soup from the night before—anything and everything went into that stew pot. Groups of men would come to the back door and sit on the stairs late in the day, tired, despondent, and hungry after another day of looking for work. Mother and Millie would dish out large bowls full of the soup, and the grateful men would then return home to their families, strengthened, and not having to partake of the pitiful supply of food available for their own families. I remember people often asking Mother, "Jean, how did you come to take this on? How can you manage it?"

"Someone has to do it," she would answer. " It has to be done, so you just *do* it." It was wonderful for me to have such an in-house role model.

Despite the depression, I had a childhood rich in things other than money. The Baldrige house and yard were the meeting places of neighborhood kids all weekend long, and from 3:30 P.M. to 6:00 P.M. during weekdays. In the summertime our yard was operational until seven at night; our father was all for children getting their exercise every day. There were broken roller skates, battered footballs, baseballs, bats, and mitts in the mud room for the use of any kids who wanted them for play and who could make do with them in their sorry shape. My father and other young lawyers in his firm would referee the games on a rotating basis. Their presence in the Baldrige backyard kept the kids working hard on their team games. Every kid who showed up played—no one was left out because of inferior ability, age, or size. Even kids from other neighborhoods were welcome to come over on their bikes to the "Baldrige Athletic Club."

Poor sportsmanship was absolutely unknown. My brothers and I were fully aware that we had the best parents in the world, who often served as surrogate parents for our friends when they were in trouble. There were always sodas in the icebox, and on special occasions, plates of glazed doughnuts and bowls of popcorn. Three afternoons a week there would be neighborhood games after school—Statue, Green Light, and plain old tag—with ten to fifteen kids at a time. My girlfriends and I felt the older boys were constantly overpowering us, but my brothers had uncanny instincts about when it was proper to stop because things were getting too rough. They knew that our father would come thundering out into the yard to set things right, but by the time he arrived, he would see a group of angelic-looking boys, playing quietly among the girls, no social crimes being committed.

Mother, who had never had an athletic moment in her life, had no sympathy for the girls when they were pushed around by the boys in the yard. With disdain she would ask, "But why are you trying to play with them [meaning those dirty, loud boys, including her own sons] in the first place? Why would you want to be out there? Why don't you come in and read a book, play with your dolls, or something?"

The Baldrige kids and their friends managed to take over the attic floor, and the boys played pool on the battered green felt table my father had had since his teens. The girls fought for position in front of the tall standing mirror between the attic closets, where old clothes had been saved in steamer trunks. We were given permission to play dress-up with the most marvelous array of what today would be called costumes, but back then were simply Bawa's lavish Paris evening dresses, slouchy velvet capes, ostrich feather fans, and headbands encrusted with brilliants.

The gang moved over into the Harding backyard a block away when it was ice-skating season. Mr. Harding, publisher of the *Omaha World Herald* and father to many children, was kind enough to make an ice rink for us and keep it flooded. He laid down firm rules, which included the command to the boys to keep the ice smooth and scraped, and to the girls to give way to the boys on who had the priority for ice time. The boys' ice hockey practice was constant, and when the girls were finally let on the ice for the first time each day, usually at dusk, out the boys would come, zooming onto the ice again, whooping, swinging their hockey sticks, and demanding more practice time. Who ever said it was an equal world?

The meetings for the high school girls' Odix Club and the boys' Les Hiboux (owls) Club were often held in our house, perhaps because we had so much space, but probably more because our parents were the only ones who agreed to it all the time. In eighth grade, I happened to walk into the house during a meeting of Les Hiboux, my brothers' club. I found the entire group in the living room, doubled over with laughter while Mac read aloud my diary. My brothers had picked the lock on this secret outpouring of love for certain of their high school friends—all of whom were sitting listening intently. In an Italian court, if I had murdered my brothers, I would have won immediate acquittal.

I eventually settled in at the convent and became a strong student. One of my most triumphant moments came in eighth grade, when the head of the entire order of the Mesdames du Sacré Coeur came to visit the nuns in Omaha. As the number one English student, I was invited to sit next to Reverend Mother at Sunday lunch. It was a thrilling honor. Without anyone in my family aware of it, I had purchased a pair of false eyelashes at Green's drugstore the Saturday before. I wanted to look really smashing at this event at the convent, so I decided to try them out. I believed they would make me look mature, beautiful, sophisticated.

The first course was cream of pea soup, ladled into soup plates by the tiny "Sisters" who served the food. One of my eyelashes, which had not been properly glued into place, fell off and into the soup. It looked like a cockroach floating there on the sea of green. Reverend Mother looked down and saw it before I did.

"Holy Mother!" she exclaimed in a disgusted whisper. A cockroach did not belong anywhere near the convent, and certainly not in the food. She jumped up, obviously startling the entire assemblage, and rushed the soup plate out to the kitchen. I quickly peeled off the other eyelash, knowing that if anyone looked me in the eye, all would be revealed. That was traumatic enough to remove from my life the possibility of ever wearing fake eyelashes again.

Adolescence is tough on most people. For some, and I am included in this group, it was excruciating. The subscription dances Friday night at the Clermont Ballroom were to me the closest thing to torture that could ever be designed. If you didn't have a drivers' license, and few people did, you were dropped off by your parents. Boys had to ask the girls to dance; it was unheard of for a girl to ask. Parents made certain their sons had a duty list of girls, daughters of their friends, who must be invited to dance at least once. My brothers had a long list of duty dances, their little sister included. Little sister? By the age of thirteen I was six feet, one inch tall.

The boys stood entrenched in the comfort of their stag line, from which they could observe the girls on the sidelines, waiting to be plucked for a dance. It was awful. A boy would even come over to where the girls were, stare one straight in the face, and then walk on without saying a word—rejection at its most painful!

If a boy was stuck (meaning he had been dancing for more than ten minutes, and none of his buddies had cut in), he just might start to dance with a dollar bill visible in his hand on his partner's back. None of the boys who danced with me dared try that, because my brothers would have made them pay for that humiliation. I knew that the only ones who danced with me were my brothers' friends, who were afraid not to—a bit of physical intimidation, one might say, because my brothers were the biggest of their school. The girls who were danced off their feet were all small, cute, big-busted, and peppy cheerleader material. Mother kept trying to comfort me. "Just wait, when those boys grow up and become more mature, they'll appreciate a tall, beautiful woman. They'll come running." Just when was this transformation into a beautiful woman going to take place? I wondered.

I towered over those boys. They all wore a lot of hair grease, which emitted a kind of repulsive fragrance but gave their hair a desirable patent-leather sheen. It was customary to dance very close in those days. Except when jitterbugging, we were always clutched together, and my chin would be resting on the top of my partner's head. After each dance I would retire to the ladies' room and remove the grease from under my chin with a paper towel.

If a dance was particularly mortifying for me, I would telephone home, and my heroic father would be there in fifteen minutes to spirit me away. We had rehearsed it: I went out the back entrance, where no one would see me leave or my father picking me up. When we arrived home, I did not have to talk about the dance. My parents knew.

On successful evenings the high school dance would end with a big group staging a grand finale elsewhere, such as at the Blackstone Hotel Coffee Shop on Farnam Street. Here, at the late hour of 10:00 P.M. (many kids had eleven o'clock curfews), the standard choice would be an individual order of french fries, dripping in catsup, and a tall glass of Coke with marshmallow syrup poured on top. When stirred with a spoon, it sent a geyser of fizzing, gushing, creamy foam into the air. No champagne or gourmet cuisine of the future would ever surpass the joy of those coffee-shop feasts.

You could tell who the fast girls were in school. They would come back into a party, their hair and lipstick all mussed up, and bits of the pastel angora wool from their sweaters would be covering their dates' dark sport coats. But the truth of the matter was that virginity was highly prized, and most young girls successfully stopped the boys from going too far by pleading, "I have to wait until I'm married," or "I don't want you to lose respect for me." I eavesdropped on my father's conversations with my brothers before they went to pick up their dates.

"Remember, Mac, no rough stuff tonight. You treat that girl gently. Don't make her do anything she doesn't want to do. Never try to overpower her, and remember you don't want to be the person who makes her lose her reputation.

"When you kiss a girl, Bob, do it sweetly, and learn when to stop."

My brothers would die of embarrassment at these little lectures and utter many protests—"Ah, gee, Dad"—but I'm sure his words came echoing back to them when they were parked with their dates in a car, or sitting rocking on someone's front porch.

I was so naive and inexperienced as a freshman, I longed to know what really good kissing felt like. I wondered what it would be like to sit in a car with a boy with the lights off, necking, out in Elmwood Park, which is what the older kids did. How did people get enough oxygen for hours on end? I tried kissing my closet door's full-length mirror for a while, because it was a cool, smooth surface, but all I got out of it was smeared lipstick on the mirror and tired mouth muscles.

I could not discuss sex with Mother. Finally, at the age of sixteen, I was desperate enough to ask my father what a soul kiss was. He explained that it was "just a silly thing a boy does when he puts his tongue inside a girl's mouth."

I almost gagged, and told him I had never heard anything so repulsive in my life. He laughed and said, "You don't have to let a boy soul-kiss you, if you don't want it. Remember that. Just push him away."

"What if I want to give *him* one, and he doesn't want it?"

"I think that is highly unlikely."

"You mean, guys really like to do it?"

"Guys really do."

"Did you give Mother soul kisses?"

"When we got engaged, yes."

"Can I see you two doing it together, so I'll know what it looks like?"

"No, you just wait until it happens to you—maybe years from now."

The first time I was the recipient of a real soul kiss, when I felt the pressure of the masculine tongue, I was so surprised I almost bit it off. Whatever was he doing? I had forgotten my father's explanation. The young man cried out in pain; I felt terrible and apologized profusely, wondering if I should go with him to a hospital or something.

He had the courage to try again on the next date, and it suddenly felt good. Nice, very nice. He went off to war, and I never saw him again or heard about him, but I'm grateful to him for my first lesson in soul kissing. Maybe he bears a little scar on his tongue. In any case, he was a good teacher.

My adolescence seemed to come to a screeching halt one Sunday in December, when the nation of Japan attacked the United States at Pearl Harbor. My parents had forced my unwilling brother Bob to take me that day to the Paramount Theatre to see the popular movie *Sergeant York*, with Gary Cooper, a film about World War I. Bob and I came from the theater into the quiet Sunday-afternoon streets to see newspaper boys yelling "Extra! Extra!" up and down Farnam Street. The world changed drastically that day. Everyone suddenly began to grow up, move around, come and go, my father and brothers among them. Within two years they would all be in uniform and headed overseas.

The house on Thirty-ninth Street was sold, we left Omaha, and I became the first full scholarship student in the history of Miss Porter's School, Farmington, Connecticut. It was a lucky break for me. We never could have afforded the tuition of this famous private school, but the head, Robert Keep, had taught my father at the Andover Phillips Academy in Massachusetts. He knew my father had served with distinction in World War I, he knew the minuscule salary my father would be earning as a major in the Army Air Corps in this war, he knew I longed to go to Farmington. He decided to help out the young football player he knew from his teaching days, who was "eager and polite, cheerful, kind, great in sports but terrible in class." The deal was that I had to keep my grades up to A's and B+'s. Scholarships were unknown in those days at places like Miss Porter's. Therefore it was to be kept secret, so that I would not be discriminated against.

I would attend single-sex schools all my life—the convent, Miss Porter's, and Vassar College. It was not an accident. I wanted the best education I could get in the most nurturing environment. Enrolling in institutions that were dedicated to teaching women was what I wanted. They were meant to bring out the best in us. They would teach us to reach—and reach high—in our lives, in whatever we chose to do. I knew from experience with Mac and Bob that boys had the upper hand everywhere, so why not learn in an atmosphere where there were none around to interrupt, distract, persecute, and infuriate? I had friends at coeducational universities who confided in me in those days that "guys don't like girls who are too smart, so the thing to do is play down your brains." That is something I would never do. Whatever brains I managed to accumulate, I would prefer to play up, not down.

Going away to boarding school in wartime was an escape from worrying about my social life. No one had a social life then; we could only talk about what used to be. It also brought me closer to my brothers; we were suddenly in a totally new relationship. They thought I was "really very okay," and I now frankly adored them, considered them to be my best friends, and bragged about them to anyone who would listen. We had reached the point of laughing about our childhood rivalries. We were not, in the face of war good-byes, embarrassed to profess real affection for one another. Good-byes were said at school with immense sadness, but with the certitude that these men were coming back. *Nothing was going to happen to them.* Thoughts of their being harmed were stamped out with tremendous thrusts of willpower.

Farmington was a lovely, quiet town nestled in a valley near Hartford, Connecticut. The school was named Miss Porter's, or MPS, in 1843 for its founder, Sarah Porter, a very advanced feminine educator, whose brother was president of Yale University. As the school expanded, she kept buying the wonderful historic houses that lined Main Street. These houses served as sleeping quarters for students, and as classrooms as well. The red brick Federal houses, the white shingled ones with dark green shutters, and the famous Congregational Church form the main part of the town's historic district, and were visited annually by those interested in eighteenth- and nineteenth-century America.

An all-important part of MPS was the housemother who lived in each house, coping with all the emotional problems of adolescent girls, including the absence of their fathers and brothers in military service. There were several millionairesses at school, but no one made note of it. Students were no longer stabling their own horses there during the war, although Jacqueline Kennedy, who followed me by three years, kept her horse there and rode it every day. Every student wore the same Brooks Brothers double-breasted polo coat with big white pearl buttons, knee-length cable-stitched socks, and brown moccasins, and was allowed to bring from home only four skirts, four blouses, and six cardigan sweaters. We all looked alike. The only jewelry allowed was a gold Miss Porter's signet ring, worn senior year, a string of pearls for dinner at night, and a wristwatch.

Strict rules forbade leaving campus. We were allowed one weekend away a year. We could not go into the village without a very special permission. Miller, a tall policeman, a paragon of patience with silly adolescents as his clients, served for over three decades as the school's guardian angel. He directed traffic on Main Street and kept the Farmington girls not only safe but also morally virtuous. He would not allow students and their male visitors to go off campus alone for one minute.

My roommate was a beautiful Hungarian girl, Marika Ross, from New York. Much to my annoyance, she was a perfect size 4, and one of the last students at Farmington to enroll in the "finishing program," as opposed to the college preparation program that had become the norm. Marika did her nails every night, put up her hair on rollers in a special bandanna, covered herself in oils and creams, and read movie magazines, while I studied under the bed every night with a flashlight. We had lights-out at ten. Since I was never finished with my heavy load of homework, the dark space under my bed became my study hall, the flashlight undetectable by the housemother, who looked at the cracks under the doors to see if there were lamps lit.

Attending Miss Porter's School did not teach me any social graces that my mother had not already instilled in me, but it reinforced their importance. I did have a rag doll I had jocularly named "Suzy Civility." (Later in life, I could have used a few of those dolls to give as presents.) Most of the other students were from wealthy families, relatively untouched by the depression. They spoke with eastern accents, talking incessantly about their clubs and vacation spots, of the debuts they would make when the war was over, and of the parties in Greenwich and places on Long Island that had always been a part of their lives, as well as those of the generations preceding them. What absolutely amazed me was the number of girls whose parents were divorced. I had never had any experience with that in Omaha, but here it was commonplace. My mother's friends in Omaha warned that I was walking into a den of snobbery where I would be ostracized because of my midwestern roots. I was determined to make my classmates like me. I succeeded, I think; at the end of the school year everyone could sing the song "Omaha, Omaha, greatest place you ever saw." They also learned the Cornhuskers' corny theme song, "There is no place like Nebraska, dear old Nebraska U." Although they knew that Henry Fonda and Fred Astaire came from Omaha, many of the students thought Omaha was the state, and Nebraska the city. This was an era in which people did not travel much domestically; American geography was little studied, and people stayed in their own part of the world.

This New England town was so different from Omaha, I was homesick when I got to school—for about twenty-four hours. I looked at the 220 other smiling and laughing students walking around and reached an important conclusion. If they weren't homesick, why should I be? Of course, each of them had come to school with a friend, or two or three. I had come alone, but the strength of women's friendships in a school like this was immediately, comfortingly apparent. Our classmates were our families. They were who we lived with, not just our social friends. The war bonded us in an incredible way. Our classmates supported us in our down periods and rejoiced with us in our up ones. We played team sports hard, each of us playing either for the "Mink," "Possum," or "Squirrel" teams. The competition was real. I had never seen that before, certainly not at the convent. We didn't have any boys around us "to make us look fragile" or to take the ball away from us and not let us play. Boys had no priority in sports here. No one had any brothers around to argue this point—though we wished we had, of course.

We had prayers every morning at Farmington. The food was terrible, but it was served on nice china; the crystal and silverware were first-class, and the napkins were real. We had a strict honor system, called "Little Meeting," in which student members, not teachers, secretly doled out punishment for infractions of the rules. I didn't feel different from the other students; I was doing well, all by myself, far from my parents. I could feel the self-confidence building within me—a delicious brew of accomplishment for a young woman to savor before she even gets to college. Farmington was very important in my life.

We graduated in demure white dresses in a ceremony in the Congregational Church, attended mostly by mothers, grandparents, and little brothers and sisters. I cried for twenty-four hours to be leaving that beloved school, but seven of my classmates were heading to Vassar with me. We never had a doubt that great things lay ahead.

My young friend from Washington, Jackie Bouvier, would graduate three years later and head for Vassar, too. She would catch up with me—in more ways than one. My favorite Farmington teachers would be hers, too: Miss Watkins in English and Sarah McLennen in history of art. One remembers one's school friends, but particularly the teachers, who are, after all, sculptors working on us like raw clay.

The war moved closer to my family—or rather, my family moved closer to it. For a while we lived in Boston, where Major Malcolm Baldrige assumed command of The Early Warning System of the Eastern Air Defense Command, supervising the large network of volunteers who watched for enemy planes and submarines up and down the coast. Mac left Yale a year early, having received his B.A. degree in 1943 instead of 1944, went to officers' school in Fort Sill, Oklahoma, and was off to the Pacific theater as a second lieutenant forward observer in the artillery. Bob left Yale in his freshman year, became a private in the artillery, and was shipped to England in his eighteenth year to participate in the Normandy invasion, and to receive a battlefield commission of second lieutenant, also as a forward observer in the artillery. Too many of their buddies were not to come home again.

Poor Mother, now alone, moved herself into a two-room apartment in the Shoreham Hotel in Washington. I was away at school, her men were gone, and she went to work with a vengeance for the Red Cross, setting up canteens at Union Station and running volunteer bandage-rolling units. She was once again a wonderful role model. Lonely and worried about her husband and sons, she did her considerable weeping at night, when no one could hear her. During the day she worked like a tiger, proving that her excellent household-managing skills could easily be turned to account in the war effort. She wore a very smart powder blue uniform with epaulettes and a visored hat, bearing the Red Cross emblem. She was at her best cheering up the wounded, most of whom had been flown back from action with limbs missing and were in the wards at the big Walter Reed Hospital. She laughed, flirted with them, held their hands, soothed their brows, read them letters, and even sang to them. The GIs whistled at her when she arrived in the wards. My mother, whistled at! If some of the boys never received any mail from home, she rounded up college girls to write them letters and send them pictures.

I loved school vacations in wartime Washington. No beach sitting in those days. The beaches I had been on in earlier vacations—Long Island and the coast of Maine—were now filled with Coast Guard units and "No Swimming Here" signs. In fact, on the beach of Cape Elizabeth outside Portland where I had sat with some other children in 1941, an excited group of mothers suddenly clustered together. The Coast Guard abruptly appeared and closed the beach, sending us all home—but not before we had witnessed a German submariner's body washed up on our beach, repulsively bloated like a giant jellyfish. The navy had good reason to wonder just how many submarines were prowling nearby.

It was exciting and glamorous in Washington—filled with handsome men of all the services, including officers from other countries. It was a city of nonstop action, everyone wanting to serve, to do something, in some way. There might be no tomorrow, we all felt—so live it up today, at least.

I entered Vassar in 1943. It was the opposite of what I had always dreamed college would be—a carefree place of hallowed halls, wild weekends, dances, boyfriends swarming happily over the campus, and an occasional cracking of the books. The men were at war, and we were expected to do our part. We were accelerating, which meant carrying five or six major subjects at a time.

There were classes all day six days a week, causing us to fight over the same books in the library all day Sunday. We didn't complain. We knew we were getting the world's greatest education, with nothing to distract us. Four years of education were compressed into three, to get us through quickly so we could help our country with the war effort. We received ten days' vacation at Christmas and three weeks off in the summer. It was pulverizing.

We were quarantined on campus during two entire autumns because of the polio scare. There was no gas to enable us to drive off campus, and the trains and buses away from Poughkeepsie were jammed full, often with servicemen. The war was forever on our minds. We were high-spirited, patriotic, and dying to do what we could, but the result was that the accelerated class of '46 had the highest number of mental breakdowns of any class anywhere in that period.

Four of us were jammed into accommodations for two in a house called Josslyn. During this time my roommates consisted of an all-round peppy girl from Philadelphia, Peggy Ritter; Nancy Baxter, who was a math whiz and a terrific sailor from Sioux City and Lake Okiboji, Iowa; a striking blonde from Lancaster, Ohio, named Molly Welles; a tiny blonde from Akron, Martha Firestone (who was later to marry William Clay Ford and thus merge two of the greatest automotive fortunes in the world); and Nancy Millbank, a great-looking brunette from New York, whose father, Jeremiah, was a Republican leader and a famous New York investment banker. Nancy had roomed with Martha ("Stonie") at the Foxcroft boarding school. Stonie's mother, who had gone out with my father many times when both were courting different people after World War I, was a small, very good-looking woman. When she brought Stonie to Vassar, she looked up at me and said, "Good God, to think you could have been my daughter!"

We were a simpatico group; I considered all of them "great women" (we now talked in terms of women, not girls). If the war had not ruled our lives, my roommates would have been away every weekend at men's colleges or in New York, dancing at El Morocco or LaRue. Heaven knows where I would have been!

Many more students had been accepted by Vassar at this time, to provide womanpower for the war effort. Living accommodations were spartan, to put it kindly. We did all the housework in the dorms and slept in double-decker bunks meant for tiny adults. About the only diversion we had was going to "The Pub" on Main and satisfying a throbbing sweet tooth with a "Vassar Devil," which consisted of a brownie topped with vanilla ice cream and fudge sauce. A Devil compensated in a major way for the typical lunch we had just been served: a cup of flour-soaked cream of mushroom soup and a plate of shredded carrots embedded in a slab of Jell-O, atop a few shredded pieces of iceberg lettuce. The Vassar Devils and our frustration accounted for a record-breaking weight gain for our class (one ton in our freshman year alone)..

I served as the class treasurer and then president. It's easy to become president after being treasurer, because you spend your entire time as treasurer tracking down delinquent classmates who have not paid their class dues. You learn everyone's name this way. I had only close to six hundred names to learn.

One of the experiments carried out with wartime Vassar girls was to whip us into military shape by teaching us drill two mornings a week. A second lieutenant and two sergeants arrived on campus one morning to find themselves facing as shaggy and undisciplined a brigade of women as they could ever imagine. This assignment was repugnant to them, and they let us know it. An assignment to the brig would be more palatable than trying to teach Vassar girls how to march—and look sharp about it. The toughest of them all, the sergeant who trained my section, was really disgusted with our sloppy appearance (men's shirts hanging out of our jeans), our casual posture, and our failure to pay attention. The sarge's constant commands to stop talking reminded me of the nuns at the convent a few years back. At the beginning of the training sessions he would spit on the ground and then say sarcastically, "Oh, excuuuse me."

But like many things in life, we suddenly became a great surprise to the lieutenant and the drill sergeants. We started looking sharp. We had rhythm, we kept neat lines, we loved marching in cadence, singing along, and we did better and better. Our sergeant finally confided to us that we "trained up better than his men back on the base." We were getting ready for a big parade—probably in downtown Poughkeepsie, although my group wanted to go to nearby West Point to show them how to drill. Then along came trouble. The second lieutenant ran off one day, eloping with one of the richest, prettiest students in the college. Her parents were not enthused. President MacCracken was livid. That was the end of military drill training.

I had such a trauma over my chosen major field of English. I had come to Vassar because of its English department, which was world famous. I had been an A+ student in English all through school. At Vassar the head of the English department was a brilliant scholar, Miss Lockwood, who in my opinion had a heart the size of a pea. Everything I said or did grated on her. She hated the very idea that I had chosen English as my major subject. She wanted only intellectual majors who wrote lofty tomes that would win literary prizes. I was "commercial," like a magazine. In the middle of my second year, she called me in and fired me from my major subject. She said I talked too much in class discussions, that I was superficial, that I tried too hard to be funny, and that I wasn't. She said she disliked the Midwest, from whence I had come, and she found Catholics unacceptable for their beliefs. She also didn't like overly tall people. She reduced me to a melted stain on the floor of her office.

I went back to Josslyn and cried for three days. My roommates told me I was extremely unappealing crying all the time and to snap out of it. I did. I changed my major to psychology and plunged myself into Rorschach inkblots. One of my teachers, a delightful Greek anthropologist, was kind and understood the trauma I had just been through. She was a radical and as antifamily as I was pro. I would repeat everything she said in class on our exams, and then add at the bottom, "You know, of course, Miss K., that I do not agree with one word of this." She gave me an A every time, because she said I had "spunk, and that deserves an A."

Revenge is sweet. I was later to send Miss Lockwood every one of my published works, hot off the press, first printing. By the time she had received my seventh book, she wrote me a letter saying she was sorry she had dismissed me from her department, but that I was not a good writer. I was, however, "an excellent communicator." I accepted that. I was and still am a "communicator."

At a certain moment I began to chafe at the confinement of a campus we could not leave. I wanted to fight for my country overseas, like the men in my family. The idea was so romantic, I could hardly wait to make it come to fruition. My cousin Barbara Connell had graduated from Vassar and gone overseas with the American Red Cross, as Bawa had done in the last war. I became determined not to sit out the war in Poughkeepsie. Without telling anyone where I was going, I took the train to New York one Saturday, went to the recruitment offices of the OWI (Office of War Information), and filed an application with a blatant lie about my age. I gave my age as twenty-one, the youngest age to be accepted for overseas service, when I was at the time barely eighteen.

I wrote on the employment form that I spoke excellent French and had "other skills." The recruitment officer was impressed by my family military service, if by nothing else, and so he began the first step of processing me and starting the security check to induct me into the agency for service in Europe.

It was proof of my immaturity that I believed I could get away with a lie of this gravity. The OWI personnel officer called me at Vassar and lectured me for fifteen minutes, stating I had perjured myself on a government document, a serious offense, and that this would be a black mark forever on my government record. The officer notified my mother in Washington, and she became hysterical with anger; the word went from the Pentagon to my father at the Aviano air base in Italy, and to Bob, somewhere in France, and to Mac, somewhere on Okinawa. All of them managed to send me angry messages that had to be coated in asbestos before reading. Mac even sent word from the Pacific that I had "over-assessed my qualifications by 300% to be useful to the OWI."

That really hurt. Brothers always know how to put their sisters in place.

My father in the meantime was having his own fascinating experiences. He was now head of the Italian air force, which, considering the size and condition of the planes, was a bit of a contradiction in terms. "These planes are unflyable," he wrote us. "The only thing they have going for them is fuel, library paste, and St. Christopher medals." Colonello Baldrige was bigger than the cockpit of most of the planes in which he flew. On many flights he claimed to have closed his eyes and prayed the entire time while the young Italian pilots gleefully did their daredevil stunts to impress—and scare—him.

General Ira Eaker sent my father to Bulgaria to serve on a military tribunal with the English and the Russians. Their mission was to find and try the Bulgarians who had mistreated or killed downed Allied pilots, and to reward with gold pieces those in the local populace who rescued and helped our pilots escape.

While my father was in Bulgaria, he befriended King Simeon and Queen Mafalda, at this time under house watch by the Russians. Queen Mafalda felt the Soviets were about to move in on them, and in great secrecy, she asked my father to do her a favor—smuggle a box out of the country and back to Rome on one of his monthly trips. She asked him to take this box to her brother, King Umberto, at the Quirinale Palace, which my father innocently agreed to do. The Soviet guards tried to inspect the package at the Sofia airport when he was about to board his air force plane for Rome, but he became so enraged that he frightened the Russian soldiers with his threats, so they backed off and let him go.

He delivered the wrapped parcel to His Majesty personally at the Quirinale. Umberto immediately knew what it was, and with tears in his eyes, he opened the contents to show my dazzled father the crown jewels of Italy, which Mafalda had taken from Rome years earlier to keep safe from the Nazis. The king left my father alone in the *gran salone* while he went for an appropriate gift to thank my father for his dangerous and brave act. The *colonello* began to picture my mother in the sapphire-and-diamond necklace, or maybe one of the emerald rings he would take home to her. With great fanfare, the king appeared with a handsomely wrapped box. It *had* to be a necklace, my father decided, from the shape of it. Alas, no. It contained a signed photograph of King Umberto, in full dress uniform, in a handsomely gold-tooled dark blue leather frame.

The joy that erupted in our country—in the world—when the Japanese surrendered was incalculable. Vassar was in session on that August date. We wept, laughed, and wept some more, along with the whole nation. The men were coming home again. The famous *Life* photo of the sailor kissing the girl in Times Square was posted everywhere on campus. My mother purchased three new nightgowns, now that her Mac was coming home. I would imagine the lingerie departments of all stores were enjoying a great business. My brothers had never intended to wear their uniforms again, but Mother forced them to do so for a photograph with their father in uniform. They were in top shape and incredibly good-looking. Bob was the first to be married—to Nancy Bierwirth of Cedarhurst, Long Island, and a graduate of Bryn Mawr, whose brother Jack had been a friend of Bob's at Yale. Later Mac was to marry Midge Murray of Pittsburgh, a lovely Smith graduate redhead, also the daughter of friends of my parents. That was how it was done in those days; people married within their social circle. In those days, as well, the Catholic bishop in charge of the area could make things very tough for interfaith marriages. He did so in the case of Mac and Midge. The Murrays were Protestants, and the Catholic bishop caused incredible animosity by placing restrictions on the ceremony—forcing them to be married in a tiny side chapel, for example, rather than the main church, when there were hundreds of guests in attendance. It was the beginning of a great marriage, but also the end of Mac's Catholic faith. The word *ecumenical* was practically unknown in those days. Thank heavens that is no longer true.

There was not enough room for the returned servicemen in men's colleges during our last Vassar year, so each one of the women's colleges took a share of the GIs who had no other place to study. The GI Bill of Rights would pay for their tuition. We were not very nice to them. If we had still been at war, we would have treated them like national treasures, but as it was, we felt they were invading our privacy; now we had to at least think about how we looked and what we were wearing, with men around. They lived off campus, so we saw them only in class, and then we mostly ignored them.

Then it happened—graduation. Free at last! Free from the terrible pressure of acceleration. I was nineteen years old. Europe was still smoking from the gunpowder of war, the Baldrige men were home, and many of my classmates had made plans to go right from Poughkeepsie to New York City to find their wedding dresses. I had other plans.

My close classmates and I realized that now that we, not our parents, were going to be in control of our lives, we could resolve not to allow these friendships to lapse. The Washington group of friends would last forever— Lucy Galpin Moorhead, Janet Grayson Whitehouse, Emily Malino Scheuer, Nancy Gray Pyne, Kay Winton Evans, plus other stalwarts from elsewhere— Nancy Bush Ellis, Mary Matthiessen Wheelwright, Anne Curtis Fredericks. No group of male alumni would remain more in touch through a half-century of time than our group.

At a cocktail party in the garden outside Main the evening before graduation, my parents mingled with my friends' parents. It was like a lovely English garden party. We even wore nice dresses, something we had never needed at college in wartime. Our hair was washed, and we wore makeup. It was the beginning of a new life. When Mother said hopefully, "Well, now I suppose you're going to throw out all those awful blue jeans," I replied yes without hesitation. Jeans could never be part of my future lifestyle, particularly considering the way I looked in them.

During the party I noticed Edward (Ned) Curtis, a distinguished Bronxville lawyer and friend of my father's, leading my father purposefully away from my mother. At this, his daughter Anne and I winked at one another. We moved closer in their direction so we could overhear them. This was the moment when Ned Curtis was supposed to convince Mac Baldrige that their two daughters should, in two months' time, go abroad to the University of Geneva for graduate school. This was the moment Anne and I had been planning since the beginning of the January semester. Jean Baldrige should be nowhere near this conversation, or she would put the whole idea in the city dump within five minutes.

"Mac," Ned Curtis said, "I know that Tish has been lobbying you, just as Anne has me, to let them go to Geneva this fall. Her mother and I have given the matter of Anne's becoming a foreign exchange student a lot of serious thought. We know about the dangers of postwar Europe, but we also know this is the greatest moment to let her experience it. There are no tourist visas being issued yet, no Americans going abroad who are not on military assignment or a foreign exchange student. She will be in a unique position to see, hear, study, and learn."

My father had to interrupt. "Ned, I'm sorry, but there's no possibility we would let Tish do such a thing. She's so young, so inexperienced—"

It was Ned Curtis's turn to break in. "It will be a great feather in any young scholar's cap. Very few Americans are over there, and remember, the cost of supporting a graduate student in Switzerland is three times less than if she were studying at a New York university. But think what the girls will learn!"

"Ned, we can't possibly let her go."

"Do you realize she's now a grown young woman? A college graduate? We've given Anne the best education anyone could have. We have no right to keep her as a little girl by our side anymore. We've raised her with good values and to have common sense. We've taken into account the fact that she is a levelheaded, serious-minded young woman who has always made us proud of her decisions."

I could hear the defensiveness rising in my father's voice. "Well, we're proud of Tish, too. I mean, she's able to take care of herself anywhere, anytime."

"I feel Anne has a great deal of maturity, Mac. Do you feel the same way about Tish?"

Malcolm Baldrige rose to his full height, like the proud, recently discharged air force colonel that he was. He relit his pipe and said, "Where are all the papers, Ned, about visas, applications, transportation costs, tuition, and everything?"

Anne and I winked at one another again. It was a done deal.

And so, good-bye Vassar and on to the University of Geneva. We were a motley group of students jammed into impossibly small quarters on the SS *Washington*, an unreconverted army troopship. There were eight bunks piled high in each stateroom meant for two. The portholes were locked, and the air was fragrant with the last load of unwashed GIs the ship had carried home from France. We were all young and eager. We would survive the constant storms on this September crossing. The food was meager and bad-tasting, but that didn't matter because many people never made it to the dining room anyway, there was so much seasickness. I wrote a note to my grandmother, Bawa, that I had followed her advice and had drunk Fernet Branca every day in the bar. It was the foulest-tasting Italian liqueur I had ever tasted, but it was medicinal salvation for seasickness.

There was a bunch of boys from Harvard on board, bound for English universities as "Henry fellows." We flirted in between trips to the wet main deck above, seeking some air relief from the storms and sickness. Their presence was to result in delightful reunions later at their universities as well as at some barely reopened ski resorts in Switzerland.

We disembarked at Cherbourg, France, a whole day late. I was now on my own, with a footlocker, a large suitcase, my polo coat, my handbag, and no porters or friends to help. General Lewis's driver, who was supposed to meet me, did not—I was unable to warn the Lewises when I was arriving or at what station, having lost their telephone number. It was two o'clock in the morning. I had not eaten since six o'clock the morning before. It was either expire or move ahead.

I hauled the trunk and baggage behind me in the darkened streets and ended up crying "Au secours! Au secours!" in the only place where a light-bulb pierced the darkness. It was a bar full of Algerians, mostly men. They were astounded to see this young woman burst into their midst wearing weird preppy American clothing and shouting "Help!" in French. Chivalry was not dead. They were kind. Five of them came forward at once to help me. They fed me, gave me a stiff drink, and walked me through the dark streets to the Hôtel Louvois, which was completely shuttered for the night. We woke up the concierge; he opened the big door, rubbing his eyes, and put me in a room. I will never be able to express my gratitude to those Algerians. They literally saved my life.

I stayed with the Lewises for two magical nights in Paris on my way to Geneva, staying awake the first night by standing on the balcony off my room, watching the rooftops bathed in shimmering, silvery moonlight and making a promise to myself to return to live in this city. General and Mrs. Alfred Gruenther, General and Mrs. Eisenhower's closest friends, took me out to Supreme Headquarters Allied Powers Europe (SHAPE) in a suburb of Paris for dinner. I found myself eating a blissful real American steak (from the commissary), sitting at the table not in the Gruenthers' home but in the Eisenhowers', and then kibitzing their bridge game after dinner for two and a half hours. General Eisenhower! If only my father and brothers were here. I felt as though I was in St. Peter's with the pope, although this man was only possibly the future president of the United States.

General Eisenhower was a very serious bridge player. He told me I could watch his hand and study how he played the cards, provided I did not make one sound. It was not like a Vassar game. It was like planning an invasion, and there was no way I was going to disobey the general's orders. Even my breathing went into a quieter mode.

I finally arrived in Geneva in a dilapidated taxi in the fifteenth-century place du Bourg de Four just as the bells of the ancient Cathedral of St. Pierre tolled nearby. There in the Pension de Crue among the foreign students were Vassar friends Peg Ritter and Anne Curtis, as well as Mary Jane Brock, Ensign Carolyn Clothier, and Pat Carnal.

It was a true potpourri of international students. We spoke French at the table and in classes, and we had rabbit every night for dinner. I felt excited to be in a new place, experiencing a new culture, but I chafed at the way the de

Crues showed their anti-Americanism so flagrantly in conversation. The Swiss were very defensive over having been neutral during the war. I had barely settled in at the pension when the situation became unbearable. No longer able to hold my tongue one night, I praised the American soldiers in face of the de Crues' snide remarks. To my surprise, the mild-mannered, boring monsieur erupted in a total rage and told me to leave the pension—now. It was nine o'clock, and he announced I had exactly until midnight to get out, baggage included, and make other arrangements for myself.

At midnight I was out, sitting on my footlocker by the Bourg de Four fountain. Everyone was in a state of shock. After a night's sleep in a hotel, and assisted by Mary Jane, I found a new pension that was far preferable to the de Crues'. I still clung to the philosophy that everything happens for the best. There was a young, very handsome German among the *pensionnaires,* named Wilfrid. He had escaped from an American prisoner-of-war train the year before as it was traveling to France. He jumped from the train as it passed through a Swiss tunnel, and because of Swiss neutrality, he was welcomed as a student at the University of Geneva. In conversation we discovered he had fought at the Remagen Bridge in Germany in 1944, in one of the bloodiest battles of the war, against my brother's Thirty-fourth Field Artillery Battalion. When I wrote my brother a letter, a kind of "Imagine this—isn't this an amazing coincidence?" my brother fired back a fiercely angry missive, describing how many in his battalion had been lost to the enemy, close friends all; what was I doing consorting with the Germans on such a palsy-walsy basis? Of course, in the mail the next day came a totally different kind of letter. Bob apologized and said of course we must forget the wounds of war and move on, and he even sent his regards to Wilfrid. Brother Bob was growing up, but that helped me, too.

Life in Geneva catapulted us along happily at top speed, although a few things did take getting used to—no heat that winter, four layers of clothing worn at a time. One bath a month was all that was allowed, and a very shallow one at that, in an unheated, bitter cold bathroom. The sheets were so icy we had to slide a series of hot water bottles up and down inside them before we could get into bed at night. How I longed to be married, and to have a husband instead of hot water bottles to keep me warm at night.

The university gave us a long winter break because the administration could not afford to heat the buildings over the holidays, and kept us in classes until mid-July to make up for it. Our Harvard and Princeton friends came over from their Cambridge and Oxford universities to join us for the holidays. We stayed in the best hotels in St. Moritz, Gstaad, and Davos; since there were no vacationers, we were given the maids' rooms for a pittance. We had sumptuous meals free in the big dining room, because management wanted some bodies around. We were young, spirited, and, well, at least cleanly dressed, a harbinger of things to come—actual paying customers. We also gave some practice to the rusty wait staff. Occasionally we would be joined in the dining salon by some legitimate paying customers, like Prince Aly Khan and his entourage.

And then, of course, there was my memorable leg-break incident skiing in Gstaad, at the very end of our Christmas vacation. I was skiing foolishly alone, at eight in the morning on our last day. It had rained the night before and frozen over, the lifts were not operating, no one was out and about, but I had to have a last run before returning to Geneva. As usual, if there wasn't a guardian angel watching over me, there was a pretty good substitute—in this case, a German shepherd. A farmer's dog, he herded sheep and had not been trained in any ski rescue work. But he saw me, high on the slope, helpless, almost unconscious and half-frozen. He climbed the slope, grabbed one of my ski poles by the leather handle, and dragged it the rest of the way down the Wassengrad slope and into the one hotel kitchen door he could find ajar. The cooks realized he had brought a sign of trouble; they called the ski patrol, and saved me just in time. I also lived to tell the tale of having my leg set by a Swiss-German orthopedist, then rebroken with disdain by a Swiss-French orthopedist, who then had to reset it—all without a sniff of anesthesia. Talk about rivalry between the French- and German-speaking parts of the country! Talk about Letitia's bravery!

During those fourteen months of study, I became fluent in French, picked up some valuable education in psychology at the Institut Jean Jacques Rousseau, where I attended most of my classes, attended symphony concerts conducted by the legendary conductor Ensermet, ate quantities of Swiss fondue in restaurants where we were always the guests of rich families, learned how to pour any liqueur over canned American fruit to make it taste like ambrosia, read Swiss history while gazing at the blue water from a terrace overlooking Lake Geneva, played tennis in the suburb of Champel on the court next to that of the exiled queen of Romania, and finally learned how to defend the policies of the United States without blowing up whenever my country was attacked. On spring break, four of us went to Italy on a fake visa, representing "The Italo-American Students Friendship Society," and had many lucky adventures. In the Pitti Palace museum, closed during the war, we were given a special private tour and ran into a glamorously dressed couple, also being given a tour. It was Vivien Leigh and Laurence Olivier. She was still as beautiful as she was as Scarlett O'Hara in *Gone With the Wind*, and he looked like a Shakespearean version of a Greek god. Greatly amused by seeing such worshipful young student fans, the Oliviers took us to dinner that night in a Florentine bistro. They also invited us to visit them on producer J. Arthur Rank's sets of their respective movies the following summer, when we would be in London.

When I developed the flu and had a temperature of 103 degrees, my friends walked me through the streets of Florence to a building that had an American Red Cross flag flying in front of it. There was no medicine in Italy in that postwar period, just aspirin, but when the military clinic tried to turn us away, I told them my father had been decorated in this war as well as the most recent one—how could they reject me? Luck and brashness worked again. The major in command gave me a strong shot of precious penicillin, which literally saved my life. We shortly learned that the reason the clinic was so uncomfortable having four girls in polo coats sitting there with all the GIs waiting to see the doctor was that it was a venereal disease clinic.

At Monte Carlo we stayed in the Palace Hotel, gambled in the Casino, and managed to pay our hotel bill with the winnings from betting a red at the roulette table. There we meet a Greek man named Aristotle Onassis. We had an hour-long cruise on his yacht, again because we amused everyone with our presences, our naïveté, and our enthusiasm. I decided Onassis was the homeliest man I had ever seen, but also one of the most charming. Then I chatted with a redhead from Kansas named Pat Wymore, who was about to marry on board another yacht. The owner and her future husband was Errol Flynn, and in a gesture of great midwestern friendliness, she invited me to the wedding. By now I was in danger of becoming blasé, after all these escapades with famous people, but that never really happened.

The following summer, when classes were over at the University of Geneva, I visited Ambassador and Mrs. Lewis Douglas and their daughter Sharman in London at the embassy residence, 14 Princes Gate. The famous annual presentation of the debutantes at court had been suspended, obviously, during the war, but now in 1947 the king and queen decided it was time to take it up again. They decided to hold it in the garden of Buckingham Palace because there were so many debutantes to present. Sharman Douglas was invited to be one of them, and the Douglases very kindly used their diplomatic pull to have "Mac and Jean's daughter" presented, too. I had a flowered silk calf-length dress made, bought a big hat with flowers on the brim, put on white suede gloves, and was off to the palace along with Sharman. As usual, I made my mark at the proceedings by turning abruptly around in the crowd at one point, upending the man coming up behind me. It was Sir Winston Churchill. His aides scrambled quickly to get him upright again and brush him off, and he looked me straight in the eye. "Young lady, you should really learn not to do that," he said, and I lowered myself mentally down under the grassy lawn surface, joining the worms that lay beneath. The only thing that saved me that night was realizing that if one has to make a major gaffe, one might as well do it in a historic, grand place like Buckingham Palace rather than on Farnam Street in Omaha.

After fourteen months, it was time for me to go home to America. I was twenty-one years old, and the carefree, frivolous part of my life was over. I wanted to get a job and get my hand out of my long-suffering-father's wallet. I threw myself excitedly into the task of earning my own living and becoming a part of that exotic world called "business."

Employée à Paris

$\mathcal{M}$aybe I had a touch of a superiority complex when I returned from Europe, speaking fluent French and with most of a graduate degree under my belt. I felt so eminently qualified for a job, I couldn't stop smiling a know-it-all Mona Lisa smile. My female friends were either pregnant or already busily pushing buggies in the park. They thought I was a little weird; I thought they were a little pedestrian. As one of the few Vassar graduates in the working world at the time, I knew I would be snapped up quickly by any company with international connections.

What a dreamer!

I tried to apply at every logical bank, travel company, and Franco-American business firm, but they wouldn't even let me fill out an application. I looked around at all the young men being recruited with speed, without language skills or any experience abroad, except perhaps at an American military base. My problem was not that I wasn't qualified—it was that I was female. The patronizing attitude was obnoxious: "Stay home, young lady, get married, have babies, and do what you're supposed to do."

Frustrated, I decided to refocus my energy and pursue a career in retail. I remembered all my nap times in my room as a little girl, when I pretended to buy and sell the contents of my bureau drawers. I also remembered my success at selling sportswear in the College Shop at the Brandeis store during one of my summer vacations. My new goal was to become the president of Saks Fifth Avenue or Bergdorf Goodman, a job requiring obligatory visits to Paris two or three times a year for the collections. The pathway to this goal in the 1940s was obvious: a place on Macy's training squad, the world-famous executive training course for retailers. Many of the most famous people in fashion—store presidents, designers, and magazine editors—were graduates, inevitably assured of a fast-track job with any retailing company they chose. I was jubilant over being accepted on the training squad, but I lost my place on it by breaking another leg skiing the weekend before the job was to begin. When I begged the head of the squad to let me join the next training session, three months hence, he angrily replied that people "fortunate enough to earn a place on this squad do not go skiing the weekend before and mess up the way you did." He showed me no mercy. It was good-bye to Macy's—forever.

I no longer had any doubt that I would only meet disappointment in my career plans in the United States. I had to get back to Europe. Memories of Bawa's colored postcards from Paris kept breaking into my thought patterns. I decided that finding a job in Paris, living there, eating, breathing, and sleeping its culture, was the only way I would find happiness.

I quickly realized that the U.S. Foreign Service was probably the only way to do it. The French were unable to provide jobs even for their own citizens after the war, much less for me. A job at our embassy in France was a nice, neat solution, but there was the usual problem: only men were being hired by the Foreign Service and sent over. I was told I was unqualified because I couldn't type, take dictation, or even file. Then, too, I would never be able to select my foreign post. Everyone wanted Paris. Before landing a plum like that, I would have to sweat it out in a mosquito-infested Third World country where the water needed to be boiled three times before drinking it. After the Macy's debacle, it was not pleasant being rejected so often by the State Department. I decided I could win anyway, with determination my only weapon. They would get tired of seeing my face regularly in the Foreign Service personnel section, like that of a pushy, irritating mendicant, but I would get the job.

Still on crutches from my skiing accident, I enrolled with a bunch of high school seniors at the Temple Secretarial School in Washington to acquire the secretarial skills I was told I lacked. It was a humbling experience at best. I hated it so much that I finished the year's course in eight weeks by taking private lessons. I learned to take dictation on a funny little Stenotype machine with keys and a rolling tape that printed out what looked like Egyptian hieroglyphics. Nothing can accelerate the learning of secretarial skills faster than being immobile. Because my broken leg kept me confined at home except for the daily trip to the secretarial school, I had no diversions, and in no time I was typing an impressive 100 words a minute.

As in many other times in my life, an initial negative response proved to be just what I needed to become motivated. Now I was the only bilingual American citizen–college graduate–stenographer with foreign experience trying to get a job in France at that time; they had no other choice but to test me and, when I passed, accept me.

My father was delighted, and my brothers thought I was nuts, but my mother was tearfully distraught to be losing me so quickly again when I had just returned from Europe. I heard her telling my uncle Jim over the telephone that I would probably come home the next time with a French Communist husband or, even worse, a Latin lover. Out came the rosary beads from her bedside table drawer as she began reciting novenas once again for her nonconformist daughter.

It was now September of 1948, and as a member of the Foreign Service with a U.S. diplomatic passport in hand, I was booked first class on one of the proud steamships of the U.S. Lines. It was a luxurious trip, a far cry from the army troopship that had taken us to Europe to graduate school.

The Paris of 1948 had certainly improved in creature comforts since the Paris of 1946, although some of the same difficulties endured. Gasoline was at a premium, but with my embassy job, I could have all I wanted, thanks to the military supply. Good food ingredients were still hard to get, but the French could make a magnificent meal out of very little. A little *fromage,* a *baguette de pain,* a bowl of hot, nourishing soup, a couple of slivers of *jambon,* and a superb supper was at hand. With each passing year since the end of the war, the food, one of France's greatest attributes, was getting better and better. Liquor was still incredibly hard to come by in 1948, but good wine was not, and our PX supplied me with the best of all liquor brands at absurdly low prices, and no tax, of course.

Electricity was still as expensive as caviar, but much less reliable. It went on and off like a moth hovering around a candle, and we had to learn how to deal with it. If you were on a date at night, it was terribly romantic being plunged into darkness. If you were trying to do a mundane chore, it was exasperating. We also learned to endure the daily *coupure d'électricité* from noon to three, when you had to do without any electricity and therefore avoided making any appointments requiring an elevator, on the upper floors of tall buildings. This was a whole new, independent world for me, a grown-up one. I felt so lucky. If I hadn't broken my leg in Stowe, I would probably have been in Macy's on Times Square right now, learning about mark-downs on holiday merchandise.

I was assigned temporarily to a former Office of Strategic Services (OSS) official, W. Lane Rehm, in the Economic Cooperation Administration (ECA) offices until a permanent position was found for me. The ECA building was the headquarters of the country mission for the Marshall Plan, right next to the embassy on the avenue Gabriel. Mr. Rehm was terribly old (about fifty-five), and he wore wonderful thick tweed suits, having been prepared for French winters, and always a natty bow tie that mesmerized the French. He was delightful, had a haircut like Napoleon's, and had been formerly married to Janet Flanner, the famous *New Yorker* magazine writer who was a prominent part of Ernest Hemingway's Lost Generation. Since my friends and I now felt we were part of the "New Lost Generation," she was a real celebrity to me.

My ECA job meant assisting Lane Rehm as his executive assistant, and also doing PR jobs for the mission with the local press. I had to start working twelve-hour days immediately, so I rushed to find myself an embassy-recommended rented bedroom suite. I found two large, shabby, but grandly furnished bedrooms with a bath on the avenue de Villiers in the home of Madame Meunier, one of the remaining survivors of a well-known family in the chocolate business. Madame and her husband were typical of the bourgeoisie who had come upon hard times and were forced to make money any way they could. A close Swedish friend of mine from the University of Geneva days, Gunilla ("Ian") Turitz, took the other bedroom, and we closed the deal. Madame Meunier obviously disapproved of us, but we were able to laugh about it. We knew that the money we gave her outweighed her hatred of brash, heathen foreign girls.

The winter of 1948–49 was another brutal one in France without heat, so we froze in Beaux Arts splendor. Faded red damask covered the walls, complemented by shabby oriental rugs and giant gilt mirrors. The bathroom had a thirty-watt lightbulb, so we put on our makeup at night by flashlight, and by daylight held a hand mirror at the window. (It is not recommended to apply eyeshadow by flashlight.) We had already survived one of the coldest winters ever experienced in Europe during our year in Geneva, so we acclimated ourselves to this hardship in Paris without complaint, equipped with hot water bottles.

Ian and I sometimes went to dinner in our neighborhood *bistro de chauffeur* (as these unpretentious little restaurants with great food and low prices were affectionately called). For five dollars, including tip, we would have a *bifteck,* crisp french fries, a salad of endives and arugula, a half liter of red wine, and a freshly baked fruit tart. After everyone had finished eating and only a few diners were left, the owners, traditionally a married couple, would come out of the kitchen, remove their aprons, and talk politics with whoever was around. Good Communists that they were at our bistro, they particularly enjoyed arguing with me. They knew "la grande américaine était une diplomate." It was all in good fun because I knew how to defend myself. I would stop by the U.S. Information Service (USIS) in the embassy on a *bistro de chauffeur* evening and arm myself with American government position papers on certain hot topics of the day. Every time anyone in the restaurant made an anti-American government remark (it was never against me personally, just my country), I would whip out some material in the USIS press releases and impress them with facts and written truths. "You have a lot of gall doing that, Letitia," I remember a USIS officer telling me. "The French don't like being corrected, or even worse, lectured to." I felt like a one-woman propaganda warrior for my country. I had a mission.

Transportation to my new job was a problem that needed solving. I couldn't get to the embassy quickly at rush hour (each Metro train and bus was filled over capacity), so I purchased my own little Peugeot 203 ("Le Deux Cent Trois," as it was called). I christened it Titine, "my sweet little one." My first drive to the embassy from the Meuniers' was a historic one. Frightened by the dangerously fast motorists circling the Arc de Triomphe on the place de l'Étoile in the morning rush hour, I sat and studied the traffic pattern for several minutes before venturing forth from a side street. I knew this giant circle was famous for its accidents that killed and maimed, but I was resolved to be strong and prevail, even if there had been no driving situation in Omaha, Nebraska, to prepare me for this! I ventured forth in a panic, shouting "Vive la France!" out the open window to give me (and the neighboring drivers) courage, and drove straight to the center of the circle, where I was trapped, going around and around for fifteen long minutes. As I kept circling, waiting for someone on the right to let me in, an incident of Gallic chivalry occurred. A gendarme on the Champs-Élysées corner where I was ultimately headed had been watching me—and my diplomatic license plates—from the beginning of this scene. He simply walked out into that tremendous rush-hour traffic in the circle and stopped it—cold. There was a mad screeching of brakes, but the drivers couldn't curse at him. He was the law. He adjusted his cape on one shoulder, defiantly held up his white baton, and gallantly motioned me to cut a path right through the immobile traffic to the Champs-Élysées. This magnificent boulevard was already a place of great emotion to me—bringing back memories of the stirring parade of French and American GIs marching down it at the conclusion of the war with the Nazis. I opened my window and shouted my gratitude to the policeman, who bowed and shouted back, "Only this time, Mademoiselle, not again."

Whenever I recounted that story, both my American and French friends remarked that this gendarme must have served with the Allied forces and wanted to repay the Americans in some small way. Otherwise, I might still be circling the Arc de Triomphe to this day.

* * *

Slowly but surely, I found myself immersed in the social circles of Paris. I made friends in the embassy, and French friends, too, who were very welcoming and invited me to meals in their homes. I was asked to dinner and dancing among the glamorously dressed at Monseigneur by some rich Frenchmen in their thirties; I was invited to dinner at humble bistros and long nights of conversation by "economically challenged" Frenchmen in their twenties. The French seemed amused to have a young American diplomat around. I was a curiosity to them. They were just as much a curiosity to me.

In due course my roommate left Paris to be married, and I rented an apartment on the rue de l'Assomption off the busy place de la Muette, in the Sixteenth Arrondissement. It was a cozy apartment, with four original good-size paintings by Maurice de Vlaminck hanging on the walls. As I had briefly studied the artist in a Vassar history of art class, I encouraged friends who came for cocktails to be careful not to bump into the canvases when they were standing near them with drinks in their hands.

The owner of the apartment was a woman who was always glimpsed through a heavy veil of Gauloise cigarette smoke issuing from the holder eternally clenched in her teeth. She had divorced one of the Vlamincks, and in the settlement she received several of the Impressionist works. In a moment of financial need, she offered me one of the paintings right off the wall of this apartment for a negotiable thousand dollars in cash. At this point in my life, a thousand dollars and a million dollars were identical—out of my reach. I stupidly turned down her offer instead of borrowing the money, and years later, when I told my friends at Christie's and Sotheby's auction houses about it, they could only conclude that I was one of the dumbest young girls who had ever gone to Paris.

A few months after I began my job in Paris, David Bruce, the head of the Economic Cooperation Administration Mission to France, was chosen to move up to the position of ambassador to France. We all rejoiced at the news. He was an aristocratic type, the epitome of a polished diplomat, and was eminently qualified. His French was fluent, even if he seemed to be speaking through a stuffed-up nose. He had been a hero in the war and was an enthusiastic student of European history, a true Renaissance man in his interests. In those days France was number one in international importance to the United States, and Great Britain number two.

An OSS colonel during the war, Bruce had headed up the Western European operations in London. His work was top secret, involving parachuting men behind the lines into France, Italy, Germany, Austria, Albania, Greece, and Yugoslavia. The OSS covert agents undertook their perilous work in great secrecy and properly earned their nickname of "the glamour boys" of World War II. Their lives were exciting and mysterious, except for when they did not return.

In 1948 General Marshall made his famous Marshall Plan announcement before Congress, calling for America to undertake a historic economic recovery program for Western Europe, the purpose of which was to save that part of the world from falling into the hands of the Soviets. Ambassador Averell Harriman immediately went to Paris to open the Office of the Special Representative to head up all European operations of the Marshall Plan, in a historic building called the Hotel Talleyrand. David Bruce, with the diplomatic rank of U.S. minister, took over the ECA, with offices in a dingy building at 4, avenue Gabriel, next door to the American Embassy building. Within a very few months, President Truman promoted him to ambassador to France, succeeding Jefferson Caffery. I knew Mr. Caffery because his wife, Gertrude, had gone to the Convent of the Sacred Heart with my mother in Omaha. One night I found myself at a large party given by the Cafferys for the Bruces. Ambassador Bruce had also met my father in Washington in days past, through personal friends, and they had lunched a couple of times. Through these connections and my usual good luck, I landed the coveted job of working for Ambassador Bruce and his wife, Evangeline. When I asked Lane Rehm just how I got this fabulous job handed to me, he said, "Because they watched you in action at Jefferson Caffery's large reception the other day and saw that you knew your way around. I told them you'd be easy to find in a crowd because you're so tall. Vangie Bruce said she wanted someone cheerful who spoke good French. I told them you knew the difference between red and black caviar, and between a patriot and a spy."

Brother Bob wrote me a congratulatory note: "It's good to see that all the time I spent teaching you how to use a knife and fork properly has paid off." My father wrote that I should work twice as hard as someone who had not met the Bruces through family connections, because they would demand much more of me. "Don't think of them as personal friends. You are their junior assistant. You will be twice as easy to fire because of incompetence than anyone else." Wow! A little reality check there.

At our last conversation before I actually started working at the embassy, I professed a certain amount of nervousness to the ambassador himself. "There are so many things I need to learn, that I don't know about, that I need to know about."

"Forget about that," he said reassuringly. "There isn't anything about this business that my wife doesn't know. Just ask her."

He was right. There wasn't anything Evangeline Bell Bruce did not know about in the field of diplomatic service, entertaining, and protocol. I should have hung a permanent tape recorder around her neck to catch all of her pronouncements. Everyone asked her questions, including the *chef du protocol* of de Gaulle's government. She was a tall, beautiful, long-legged, chestnut-haired size 6. She was also very young, and had married David Bruce, eighteen years her senior, when she was his secretary in OSS. He had been previously married to Ailsa Bruce, sister of Paul Mellon, scion of one of the great fortunes in America. An amiable divorce from Ailsa followed his love affair with Evangeline; then came their simple wedding. It was one of the most talked-about romantic pairings of all in a city under a Luftwaffe bombing siege. The reception was attended by the top British and American diplomatic and military brass in London. The wedding cake was flourless, and almost sugarless, but at least a quantity of good French champagne was on hand. It had been stolen by the Germans in France, and then restolen from the Germans by the GIs.

Multilingual, Evangeline Bruce had been born and raised in the diplomatic service herself. Her father, Edward Bell, was a diplomat, and the family had lived abroad most of their lives. What luck to have her as my teacher and mentor in the high-powered profession into which I had suddenly plunged! Life was beginning to be a far cry from Thirty-ninth Street in Omaha, Nebraska. Working for the Bruces at the avenue d'Iéna embassy residence was from the start never-endingly amusing, hair-raising, and charming.

Two children had been born to the Bruces before he became ambassador—five-year-old Sasha and three-year-old David. (Alexander, alias "Nick," was to come along later, in 1951.) Their domain was the nursery on the top floor, managed firmly by Nannie (Winifred Sawyer). The house was always filled with action, noise, and an air of excitement. Embassy officers and diplomats from the Ministère des Affaires Étrangères would be coming and going at all hours. Wives of ambassadors would be paying formal diplomatic calls on Mrs. Bruce, and lunches, dinners, cocktail receptions, and teas were in constant planning stages. The chef and his kitchen staff were very much in evidence when entertaining was in progress, as was the all-important, imperious butler and his young footmen waitstaff, who believed, perhaps rightfully, that they were the most important elements in the tableau. The woman in charge of pressing the linens would be trying out the cloths and place mats for size; the gardener would be everywhere at once, removing dead flowers and putting new ones in their place, adding some greenery here and some water there. There was, at least eight hours a day, someone polishing silver in the main salon and the dining room.

Odette de Wavrin, the housekeeper, was always in evidence. A wellborn Frenchwoman with a superb sense of humor, she knew all the scandal in town and loved to discuss it. She was also completely professional in her duties—which included buying the food and supplies, keeping the gardeners in check, overseeing the chef's expenses, waging a perpetual war with the butler over who was cheating on the accounts, and keeping the liquor locked up as though it were the crown jewels. Odette's well-secured liquor closet was our Tower of London. Not even David Bruce was able to get a bottle of special wine from it if Odette and her giant keychain were not around.

Adding to the general din was the sound of three adorable floppy-eared, black-and-white English springer spaniels, who raced up and down the stairway, always together, as though on an Olympic relay team. When they moved from one floor to the other, the entire neighborhood probably heard the sound of their pounding paws. The children, always running themselves, laughing and chasing the dogs, added another level to the noise. This was not a calm household but an orchestra of sounds, and it made a warm, melodious kind of music. Nevertheless, when an important occasion demanded an atmosphere of formality, it was always there. Evangeline Bruce saw to that.

The avenue d'Iéna residence was an imposing mansion near the Palais de Chaillot, with tall French doors leading into a lovely garden off the grand salon, perfect for summer receptions. My office on the first floor of the residence was unique, if you stopped to think about it—and I often did. It was really a formal room, right inside the front door, to the left, so that I did not miss anyone coming or going. Marie Antoinette never had it better. No government-issue gray or gray-green metal furnishings in evidence here, but warm oak-paneled walls, a carpet of deep velvety green, and a deep sofa and chairs upholstered in French damask or velvet in cream or green shades. My desk was a large inlaid Louis XV rosewood antique with intricate ormolu mounts and pulls on the drawers. I wondered which member of King Louis's court at Versailles had used this desk before me. My desk lamp was an eighteenth-century bouillotte with a black tole shade. My pens and pencils resided in an exquisite porcelain mug from the Sèvres factory—I like to think from the same place where Marie Antoinette got hers. A table flanking my desk on one side held my Royal manual typewriter, and my Stenotype machine sat on another much smaller table to the right. They were definitely not of the Louis XV era, but they brought reality into this extraordinary office.

It was nerve-racking to stay on top of the perpetually ringing phones. So many people who had been turned down at the Chancery tried to reach the Bruces through me at the residence. Knowing when to interrupt an impromptu conference and when to keep the grand salon doors closed no matter what became an art. The Cold War was always with us now. Prague had fallen to the Nazis in 1938. The Berlin Airlift commenced, bringing food and supplies into a beleaguered city. It was a tense, scary time. Senior aides would appear at the residence, ignore my command of "Please do not enter that room," push me aside, and usher themselves into the ambassador's closed meeting in the living room across from my office. At times they were ushered right back out again, cheeks flushed with embarrassment, having thought themselves more important than they were.

At times there would be a conference going on late into the night, and I would be called in with my Stenotype machine to take down an urgent top secret cable for SECSTATE (secretary of state). The secretaries down at the embassy would have all gone home for the night. The ambassador would say, "Tish, remember, this is highly confidential." I did not have to be told this. A Marine guard would take the dictated and typed cable from my hands and rush it down to the Code Room, where clerks with special security clearances were on all-night duty, and where it could be processed and sent to Washington.

Ambassadors in those days were in a position of power and enormous responsibility in transacting confidential, emergency measures with their foreign counterparts. They were like a wartime cabinet. (The time would come later, of course, when the age of instant information and computers would make an ambassador's job almost obsolete, except for formal symbolic functions and public relations on behalf of his country to the host country.)

The typewriter became my alter ego. I had to learn with haste the stiff, standardized way of writing to a French *fonctionnaire*. You didn't simply sign off your letter with a "Sincerely." You had to write something like "Veuillez agréer, cher Monsieur, l'assurance de mes sentiments les plus distingués." What a mouthful of politeness! I put myself in Mrs. Bruce's place and wrote draft letters that I thought were the kind she would write to answer her official mail, even personal letters. I would type them for her signature on beautiful, personal engraved stationery from Cassegrain, the Parisian shop where government leaders, princesses, and opera stars bought their stationery. I think this is when I became a stationery snob, spending much too much money on fine papers and engraving, which forced me to become an avid correspondent myself.

I had no choice but to learn my job quickly. There was no time to ask questions. I handled the telephone with aplomb, at least insofar as any aplomb could exist with the constant, infuriating interruption of the line in those days. I would give my ambassadress's name as the caller—"C'est de la part de Madame David Bruce"—and there would be an immediate reverential response, "Ne quittez pas, Madame" (Right away). Frustratingly, many times the line would be broken, we would be cut off, and I would plead an ago-nized, fruitless "Ne coupez pas, ne coupez pas!" to no avail. When I called back immediately, the line would be busy. When I complained furiously to the telephone repair people, I would hear by way of explanation, "C'est la guerre, Mademoiselle, il n'y a rien à faire" (It's the war, nothing can be done about it)—even though the war had ended three years before.

If it was difficult dealing with the local French telephone system, placing a call to another country was an exercise in mental torture. Often one had to go through the operators in four countries, trying to make contact. You had to speak each operator's language, win her over with charm and patience, soothe her if she was having a bad day, and apologize when things became hopeless. You also had to be able to express your fury in the operator's lan-guage if threats were the only avenue left open to you. A friend of mine, vis-iting from New York, sitting listening in my office one day at the avenue d'Iéna, was so struck by my telephonic frustrations, as call after call was inter-rupted by cut-offs, she sent me a thank-you hostess present from New York upon her return. It was a handsome telephone and address book with the ex-pression hand-embroidered in needlepoint on the cover: "Ne Coupez Pas, Je Vous En Prie" (I beg you, don't cut off the line!).

The Bruces were number one on the social scale in France. They were in-vited everywhere, and when they appeared on the stairway at the residence, about to embark upon some official or social function, we, the hired hands, would just stand looking at them with pride, like a bunch of awestruck fans. It wasn't only that they were beautiful to look at. David Bruce was one of the most brilliant and influential diplomats in the American Foreign Service, and Evangeline was the only diplomat's wife who spoke five languages fluently, wrote for French intellectual magazines (in French), and was considered his assistant as well as his spouse.

Evangeline was poetry in motion, even in the smallest gestures. She would sink down into one of her Louis XV fauteuils in one graceful move-ment, her back straight against the back of the chair, one leg folded over the other at the knees, affording her guests a perfect view of her long legs and in-evitably high-heeled kid or satin pumps from the latest collection of the most famous French *bottier*. Her French maid prohibited even the suggestion of a scuff on those pumps or crocodile handbag. Every couturier in France tried to dress her, because she made their creations much more dramatic than they actually were. Often she knew about the makeup of upcoming art exhibitions before the museums involved did, because she was in on the diplomatic discussions that led to them. Everyone in Paris talked about her skill at making each guest feel individually appreciated. She would lead an important woman off to one side of the salon for a private, four-minute chat, but everyone at the party would see it and be impressed for the woman guest's sake, and the woman herself would feel singled out and important. Then Mrs. Bruce would move to another side of the room and take another person off for a four-minute conversation—all deftly done, requiring great social and diplomatic skill.

The ambassador was obviously born under a special star as well; later in his career he would be appointed ambassador to the Court of St. James, Bonn, the Peoples' Republic of China (the first there since before World War II), and many other important troubleshooting diplomatic missions. Immensely attractive—tall, slim, silver-haired, and an impeccable dresser—he loved books, history, art, politics, the decorative arts, wines, and great cheese with an unlimited passion. He knew as much about eighteenth-century court furniture as most curators and *antiquaires*. The French were eager to deal with him.

The Bruces took me with them antique-hunting on the Left Bank on a few Saturday afternoons, where I experienced firsthand their knowledge of the eighteenth century (as the ambassador described it, "the era in which there was no bad taste"). He would turn over the top drawer of an antique dresser to show where it had been repaired on the bottom side with a small insert of twentieth-century wood, while the corner of the top drawer had been chipped and repaired with a tiny piece of nineteenth-century wood. Mr. Bruce would then buy it at a suitably reduced price, because it was no longer considered in "perfect condition." My eyes were opened to a new pursuit. The next best thing to owning antiques is knowing about them.

In a grand gesture, the French government invited the Bruces to use one of its most celebrated historic properties—Le Pavillon de la Lanterne, in the Parc de Versailles—as a weekend home. This loan was a special gift, never before afforded any diplomat. Le Pavillon de la Lanterne was a true treasure, a small, perfectly proportioned Louis XV royal house, which had been the playhouse of Marie Antoinette, built near the big chateau. The young queen turned it into a *laiterie,* a dairy, and would escape to it from the big palace almost every week. She would change into a milkmaid's costume on these occasions and actually milk a cow or two. It was her fantasy played into reality.

I loved going out there to work on correspondence with Mrs. Bruce, sitting in the small sunlit dining room, which was like a French garden in itself. We would often eat a cheese soufflé and green salad for lunch, served with a cold white wine, and then get to the business of the in-box contents when coffee was served. Life at La Lanterne wasn't exactly like life on any other dairy farm.

I was well aware that my boss was considered an intellectual, but also one who made the best-dressed list every year, a highly unusual combination. When she was elevated to the "Best Dressed International Hall of Fame," she pretended to give it no importance, but I realized that secretly it meant a great deal to her. As we discussed this, she was going over her House of Dior haute couture bills, frowning as she turned the pages. "The ambassador," she said, "will be happy for me now that I'm a member of the International Hall of Fame, but when he sees these bills, his pride in that will quickly evaporate."

The Bruce children were fully as scenic as their parents. Dark-eyed Alexandra (Sasha) was the oldest, and always wore beautifully smocked Liberty lawn-print dresses. David came next, an enchanting little blond-haired boy in shorts and wool kneesocks in cool weather. (Their baby brother Nick, who was to be born in 1951, was dark-eyed and handsome, too.) They wore matching double-breasted blue coats with blue velvet collars and cuffs and buttons from the famous children's store in London, Rose's. Their English red leather Mary Janes and white socks were worn by English and American children to parties for seven decades, including Caroline and John Kennedy when they were little, and including my own children, too, many years hence.

The busy Bruces were hard put to find time to spend with their children. Every afternoon at five o'clock was "Nursery Hour" up in Mrs. Bruce's sitting room, where the children would have their supper and play with their mother. On weekends the children would often go with their parents to Le Pavillon de la Lanterne to play in the gardens of Versailles. They had a busy social life with other children of the French aristocracy and diplomats, supervised as always by jolly Nannie Sawyer—she of the perpetually rosy cheeks, wearing a blue-and-white nannie's uniform and apron and a broad-brimmed straw hat for sun protection whenever the outside temperature rose to 55 degrees.

The French public wanted to see and know every detail of the Bruce children's lives as the months passed by. What do they eat? Do their clothes come from French children's shops? What are their favorite games and books? The Bruces made sure that their children were not photographed or hounded. Actually, French intelligence quietly saw to it that the children were left alone. The children's one really liberated activity was a trip in an embassy car with their mother each week to the American PX, on the outskirts of Paris, for a "look around" at American products and a cherished stop at a soda fountain for a hot dog and a chocolate soda.

I loved watching them grow up in this ultra-refined atmosphere—attractive, well behaved, beautifully dressed, and well mannered—a far cry from the Baldrige kids, but a lot of fun to observe.

One evening in the third month of my job, Mrs. Bruce sat me down in her gray satin boudoir (Americans think of this as a bedroom, but the French call it their home office) to help me understand the parameters of my job. Her description of my duties was so fascinating and exotic that I had a hard time concentrating, and she had to keep prompting me to write it all down in the notebook on my lap.

I was to draft as many letters as possible for her signature. I was to try to write in her voice—a brief, chatty note saying what an experience Paris was, and how fast the children were growing, and yes, they hoped their friends would come stay with them when they reached Paris. (The latter sentiment was expressed only for a year, creating as it did a veritable stampede of visiting friends.)

I was to keep track of all of the invitations sent out or received, keep track of the RSVPs (in those days, you did not have to beg for them; you received them automatically), and keep the guest lists in shape for inspection and additions at all times.

I was to think of the ways in which the Bruces could remain in fruitful contact with the leaders of the American colony residing in Paris, without being cannibalized by them socially. Early in my Paris experience I created a public relations disaster with a prominent member of the American colony, a woman who had been brashly trying to get on a Bruce dinner list by any means possible. As ugly, pushy, and rude as she was, she was also very important because of her money and support of local charities. Mrs. Bruce relented and invited her to a dinner to take the pressure off me. On the day of this large event, while retyping the last updated copy of the list of dinner acceptances, I made a major Freudian slip. I inadvertently omitted this obnoxious woman's name from the final list. That evening she arrived in her chauffeured Rolls, bejeweled to the extreme, only to find her name missing from the door list. She was not on the seating chart, nor was there a place card for her on the dinner table. She felt furious and humiliated, for which I don't blame her. The Bruces knew just what to do. They simply slathered her with an oil bath of deep apologies. The butler saw to it that a place at the table was set for her within three minutes. The official seating was now out of whack; officials were sitting above and beneath their rank, and I hid in my office all night so as not to be burned alive by the furious guest's glance. The ambassador reminded me the next day, "Remember, Tish, if you do that to someone we happen to like, you'll be in *real* trouble!"

Everyone wanted an invitation to avenue d'Iéna, and Mrs. Bruce explained that it was up to me to see to it that personal requests from their friends at home that the friends of their friends be invited to a party at the residence were accommodated. There would be requests for tickets to a visiting American symphony orchestra's concerts (free, of course), pleas for help in getting an American child into a private French school, and a barrage of requests for information, including questions of major portent like "Where should we go on the Riviera where we will have the greatest chance of running into people like Brigitte Bardot and Maurice Chevalier?"

The houseguests required elaborately detailed attention: what would they like for breakfast, and at what exact hour? What flowers would please them most in their rooms? When would they need a car, and for how long? Pressing to be done? Appointments to be made with a couturier? Reservations to be made in the restaurants we recommend? Need to know the best bookstore in Paris? Lingerie shop? Revillon furs? Handbags? Hermès scarves? Chanel costume jewelry? Cartier real jewelry? The name of the best facial specialist? This responsibility turned me into a walking yellow pages. I knew the luxury side of Paris like the back of my hand.

A very important part of my job was handling the seating at our lunches and dinners, which had to be done according to strict protocol. The French government had its own strict protocol requirements, and so did the American. The foreign embassies had another. The military had its own rank requirements, and so did the aristocrats—the French dukes, princes, counts, barons, and so on. People really cared where they sat at table. It was proof to everyone present of where they had arrived in life, and how high their position was. If a person was given a seat inferior to his or her perceived place in the hierarchy of life, that person would be deeply insulted—a silly fuss to an American, a dastardly deed to a European. I would have to juggle all of these sets of standards, trying to embarrass the American government as little as possible with my decisions.

Women and men were to be seated alternately, and husbands and wives were not supposed to be seated next to one another, unless the table was small and it couldn't be helped. Many American guests complained loudly at this. They wanted to sit next to their spouses and demanded to know why they could not. I would look them coldly in the eye and say, "We separate spouses, so that they can work their considerable charms on new people and help build their social contacts."

Mrs. Bruce would give me imaginary protocol problems to see how I would solve them. For example: What do you do if a very revered patriarch of the Eastern Church is your guest at the same dinner as a very revered archbishop of the Church of England? Answer: Call the office of the *chef du protocol* for this answer, because the answer may differ country to country.

What do you do if a brash thirty-year-old guest outranks an eighty-year-old retired gentleman who is loved by everyone? Answer: Seat the older man ahead of the younger one, but call the office of the younger one to explain that, since the older man is being saluted at this dinner, the hosts hope the younger guest will understand and forgive this exception to protocol rules for this one occasion.

I did make mistakes; in fact, my first great blooper in seating almost railroaded my career as a social secretary. I had been on the job for only a couple of months. The Bruces had been in Germany on an official visit, and their flight back to Paris was seriously delayed because of weather. They almost did not make their own party, and consequently they did not have time to check my seating plan for this huge, very important dinner. I had done it as best I could without Mrs. Bruce's assistance. There were several extra men, so I had to seat men next to one another in several places.

The Bruces rushed in from the airport and ran up the stairs to change for dinner, and we held off the guests from going into the dining room as long as we could. Finally we ushered them in, and down the stairs came the Bruces in evening clothes, on the run, to join their guests. A hush fell over the room as people took their seats. I had managed to seat a top French Foreign Office official next to another equally important man—his wife's lover! Our French guests immediately thought it had been done on purpose, to embarrass the Foreign Office. The turtle soup course was on the table. David Bruce looked up, saw the two men glaring at one another, and, realizing what I had done, immediately rose. He went over to them, greeted them warmly, and in an absolutely silent dining room, took them to new seats, asking the people already in those seats to exchange. He reseated the dinner on the spot, apologizing to everyone, and then returned to his own place and his two-handled fine porcelain bowl full of turtle consommé.

Because I had no idea who was sleeping with whom in Paris (they didn't teach me that in my University of Geneva International Relations course), I had made this major mistake quite innocently. It was then that I realized that when you have a job like mine, there's no excuse for not knowing who is sleeping with whom in officialdom. It's something I had to learn. I was lucky to have the Bruces forgive me, and to keep my job. Believe me, from then on I made it my business to learn every VIP scandal of importance in the city almost before it happened.

Cocktail receptions were much easier to arrange. No seating! At each one, government officials, business luminaries, and famous socialites attended. I witnessed the best and the worst in behavior on these occasions. I had been on the job for about three months when the guests of honor were a glamorous young newlywed couple from Hollywood: Elizabeth Taylor and her first husband, Nicky Hilton. They were only a few days into their honeymoon, but in most peoples' opinions that did not give them an excuse for being so late to a party in their honor at an official place like the embassy. They emerged from their limo battling like a pair of noisy roosters. He was loudly berating her for her "constant tardiness." She told him it was "none of his d—— business." I shook hands with them and attempted to calm them down, and by the time they hit the receiving line inside the grand salon, they were doing a great acting job, looking all smiley and affectionate for her fans. I was glad they had not ruined everyone's evening, but I was crestfallen, disappointed by their terrible behavior. I remarked to Odette de Wavrin, who happened to be nearby, "Ce mariage ne durera pas" (This marriage won't last). And later they did split. So much for Hollywood glamour.

Odette, a gentlewoman of good family who had been forced to work to support herself, mothered me, and I enjoyed the attention. One day when I professed my jealousy of Evangeline, of her beauty and position, Odette would have none of my whining. "You are a fine American girl. Be what *you* are better than anyone else, and let the ambassadresses of this world be who *they* are."

I wanted to speak graceful French—not poorly accented French, not ungrammatical French. I read easy things in French, like movie magazines, then harder things, like novels by Colette. I began to feel the rhythm of the language. I read *Le Figaro* every morning, at first regarding the political essays as boring, then finally fascinating, as I began to understand the French spirit and its complicated government system. After six months on the job I could hold my own with the language anywhere, including in the little nightclubs in the Étoile district, where my French friends and I would often go to have an after-dinner cognac and listen to the clever lyrics of "Les Chansonniers [song makers] de Paris." We spoke only in French, because their English was not as good, and making them strain to communicate with me was no way to earn their friendship. The Chansonniers were political wits who made up most of their lyrics as they went along, summing up the political gossip and satire of the day in the cleverest of ways. I felt welcomed and definitely part of the group as I sat there with five or six French friends, mostly my age, but politically more sophisticated.

I was evidently a curiosity among my peers at the embassies and government offices in Paris. Traditionally these women and protocol officers were supposed to be cold to one another, never joking or, heaven forbid, teasing one another. They were afraid to unburden themselves of tales of unjust treatment on their jobs. The duchess of Windsor's private secretary finally broke down and cried one day. As she requested, I never passed on her story, but so many years have gone by that I feel I can now. After more than a year of never having any time off on weekends, she was finally allowed to go see her mother who was coming from abroad. The duchess at the last minute made her cancel her visit, saying she was needed for important reasons at the Windsors' house in Neuilly. The secretary then found out that the "important reason" was two ladies coming to see the duchess for a one-hour tea visit.

I thought my paltry salary of $4,800 a year in Foreign Service as social secretary was bad enough, but most of my colleagues in other embassies made half of that. It was considered an honor to hold a position "so clearly important to the function of international diplomacy," but their perks on the job were few, and mine were legion. (As a young woman from the Irish Embassy said, "I'd give all the champagne and foie gras in the world for one hamburger and a chocolate sundae at your PX.")

I was ambitious and determined to make big things out of this job. It meant wandering far beyond the boundaries of my job description. John Lackey Brown, a distinguished professor, poet, and at that time the head of the U.S. Information Services in Paris, was scheduled for a major policy address on the Marshall Plan—in French—to the membership of the France-États-Unis organization, an important French group involved in trade and cultural relationships between our two countries. The speech was to be given in Reims, the historic spot where the treaty ending World War II in Europe was signed, though perhaps more famous for the region's number one product: champagne. Two days before he was scheduled to speak there, John was pulled back to Washington on urgent business. He called me at my office, despair and Gallic charm mixed in his voice.

"Tish, this marks the first visit of an American diplomat to this historic region of France since before the start of the war. They have built up my appearance there far beyond its real importance. And now that I've been called to Washington, they will be terribly let down. I need an American of stature to go in my place."

"Who have you suggested to them, John?"

"You."

"Me?" I screamed. "What is all this bull about stature? I'm on the bottom of the embassy totem pole."

"At this moment, you're the only American around here, other than the very senior officers, who speaks fluent French. Your audience will find you immensely imposing. I've written the speech."

"I probably don't even understand what the speech is all about."

"You will," he said conspiratorially. "I'm going to give you my remarks, neatly typed in French, on the role America has played in the economic progress of France since the launch of the Marshall Plan. Just think back on your economics course at Vassar."

"That's all very nice, John, but I plan to be in Deauville, playing roulette in the casino, that day."

"I've already told them that we're sending you, a top-ranking American official, to sub for me."

"Mrs. Bruce needs me that day," I interjected lamely.

"I've already checked this out with the Bruces. They agree that you will be a big hit with the French down there, and that this will be an important stepping stone in your career."

"I will be completely humiliated. I don't need this—"

"You will be *formidable*. Stand up tall, and they'll think you're a living Statue of Liberty. I'm sending you down to Reims in an embassy car with a chauffeur, and I've assigned Betty Schasseur [a French-born embassy employee] to help you with your nerves. Just read the speech slowly and distinctly. Your accent is better than some of theirs. It's a dry, boring speech, so smile a lot, enjoy the champagne, and always pronounce every taste of it to be excellent. They are very competitive about their champagne." Naturally, his flattery had soothed my protests. In one minute he was gone from his office, briefcase, coat, and passport in hand, on his way to Le Bourget for the flight to Washington.

In the embassy car headed for Reims, Betty Schasseur tried to calm my understandable jitters. She told me that the most important thing I must now remember is to take a sip of champagne every time it was offered to me, that it was protocol never to reject it.

"What if I never touch it?" I asked. It was true, I drank almost nothing, and never champagne. I was beginning to feel rebellious.

"I have news for you," she said with Gallic firmness. 'You *will* drink champagne every time it's offered. Otherwise, you will be committing an unpardonable gaffe."

The mayor greeted us officially on the main square. I was now beginning to feel a bit important. His Honor was also the president of France-États-Unis for this region. When the first *vin d'honneur* was offered in the traditional silver tasting cup, I made a face, swallowed it, and managed a fake smile of approval.

Betty Schasseur's fist was in the small of my back as a reminder to follow the script. Then I was taken through the champagne *caves* of the Taittinger family, where the more I tasted the offerings in my tasting cup, the more attractive I found my host and guide, the handsome dark-haired son of the family. He was in tennis clothes and was on his way to a match, dressed in white trousers, a white cotton sports shirt, and a white cable-knit pullover, its V neck outlined in red and black, just like the legendary American tennis star Bill Tilden's. The wine was definitely beginning to take effect, because I was trying to figure out how I could go play tennis with Monsieur Taittinger instead of giving a speech at the banquet.

By the dinner at eight o'clock, I had been quaffing champagne continuously since three o'clock. Oh, yes, there were hors d'oeuvres, but the hated taste of champagne now didn't register at all. By the time dinner was finished, accompanied by two more *marques* of champagne, it was time for me to speak. I looked at the typed pages in my hand and saw nothing but dizzy words. I heard the mayor introducing "this distinguished diplomat from Washington, D.C." and thought to myself, "Who's that?"

At the last minute, I changed my lecture topic, fearful that my speech was unforgivably boring. I talked about what young Americans were doing for amusement these postwar days. I talked about how the young people of France would soon be able to have fun again, too, without the specter of war hanging over their heads (applause at this point). I talked about what proms were like at Cornell University, and what people liked to eat at the soda fountains in drugstores, which I could tell my audience found quite unbelievable. I demonstrated a few jitterbug moves so my audience would understand the subtlety of the dance, explained what happened on a Yale-Harvard football weekend, and compared Frank Sinatra's love songs to Edith Piaf's. I even sang a few bars of Edith's "Les Feuilles Mortes" for good measure. I looked over at Betty Schasseur only once; she was holding her head in despair, her copy of my speech dangling from one hand. I had not once referred to the script, had not once mentioned the Marshall Plan.

It didn't matter. The audience gave me a standing ovation. Everyone was on his feet at the end, shouting "Bravo!" They loved me. I was thinking to myself, Score one for American culture! Betty told me in the car going back to Paris that she marveled at the fluency of my French, that never had I pronounced the words more accurately and smoothly. However, she ruefully reminded me that I had not pronounced the words "Marshall Plan" once. She told me she had judged me that night in Reims, if not already there, at least well on my way to being *complètement noire* (completely drunk).

* * *

Most young women in my home country would have killed to be where I was—at what was probably the social peak of Western Europe. I had the best springboard into the middle of things of any foreign young woman in Paris—the American Embassy. If you wished to make anyone appreciate your social success in Paris, all you had to do was to toss out in casual conversation, "Well, *at the Bruces'* the other evening . . . "

I met all the eligible young titled people in their twenties and thirties at the receptions the Bruces gave and the ones to which I was invited, simply because of my diplomatic entrée. Sons and daughters always accompanied their parents to important receptions in those days. I found the young Frenchmen who were impressed by all this show to be terrible bores and social climbers. On the other hand, I found the few who were unimpressed, forced into coming by their parents, to be very desirable.

I had to have my own life, apart from my official one. Even after four years, I had not become blasé about the functions at the embassy or the ones to which I was invited by the leaders of Paris society. I knew why I received so many invitations. My hosts were hoping (perhaps even praying) I would insert their names into the guest list for a dinner at the most, or a cocktail reception at 2, avenue d'Iéna, at the least.

I quickly joined "Le Racing," the private club du jour in the Bois de Boulogne. All of Paris's café society seemed to hang out here, including movie stars, playboys, and fortune hunters like "Baby" Pignatari and Barbara Hutton's swain, Porfirio Rubirosa. I was so busy, the only facility I could use at the club was the tennis courts at seven in the morning, but every day that I could, I would play tennis with a male friend. We would finish playing at eight, and I would be at my desk at nine. The Bruces thought I was stark, raving mad to rise at five-thirty on my tennis-date mornings, down some *caffé filtre,* and be off to the courts, but the Frenchmen I played with were well worth rising for at an early hour. In those days we didn't call delicious men "sexy," because that term was demeaning and cheap. We called them "attractive." I went to Le Racing occasionally for lunch in the summer, but I never got over the shock of seeing the almost nude girls promenading around the pool in ultra-high-heeled sandals, Carmen Miranda–type sunglasses, and the briefest of bikinis. This was as yet unheard of in the States. I thought this type of swimsuit was nothing less than disgusting (the nuns certainly would have said so), but then remembered that one reason for my strong moral opinion was that I would have looked terrible in a bikini.

I attended my first French ball at the Pré Catalan—a renowned Art Nouveau restaurant, surrounded by endless expanses of terrace—in the center of the Bois de Boulogne. Part of the movie *Gigi* with Maurice Chevalier would later be filmed here. My escort for the ball was an Englishman. Mother insisted I write her in intricate detail about my ball gown, made by a couturière, with special silk fabric from Lyons. Yes, I reported, I had worn the proper long white kid gloves, and yes, the dress was spectacular, made of the most heavenly shade of pale blue brocade, off the shoulders, with a tight waist and a huge, billowing skirt. A real ball gown, a lifelong dream. Mother wrote back, aghast. How could I have had the dress made that way? I must have looked like a floating blue balloon, she lamented. What I described was fine for an undernourished fashion model, but for me, with my hips and waist, it had to spell disaster.

"Mom," I wrote back, "you are treating me like a child again. I'm a grown woman, earning my own living. I don't think you have the right to blast off like that at my fashion decisions." I was just a little girl to her. I loved her so much, I took it from her—but not without a protest. Of course, she was always right, but I would discover this later.

When I went back to Washington on home leave that fall, I took the precious custom-designed ball gown with me to show the family. I looked at myself in the full-length mirror in our apartment and immediately took off the dress without showing it to them. Instead, it went to the Junior League Thrift Shop to be sold for charity, and I never again purchased a tight-wasted, full, billowing dress. As my mother had predicted, I truly did resemble a perfectly beautiful pale blue brocade-upholstered sofa.

One young count was forced by his mother to ask me out to dinner and the theater, in the hope I would rush to get an embassy dinner invitation extended to his parents, who were feeling out of social sorts because they had not yet been invited by the Bruces. He was movie-star handsome with an ego to match. I discussed the situation with Odette, who was horrified at the thought of my refusing his invitation.

"But you can't! He's a great catch. He has every girl in Paris after him."

"Not me. He's a terrible snob, Odette."

To her, that made him even more prized. "To be seen with him—to be taken to dinner at the Theatre des Ambassadeurs to a Jean Marais play—that's, well—" She was sorely disappointed at my lack of social understanding.

At lunch that day, Marlene Dietrich was on our guest list. I told her I was absolutely thrilled to be meeting her, that I had been a big fan all my life.

"At Vassar, you know," I said, "we used to try to imitate you singing 'See What the Boys in the Back Room Will Have.' You were the best!"

The butler, Odette, and all the footmen were standing and gaping at the actress, who had kept every inch of her early days' glamour and figure, positively reeked (in a nice way) of French perfume, and wore a cream-colored suit with a blond fur collar on the jacket. The skirt of her suit was suitably short to show off the famous legs and her small feet in cream-colored kid pumps. Even her stockings matched.

Obviously pleased with the tales of her Vassar fan club, she chatted with me. She told me that she was going to a Jean Marais play that evening, and I told her I was, too. Then I mentioned my escort, the obnoxious count, and she said, "I'll see you at intermission tonight. We'll see what we can do." I had no idea what she meant.

That evening, conversation at dinner with the count was even more difficult than I had envisioned. He would only answer me and pick up on the conversation if I said something flattering about him. Going to the play was a welcome diversion for me, and at intermission we went out into the lobby to have a fruit juice. Suddenly I got a familiar whiff of that strong perfume from lunch. There she was across the lobby, in a white-sequined crepe dinner dress with white fox furs draped across her shoulders, glamour personified. The count caught his breath. "Do you have any idea who that is over there? I don't believe it! It's La Dietrich!" His jaw dropped and remained locked in that lower position.

The actress saw us and immediately crossed the lobby to where we were standing. "My dear Letitia," she said warmly, body-blocking the count to turn him away. "How lovely to see you again! What do you think of the play?"

The count was beside himself. He had not been introduced, and he had been body-checked by the woman of his dreams. He broke into our conversation.

"Madame, may I introduce myself? I am the comte de—"

"Really?" she said wearily. "You must allow me to talk to my friend Letitia. What did you think of Madeline Renault's performance? And Jean's? Weren't they superb?" We chatted for a few minutes more until the buzzer sounded, signaling the end of intermission, and off she went across the lobby, trailing her furs and scent behind her. I never saw her again, but I will certainly never forget her. She did me a real favor that night and raised my self-esteem every bit as much as she clobbered the count's.

Because the clothes industry had obviously collapsed in Europe during the war, the years following it became a dress-up era. Young women wore white kid or cotton gloves in the evening, with little black cocktail bags made of peau de soie or velvet. American girls used enough good French perfume to pervade a large area and reach a number of nostrils. More than once a taxi driver said to me as I was paying and leaving, "Please, don't get out of my taxi. Stay awhile. You smell so good." Frenchmen knew how to appreciate the scent of their own perfume.

Every girl I knew spent a long time getting ready for a date. If it was a Saturday or Sunday evening, we would spend over an hour in preparation. During the busy workweek the process was speeded up, but it never took less than forty-five minutes plus bath time.

We were young and well dressed—the girls in black dresses and pearls, the men in dark suits, white shirts, and silk ties. Because of this, the management let us sit at the best tables in nightclubs, where we subsisted on one cocktail each because no one had the money to drink more. We danced all night, close and closer, to the violins at Monseigneur's and the orchestra at Carrère's. We clutched one another, body to body, when romantic music played. We danced to the hot new rhythms of the samba, and held hands and touched and sighed in darkened corners.

American men visitors inevitably wanted to go to the Folies-Bergère to see the girlie-girlie musicals with towering feather and sequined headdresses and glittery, almost nonexistent costumes. The show was scandalous for its time. I was taken (forced, really) to see the show at least twenty-five times during my four years in Paris. Visiting American male friends would buy the tickets to the show without asking us, their American dates. We were bored out of our minds by the parade of beautiful girls and the comedians' terrible jokes, but the visiting tourists thought it was the greatest thing since the end of Prohibition. I am my mother's own child. I would sit there and laugh, applaud, and say with great enthusiasm, "Isn't it fabulous?" If a date was spending money on you, you were supposed to act delighted and enthusiastic. It was the right and the polite thing to do.

During my first Thanksgiving in Paris, overcome with the spirit of giving and the true meaning of hospitality, I decided to invite seven close French friends to a real Thanksgiving lunch. Paris did not have the proper fixin's in those days, but I found them at the American PX outside Paris—a big frozen turkey, stuffing mix, canned cranberry sauce, and canned sweet potatoes. I had never cooked a turkey before, not even a chicken, but I had a Junior League cookbook of Mother's from my Omaha days, with very simple directions. It was going to be a snap.

However, that afternoon, when I started to roast the turkey, I realized that it was far larger than my oven. I did not have the proper pan, rack, or anything for it, and I couldn't even get the thing inside the oven door. I had not even asked how long a cooking time such a bird required. ("Millie, where are you?") I made some other discoveries, too, of things I could not possibly prepare in my small, antiquated French kitchen. I called my seven guests and told them it was now Thanksgiving dinner at eight o'clock instead of Thanksgiving lunch at one. Amused, they said they'd be there.

Now truthfully on the point of tears—even past it—I took the breast of another still-frozen turkey that would have taken a long time to thaw to the embassy residence. I snuck in the back door, found the chef, and explained my plight. He was busily preparing the dinner for the Bruce family and a few guests. Maybe it's part of the female advantage, but when Chef saw my highly emotional state, he was overcome with pity. Quickly he presented me with a freshly roasted, just-out-of-the-oven turkey, which he said was extra, because he always made another one for the family's dinner—"just in case." (He probably gave me the one he had roasted for his own family.) It was manna from heaven.

Along with the bird came a cream of oyster soup, a container of gravy, a casserole full of stuffing with chestnuts, tiny fresh green beans, dinner rolls, a casserole of sweet potatoes with marshmallows, and a plum pudding with hard sauce. An all-American menu!

I kissed the chef on both chubby cheeks in gratitude, warning him to remove the lipstick before going home to his wife that night. "Absolument pas" was his answer. My dinner, needless to say, was a smashing success, even if my French friends had been waiting for it since noon, and it was now ten P.M. They admitted they had a tough time eating sweet potatoes with marshmallows because it seemed a culinary crime to their tastebuds. But the rest—it was perfect.

I ran my own little mini-embassy of sorts in the apartment I moved into in 1950, on the top floor at 8, rue du Conseiller Collignon, in a most elegant *quartier* off the avenue Henri Martin, the Paris equivalent of New York's Upper East Side. Everyone, and his or her sibling, spouse, lover, and business associates, was given my name to contact in Paris, as the opener of all doors. Friends and strangers both admitted they had been told I would invite them to my apartment for drinks, and I would most likely get them invited to a reception at the embassy. I didn't mind, and the Bruces did not mind either. In fact, they enjoyed seeing attractive compatriots at their receptions. These were "scenic" guests, and they gave the flavor of young America to the Paris of that decade. At the same time, my friends were delighted to be sent engraved invitation cards, with the gold U.S. seal embossed on the top, to the imposing embassy residence, to meet the famous Ambassador and Mrs. Bruce, and to enjoy all the really good food and free booze it was proper to consume in such awesome circumstances!

I never knew, when I gave a cocktail party in my apartment, if there would be ten or eighty people in attendance, because the invited guests would always bring along others. The top floor of the house on the rue du Conseiller Collignon, which I had rented, had been designed as a small concert hall, suited to the needs of the late owner of the house, a concert pianist and composer. Most of the people who rented the apartment since his death had used the empty space where the audience chairs used to be as a living room. There were four steps to an upper level—the stage for the concert performance, if you will. All of my guests kept going up on the stage and staying there during the party, drinks in hand, because it was an unusual space to which they were drawn. When they imbibed too lavishly, they occasionally fell off the stage, so an embassy lawyer helped me get accident insurance for this very problem.

There was a small dining area and tiny bedroom off the stage part of this concert hall. In the small back hall was a bathtub, basin, and toilet—as well as the stove and mini-icebox. How many people have a bathroom and kitchen combined? My *femme de chambre,* Marguerite, managed to turn out lovely dinners in this impossible situation, cooking on a miniature stove, often while I sat soaking in the bathtub four feet away from her. One day the wine merchant made a delivery up the back stairs and into my hall (which could not be locked), bursting in upon me in the tub, as Marguerite stirred her *escalopes de veau à la crème* nearby. He almost had a heart attack, and I made plans to have a sign made, in French for delivery people, to post at the top of the service stairway when I was in the tub: "ATTENTION, FEMME NUE" (Warning, Naked Woman).

By 1949 the political situation was anything but tranquil. The Communists tore up sections of pavement on the sidewalks of the Champs-Élysées and threw them like missiles at anti-Communist demonstrators or anyone who happened to get in their way. The embassy called in the staff for emergency evacuation briefings, in case things became really serious. We were given maps showing us how to drive to the Spanish border and make it to safe territory. We were given ten-liter jerry cans of gas to store in the trunks of our cars for emergency use. It was a toss-up which was more dangerous: an explosion from the gasoline, or the threat of Communists in hot pursuit. The French seemed totally unperturbed as the demonstrators had regular violent encounters with the police.

One night after a particularly scary day at the embassy, I attended a ten P.M. "Musicale" at the home of the parents of my good friends François and Mary Vaudoyer. I was told I should be very proud of the fact that I was the first American invited to this entertainment in their house on the Boulevard Pereire. When I casually mentioned that these were worrisome times, François's father laughed and told me not to worry; the ballet performance tonight would take my mind off serious preoccupations. The Vaudoyers were delighted that their famous family member—Jean-Louis Vaudoyer, one of the most erudite members of the Académie Française. was with them this evening. Mary Vaudoyer informed me that the French regard the members of the academy as celestial figures, certainly eclipsing other intellectuals, such as Nobel Prize winners.

The audience was elderly and distinguished. We sat on spindly little chairs in neat rows in the living room and watched a two-dancer ballet, accompanied by someone playing on a piano "that had not been tuned," as Mary said, "since the time of Louis Philippe." Two clumsy dancers of a certain age performed in pink tutus, and it was all I could do to keep from bursting out laughing. It would have made a great Charlie Chaplin movie. After an interminably long time of watching the figures jumping up and down, often not in sync and never in rhythm with the piano, we applauded politely, retired to the next room, and were served canned orange juice in delicate cut crystal goblets, when what we really needed was a drink—at least, I did. We were presented gravely to each of the dancers. No one cracked a hint of a smile. Mary and François explained that this kind of event was taken very seriously by "the musical elite," and I must never make fun of it. Odette reiterated this fact the next day. "How fortunate you were to have been there for a Vaudoyer evening," she said, solemnly. "That's something *I* would have enjoyed."

Mama Rose and the Kennedy sisters—Eunice, Pat, and Jean—were famous for showing up in Paris all through the late 1940s and '50s. They expected to be entertained by the embassy, and they were. After all, Joseph P. had been an illustrious ambassador to the Court of St. James, so they were automatically invited to any embassy reception on the ledger. Mrs. Bruce would receive a cable from Ambassador Kennedy from his New York office, giving details on who was arriving next, "and would the embassy make a reservation at a good restaurant for his girls, where there's dancing, and invite some eligible young Frenchmen?"

"This is your department, Tish," Mrs. Bruce would say. "Get them some dates—you know the best nightclubs in town—and go with them. Have a good time!" I set up two such evenings, at expensive, glamorous restaurants and boîtes, and twice the same thing happened. Their French escorts—my own friends, with nary an extra sou to spare—got stuck with the tremendous bills for the evening. I had thought, of course, that the Kennedy girls would have a wad of cash with them for this purpose and that the Kennedy brothers would have educated their sisters about how this was not the way things were done. I finally called the Kennedy office in New York and said this was inexcusable. The ambassador's secretary immediately sent me American Express checks to reimburse the men, but that was the last time I tried to arrange an evening out for them. The Kennedy girls eventually became very good friends, in spite of it!

In the meantime, I received a letter from Jackie Bouvier, announcing she was coming to spend a year at the Sorbonne. There had been a recent surge of applications from American students to European institutions. I was delighted to realize she was coming, as she was such an attractive, pleasant, vivacious girl. She had found a nice French family with whom to live, not too far from me, a situation that would be cheaper and safer than staying in one of the decrepit dorms at the Sorbonne.

Our parents had been friends in Washington so I had come to know her well. Jackie had graduated from Miss Porter's three years behind me and then gone to Vassar, too. She still had another two years of college before graduating, but she had also already caught the eye of the leading society and fashion editors of the time. Gossip columnist Gigi Cassini (aka "Cholly Knickerbocker") and his brother Oleg Cassini, a dress designer, had already picked Jacqueline Bouvier from the crowd of debutantes as being head and shoulders over the other girls of that year.

Once Jackie was ensconced with her French family and enrolled in her courses at the university, we managed to see each other several times a year. I was extremely busy with my job, and it was a relief to spend some time with her and gossip about everyone from home. She very quickly seemed to major in men, but at the same time attended every opera, ballet, play, and opening museum exhibit for which she could get a student ticket. She chafed under the tight financial controls set by her mother, which inhibited her from purchasing the many delectables her sharp fashion sense unearthed in Paris. Everything was exorbitant. So much to choose from, so little a capacity to buy it! When we met for Saturday lunch, we would go window-shopping afterward on the Faubourg St.-Honoré, on the Place Vendôme, and down the avenues where the *grands* couturiers had their big *maisons de couture*. Coco Chanel was reintroducing her remarkable costume jewelry of the 1930s (a first for Parisian women); Madame Grès was producing once again her ravishing Grecian drapery-like jersey evening gowns; Revillon Frères was back to selling the incredibly chic little black broadtail jackets with sable collars; and Hermès was, as usual, at the center of the world of expensive leather saddles and alligator handbags. Jackie and I ran into Hubert de Givenchy at lunch in an outdoor café with "Bettina," an incredibly good looking reddish-haired young model just beginning her ascent to fame as Hubert's favorite. The young Yves Saint Laurent was very visible. The older lions of fashion, Christian Dior and Balenciaga, were beginning to feel the young talent nipping at their heels. It was exciting to be in the midst of it all, even if neither Jackie nor I could be purchasers. Some day . . .

Early in my Paris days, I learned that the place to be once a month on a certain Thursday evening was at Marie-Louise Bousquet's apartment. Marie-Louise's *Jeudis* were legendary among, as she described it, "les gens qui comptent" (the people who matter). She was the Paris editor for Carmel Snow's *Harper's Bazaar* magazine. Once a month, in the social season, she would invite an eclectic group of people living in or passing through Paris to one of her Thursday-evening receptions, from seven to nine P.M. She was old, short, whiskey-voiced, and admittedly ugly—yet mesmerizing—and she considered herself the rightful queen of the artistic, business, and fashion celebrities of Paris. Playwrights would rub shoulders with American CEOs at her parties. Actors like Jean-Louis Barrault, playwrights like Jean Cocteau, interior designers like Boudin of the Maison Jansen, couture designers like Balenciaga and Jacques Fath, cabaret stars like Edith Piaf and Maurice Chevalier, American designers like Normal Norell and Pauline Trigère, actor Henry Fonda, government ministers, U.S. bank presidents, and intellectuals of the Académie Française all mingled amiably in her apartment, bumping into fragile little chairs, overturning small tables, and hitting heads, if they were tall, on the low-hung Regency chandeliers. The scene was a potpourri of whoever happened to be in Paris at the time.

Marie-Louise's was always crowded with talented gays. When the American executives would ask them about their Bourse investments, raise a question about agricultural reform in France or gross profit, or ask them about their wives and children, the gay guests would shrug their shoulders and jump to another topic—"Have you seen the latest exposition at the Jeu de Pommes museum?"

One night Jackie and I closeted ourselves for an hour in Marie-Louise's little bathroom, learning eye makeup techniques from the world's most famous model in that era, Anita Colby (aka "The Face"). She had brought a sackful of new products with her and gave us lessons in how to apply them. We were so far removed from American products in those days that to be exposed to all of this in excess was as much fun as going to the opening of the opera. It made us a little homesick. We longed for the American drugstore and its counter displays of Revlon lipsticks. We emerged from the bathroom that night at Marie-Louise's with glamorous, colorful eyes (Jackie's color palette was "blueberry," and mine was "sangria"). By the time we were finished, there was a line outside the bathroom, and the guests were muttering at us—"Quelle manque de politesse!" (What bad manners!)

I wrote a letter that night to my grandmother, Bawa, describing as usual all of the wonderful things I was experiencing, not to mention that I now knew how to apply my eyebrow pencil "so that the top of the curve is centered over the iris of the eye." Bawa wrote back that she was delighted I had learned about the proper use of my eyebrow pencil, but had I by chance learned anything new about French literature?

One of my men friends (I hate the word *boyfriend*) was Mike Forrestal, one of Ambassador Averell Harriman's right-hand men in the Office of the Special Representative for the Marshall Plan. Their offices were close to the embassy, in the ancient Hotel Talleyrand. A Princeton graduate, two years younger than I, Mike had lived a fascinating life, including service in Moscow with Ambassador Harriman. His father, James Forrestal, was the legendary secretary of defense who tragically committed suicide in 1949 by leaping from the tower in the Bethesda Naval Medical Center. To me, Mike was a person of a sharp intelligence and a zest for life, which included excellent food and wine, but he also had something nonexistent in all our lives—a new black convertible with red leather seats. On one Sunday we had lunch in a little inn near the king's hunting chateau in Rambouillet and hatched a plan that would have fascinated Louis XV, if he were alive. We sketched out a dream of a trip, and surprisingly, it all happened, instead of remaining on the drawing board. We were going to be the first American tourists to enter postwar Yugoslavia, a country still in the grip of an unforgiving dictatorship. It was now 1950, times were very hard in that Communist country, luxuries were unheard of, but the government was desperate for American dollars. Mike and I both had a month in leave coming to us, not having had a vacation in two years. Since Yugoslavia was supposed to be a perfectly beautiful country, with vestiges of ancient Greece and Rome, we decided we should go. I did not tell my parents—why get them all upset when our visas would very possibly never materialize?

We had waited three months for those visas, but much to our surprise, they finally came through! Mike called me from his office late one evening in March with the good news: "It's a go!" I let out a war whoop of excitement that startled our houseguest at the avenue d'Iéna. Secretary of State Dean Acheson was sitting in my office, slumped in a comfortable chair, his eyes closed from fatigue. He was now, of course, awake.

"Mr. Secretary, guess where Mike Forrestal and I are going? Yugoslavia!"

He straightened up at this. "My dear Tish, I hate to tell you this, but Yugoslavia is still one of those countries to which Americans are not permitted to travel. The embargo on travel there is stamped right on a page of your passport. The State Department will not let you travel there because it's not safe, and I'm sure the Tito government wouldn't let you into their country anyway."

"Mr. Secretary," I countered, joyful at the historic opportunity I had to correct one of the most highly placed members of the U.S. government, "we waited several months for our Yugoslav visas—we never thought we would get them—but now Mike says they have come through. We'll be the first Americans to be admitted since before the war. I guess you hadn't heard that the State Department has lifted the embargo on travel there."

He frowned, and then he laughed. "I'm sorry I didn't hear about this first from my own State Department, but I'm happy to hear about it from my old friend Mac Baldrige's daughter. Is there anything else I should know about and don't?" He went upstairs to change into his evening clothes and prepare for another official dinner and speeches of praise for the success of the Marshall Plan in its quest to save the western European economy. If my parents had known their little girl was planning a trip alone with a man into a war-torn Communist country, they would have arrived the next day by any means possible, including a blimp, to rescue me. In my parents' logic, a young lady never went off with a young man on a trip like that, unchaperoned, no matter how well educated and polite the young man was, unless she was a brazen hooker. If my mother had found out, I would have sworn to her that should Mike and I ever have to share the same bed, I would put a bundling board between us, as they did in eighteenth-century America. I kept mentioning "our group" of several friends. But if my parents had also known how I was going to finance my share of this expedition—by selling the oriental pearl necklace that had been given in payment to my father for big legal fees in Nebraska during the depression—they would have exploded. If they had known their daughter would have accepted only $500 for the necklace from Monsieur LeBellec, a distinguished Parisian jeweler, they would have denied that a daughter of such stupidity could have emerged from their gene pool. Large natural oriental pearls were by now exceedingly rare. They had been possessed, worn, and worshiped by women of wealth around the world since the days of the Italian Renaissance, and later by the robber barons' wives in America until World War II made them seem archaic. Cultured pearls were on their way to becoming a fad. The natural ones, the real gems, were becoming extinct.

Sitting in Monsieur LeBellec's salon, I heard him say to me, "Are you SURE you want to do this, to give me this *parure* for this amount of francs, which is all I can give you at present? This necklace will probably become extremely valuable again in time."

I couldn't wait for time. I wanted to make this trip. Good-bye, pearls.

Mike and I drove from Paris to Frankfurt to spend the weekend with High Commissioner John J. McCloy and his wife, Ellen, in their fairy-tale castle in Bad Godesburg. It was free lodging, but more importantly, palatial lodging. Our parents were friends of the McCloys', and their children were also our friends—it's called lucking out. There was a battery of army stewards to wait on us and pack gourmet feasts for lunch on the road when we went sightseeing around to museums, *Schlosses, Bierstubes,* and bombed cathedrals. The May weather was perfect the entire time, so the top was always down on Mike's black Mercury convertible, a movie-star car without a movie star. We never put up the top when we parked it. We never gave a thought to any of the locals stealing anything, leaving anything and everything on the seats. Wherever we went, the car was universally admired by the local populace. Mike let them open the hood and lovingly inspect every inch of the motor. We drove to Rothenburg, an exquisite medieval town Jack McCloy had saved from destruction by the American forces. At the mention of the McCloy name, the townspeople burst into applause, some of them crying. "We love him so much," we heard from all sides from people who barely knew English. I have never seen such emotion, and I told the high commissioner afterward that he should allow the townspeople to put him up for sainthood.

We drove to Berlin, a city in ruins, still gasping for air after the air war damage. I kept thinking of the Berlin Airlift—such a short time ago, but now it seemed as if an eternity had passed. One could feel the beauty of the city, driving from a handsome apartment district surrounded by neglected parks, still green with the hope of spring, and then driving into the war-damaged sections, with fragments of buildings standing like jagged works of art in a modern sculpture garden. We covered the nightclubs, too. One club consisted of a series of modern circular Lucite terraces, allowing each person to have a clear view of everyone else. There was a telephone on each table. "Hello. Are you the girl with the red hair at your table, in the dark blue dress? Would you like to come have a drink with me?" It was all very naughty, racy, and advanced technology for its time.

Then it was on to Vienna, mysterious and scary in the eyes of those of us who had seen Orson Welles's movie *The Third Man* about ten times. I even found a gold charm of a Ferris wheel in Vienna to add to my charm bracelet, which had now grown heavy with items, each with its own story. Mike and I sat on the open-air terrace of the famed Hotel Sacher and drank cups of dark, strong coffee, pretending to read the German-language newspapers that sat on racks, hanging from large wooden rods—a surefire way of ensuring that no one could absentmindedly walk off with a paper. Every international spy in the films I saw in that era sat in that same place, hiding behind a paper, at some point in the movie. Vienna was the center of spying in those days. One saw many men on the streets, their fedoras pulled low over their brows, their gray trench coats tightly belted at the waist, and perhaps wearing dark glasses, too, particularly on a dark, rainy day. *Sinister* was the prevailing description of the atmosphere, and one could hear the theme song from *The Third Man* in one's head all day long. If there was a *Paris Herald Tribune* among the papers on the rack at the Sacher Hotel, even if it was ten days old, we were thrilled. We devoured every single word.

We left the cultured refinement and beauty of Vienna and drove down into the wholesome atmosphere of the Austrian lake country. Mike had been boasting of his sailing prowess a bit too much. When we reached the town of Velden on the lake, we stopped at a little marina to go sailing. Mike was ready to show off, but I was worried. "You don't know this boat, these waters, these winds," I said testily. "Wouldn't it be wiser if one of the men who rents these boats skippered ours like they do for everyone else?" His ego was bleeding at this. "Absolutely not! I know a hell of a lot more about handling these boats than they do," he protested, so of course we shoved off by ourselves, and within twenty minutes on a beautiful, sunny day, the boat had capsized. As we trod water, waiting for a rescue by one of the motorboats that only rarely went by, Mike said, "This is just awful, just *terrible.*" I knew he was upset, so I tried some comforting; "Mike, this isn't serious. It could have happened to anyone, to the most skilled of sailers. The choppy, sudden winds that arose were killers. Besides, our boat was old and creaky." (Mother had always told me that when a man is distressed because something athletic in his life goes awry, always blame the equipment immediately.)

He almost took my head off. "This isn't serious? What would you say if I told you that I was carrying all of my American Express checks for the entire trip, plus my passport, and that they have all fallen out of my pants pocket and are somewhere at the bottom of this vast lake?"

"I would say that we are going to be spending an awful lot of time at the American Embassy in Vienna on crisis control for the next few weeks," I replied, worried that now we'd never make it into Yugoslavia. The visa gave us only five days to make entry into that country.

I felt that if I drowned in the lake at Velden, it would make a terrific obituary headline in the next day's *Paris Herald Tribune:* "David Bruce's Social Secretary Letitia Baldrige and Diplomat Michael Forrestal Killed in Boating Accident in Austria." Juicy for the tabloids.

Saint Anthony, the Finder of Lost Articles, was on our side. Mike hired a couple of divers, and they went to the bottom of the lake for a couple of hours and came up with his passport and the traveler's checks. The American Express Company in Vienna issued him new ones immediately. Mike's passport, now unusable, faded and ink-smeared, caused a two-day delay in Vienna to get some fake, freshly stamped visas onto its lacerated pages. In those days, you could not get a new passport just like that. There were many restrictions, a gigantic amount of red tape, and a hurry-up-and-wait attitude about it all. The Cold War was on, and the Russians as well as the Allies were stationed in Vienna. There were "incidents" every week. American passports were very marketable and brought many thousands of dollars on the black market, so a lost or damaged passport was a serious problem.

Mike got the American ambassador to Austria to help him out on that one, and cabled Averell Harriman, too, to lend support from Paris. With a distinguished name like Forrestal, he could get anything he wanted, but there was still the problem of the totally washed-out Yugoslavian visa he had waited so long to obtain. No one seemed to be able to duplicate that one. We found a graphics artist in Vienna who had been in intelligence, and he painstakingly copied in Mike's passport a fake visa in the same colors of ink as the Yugoslav original in my passport. When the artist asked what visa number to put on it, none of us had any idea, so he took a chance and made it one number lower than the eight number figure in my passport. As it was, the border guards on the Yugoslavian side were so nervous about our crossing into their country, and so suspicious, they never put down the visa number in their records, only our passport numbers and the dates and places of issue. They went through all of our luggage three separate times at the border, which worried me. I felt prison gates shutting in around us, but Mike whispered, "They're just damn curious. They haven't had anything like us come across the border ever, so they're going to make us hang around as long as possible."

When we opened our bags for them, their eyes popped out. There were real treasures packed in our bags—toothbrushes, hand cream, shaving cream, pajamas, candy, stockings—and they wanted any excuse to keep poking through our belongings.

A tall, delightful, ruddy-faced Brit named Charlie, a BBC broadcaster, crossed the border in his dilapidated Morris car right behind us. We were held up so many hours at the border in Trieste, we became good friends in the interim. He decided to join us, so we now became a two-car entourage. Then another person joined us, Aldo Stovasser. As a member of the newly formed tourist bureau, called "Sputnik" in a tribute to Mother Russia, he was to be our government guide. Small, slim, and of course mustachioed, as all the men seemed to be, his one credential for this lofty job of heading up tourism was the fact that he spoke English. He had never traveled anywhere, but no matter. He could talk the talk and walk the walk. He announced that he was assigned by the government to stick to us, and whether he was a Yugoslav spy or policeman, I cared not. He was someone who could translate for us and find a proper bush for me to pee behind when we were touring around. It was plain to see that bathrooms were not included in the price of accommodations in this country.

We saw the historic sights of Belgrade and then boarded a cattle boat to "cruise" down the Dalmatian Coast. I told Aldo a rowboat would have been a more comfortable solution. The boat did not have room to sit for most of the crowd, who stood upright, pressed against each other, for the entire trip of several hours. It was an accident waiting to happen, but thank God, it didn't. We drank in the overpowering beauty of this coast from the deck and walked through the historic port town of Dubrovnik for almost twenty-four hours. I had mistakenly thought we were being given staterooms. There was one stateroom, which was given over to Communist Party wives, just to hold their tote bags and luggage. I put my suitcase and handbag in there, too, and when I went below deck to the "stateroom" at one point, I found my bags opened and all of their contents spread out for inspection, to the sound of oohing and aahing, even cries of delight. These women had been through the war, and no consumer luxury goods had been imported since. They had never seen nylons, good soap, or American chocolates and underwear. They could not believe the contents of my cosmetics bag. They had not seen face creams, Kleenex, lipsticks, compacts, perfume, anything of that kind. When I burst in on them inspecting my things, definitely a traumatic shock to them, one woman was standing in front of the little mirror, pinching the end of her nose with my eyelash curler. The women, inspecting this object with its scissorslike handles, had decided its purpose was to curl up the end of the nose—to make a perky American nose, like that of Katharine Hepburn, Doris Day, and all the other American movie actresses. I decided to show them how to curl their eyelashes with this appliance and then leave them alone for the next hour or two so they could continue to try out everything in my makeup kit without embarrassment. I had to help them with the eyeshadow, too, because they didn't know exactly where to put it, and were putting it on their brows instead of lids (green eyebrows—not good.) They had never seen fine soap, so I let each one of them put some on their hands under water. They kept smelling it as though it were the finest of perfumes. I let each one of them apply lipstick to their mouths, and when I finally came into possession of my three tubes again, there was almost nothing left in them. Time and time again in life, I have realized how lucky it is to be American.

Since there had been no tourists in Yugoslavia since 1939, when we asked the prices of our hotel rooms and meals, we received astonishing and unacceptable answers. They had not quite thought it all out. A single room in dinars cost $1,000 a night. We quickly taught Aldo the realities of life, and he recalculated every price for food and lodging as we went along, according to what we felt Western tourists would pay. This was "adjusting to the market" at its most powerful: our prices became the standard for all tourists for that year. The Yugoslavs were unable to buy any luxuries themselves, so the imported necessities for us westerners, like soap and paper tissue, had to be reasonably priced. Otherwise, any tourist faced with the prices they had originally decided to charge would have left the country immediately.

Aldo and the other Yugoslavs we met kept bragging about their national drink, slivovitz, a fiery plum brandy made from fruit left on the windowsill in the sunshine for months on end. Aldo took us to his little house in the country so we could taste his homemade "fire in the belly brew." After a supper of roast chicken, bread, fresh pears, and coffee (a gift from his Communist superiors), out came the little slivovitz glasses. The three men watched me in fascination as I downed two glassfuls of the strong, delicious brew in rapid succession. It tasted so extraordinarily good! After years of moralizing about how women must watch what they drink so they don't put themselves in sexual danger, I was out cold. The men let me sleep it off. It took my head and stomach three days to recuperate from it. I was too surprised to be ashamed.

Aldo disappeared on us without explanation near the end of our travels. Mike and I were perplexed, and worried too. Mike felt that in the eyes of Tito's government, Aldo had grown too close to us. The secret police were always watching us; it seemed as though they went through our papers and suitcases every time we left the hotel rooms.

Mike and I were the first to leave the country. We had been gone from Paris a full month. Charlie, in the meantime, who had promised to write every week until he could make it to the States on assignment, which would be soon, never answered my letters when we left him behind in Yugoslavia. That angered me, because I had a bit of a crush on this strong, muscular, funny Brit, who had done everything and been everywhere in his life. Charlie had professed a similar bit of a crush on me, too.

An extraordinary thing happened in London two years later. I was having tea by myself in one of the Lyons Corner Teahouses. A woman was sitting two tables away, and I became aware that she was staring at me. Finally she arose and walked over, holding out her wallet, which held a snapshot encased in plastic. The snapshot had been taken by Mike with Charlie's camera on the

Dalmatian Coast. It showed Charlie and me, sitting on an ancient stone wall in Dubrovnik. "You are this woman, aren't you?"

Yes, I was. It was a coincidence, one in a million. This woman was Charlie's mother. Her son had never been seen again after he entered Yugoslavia, she said; she had received the snapshot in the last letter he sent her. A lot of mystery was solved when she said, with terrible grief in her eyes, "He wasn't with the BBC, you know. He was with MI-5 [British Intelligence]."

All of a sudden the happy, sunny memories of Yugoslavia—young travelers celebrating the beautiful month of May, dancing around a Maypole—disappeared. Our two friends Aldo and Charlie had disappeared without a trace.

I still had a couple more years in Paris, and more years after that in Rome, on my horizon, but fate was calling Jackie home from France for good. There was a college degree to finish at George Washington University, and a romance with a U.S. senator to bring to its conclusion. On my occasional trips home after she had returned to Washington, Jackie and I would have Saturday lunch for old times' sake at La Salle du Bois, what we considered to be a glamorous restaurant on M Street off Connecticut Avenue, where we would order a glass of white wine and the cheapest thing on the menu, like creamed chicken in pastry shells and peas. M Street Northwest in D.C. was a far cry from the avenue Matignon in Paris. During these lunches, Jackie would make coy references to Senator John F. Kennedy, whom she had met at Charlie Bartlett's house. Of course I knew who he was. Who did not? He was the most eligible bachelor in America. In Congress he looked like any other sincere young politician, but American women absolutely swooned just glancing at a picture of him. This was the talk of America. At one of those Salle du Bois lunches, before I returned to Paris, I said good-bye to Jackie and added in a hushed voice, "I really hope you get him, Jackie."

"You mean, you really hope he gets me," she replied.

I have missed few things in my life that have absolutely devastated me, but missing the outdoor seaside wedding in Newport of Jacqueline Bouvier and John F. Kennedy ranks high on the list. I could not be there. One did not flit back and forth across the Atlantic for a weekend wedding in those days. One did not flit anywhere on a social mission when one was on a government assignment. I have to laugh, remembering how Jackie's family place in Newport was always rather snootily referred to as "the Auchincloss place" or "house," in comparison to being called an "estate" or a "Newport mansion." In marrying Senator Kennedy, she would be assured of an exciting, well-heeled life, but she also loved him. And, yes, her good breeding, beauty, and intelligence would enhance the Kennedy name and place in history. Each had much to gain from the other, but what must never be forgotten is that they loved one another. If you saw them together, it was undeniable.

My family pulled me back home in 1952, worried about my having become too Europeanized. I knew they were right. It was time to go home again. They put the pressure on me. I had become, and still am, a Francophile. While I was on home leave, back in Washington, every man who asked me out was sorry he had. A new acquaintance would take me to dinner in a French restaurant to please me, and in return I would criticize the way he pronounced the French courses and wines on the menu. Any man who asked me out soon found out that he did not know anything about my life in France and didn't necessarily want to, but on the other hand, I did not care anything about his life in the United States. My brothers informed me that I was a total loser. Luckily, I knew inside me that they were right.

So I came home. But not for long.

Viva La Luce!

It was wonderful coming home again to Washington, and to my family. My parents were living now in an apartment at 2101 Connecticut Avenue, and although the family was shrinking in one respect, with my brothers gone, it was growing in another. Bob and Nancy and Mac and Midge had begun producing granddaughters for my parents, and beautiful nieces for me (Alice, Jean, Megan, and Molly). I actually stayed home for a year and a half, even if I did spend the whole time plotting to go back to Europe, this time to Italy. It was another dream I longed to fulfill.

In my job for the Bruces, I had used every possible opportunity to visit Italy, even if it was only for thirty-six hours over the weekend in the air attaché's plane or on a free ride on a special Pan American Airways tourist promotion flight. Something about the endless sunshine (in contrast to the endless rainy, gray skies over Paris), the constantly smiling, beautiful people, the music that I heard everywhere in the streets (guitars, violins, and the human voice singing), the streets fragrant with a mixture of strong sausages and cheeses, and the warm figs and plaques of chocolate lying on open counters was so intoxicating, I had to be there. This country had enthralled the playwrights and romantic poets of England and the great painters of the world for hundreds of years. I wanted to shout from the rooftops of Rome, "Me, too, I'm enthralled, too!" Italy in the 1950s was indisputedly the most romantic spot in the world. My love for France had not abated, but there was this additional unfulfilled passion to pursue. I disliked unfulfilled passions. I liked being in the middle of them.

I devised a scheme, and it revolved around learning the Italian language. I knew I couldn't get sent over to Italy without a job and without someone other than my parents paying for it. The endless pocket of parental cash had dried up. I lived with my parents, and I realized that was an enormous financial help, but I had now entered that frightful state of being known as "self-supporting." I couldn't believe it, I felt so overladen with education, but I had to learn a new language so that I could realize my dream of working in Italy.

If the Italian language was a necessary skill for employment, I would have to learn it on the side, extracurricular to a regular job. The State Department officials told me that after having had Paris as a post, I would have to go to Afghanistan and then to Moldova before they would post me to Rome. Three weeks after I had returned from France, and thanks to a long conversation at a cocktail party with Frank Lindsay, formerly of the OSS and now high up in the Central Intelligence Agency (CIA), I got a job—in the Psychological Warfare Division, Eastern Europe, no less. It was fascinating business, learning to be a "spook," and the agency was full of colleagues of David Bruce from the wartime London OSS operations, most of whom I knew. Our CIA offices were in temporary buildings flanking the reflecting pool in front of the Lincoln Monument. The buildings resembled large, dilapidated, un-air-conditioned Quonset huts, and managed to completely destroy the aesthetics of the Washington Monument and its surroundings. No more avenue d'Iéna Louis XV splendor. *Fini.* I laughed when I looked at that reflecting pool—because I remembered the area when there were no temporary buildings, and when, in first grade, I had sailed my sailboat in the pool on many Sundays, firmly holding on to the rope as I ran up and down alongside. I also remembered my brothers' attempts to push me into the pool. They were successful only once.

The buoyant camaraderie of working in "The Agency" in the early 1950s made up for the long hours and low pay. Stalin's shadow covered all of Eastern Europe at this point, and it seemed impossible that the millions of people enslaved by him would ever be free. My division had indigenous agents everywhere, including Hungary, a country that would soon give America its blackest mark in history, in my opinion. We encouraged the people there to revolt, promising immediate help. When they did, America did not provide the promised backup, and many lives were lost.

My boss was the brilliant Frank Lindsay, a wartime OSS spy hero. The head of the agency at that time was General Walter Bedell Smith, and later Allen Dulles. We, of course, could not talk about what we were doing. Many people could not even say where they were working. Some were undercover, working at other agencies of government. Some young people went around being mysterious just so people would think they were in CIA. The plethora of young, attractive people in Washington gave the agency the reputation of being a country club. Believe me, it was not.

What I learned at Vassar in psychology class had been invaluable, as had what I learned in the Psychological Warfare Division of CIA. (What I would later do in public relations in the business world would mainly be a repetition of all that had gone before—swaying public opinion and inciting people into action.) In wartime, the purpose of psychological warfare was to teach the oppressed how to fight the enemy in silent ways, and to incite them to be ready to act as a united group when liberation from Communist domination was possible. In peacetime the goal of public relations was to create attitudes favorable to certain companies and their products or services, and to inspire the masses to buy those products or services. Propaganda in wartime is called promotion in peacetime.

In the meantime, the goal of Rome was ever in my mind. Through the Italian Embassy, I found a patient Italian woman, Signora Sera (her son called her "Contessa" Sera—who knows?), who gave me Italian lessons on Sundays during my year and a half in Washington. Berlitz it was not. Her son was attached to the Italian Embassy, and every Sunday I would go to the Sera house on Decatur Place in the Kalorama area at eleven A.M., to help the Signora cook a huge family lunch. (How ironic that my own family and I would end up living on this same little street fifty years later, after returning to Washington to live permanently.) It was a painless way to study a foreign language. I helped her cook, and afterward joined her family to eat a great feast that would have satiated the appetite of Henry VIII. I learned the vocabulary of an Italian gourmet. My language ability therefore strictly pertained to gastronomy, but it made me feel confident that I could bluff my way along in other directions. Doesn't everything in life start with food? "Abbacchio arrosto con verdura" would roll off my tongue with the greatest of ease, but I would then have to add, "Please don't expect me to discuss foreign policy in Italian right now." At night I went to sleep with a tape recorder playing in my ear. "Buona sera, Signora. Come sta? Sto bene, grazie, e Lei?" I went into a deep sleep hearing the proper pronunciation and rhythm of the language playing right into my ear.

A year later, it was time to act. I took my two weeks' annual vacation from the agency to fly to Rome, on a secret mission to job hunt. I tried first at the American Embassy, but the State Department had a job freeze and was further downsizing employees everywhere (they called it "riffing"). President Eisenhower had commanded it, and the only jobs available anywhere were for locals, the Italians, who would accept low salaries paid in lire, not dollars. I could not afford to do that. The country was poor, in a deep recession. I knocked on the doors of every major American company in Rome, including the offices of Time-Life, looking for a job that paid a proper amount of dollars. The *Time* bureau chief, Bob Neville, and I had a long chat that we both knew would lead nowhere, but he loved the city and succeeded in firing up my enthusiasm even more for living there. During my job-hunt period there, I stayed with Ambassador and Mrs. Ellsworth Bunker, great friends of my parents', in a place of great beauty and history, now the American Embassy residence but formerly the Villa Taverna, built in the sixteenth century.

It was luxurious, no doubt of that. Painted tile ceilings, porcelain tile floors, eighteenth-century brocade bedcoverings, massive carved stone fireplaces, stately blue velvet chairs in the dining room—it was certainly fit for cardinals, or even the pope. Little did I realize then that with the next change of ambassadors, I would be returning in an amazingly short time to manage this very same house for the ambassador of the United States of America to the Republic of Italy.

When my two weeks of unsuccessful job hunting were up, I had to go home. I felt like a dog with its tail between its legs. Total dejection. No more vacation time left, no more money left. Just before plane time, I sat in the sun sipping a double espresso in the Piazza Navona, then, as now, my favorite piazza in the whole world, but I was returning to Washington without any hope of a job in Rome. Luckily my friends and colleagues at the agency hadn't even known my purpose in taking off those two weeks, so no one knew the reasons for my dejection.

Then came the magic again. I received a call at home one evening from a very important-sounding man from Time-Life in New York, a Mr. Allen Grover. "I have just returned from Rome," he said in a rich, cultivated baritone. I could tell from the voice that this must be an incredibly attractive man. (He was—and he was also Henry Luce's right-hand man.)

"Bob Neville told me at lunch in Rome two days ago that you were dying to work there." My heart jumped up into my throat and stayed there for the greater part of an hour's conversation. Grover had been present at a meeting with Henry and Clare Luce and Bob Neville at the Villa Taverna in Rome. The Luces had just arrived. She was to serve as the first American woman ambassador to a major foreign country (another Eisenhower appointee, Perle Mesta, had been the ambassador to tiny Luxembourg before her, but that was hardly comparable, to put it politely). Mr. Luce planned to live in Italy half the year, running his publishing business from there (*Time, Life, Fortune, Sports Illustrated,* etc.) plus doing a reporter's job—interviewing heads of state for *Time.* This was traditionally the job of the bureau chief, but now he could do it again after decades of leading the CEO's life. He was to experience a rebirth—being a young reporter again. His bureau chiefs were less enthusiastic at this turn of events; they wanted to do those interviews themselves, and felt intimidated by the big boss looking so earnestly over their shoulders.

"Bob Neville spoke very highly of you," Allen Grover explained during that initial telephone call. "We were discussing how we could help the Luces, who had just arrived on the SS *Andrea Doria* in Naples. They are helplessly trying to cope with managing their residence, the Villa Taverna, because they don't speak Italian, and the large household staff is unable to speak a word of English. Everyone is frustrated, whether it's a question of handling telephone messages or instructing the chef to prepare someone's eggs once over lightly. Mr. Luce tried to order a grilled cheese sandwich when I lunched with him at the villa two days ago, and he got a grilled ham omelet instead.

"The Luces," Grover continued, chuckling at the memory of this lunch, "do not handle frustrations well. Anyway, Bob Neville went right over to his office that Sunday afternoon, got your job application out of his file, and brought it back to the Luces. It seems you know well the whole business of managing an ambassador's official ceremonial duties, and you are fluent in Italian—a major requirement."

"Oh, yes," I replied without hesitation, "I can do all that." Yes, sure, said I to myself, I'm fluent in discussing the ingredients of spaghetti *alla carbonara*, perhaps, but not in expressing intricacies of protocol. But wasn't I an expert in bluffing? A little voice within me warned me not to admit my shortcomings; I could usually correct them before others even became aware of them.

Allen Grover explained that there were bilingual staff people down at the embassy office, of course, but the place was seriously understaffed. No one could be spared to help at the residence, because the State Department had already fired a third of the staff. Before Mr. Grover rang off, he asked me to fly from Washington to New York the next day, on a Saturday, to discuss the possibility of my transfer to Rome.

He called me on Monday after that meeting. "I've talked to the Luces. We're going to give it a try," he said, "and if it doesn't work out, we'll send you right back—first class." It took me all of two weeks to resign from the agency, pack, and fly to Rome. It happened so fast, Mother didn't even have time to object, since she had to help me pack for life in another country. She managed to get in a couple of complaints ("How are you going to meet any nice men over there? How are you going to find a husband in that unlikely foreign place?")

My agency friends were surprised but elated for me. I was to be paid temporarily by Time-Life in New York until the embassy could afford to put me on its payroll, but I was to have diplomatic status anyway. I had my diplomatic passport, all my shots, and a firm determination to make this work. The minute I announced in K Building that I was going to work for Clare Boothe Luce—famous beauty, wit, congresswoman, playwright, author, politician, and now ambassador—everyone seemed to react with amazement that I had the guts to take the job.

"She's tough," said one person.

"She'll skin you alive," said another.

"Better keep your job open at CIA. You may need it shortly."

"She's a real dragon lady. Breathes fire. Eats little children."

I had heard only exciting, laudatory things about this woman all my life, but by the time my plane had landed at Ciampino Airport, I was really worried. She had elicited such negative reactions when I proudly informed people I was off to Rome to work for her. My parents had backed me up, of course. Mother was proud that her daughter was going to work for one of the world's most famous, distinguished women. My father had met her at a stag house party of important Republicans at Dave Ingalls's house in Cleveland just before she and Henry Luce were married. Mr. Luce had brought her along as a "surprise." My father had been impressed, first, by how well she looked in a bathing suit, and second, by the fact that she beat every man there in swimming races in the Ingallses' pool. Henry Luce had taken bets on her from all the men who believed a fragile blond could not possibly swim stronger and faster than they—all strong men and "in perfect athletic condition," as they considered themselves

Mother kept saying, "You come right back if Rome doesn't work out. We'll pay for your return plane fare, don't worry. Don't be a martyr over there." (Ah, the comforting protection of family, even in one's mid-twenties!) Mother, too, had heard the scuttlebutt that Clare Luce was, to use some of the critics' language, a "bitch," although my mother would never use a word like that.

I was justifiably uneasy when I finally arrived at the destination I had tried so hard to reach. The Luce job had happened so fast. But then, in the car on my way to the hotel with Kip Finch of Time Inc., who had been dispatched to fetch me at the airport, I took note of the color of the Roman sky, the abundance of trees and flowers already in bloom, the beauty of the people passing on the street, the splashing waters of the fountains with their stone or bronze ornamental animals, and the majesty of the fragments of Roman ruins, tucked casually into the façades of modern buildings, with greenery springing forth from the cracks in the ancient stones. My grandmother, Bawa, would have said, "You're a lucky girl. Now, whatever you do, don't mess things up." I decided I definitely would not. Besides, think of how much I would be learning, I told myself, banishing any thoughts that this Roman experience would fail. I always had an endless desire to learn—that meant pure joy for me, and there was so much more to be experienced in life.

After a night's sleep spent fighting my jet lag (trips were longer, airplanes went much slower in those days, and made stops in more places), Kip Finch escorted me to the villa for my initial meeting with the ambassador. Even Kip was nervous for me. I had been brought all this way from the United States, sight unseen, and Mrs. Luce was known for her quick dislikes. My job was to hinge entirely on the success of our personal relationship. It was like playing roulette: "Faîtes vos jeux, messieurs et dames. Rien ne va plus." It was Sunday afternoon. We were ushered through the front gate by Ferdinando, the *portiere* (who looked more like a diplomat than a gatekeeper), and down a driveway lined on both sides with tall cypress trees, standing at attention like honorary guards. I was familiar with this rosy stuccoed villa from having stayed there with the Bunkers a couple of years before, but I certainly looked at it now with a new pair of eyes. It was not just a pretty piece of historic Italian architecture. It was to be my workplace, where I would spend more hours in a day than in my living quarters.

Built in the sixteenth century as a seminary for rich young Italian nobles, the villa was surrounded by acres of disciplined gardens and fountains, which were destined to become the perfect series of outdoor dining rooms for the Luces' entertaining six months of the year. Gnarled intertwining ilex trees formed a natural vaulted ceiling over the walkways.

I was ushered up an enormous stairway to the second floor (*primo piano,* in Italian) by the very proper butler, Pellegrino Capitani, who eyed me silently but carefully with every step. Capitani, the most famous butler in Rome by virtue of working in the most prestigious post—for the American ambassador—knew that if I was to be accepted as the assistant of *Sua Eccellenza,* he and I would be either very close or at one another's throats.

Mrs. Luce had been napping before I was ushered into her boudoir. She was wearing blue bedroom slippers and a pale blue peignoir over her blue nightgown. With that amazing white skin, sparkling blue eyes, and white-blond hair, she looked like a diminutive and surprisingly young Alice in Wonderland. She looked up at me in wonder—no one had prepared her for my height, particularly in heels. "And do you mean to say you can type?" she asked incredulously, and then laughed at her own question. I sat down across from her, on one of the pale blue satin *bergères.* An oversized square inlaid marble coffee table separated our chairs. The table was covered with magazines that had been airmailed over by Time, as well as straw letter baskets full of embassy work and writing projects. The table was littered with almost every electronic gadget that had been invented: dictaphones, minirecorders, tape recorders, record players, and the most important part of anything electrical in Italy—generators to transform American electrical voltages and watts into Italian. (Of course, nothing would work—ever—which was to be, as she described it, "my greatest cross.") This surprising jungle of electronics was in her bedroom, but it was also her workroom. The scene was one of neatness and tidiness, luxurious but incredibly work-oriented. There were ten or fifteen yellow legal pads neatly stacked and two enormous antique silver mugs full of Time Inc.'s famous red editors' pencils.

We talked for two hours. She was absolutely fascinating. That voice! It was so smooth and silky, coming from a magical throat. Since she did all the talking, I had no idea how she was reacting to me. Her grammar was impeccable, her vocabulary intimidating, her diction perfect, her laughter irresistibly contagious. She told me about the Luces' experiences in arriving at the port in Naples, with cheering throngs there to greet her. She was obviously given movie-star treatment, with the Italians throwing kisses to her and shouting, "Bella donna! Bella donna!"

"Those are two words I've learned since I've been here," she said, chuckling as she repeated them. "There was a contingent of American military in parade formation to greet me," she continued, "embassy officials, Foreign Office officials, the dean of the Diplomatic Corps. There was a band playing somewhere, children waving little flags, and, oh, yes, two or three guitar players strumming nearby, barely heard. Harry was so used to having all this pomp for him, he was surprised, but this time it was for me."

I thought she would ask me some questions, but she did not give me a chance to enter into the discussion. She was accustomed to having people vetted before they saw her, so I had no need to tell her anything. Later I was to find this was her way. She was destined to do all the talking, and I was more than an appreciative audience. She recounted her exciting times as a *Life* correspondent during the war, her life as one of the first women in the U.S. Congress, and her love of—and success in—writing plays and books. I was fascinated. How could anyone so beautiful be so sharp and witty? Then she told me about her daughter Ann, who was killed during her college years at Stanford in an auto accident. A great cloud seemed to lower itself over her. The voice changed, becoming lower in volume and in tone, and her eyes were now half shut. She explained that she welcomed working like a demon at this embassy job because she did not want to give in to the grief she felt.

"You are very close to what would have been my Ann's age," she said, and I realized this was obviously part of the reason I had landed this job.

Early-evening shadows now covered the grounds of the Villa Taverna as I glanced out the window. It was time to go. She bade me good-bye, never once mentioning whether or not I had the job. It was simply a fait accompli. The chemistry between us had been right, and besides, I was "so perfectly fluent in Italian," as my résumé had said. She told me to sleep well tonight, "because tomorrow, Monday, your first day on the job, all hell is going to break loose. Hell has been waiting impatiently for your arrival."

My first day could very well have been my last. Mr. Luce had some extra time that afternoon and Mrs. Luce was down in her embassy office, so he kindly asked me if I would like to explore the villa's grounds with him. I welcomed a chance to leave my messy office, full of cartons and boxes to unpack. He wanted to explore the catacombs in the garden that supposedly led to the Vatican—a very special escape route for the clergy living in the villa. I was quickly disenchanted by this idea once we had gone behind the ramshackle door and begun our descent into a very cold, wet passageway. Mr. Luce had the only flashlight, and as I clunked behind him in the mud, I felt I was treading upon worms, too. Worms from the bodies of failed escapees? After fifteen minutes, I had had enough. I was catching cold. There was nothing to see. The "catacombs" had collapsed partway. I had a lot of work to do back at the villa, so I made my excuses and left Mr. Luce. I did not notice that the crude door had swung shut behind me. The publisher of Time-Life was now imprisoned, unable to free himself from the inside. His cries for help went unheeded for forty-five minutes until Nicola, the gardener, heard human, muffled sounds, opened the door, and went down after him. Mr. Luce's flashlight batteries were almost dead. He could not tell where he was or in which direction he was headed. One does not lock Henry Luce in a dank, wet underground place. He was raging mad, like a bull that has just received the thrust of a bandillero. I apologized in my usual overblown way, but it fell on impervious ears. I wrote him an emotional note of apology, left it in his bedroom, and begged Mrs. Luce for advice on what to do next, short of taking a taxi to Ciampino Airport to fly home.

Her advice was simple. "Avoid him at all costs for the next week. There's another way of putting it. Hide."

"Of all the terrible things I could have done on my first day on the job!" I moaned.

"Cheer up," she grinned. "I'll tell you one thing you could have done that would have been a lot worse for you. You could have locked me in the catacombs instead of Harry!"

La vita Romana thus began without my being able to catch my breath. It was always going to be like that around Clare Luce. That Monday morning she gave me a schedule of seven parties we were to give within the next two weeks. I felt as though the Luces had been waiting for me, like tigers crouched in the underbrush.

"I don't want to be consulted about any of these parties," she said, "linens, menus, wines, anything. I just want to attend them. I have enough problems down at the Chancery. I don't want any more here, at the house, but I want our entertaining to be distinguished and flawless. Your job is to accomplish that independent of me. In fact, your job is to be my wife!" I thought that one over quite a while. "The wife of." This was going to be a wild ride.

I rented a furnished apartment on the Via Serpieri near the Villa Taverna that very afternoon and moved in, and at six in the evening interviewed an embassy-recommended hefty peasant woman from Abruzzi to live in, keep the place clean, and even cook dinner. Her name was Brandina. She had one whisker on her chin, only three teeth still in her mouth, and the biggest bust I have ever seen on a woman. She also apparently had a will of iron. No nonsense. She was heaven-sent.

I knew from my Paris experience that the first friendships to forge in an embassy are not with high potentates like minister-counselors and political attachés, but with the secretaries down at the offices in the Palazzo Margherita on the Via Veneto, and with the household staff out at the Residence. They would either make or break me in the performance of the job. In the world of diplomacy, if you start in the basement with the people there and earn their trust and affection, you'll get up to the penthouse with everyone's support. There were eighteen Italians on the regular staff at the Villa Taverna, with another six who came in regularly to help with parties. The big cheese was Capitani, the butler (*maggior d'uomo*), and his retinue of footmen in livery. There was also Rocco, the chef, and his sous-chefs. Rocco spoke in his own dialect, but we understood one another anyway, as long as I flattered and praised him enough. When I would mention that today's *osso bucco* at lunch was *delizioso,* it was sufficient to inspire him to venture beyond perfection for his next meal.

There was a noticeable amount of flirting among the young footmen and the pretty young maids on the third floor, the work floor of the villa and the site for not only all the pressing, polishing, and sewing, but sexual trysts among the staff. I joked with some of my friends down at the embassy by referring to it as the sex floor. "I would never go up there," Mr. Luce, the son of missionaries, said gruffly one day, after hearing some noise on the servants' stairway. "I would expect to walk in on something outrageous. Clare and I consider it off limits to us." Little did we know then that a few months later, hearing terrible noises, the ambassador would appear in her nightgown on the top floor to stop a fight between two of the footmen over one of the maids. One of the protagonists of this operatic scene had a large knife from the kitchen. Mrs. Luce managed to wrest it away from him by yelling in English with such formidable anger, she must have scared the animals in the zoo nearby. There were no more knives that we were aware of, ever again, and the staff was in admiration and awe of her. "Don't mess with *her*" was obviously the staff slogan. She was delighted when the whole episode was over. "Now I know where the opera comique got its foundations," she said.

I had to laugh at Mr. Luce's being so shocked that there could be sex in this U.S. Government–owned house. It was a manifestation of his Presbyterian prudery. "Mr. Luce, we're in Italy, and these are Italians. They love to make love. It's part of their tradition."

"I should think it would greatly interfere with their work," he said sternly. Mr. Luce was obviously against anything of that nature.

"Actually, it doesn't," I replied, "and we should take into account the hours they work, too, from sunrise to past moonrise, six days a week. What Americans would work on a schedule like that? Thank heavens there aren't any American-type labor unions here to investigate this."

Henry Luce thought that over for a minute, still couldn't find the logic in it, shook his head, and went back to his economic report.

The autonomy that the Luces gave me in my job made me rather smug to have such a free hand in organizing events, with no one criticizing me unless I made a terrible mistake, so naturally, I did make terrible mistakes. The ambassador gave me the simplest of instructions about the parties the Luces were to give. "It's up to you," she said, handing me the copy of a page from her State Department briefing book, which I was supposed to read and digest, right then and there. "The purpose of official entertaining is to make friends for the United States, and to help spread the knowledge of and support for American foreign policy. Social contacts can become very important in the conduct of official business. Guest lists are to be composed of the leading officials of both countries, the top Italian government figures, ambassadors from other important countries based in Rome, and senior American officials based in Rome." Mr. Luce had mentioned that he would also enjoy meeting the leading Italian industrialists and members of the financial community, and he added with a chuckle, "and don't forget members of Roman society."

Mrs. Luce admonished me to be sure to do these parties so well, everyone would think that she was the one who planned them. How different she was from Mrs. David Bruce, who went repeatedly over and over all details of every party, tightening up every aspect of the plan to make it perfection. Thank God I had been fortunate enough to have been trained by Evangline Bruce, so that I could be of more use to Ambassador Luce.

When I was planning our first party—a dinner for forty-eight people—it became quickly apparent that the inventory of equipment on hand was lamentable. The linens were torn and frankly unusable. Help was at hand. After a one-hour interview, the Duchessa Lante della Rovere, a woman of noble birth, a member of the papal aristocracy on both the Lante and Rospigliosi sides of her family, and the impoverished wife of a noble who was having an incestuous affair with her sister (nothing in Italy was ever simple), was anointed "housekeeper." Her friends called her Nelly, which was a lot easier than using all this *marchesa* stuff. She accompanied me to the best linen house in Rome to buy fifty place mats with matching napkins, eight large tablecloths, and a hundred and fifty beautifully embroidered napkins for buffet parties. Evidently money was no object with the Luces. They wanted things up and running—fast.

There were not nearly enough plates and stemware in the inventory for our first party, so we sent an emergency request to the Foreign Buildings Operations (FBO) to enable us to purchase some large sets of china and glasses. They said no, there were no funds, so the Luces had me order enough of everything we needed both for formal diplomatic entertaining and summer parties in the garden. By now Nelly and I had the courage to order a full set of sterling silver flatware, too, having found only a few errant knives and forks of different patterns in the villa. Mr. Luce simply forwarded the bills when they arrived to Time-Life in New York. Done. So simple.

I saw proof that very first week that to be an ambassador to a large, popular post requires personal wealth, not just diplomatic skills. In 1953 the Luces spent, of their own money, over a hundred thousand dollars, an enormous sum at the time, to equip the villa. Otherwise, the villa with its shabbiness would have provoked diplomatic gossip. The United States would have made *brutta figura*—a very poor showing—and we would have lost face. We were perceived as the most powerful, educated, graceful country in the world. Let us do nothing to change that.

CBL (as I now referred to her in memos) did not want to bother about food ("Tish, I don't know one pasta, veal dish, or *tiramisu* from another, and I don't want to know, so just decide"). My reaction, frankly, smacked of undeserved superiority. Had I not learned about gourmet diplomatic food from Evangeline Bruce in Paris? Had I not learned well from Signora Sera during my lessons in her kitchen in Washington? Mrs. Luce, leave the menus to me. You will be very happy, I promise you.

So naturally my first two important dinners in Rome were disasters. If one learns from one's mistakes, I guess I was learning a lot. The menu for the first important official dinner was accidentally all white. Not a speck of color. White asparagus, creamed soup, white fish, veal in a cream sauce, endive salad, and a frothy white blancmange pudding. HRL asked if I was color blind. Rocco and I leaped to correct this situation: the next dinners were so colorful, every item on the menu looked like a tutti-frutti nightmare, with strident color everywhere. Mrs. Luce called a halt this time after glimpsing a neon-orange fish sauce. "Good Lord," she lamented, "I felt I needed my sunglasses at the table." Rocco and I went back into our football huddle and came up with balanced menus, with just the proper amount of color and no-color.

The second major official dinner saw the Luces being very solicitous of the guests of honor, Secretary of Agriculture Ezra Taft Benson and his wife, who had not touched one morsel of their food. The State Department had asked the Luces to put on a big blast for the secretary, since he was giving the major address to a new, very important international organization based in Rome, the Food and Agriculture Organization (FAO). When Mr. Luce, after noticing the Bensons ate nothing, suggested sympathetically that they might be having tummy troubles, he added, "We have lots of medications upstairs for this." Secretary Benson smiled and said, "Oh, no, Harry. It's just that as Mormons, we do not touch alcohol." There had been sherry in the consommé, white wine in the fish sauce, red wine in the meat entrée, and cognac in the dessert, crème brûlée.

Mr. Luce pulled me aside. "You know, Tish, if you had spent three years trying to come up with the most inappropriate menu you could concoct, you couldn't have done better than this."

His fury was softened somewhat by the flow of my dramatic apologies.

I had always thought that my office at the residence in Paris, with its carved wood panels, satin- and velvet-upholstered antique chairs, and priceless oriental rugs, would hold the record for lavishness. But my Rome office was equally sumptuous. The floors of the villa were beautifully patterned yellow-and-blue-flowered porcelain tiles, the lighting fixtures depicted flowers and branches in delicate colors of Venetian glass, and giant Venetian glass mirrors reflected the gold damask brocades of the walls. French windows opened everywhere into the gardens. The command post in the villa was not my office, however—it was Clare Boothe Luce's bedroom. She worked in bed in this feminine, pastel environment many hours a day, following the philosophy, "The more time spent off the feet, the fewer lines in the face." All of her speeches and articles were written in bed. My office was right outside her room, but in its disorder, it was such an eyesore that the ambassador considered it akin to a city dump. "It is always so messy and full of what seems like junk," she complained. She finally had the nuns at a nearby convent letter a sign in beautifully illuminated calligraphy, as the monks used to do in the

Middle Ages: "A dirty desk is the sign of a dirty mind." She had it framed and hung over my typewriter.

It would have been easier to keep up to her standards of order if she had not had the habit of piling enough work on my desk to keep three executive assistants busy on overtime. Every time I thought I would have a heart attack from the stress, I remembered what I was learning, the fascinating work in which I was engaged, and the famous people with whom I was corresponding, from literati to movie stars, and from the secretary of state to the leading theatrical producer in the world. Undue stress? What stress?

In my role of "ambassador's wife," I started in right away serving tea to prominent visitors and impressing them with the Luces' art collection, hung on the villa walls. I soothed the members of the embassy staff when they felt they had displeased the ambassador in some way (yes, they were scared of her the first year). I tried to keep good public relations going for her with the press back in the United States by writing a note for her to sign to every single journalist who wrote about her, saying how much she appreciated the article (no matter how critical and snide it had been). Then there were the parties, for endless streams of Italian officials as well as VIP Americans passing through Rome, and Henry Luce's powerful friends in government and in the press all around the world. The houseguests were difficult to keep happy: they always wanted a car when there wasn't one free, and they kept losing their passports or leaving a package behind (at the Colosseum, at that "restaurant on the Via Veneto," or "somewhere on the beach at Ostia"—and would Miss Baldrige mind tracking it down before plane time?) It was easier to coordinate the ambassador's schedule than the visitors'.

Twenty folders at once obscured my desk, each containing the plans for a separate event, jammed full of messages in English, Italian, and French. There were three suggested menus for each lunch or dinner, and stipulations for linens, flowers, seating charts, and names of strolling musicians "who might be free to drop by and perform on party night." An updated copy of the guest list was always thoroughly annotated, saying who everyone was, their accomplishments, official ties, and a hint of any skeletons rattling around in their closets. Before this ruling, Mr. Luce did not know whom he was sitting between and didn't care. One day he arrived at the table late and turned his back all through lunch on an "ugly, boring woman with halitosis." He felt chagrined about it afterward when he learned she was a member of a European royal family. He felt even more chagrined when he realized that the memo I had left on his bedside table the night before explained in detail about the visiting royal.

On top of that, I was to handle all the personal correspondence that came to the villa except for stateside personal business and family matters, which CBL's longtime faithful secretary, Dorothy Farmer, handled miraculously well, first from an office at the embassy for a while and then from her office back in New York. Chubby little Dorothy may have looked like a soft white snowball, but in fact she was a fireball of action. She had consciously assigned her own life over to CBL, juggling relations with literary agents, Broadway producers, lawyers, money managers, and the long list of widows that Clare supported in their later years.

I would arrive at the villa at 8 A.M. and leave around 9 P.M.—on easy nights, that is. During the first two weeks on the job, I understood nothing on the telephone. It did not matter much anyway because one was always cut off after a minute's conversation. Italian voices came at me over the wire with machine gun speed, rat-a-tat-tat, crackling in my ear. Everyone sounded as though their lives depended on the transmission of their message. Could all of this be that important? I kept asking myself. It obviously was to the Italians. In the first days at the villa, I made a logical guess at what each message was, and on all of the message slips, I gave the ambassador the caller's name and telephone number for an embassy secretary to act upon. I would write, "Signor Attolico wants Mrs. Luce to call him back." Signor Attolico might have been calling her to tell her a Communist cell was about to blow up the Villa Taverna, but I took a chance that was not his purpose in calling. It was a great comfort to slip my nondescript messages into her briefcase, to be dealt with down at the embassy, but I realized my American colleagues down at the offices in the Palazzo Margherita would soon catch on to my bluffing game. I had to learn the language fast and get beyond kitchen Italian, or I would be sent home in disgrace. I begged each caller to go slowly—s l o w l y—and they did. If they repeated a name ten times, I could get it, title and all.

By the end of two weeks, I had strained so hard to understand people, it worked. I thus began my journey into fluency in the language. You have to have an ear to become fluent in a foreign language, but you have to be able to work at it like a tiger.

I was also, alas, in charge of the ambassador's wardrobe, making certain, along with her faithful German personal maid Gretel, to keep her fashionably dressed on all occasions, a subject of no interest to her whatsoever. She hated having fittings, making selections, talking to designers, deciding on fabrics. In fact, she would usually send Gretel, who was painfully thin, to the fittings to substitute for her. The only trouble was that she and Gretel were two dress sizes apart, of totally different heights and body shapes!

The ambassador would be photographed by international photographers every time she stepped out of any door, and she could not have cared less. It became my job to make her care. "Everyone is dying to dress you. Fabiani and Simonetta, Eleanora Garnett, Irene Galitzine, the Sorelle Fontana, just everyone here." (This was before the time of Valentino and the Milano designers Versace and Giorgio Armani.) Clare Luce was the only woman I have ever known whose clothes wore her. She did not wear them, but it made no difference. She was startlingly beautiful and intelligent. She was always suitably, expensively dressed, even if you never quite knew what she was wearing. Clothes were an afterthought.

She finally allowed the Fontana sisters to custom-make her first Roman ball gown. It was made of what must have been hundreds of yards of layered tulle—all in rainbow colors. She wore the dress only once, complaining she could not get through a swinging door in it, and then gave it to a charity. She insisted that every designer put deep pockets on both hips in everything they made for her—even her evening dresses—so she could stuff them with eyeglasses, compact, lipstick, even a small notepad and pen (eighteen-karat gold, Cartier). She couldn't bother to carry a handbag.

The entertaining pace never relaxed at the Villa Taverna. The Luces' presence in Rome had caused a social revolution. Everyone who was anyone and everyone who was no one wanted to entertain them. They could not help but be aware of the strength of their social draw, with close to a hundred invitations arriving weekly at the Villa Taverna, inviting them to everything from a wine festival in Sicily to a sixtieth wedding anniversary in the Alto Adige. Understanding how social success can achieve business goals for the United States, they did not choose to waste their ammunition. The embassy decided which official, government-related invitations they should accept, and then the Luces would cut that number by half. On the social invitations, they had to rely on me and my network of information suppliers. To our own dinners, we invited the usual coterie of official, diplomatic, and business figures, but we added the spice and glamour of young, beautiful people, too. I would discuss the guest lists with Nelly Lante. Her word was law when it was a question of the old papal aristocracy like the Prince Orsini and the Prince Colonna families, who had been tied to the Vatican for centuries. Because they were "black papists," their behavior was always supposed to be above reproach. (It wasn't.) Then there was the café society, the jet set of Rome—people like Prince Nicolo and Princess Luciana Pignatelli; Count Rudi Crespi and his wife, Consuelo; and his brother Marco Fabio Crespi and his wife, Vivi. They were constantly in *Vogue*, *Harper's Bazaar*, and *Town & Country*. They were a decorative, essential part of every guest list.

The Luces knew that the presence of the young at their parties made them instantly palatable, decorative, and amusing, even to the most ossified and important of Roman statesmen and business moghuls. Consequently I was able to sneak onto the guest lists many of my own friends. Mr. Luce's two sons, Henry Jr. (Hank) and Peter, visited often—

especially Hank—which was always a reason for a big party. Mr. Luce's many nieces, nephews, stepnieces, and stepnephews contributed to the feeling of youth around the house. Mrs. Luce commented about her niece Libby Severinghaus that "she can unstuff any group just by the way she walks into a room."

There was usually music at our parties—never during dinner, because both Luces were furious when they couldn't hear what others were saying or be easily heard themselves during the meal. I saw to it that there were guitarists, singers, and violinists ready to play romantic music after dinner. Because of the beautiful weather, we were able to have dinners outside under the ilex trees five to six months out of the year. Imposing pink travertine marble refectory-style tables, with travertine benches to match, lined each side of the terrace. The sixteenth-century seminarians had eaten their meals on these, too. We used the newly purchased hand-painted earthenware plates and place mats embroidered in the same ferns found in the gardens. The setting was a midsummer night's dream. On the Roman fragments of walls, we set three-hundred-year-old iron pots filled with oil, which, when illuminated, shot rays of moonlight up through the branches of the ilex trees overhead. There were no bugs. The strong perfume of constantly blooming rosebushes wafted over us and the sparkling crystal reflected the candlelight. It was all exquisitely romantic, to which the music added a great deal, although some of us with observant eyes had to snuff out our laughter when the trio of rather raunchy Roman musicians hovered, bending low right over the *poitrine* of any well-endowed lady. Said lady, of course, would not notice their crude gestures, swooning as she was over the music and the attention. The musicians managed to converse with their eyes as they sang and played. I would pass by when they were being too obvious and whisper "Cattivo!" (wicked), but they were just naughty little boys.

It was necessary for me to live near the Villa Taverna, to be within five minutes of the office. Down the street from the residence was the entrance to the Roman zoo, a noisy neighbor populated with animals, strong outer fences, cages, and natural wildlife scenery—pathetic in comparison to American zoos, but striking enough. All day long we could hear the sounds of trumpeting elephants, braying zebras, chattering monkeys, and growling tigers. At night, when the elephants grew hungry again, they let the world know it, and their trumpeting got many other animals started. The sounds drove Mrs. Luce *pazza* when she was trying to sleep. Because of my theory that one never bucks the boss, we got her a special pair of earplugs to wear at night. No one could deny, either, that when the opera *Aïda* was being performed in the summer in the outdoor Baths of Caracalla, a good three miles away, the elephants, zebras, and camels marching through the streets to and from the Roman theater made for a magnificent sight. Traffic was stopped or detoured, but the Italians didn't mind the inconvenience at all; anything for art and opera.

My apartment was a little farther from the zoo than the Villa Taverna, but in any case nothing could keep me from sleeping after my average workday. The apartment had simple but adequate furniture with a flowery green-and-beige cotton fabric covering the seating pieces. A built-in illuminated niche over the sofa gave the room a very glamorous atmosphere, particularly when the other lights in the living room were turned off. The landlord had hung a painting in the niche, a dreadful Atlantic City boardwalk kind of thing. I changed it. The lighting, the scent of the flowers, the deliciousness of my stock of brandy, and my record player playing a Frank Sinatra album made this room, as one young man expressed it, "a lethal spider's web."

There were two bedrooms and two baths, and a nice little dining room in addition. For one year my chic friend Grace Mirabella shared the apartment and its expenses with me before returning to New York to become editor in chief of *Vogue* magazine. With Brandina cooking good dinners for our guests at least twice a week, Grace and I had a wonderful social life. We would give Brandina three hours' notice that guests were coming to dinner, and she would go flying out the door with her crocheted tote bag and make it up to the open air food market and back in twenty minutes. Ecco! A hot cheese soufflé, following the first course of *prosciutto con melone* and a beautiful green salad. Brandina was very vocal about her opinion of the men who came to the apartment. If she liked the male guests, we would hear a happy sort of cackling in the kitchen, and one of us would say to the guests, "You've been approved." If she did not like them, which was most of the time, she muttered dark criticisms out in the kitchen the entire time. She simply distrusted men.

There was no hiding the fact that Henry Robinson Luce, big-time editor in chief, was a focal point of our lives. The Italians had known all about him, through his magazines, long before they ever heard of his wife. Tall, gray-haired, handsome, with fierce, bushy eyebrows, he was an imposing figure to the Italians. His clothes were tailored in Savile Row in London, and he could never come around to admiring, much less understanding, the pinched-waist style of the Italian tailors, and the pointed shoes so popular at that time. He liked Italian silk ties and shirts, but the admiration stopped there.

He was unaware of what great consternation his presence caused in government circles. "Mr. Luce," I told him one day, "you are causing acute indigestion down at the Palazzo Chigi in the Protocol section."

"Put that in English," was his gruff reply.

"Even though you are the male spouse of a high official, you have no rank. You will have to sit in what is called 'a lowly place' at official meals, whereas Mrs. Luce will sit in a top seat. The Italian government is having a heart attack. They're afraid to even talk to you about it."

"Will the food be any different down at the bottom of the table?" Trust Mr. Luce's sense of humor to come through at a time like this.

"You'll have one big compensation," I replied, "because you'll probably be sitting between two young, lovely, unranked women."

"And that's supposed to be bad?"

"No, that can be very good."

"Well then, don't let the Palazzo Chigi change my nonrank status in this city, whatever you do. Leave it as it is."

He loved being unranked. Everyone paid him homage at home in the United States, "everything," he once described it, "short of kissing my hand"—but here he sat with beautiful young princesses and countesses, while his wife sat among older more important stuffed shirts.

I found out something that very few of Henry Luce's cohorts at Time-Life ever knew: their boss was at heart a social butterfly who had found a new life with the titled Roman aristocracy. Born and raised in hardship as the son of a missionary in China, he had been a big player—a genius, in fact—from his thirties on in every avenue of journalism, business, international politics, and the Republican Party. Royalty was something he had not experienced "up close and personal" before, except to greet Their Majesties in England with all the stiff protocol that surrounded such visits. Now here he was in Italy, with beautiful young royals all around—none with a kingdom, of course, but with social credentials and historic breeding intact. Mussolini had not been able to destroy that. No one appreciated more than HRL going to dine in the magnificent palazzi of Princess Pallavacini, the Aldobrandinis, the Aspreno Colonnas, the Caracciolos, or even the Pecci-Blunts. "It's frankly very different for me," he said one day, " to be invited into these historic edifices for dinner rather than ordering an excellent meal at '21' with [owner] Mac Kriendler hovering solicitously."

He and I had, I like to believe, a very special relationship. I suppose I had a kind of a crush on him. His Presbyterian character was all there in his face, and he was so dapper and classy looking in that marvelous gray tweed Chesterfield coat with the gray velvet collar! He thought I was amusing because I was not afraid of him. If he was tired, he would let me talk and talk, and it was for him a rest period. I was certainly not one of his yes men. He could be pretty rough when he didn't see the logic in being otherwise. I lectured him when he did something wrong or rude in a social context, such as not seeing a prominent guest to the door when that person left. I was also just one more source of information for him, and there is nothing he liked more than that. I kept him in touch with the actions and mood of the young Italians. High-ranking diplomats see only other high-ranking diplomats, and in a country like Italy, that is certainly no fun.

I made him ride on the backseat of a Vespa, behind one of our embassy drivers, which he pronounced very exciting—"But is it the same when you're seated behind a pretty girl, which everyone here seems to be?" (He was only half kidding, but I wasn't about to arrange that, with Mrs. Luce a room away in the villa.) I talked often about the Sunday-afternoon soccer (*futbol*) games at the Foro Romano. His curiosity finally grabbed him. He didn't know what the game was or why the Italians seemed so passionate about it, but ever curious, he wanted to go to a game with my young Italian friends and me. I warned him that it was all very "popolare," informal, and that the enthusiastic crowd was sometimes rude. I told him girls got pinched black and blue in the crowd. Now he really wanted to go, so we took the renowned publisher in his custom-tailored clothes and gray fedora to his first *futbol* game. Our seats were cheap, the kind he had not sat in for thirty years or so, to watch the Squadra Roma play the Squadra Lazio in soccer in the huge sports arena Mussolini had built for the Olympic Games. To the spectators, this might have been a game of the Mets versus the Yankees in Shea Stadium. I kept telling him how exciting and wonderful this national sport was, but he understood practically nothing going on around him—the tumultous shouting of men with short muscular legs in shorts and wool knee socks, running up and down the field, kicking a ball in a frenzied fashion, even bouncing it off their heads. At one point a Lazio fan sitting behind us, carried away with enthusiasm, smashed HRL's hat down over his ears with a joyous cry.

"You now look like one of the Three Stooges," I teased him. The fans were all to a man (and to a rare woman) really showing their emotions, which fascinated our guest; he had never shown any of his own in public.

Henry Robinson Luce never attended another *futbol* game, but at least he had experienced it once, and that is the way he approached all of life.

My ambassador boss was a stickler for details. I at times was sloppy in this regard, and she went into her "explosion mode" whenever that was apparent. I was not the only one penalized for lack of attention to detail. Her good friend, former senator Bill Benton, had shipped to her in Rome, air freight, at an unbelievable cost, a full set of more than twenty volumes of the new edition of his *Encyclopaedia Britannica*. Each book had been bound in the finest of soft Italian leathers with her name and the year hand-tooled in gold by the Florentine bookbinders. The only trouble was that her name, as usual, was misspelled: each volume had the gold letters "Clare Booth Luce" instead of "Clare Boothe Luce." She made me send the entire set back to Bill Benton, collect air freight, with a note that said, "Bill, these are very nice, but they're for someone else. They don't have my name on the covers."

I told her only she could get away with that; anyone else would have made do with such a minor spelling mistake.

"There is no minor misspelling mistake," she countered, "when it's a question of your *name*."

Mrs. Luce may have shown her toughness in many ways, but she also showed great sentimentality in her relationships with the staff. The villa went into a state of shock when our butler, Capitani, died very suddenly of a heart attack. He had served *l'Ambasciatore* with immense pride for two years now, after many years of serving the *aristocrazia* in their Roman palazzi. The ambassador announced, "We will give Capitani what is really, in the butlers' world, a state funeral, because that is his due."

He was laid out for a special journey to heaven. Every princely house and every embassy in Rome sent a representative, formally dressed, to pay their respects and sign the gold-tooled leather book for Capitini's family to keep. On Mrs. Luce's orders, refreshments were served to the mourners on the best embassy silver and porcelain by the young footmen who had served under him, now properly dressed in white tie formal dress, as Capitani would have considered appropriate.

Flowers overflowed the cottage and out onto the lawn. Every butler, chef, housemaid, and all the assistants in the service of the great houses in Rome came. Capitani had been more aristocratic than many of the most famous members of the Roman aristocracy. He lay on an antique bed in a cottage on the villa grounds, dressed for his viewing in one of Mr. Luce's best business suits and a new Brioni silk tie and dress shirt. Tall tapers in the Luces' museum-quality sterling silver candlesticks burned at the four corners of the bed, which had a magnificent Renaissance cut-velvet covering on it. Relatives kept vigil for two nights and two days. The women moaned loudly in unison, regretting his departure, discussing his virtues, and wishing him godspeed on his journey. The wives of two of the street cleaners in front of the villa came up to Mrs. Luce, shook her hand, and said, "You did it properly. You gave him the honor due." Mrs. Luce told me afterward that never before had she been involved in such a successful funeral, and she hoped her own would have as much class as Capitani's.

We had no trouble finding a new butler, even an excellent one, Mario, but the Villa Taverna would never again be the same, even if Mario had served during the war in the famed "running Alpine troops," the Bersagliere. Mario would occasionally, in times of celebration, don his black broad-brimmed Bersagliere hat, with its long, flowing feathers, and run around the villa grounds for old times' sake. To laugh at this point would be sacrilegous.

Clare Luce got all the credit in the Luce family for being religious—her conversion at the hands of the telegenic Bishop Fulton Sheen in New York had made her the best-known convert in America—but in actual fact it was her husband who paid homage to his Lord on Sundays. Clare often missed Mass, but when she did go, she caused a sensation with her black lace mantilla over her blond hair. No one could concentrate on the Mass with La Luce present. Her audiences with the pope (held to the minimum because of the political anti-Catholic harping in the United States aimed at people in government positions) provided fodder for the Italian paparazzi for an entire week. She dressed carefully in her "Madonna look"—a covered-up, floor-length black silk Balenciaga evening gown that made her look very saintly. She would wear an enormous jeweled cross hung from a gold chain. Even Michaelangelo's figures seemed to peer admiringly down at her from the Sistine Chapel ceiling. (Ten years later Jacqueline Kennedy would duplicate her ensemble almost exactly in her visit to the pope as first lady of America.)

It was Henry Luce who was down on his knees every Sunday. He did not want to miss going to church—ever. There were no Presbyterian churches in Rome, but his missionary upbringing had fixed the true meaning of Sunday worship in his blood, as well as in his heart. He did not like going to church alone in a foreign country, so he often accompanied me to the eight o'clock services at the Catholic church closest to the Villa Taverna. He sat next to me in a pew, his eyes glued to his prayer book, never looking at the altar but concentrating on his own thoughts during the entire service (including the sermon in Italian). He would respectfully stand up, sit down, and kneel with all the rest of us during the Mass. This was a House of God and an acceptable substitute until he was back home in a Presbyterian church.

When I told him I had been asked by our church administrator to serve as a professional mourner at the "pauper's Mass" (which he and I attended), he was astonished that an American embassy staffer could be offered such a job. But then again, he said he could believe it; I was completely torn apart emotionally every Sunday when there was a paupers' burial service at eight A.M. I would weep at the presence of the closed rough-hewn wooden caskets in the church center aisle, even without having a clue as to who was inside. The tiny coffins for infants really got to me. In Italy at that time, a law stipulated that every deceased person should have a mourner walking behind the casket for a few blocks from the church. Many of the people in these caskets that were parked down the center of the aisle were unknown and had no families, so I, along with my tears, seemed to be the perfect applicant for the job of chief mourner. The church administrator had no idea who I was. He offered me 500 lire a casket for each Sunday to help a poor dead person start his or her journey to eternity. I had to turn the job down because of my diplomatic duties, but believe me, if I had been able to do it, I would have. (It would have looked great on my résumé, too.) Mr. Luce was absolutely fascinated that there was such a job, and that, furthermore, his and his wife's assistant had been offered it.

The "consort," as some in Rome dared to refer to HRL, was a major influence on his wife's happiness. When he was in Rome, she bubbled with good humor; when he was back in New York, at times she would become morose and unsure. She adored him in spite of their competitiveness and her resentment of the way Time Inc. executives treated her. She was particularly lonely on weekends when he was back in the United States, and since Sunday was my only day off, her loneliness completely destroyed my good times. I would be on my way out of the city (sneaking out is more like it) with young Italian friends, and she would dispatch Wernon, the chauffeur, in the Luces' personal gray Cadillac to find me and shepherd me in my car back to the villa. He always knew where to look in the countryside. I felt hounded by CBL, but I knew there was a psychological need for me to be there "to do some work" and to be an interested listener to her latest ideas on the saga of Italian politics. She knew she couldn't get any official Italians to listen to her theories on Sundays: Elbridge Durbrow, her number two in the embassy, told her frankly that the embassy officers would revolt if she took them away from their families on the one day they could see them. So I was it. CBL would eventually make it up to me by inviting my young Italian friends to some pretty grand parties at the villa and giving them memories to feast upon forever.

Life was so much happier and better functioning when her Harry was in residence. It was terrible when rumors began to circulate our way all the way from New York that he was having an affair with the granddaughter of the English press scion Lord Beaverbrook. Her name was Lady Jean Campbell, and she had formerly been married to author Norman Mailer. It was particularly ironic because Mrs. Luce had reported several times that Lord Beaverbrook over a period of years had been trying to get into her bed, even proposing marriage. "If Harry were to leave me for Lady Jean," Clare commented, "in that instance, I would become Lady Jean's grandmother, and my former husband Harry would become my son-in-law."

Some things are just too terrible to contemplate. Thank God for the sense of humor with which some people are gifted.

When Clare Luce became Italy's number one movie star, without ever having been in a movie but with legions of adoring fans, her husband was never jealous of the attention shown to her. He loved it—after all, it was a reflection on him, the man who had won the prize. He basked in her accolades. He was also modest (and naive) enough not to think that he was responsible for her fame or success.

It was intimidating to be alone with the two of them when they were in competitive mode. Each wanted to better the other, and they preferred to have an audience, even of one, to listen and to referee. (Not that any one person would dare state that one Luce had won over the other.) On nights when they did not have a social engagement, they would sit in her cavernous bedroom, adjacent to her husband's baronial one. A Scrabble game would be set up on a fruitwood gaming table, and they would sit in comfortable chairs, armed with his-and-her dictionaries, and compete with words. Their vocabularies were naturally frighteningly advanced, but when they tried to find words to trick one another, using different dictionaries from secret sources, it was impossible not to laugh and be incredibly awed at the same time.

On one of these evenings, they had a big blowup. Mr. Luce was really angry about something. He sat on the edge of her bed, nervously eating chocolates from an antique crystal candy jar on her bedside table. I gathered up my files and tried to leave the room—it was embarrassing to witness this scene—but CBL stopped me. "No, we still have some work to do," she insisted. She wanted me there. She waited to speak to him until her agitated husband had finished his complaint and eaten the last of the chocolates in the jar.

"Harry," she said brightly, "I think you will be interested to know you have just finished the last of the poodles' [Scusi and Prego] Dog Yummies." Then she became convulsed with laughter. Those Yummies really did look like candy, but HRL admitted later they tasted like "something worse than llama dung."

"How could you let me eat those things, Clare?" he asked angrily.

"But how could *you* have eaten them?" was her answer. "It doesn't say much for the quality of your taste buds."

Finally his sense of humor broke through. He laughed along with his wife and me, but the merriment did not last long. I heard the next day he had spent the entire night being sick in his bathroom.

One of the things I admired most about HRL was his incredible, all-consuming curiosity. He also had a temper—*Dio mio,* did he have a temper—but I understood it and the terrible work pressure laid upon him. (I had seen tempers erupt before, in Paris, with the David Bruces, but it's the staff's job to let it happen, absorb the shock, and forget it ever happened.) Henry Luce always worked through the tantrum, felt sorry for having displayed it, justified or not, and apologized. When he screamed at me one day for having stolen his *Rome Daily American* morning newspaper right off his breakfast tray, he later found out from Capitani that the papers hadn't even been delivered that day. He sheepishly apologized to me with one sentence, but I knew how hard it was for him to do even that.

I had told the Luces the previous day about the "outrageously expensive" evening pumps that were all the rage among the *principesse, duchesse, contesse,* and even *baronesse* for the moment. Italy held the uncontested leadership spot in shoe couture. I had been giving my bosses a report of what young people were wearing in the best nightclubs, and I mentioned the drama of the flashing stones on the heels of the satin pumps women were now wearing on the darkened dance floor. The afternoon of the missing newspaper incident, I received a telephone call from the most expensive *bottier* (shoemaker) in Italy, saying he had received a gift certificate in my name to custom-make a pair of new satin pumps with rhinestone-encrusted heels. Dal'co, the store, said that there was a card attached to the gift certificate: "I hope this will make up for the *Rome Daily American.*" I rushed to Dal'co as soon as I could, and while the salesmen were measuring my feet ("Multi longhi," laughed one shoe salesman), in walked a beautiful, gum-chewing, even bubble-gum-blowing and -popping American woman, Ava Gardner. The casual appearance of an international star on the streets was a common occurrence in Rome. Hollywood considered this its favorite city. Ava Gardner had to wait until they had finished measuring me and writing up my order before they even spoke to her. When I asked, in a whisper, as I left, why had they not taken immediate care of *la famosa actrice,* Signorina Gardner, when she arrived, the head of Dal'co said, "Because you have a much more important job, Signorina, and second, because she is chewing gum, right here, in front of all of us. She is not *una vera Signora,* and you are, Signorina Baldrige."

I loved Mr. Luce's gift of the extravagant shoes, my nights dancing to the rhythm of the sexy new bossa nova beat from Brazil, my arms wrapped around a delicious man and his wrapped around me in the aphrodisiacal darkness. It was fun, too, when I knew my rhinestone-studded heels were glittering on the dance floor, caught by rays of light from somewhere. I had never even heard of the "women's movement" in those days, except in the most distant way. I did not really trust the concept. Where was the woman supposed to be moving? The consciousnesses of my family, friends, and colleagues in the embassy had never been raised, from the feminists' point of view, and we were all more involved with the settlement of the Trieste question than with the cause of women. But here I was, working for one of the most successful women ever to enter a man's world, a woman who had consistently rushed in where angels feared to tread—into the halls of Congress, onto the front lines of World War II, over to Broadway to oversee the production of her plays, into the smoky back rooms where political strategy was made, and onto the world's most important stages. She was one of the first women to go beneath the sea with Jacques Cousteau, the underwater explorer. She was one of the very first people to refer to God as "She." Yet she was unbelievably feminine, determined that women should not compete with their husbands but stay home and mind the children. I caught her on this contradictory philosophy many times during that sojourn in Rome, but each and every time she held fast. She would criticize women who arranged excellent child care in the home so that they could travel for business all over the world. Our conversation was always the same: "But Mrs. Luce, how can you criticize that woman for doing that when she had children? You did that yourself with Ann." "But I did it under totally different circumstances," she would retort.

When I talked about the things I was going to do in my career, after marriage, she surpassed even my mother in lecturing. "Stay home once you have found the right man." The fact that she had never done that herself never entered her consciousness. She was avidly antiabortion and generally against most of the statements of the leading feminists.

"Yet you," I protested to her one day, "scattered leaflets from the open cockpit of a little plane, demanding the right to vote for women. That was very daring and controversial."

"That was different," she answered, irritated. Anything she did at any time was all right. She had her own brand of feminism. I accepted it, too, coming from her (I certainly would not have from anyone else). I guess I was becoming what in that environment was considered a "Luce-type feminist."

Clare Boothe Luce was a natural teacher. Her thoughts were beautifully expressed. She looked at everything in terms of what is good, better, and best, and one should always reach for the best.

She did not have an easy time growing up. She had a pushy mother without a sterling reputation, and there were frankly a lot of bad times and money troubles. She was to lose her only sibling, her brother, David, as a suicide at a fairly young age, and her only remaining blood relative, her daughter, Ann, when she was only twenty. She was to become a dazzling figure in New York because of her first job at a Condé Nast magazine, leading to a wonderful job at *Vanity Fair*, where she began her rise to achievement and fame. In spite of the difficult early years with her mother, she had been born with a great many marketable assets, and she knew it. Some of them had to have come from her much-criticized mother—her looks, for one. There were undeniable attributes like her voice, describable with lots of *M*'s—melodious, modulated, and mellifluous, for starters. She never spoke too loudly. People would lean toward her so as not to miss a word (a good flirtation move, that). If they did, they would always get a delicious whiff of her custom-made perfume, one part Caron's Pois de Senteur and two parts Joy. If someone was hard of hearing, she would graciously raise her voice, but never sounded harsh or strident. Her accent was as cultivated as that of a duchess who had been raised in the great castles of England.

Her voice belied her birth. She had grown up on the wrong side of the tracks, but because of a beautiful, smart mother, she was able to follow her to the right side of the tracks—over, back, and over again, always depending on whoever was paying the bills for her mother. They would move from an unfashionable section to an elegant one as soon as some money could be found to finance it, usually from a gentleman friend of her mother's. Then they would have to move back again to a lesser address and away from the "chic" people of New York.

Her looks were never to desert her, to the unhappy end of her life. She was startlingly fair, blue eyed, and vulnerable looking, like the Renaissance women painted by Botticelli. She looked as fragile as a delicate piece of Sevres porcelain, but the word got around. "Watch out!" one *Vogue* assistant editor warned. "She is as tough and strong as a thick piece of hotel china. Forget the delicate French porcelain." I am positive she suffered because of people talking behind her back like this.

I had heard the worst about her, but I found the best in her. She knew I was impressionable, that I wanted to reach the sky, and she made it one of her projects in life to bring me back to earth, to make me realize I wasn't tough enough to reach the sky, but that down where I was, sitting on the treetops, was a very satisfactory place to be. She said over and over, "If you aim too high, you'll get shot with arrows by those who don't want you there with them. There isn't enough room for you and them. Let me tell you, it really hurts to get shoved out. Live in a world of good friends. Stay where they are, not where the enemies are."

I knew she was very familiar with the world of enemies. When I felt demoralized by the actions of people who were jealous of my own position in Rome, she would laugh and, instead of dispensing sympathy, command me to toughen up, get smart, not waste a minute more on licking wounds, and get out of whatever negative situation I found myself in.

She also warned me again and again that I was the kind who would never be rich and would never therefore have real power. I flinched at this unwelcome reading of my tea leaves. She was going over her jewelry when she told me this, having asked Gretel to lay it all out in her boudoir, so that she could decide what she would wear that night to the ball at the Quirinale Palace, given by the president of the Republic of Italy.

"I want to have money some day," I protested. "Look at those jewels of yours. I want to have jewels like that. I want your kind of lifestyle. I wouldn't mind marrying for money."

"Forget it," she said, "you're not tough enough. You wouldn't last a week. My first marriage [to George Brokaw of New York] was for money, and it was the worse mistake I ever made in my life." Social historians would disagree with her analysis, saying she never could have broken into New York society without someone of Brokaw's standing and bank account. The following Christmas, CBL gave me a pair of gold earrings studded with small diamonds, purchased from the Roman jeweler Petochi. "Now you have your diamonds," she wrote in red ink for Christmas, "so now you can marry for love." It was a double message.

I could not believe my good fortune in having her teach me about so much of what was going on—how to judge her colleagues at the embassy and at the Italian Foreign Office, what was important to read and comprehend in the vast amounts of reading material she had sent to her from around the world, and always, who were the people capable of soothing and comforting her. This was a side of her never reported in the press. She never had an audience as appreciative as I was—for her jokes, her take on the political situation, and her beautiful clothes and jewelry. I sopped it all up like a dry sponge, and took some pretty unfair criticisms from her, too. As with Mr. Luce, when the boss is under terrible pressure and becomes unkind to the staff, there's a reason for it. One must understand the reasons and forgive.

As I watched her in action, I felt I was part of a perpetual seminar, learning from a master. When journalists wrote mean things about her, for example, she would turn on the charm, flatter them, tell them what good journalists they were: "Do come to lunch with me at the Villa Taverna the next time you pass through Rome." It worked like a charm for future stories.

She knew how to take care of her fans. She sent them copies of recent speeches she'd made in Italy, glamorous photographs of her in diplomatic action, even copies of her books and plays. "You leave a little of yourself in their home or workplace," she explained, "and they feel you're there with them forever. It doesn't cause me any trouble, only you!" (It was tedious and complicated to get things wrapped for overseas shipping.)

I learned to write good letters because of Clare Luce. She made me redo my drafts of letters for her signature over and over until I got the right flavor, even the right measure of affection for each person. "Discipline, discipline, Tish! Stop writing all over the lot. Focus. Keep that charm of yours in every letter, but don't forget what I told you about content. Listen to me!"

Every day an overflowing letter box was put on my desk, full of things to do, details to take care of at once. When I saw the letters SMAT—"See Me About This"—at the top of a letter, I knew there was complicated hard work ahead. She would fire barrages of instructions at me, even as we descended the staircase or walked out into the garden, and I would find myself writing notes on anything I could get my hands on—the corner of the newspaper, the back of a magazine, a paper napkin from lunch, the palm of my hand. She always had a little notebook in one of her dress pockets, and a small pen as well, and she couldn't understand why I wasn't as prepared as she always was to spring into action.

She taught me how to say no nicely, so nicely that people think you've said yes. When the wife of the army attaché General Allen proudly ran a "Japanese Flower-Arranging Class and Box Lunch Day," she spent three months trying to get the ambassador to attend. There was no way that would happen, but Mrs. Luce made up for it. She had Rocco, the residence chef, make a huge, delicious cake, decorated with petals, Japanese style. She sent it to the lunch with a note saying, "I am so sorry not to be with you, but I have arranged some flowers for you today anyway."

She taught me how to work a crowd, political pro that she was—a skill I was to bank and use in every job in my future life. "Start on the outside of the room, put a warm smile on your face, even if your feet are killing you, and put out your hand to shake the hand of everyone in the vicinity. Say your name, and they will say theirs. Work toward the inside of the circle. It's less difficult standing in the center—it's like a safety zone, where it's difficult for people to get at you and bother you. Then, when you want to leave, go fast, jet propelled, in a straight line to the outside of the crowd and to freedom. Even if you're not the host of the event, make everyone think you are."

She knew that the "little people," the ones in the embassy who worked so hard for so little pay and so little praise, deserved recognition. After she helped resolve the Trieste dispute, when Yugoslavia and Trieste agreed to stop fighting over the territory, she threw a victory party that very night at the residence. She ordered the very best champagne and caviar and paid for it herself. The guests were not the top officials on the Italian or American sides but the embassy clerks and asssistants in the Code Room, who had been working twenty-hour shifts for days, getting the coded and decoded messages back and forth between the embassy and the State Department. She toasted her guests, who had never even seen the inside of the Villa Taverna before, for their efficiency and their patriotism. (They would never forget *that* night.)

The ambassador had a special love affair with the U.S. Navy—all of it, from gob to admiral. In a moment of enthusiasm, she invited the entire Sixth Fleet to come from Naples to Rome for a Fourth of July party. There had certainly been nothing done like this before. The delighted sailors accidentally trampled all over the gardens, just because the walls of the Villa Taverna did not expand out over several more acres. It was a mob scene—thousands of frankfurters, sodas, and chips, and of course a lot of peeing in the bushes. Not a politician for nothing, CBL wanted to reap some benefit from this party. She told me to drop a message into about ten intelligent ears at that reception, and then watch it circulate: "You know, of course, that the diplomatic achievement of which the ambassador is the most proud is the major role she played in the settlement of the Trieste dispute." Within a short time the entire U.S. Navy knew about Clare Luce and Trieste, and news dispatches all over the world carried the valiant story of her role.

That Fourth of July party brings back other memories to me. We didn't let the sailors into the house because of all the priceless works of art and fragile porcelains everywhere. To save the garden, however, we had to allow some of them to go into the powder room on the ground floor, beyond which they could not venture. Hundreds of navy men used the facility, one by one. Near the end of the party, I suddenly remembered that on the dressing table in the powder room sat a priceless Fabergé vermeil dressing table set—a large hand mirror, comb, brush, powder boxes, and manicure tray. I should have put it away before the fleet arrived. I rushed into the powder room, interrupting a sailor in the act of relieving himself, and said, "Sorry, but I had to get in here." The Fabergé set was gone from the dressing table. I immediately reported it to the navy security officers there, and they said, "Ma'am, don't worry, you'll have it back, probably by tomorrow or the day after."

Of course, it wasn't back by "tomorrow." I called the admiral's office in Naples, feeling that a specially sharpened sword was about to fall on my neck. The admiral's aide got on the phone. "Miss Baldrige, don't worry, by tomorrow you really will have it back. No discussion, this time." We miraculously did have it back by five P.M. the next day. A naval fighter pilot flew it up to the Rome airport, and a naval courier rushed it from there to us. The pieces had obviously been taken by the sailors to send home as souvenirs. They had no idea of the value of the pieces, never having heard of "this guy Fabergé."

When I queried Naples about the miraculous retrieval of the Fabergé set, I was told, and I don't know whether or not this is true, that the admiral had threatened to cancel the leave of every man and woman in the Sixth Fleet until the culprit(s) made restitution. If the entire navy was to be punished by losing leave, the thieves' buddies obviously forced them into surrendering the treasure.

CBL was like a child attending an important birthday when the beloved Sixth Fleet invited her to inspect the naval aircraft carrier near Naples. She rejected the cavalcade of limousines sent by the admiral to escort her to Naples and then onto the SS *Forrestal*. Everything had been planned, according to meticulous protocol, but CBL outfoxed them all, having made private arrangements with the commanding officer of the aircraft carrier. She simply went out to Ciampino Airport in Rome, wearing a bright orange Roman designer jumpsuit complete with helmet and goggles, and flew off with a navy pilot in his fighter plane, onto the carrier in the Bay of Naples. The cheers and whistles of the crew as the beautiful orange-clad ambassador emerged from the cockpit onto the deck could be heard all over the Mediterranean Sea. She knew how to play to her audience, but she also knew that this kind of day was worth all the hard work and sacrifice that preceded it.

Ambassador Luce used me as a willing instrument of her political manipulation. A senator, an acknowledged political enemy of hers, came with his delegation to a party at the villa. Mrs. Luce had me sidle up to him and confide, very quietly, "Senator, I wish you could have heard Ambassador Luce talking to the Italian premier the other night about you. She said you were the great hope of American politics." Needless to say, the senator quickly became one of her best friends. I was told he was even politically helpful to the cause of the State Department budget.

Another example of her "social conniving," as some people rudely called it, was when a stuffy, difficult Italian minister, markedly unfriendly to the United States, was coming for a drink. She and I rehearsed a little ruse together, and it played out beautifully. When the *Ministro* arrived punctually that evening, Capitani greeted him in the hall and took his coat, leaving him at the bottom of the stairs. At the top of the next landing, hidden from his sight, I began singing and playing on the guitar an old Roman song, "Quant' e Bella Roma." The song has some fifty verses, but fortunately for everyone, I didn't attempt that. Capitani walked quickly up the stairs and called out, "*Eccellenza,* your guest has arrived." I stopped singing at that point, and the ambassador picked up my guitar and began sauntering down the stairs. She saw her guest, greeted him, and quickly put the guitar down on a nearby table.

The *Ministro* was stupefied. "That couldn't have been you, Signora Ambasciatore? That wasn't you, surely, singing and playing those *stornelle Romane?*"

"Oh, yes," Mrs. Luce replied breezily. "I have had an amusing time learning some characteristic Roman songs. They're fun to sing." The *Ministro,* who had grown up in the Trastevere district where the songs originated, remained stunned. He told her she was the first ambassador in all his many years in the Palazzo Chigi who sang the old songs in Roman dialect and played the guitar, too. He was in awe of her. Their business conversation proceeded brilliantly, CBL later reported to me. Her fame as a musician spread rapidly in the diplomatic corps, but she modestly and wisely refused to play again upon demand.

She did not mention that in return for my cooperation, she was paying me back ten times over. It was mutually understood. She took me on jaunts to Paris and all over Italy with her. She arranged to have me meet Sir Winston Churchill when he came cruising down the Mediterranean. When I laughingly reminded him of my upending him at the garden party at Buckingham Palace in June 1947, he made no comment and simply turned away. When I mentioned to Mrs. Luce later how disappointed I was by this rebuff, she said, "You should know by now that people like Sir Winston only want to be reminded of stories that center on them, and that make them look very good. They do not want to be reminded of an embarrassing incident caused by a young person."

I told Mrs. Luce that William Faulkner was the literary idol of my life, so when he came to Rome, she invited him to a lunch party and put me next to him. I was so excited, I made a long-distance call to Washington to spread the news to my family. Boy, oh boy, would Miss Lockwood, the head of the Vassar English department, be impressed! After the luncheon was over and everyone had gone, the ambassador asked me how it had all gone. I told her that Faulkner had been awful, sullen, disagreeable, rude, and every other negative adjective I could think of.

"I know he's like that," CBL said with a smile. "Why do you think I put you next to him? I wasn't going to have him be rude to my other guests. That's what staff is for, to take disagreeable things on the chin, without complaining."

My list of literary heroes was shrinking. Faulkner and Miss Lockwood would have gotten on well together.

Both Luces equally share in the credit for giving a major assist to Italy's one struggling airline in those days, Alitalia. The State Department would pay for government employees to travel only on American airliners, but when Alitalia had a horrendous crash, killing everyone on board right before Christmas, leaving only one overseas jet in service, it looked as though that was the end; people were afraid to fly on the airline. The Luces reacted in the opposite way. They cancelled their reservations on TWA for their home-for-Christmas flight and flew Alitalia, even paying for it themselves. This vote of confidence really touched the Italians and helped Alitalia get over its disastrous accident. It was a great public relations gesture on the Luces' part, but frankly, it was not calculated to look good in the press. Their hearts were involved in this: the whole nation was in mourning because of that crash.

Clare Luce was a born public relations specialist. It was in her blood. Neither of us could predict that one day I would be running my own PR firm, but working around her gave me an invaluable education in the field. Her fearless appearance in front of a shouting Communist mob demonstrating against America outside the embassy offices on the Via Veneto impressed thousands of Italians, including the Communists. It made the front pages for days. She looked so tiny and vulnerable next to Interior Minister Mario Scelba's tanks in the street.

Even her famous poodles became a national tearjerker—that is, if you love dogs, and the Italians certainly did. One of her miniature French poodles, Scusi, a beloved icon in Italy, died in childbirth, leaving two very tiny puppies. The vet said the puppies were too small to survive; they could not be fed even with an eyedropper. The ambassador was in despair. There had to be a way to save these pups. Finally, the vet said that if we could find a small nursing bitch who had just produced her own litter, the chemical makeup of her milk might possibly be just right for our little ones. He doubted this miracle could occur—in time. The ambassador commanded me to find that nursing dog. The word went out on the radio that the American Embassy was in crisis. The media picked it up, and soon there were cameras, recorders, and citizens coming to the gate of the villa with every known kind of nursing animal—but no small dog. "The puppies must be saved!" was the rallying cry. The zoo offered us many other nursing animals—a zebra, anyone? A nursing monkey? Finally Wernon, the driver for the Villa, said, "Let's try the Canile Communale [the municipal dog pound]." No wonder no one talked about it in Rome or even admitted its existence. It was a shameful, pathetic place, but there I found a huge mutt who had just had her own litter of eight oversized puppies. Knowing this probably wouldn't do, but desperate to do something, I purchased them all for a few hundred lire, had them de-fleaed, and brought them back to the villa. The ambassador was waiting in the driveway, holding Scusi's puppies, now near death. The vet and two Italian ministers were standing with her, anxiously awaiting us. The ministers had come to the villa for an afternoon meeting, but the political discussions were on hold—the little puppies took precedence. It was a scene of sheer drama.

What transpired then was truly a miracle. CBL put the mangy mongrel mother and her brawling puppies into an empty carton for cans of soup from the PX. Then she added the tiny toy poodles. The mother knew exactly what to do. Her own big pups would never let our little ones near the drinking fountains, so with her teeth she deposited each one of her own in the corner of the box, above her head, where they were temporarily imprisoned, leaving all the fountains free for our little ones. The vet shook his head several times—"I never thought it would work, it was destined to fail." The tiny Luce puppies nursed at once, in what was to become a regular ritual until they were weaned, and they grew up to be healthy adult toy poodles. The ambassador touched the head of the mother dog and proclaimed it a baptismal moment: "I christen you Signora Snackbar." Then she touched the heads of her puppies and said, "And you two, Romulus and Remus." The symbolism of the names she chose—of the two human orphaned babies suckled by the fabled Mother Wolf of Rome—reduced the two ministerial officials to tears. The sight of that ugly big dog, lying in the carton with the two tiny gray toy poodles, was unforgettable.

The Italian press went wild over this story. Headlines popped up all over the media; "Italian Mother's Milk Proves Once Again to Be World's Best," and "Italian Canine Diplomat, 'Signora Snackbar,' Solves International Crisis at the American Embassy." Signora Snackbar went on to lead a prestigious doggy life as the head greeter at the gates of the Villa Taverna, along with her new master, Ferdinando, and the puppies eventually went back to the United States to lead very privileged and happy lives.

The ambassador brought with her from New York a reputation for stinginess, but she was anything but. She gave money quietly, privately, and constantly. I am not going to say she did not complain about it to those of us in the inner circle. She hated being taken for a ride, which people were always trying to do to both Luces. She let us know how she felt about every check that went out, like those to help her indigent friends, for example. She had several elderly widows on her payroll. She paid their medical bills, including complete operations. She paid their monthly apartment rents. She even bought them apartments. The Luces received literally hundreds of letters a month pleading for donations, many of them pathetic and heart-rending. I often wept as I was reading them and longed to send money to each and every case. CBL was curt on the subject: "It's easy to be so saintly and generous, Tish, when it isn't your money you're giving away. Let Monsignor Landi handle it!"

The Luces gave a large sum of money every year to the National Catholic Welfare Conference, and Monsignor Landi, from his office in the

Vatican, would check out the particularly worthy cases and send them money from the Luce fund. One day the ambassador got fed up with my sniveling (I would have, too), and gave me her personal check for a large donation ($500) for a poor woman in southern Italy.

"You'll see," she said wryly. "You'll learn. You'll see why we have to let Monsignor Landi handle these things. No good deed goes unpunished."

How true. Back came a letter, written on behalf of the woman, who was illiterate, thanking Mrs. Luce but asking her to adopt her daughter's soon-to-be-born illegitimate baby and to pay for four pairs of new shoes for her children, eyeglasses for herself, and an American education for their brightest child. I did not answer the letter, I was so chagrined, but the worst was yet to come. A week later the entire family, seven strong, including the pregnant daughter, was waiting for me at the gates of the Villa Taverna. They had arrived unannounced, carrying their meager possessions in paper bags, ready to move in with *l'Ambasciatore*. After all, she had so much room and such a big heart.

I listened to their wailings for a few hours, got Rocco to make up some baskets of food, and gave them some lire to return to their village on the bus. Henceforth, Monsignor Landi would handle all pleas. I made a promise not to be duped again. The Luces had the answer. A rich person needs a Monsignor Landi as the channel for funds and investigator of all heartbreaking stories. I never thought I would embrace Mrs. Luce's cynical remark, "No good deed goes unpunished." But after being around the Luces a few weeks, it became my own favorite saying.

Forget the glass ceilings of this world that women have tried to break through. The word *ceiling* meant only one thing to me—the one over our heads in the front section of the second floor of the Villa Taverna. On this celing hinged an Agatha Christie thriller of a story.

The ambassador had returned to America that summer for a prolonged vacation. She had gone home a very sick woman—her hair falling out, her nails and teeth loosening. The old Luce sense of humor nevertheless prevailed; before she left, when I came in at eight in the morning to report for work, she would give me the latest health report, by such means as wiggling a loose front tooth at me. Her condition was kept very secret, but those of us around her simply attributed it to a touch of hypochondria, plus advanced colitis—a stomach problem that had seriously affected her for years.

Back in the United States that summer, the ambassador's physical problems greatly improved. Two days before her return to Rome, I was sorting out some files in my office when an embassy officer walked in with two men who had just flown over from Washington. When the embassy official excused himself and left, the men closed the doors: one identified himself as a CIA agent, the other as a CIA doctor. Then they proceeded to lay out an unbelievable story. Mrs. Luce was suffering from arsenate of lead poisoning; enemies of the United States might be poisoning her; and as the only American citizen working in the Villa Taverna, I was to be their contact person. Then they proceeded to tell me that every person in the villa—including me—was suspect in the possible poisoning of Mrs. Luce. My American citizenship was of some help, but only some.

The men put me through the third degree about the staff, the Luce friends, and everyone who came to the Villa Taverna for whatever purpose. When Mrs. Luce returned from New York, Gretel would bring her breakfast on a tray as usual. With an Alfred Hitchcockian flourish, I would make some excuse to take in her tray myself, instead of Gretel. Once inside, I went into her dressing room, where one of the CIA men was waiting with a tray of "secure [unpoisoned] food." They would then take the tray that had originated in the kitchen and have a laboratory check every single bit of food and tea for poison.

I was frankly terrorized. The ambassador began to feel sick again. I was under suspicion, and that got to me. The men tested everything in the ambassador's suite. They dispatched to a U.S. lab in Naples, top secret, samples of her cosmetics, hair dye, vitamin pills, candy jars—yes, and the dogs' Yummies—and finally bits of the ceiling, which had been flaking down over our heads. There was fine dust everywhere from the beautiful old ceiling, repainted in the late 1880s in a mosaic pattern reminiscent of a Renaissance palace. The domestics on the third floor, constantly moving around, were shaking apart the ceiling below them. The FBO had originally refused to replace it until the following January, when it would take an act of Congress to appropriate the funds, rumored to be $10,000, to do the job. I was inhaling the same dust as the ambassador. Because it was showering down all over the front of the second floor, they also tested me for arsenate of lead. I tested very positive—but as fast as I was ingesting it, I was also expelling it. My life was very different from the ambassador's. I would sneak out for a game of tennis whenever I could. I met friends in the zoo at seven in the morning (the only time all day I could find to welcome them to Rome and give them hints on what to do), and I made dates every night from nine-thirty to the wee hours of the next morning—eating in the *ristoranti* of Trastevere, dancing in outdoor trattorias, and dining on the top-floor terrace of the Eden Paradiso Hotel, where my dates and I became conversational friends of King Farouk, the portly exiled ruler of Egypt, who dined there almost nightly. I had no time to become poisoned. I was breathing good air, except for the ceiling dust during the day, and even then I kept the windows open. The ambassador was breathing the same stale air of her bedroom most of the day and night, except when she went to her office at the embassy, and her bedroom windows remained closed. Even the windows of her limo were shut tight. She was inhaling continuous large doses of arsenate of lead, and at the same time suffering from painful colitis. But, thank God, the security of the United States of America was not at stake. There was no Machiavellian plot to get rid of the American ambassador, just an accidental near tragedy.

The Foreign Building Operations rushed to put in a new ceiling over the front of the house (never has anything happened so fast in FBO history). Time Inc. screwed up matters to the maximum by printing a story that the CIA had originally suspected, with good reason, an Italian plot to kill CBL. This *Time* story so incensed the Italians that many of the government leaders never forgave Henry Luce for allowing such a destructive rumor come into print in his publication. It made a good story, lots of drama, but to accuse the Italians of such a dastardly plot seemed ridiculous to them, and I saw Clare Luce's popularity in the country eroded to a certain extent. The Italians did not take attacks on their chivalry lightly, and the thought of allowing the murder of the American woman ambassador to occur at the hands of Italians was beyond their imaginations. After all, Lucretia Borgia had lived several centuries before.

One of the high points of my life in Italy was when I managed to deliver one of Clare Luce's most important speeches—in Italian, too—before she had the chance to deliver it herself before a large Chamber of Commerce forum in Milan at the height of the Cold War. The Communists had been making great gains in the Italian local elections; a big national election was coming up, and the Christian Democratic government, friendly to the United States, was in danger of falling. The ambassador had labored long and hard over this speech, her most important one, which clearly laid out the nature of the benefits from the Marshall Plan to Italy. She had all the facts and figures to debunk the Communists' absurd accusations that the American government interfered in local politics, and to argue that Italy's economic recovery was in fact due to American economic aid—something which the Italians did not like to admit, but which they needed to realize before the Communists took control of the government.

Perfectionist that Clare Boothe Luce was, she made me retype her speech—in Italian—over and over on my Royal portable typewriter. It was agony. I prayed for someone like President Eisenhower to appear and take her away from Rome, leaving me alone. For five days she made small changes on every page, after talking to Secretary John Foster Dulles or George Kennan, Robert Murphy, and other top State Department policy officials. For five days and nights, fourteen hours at a time, I was slumped over the Royal, re-typing the entire speech from beginning to end. Anyone who has typed something that often knows what happens—the text is transferred to the brain of the typist and temporarily stored there. I was even typing that speech in my sleep every night.

As a "big favor" (I was now calling her the Slave Driver) the ambassador allowed me to go away for four days after the speech was finally recorded perfectly on paper. I drove north in my little Morris Oxford toward the lake country, where no one would know where I was and drag me back. I stopped for the night in a small town that boasted a small hotel on the town square. I went down to eat supper in the only trattoria visible. It was jammed. I couldn't believe the unusual size of the crowd. Had I crashed a wedding feast? I was hungry and tired and didn't care. The *maggior d'uomo* looked stunned to see this tall young foreigner asking if she could get something to eat. He was so surprised he didn't say no, but ushered me to the only place left—a small table on the outer fringe. I ordered a bowl of pasta, a green salad, a liter of red wine, and some fresh fruit and then closed my sore eyes to rest them.

The volume and excitability of the voices around me were rising rapidly. A man with a microphone was urging the crowd into action. I discovered at this point I was in the middle of a Communist cell meeting, and they were making absurd accusations against America, particularly against "La Luce." My fascination began to change to anger, and my courage arose the more I listened, and the more I consumed of the Chianti. Finally I had heard enough of these lies against my government and my boss. All of me unfolded from the little chair as I stretched to my full height. All eyes were upon me. All conversation in the café immediately ceased. With short people seated all around me, I was a giant. "Ma chi è questa donna [Who is this woman]?" I heard from all sides. Maybe someone went to call the van for the mental hospital, I don't know. All I do know is that I began to address the audience, which was by now everyone in the outdoor restaurant, diners and waiters, as well as others passing by in the square. "You need to know the truth!" I shouted. I told them I was with the American Embassy, and that my father always told me that when I knew I was right, I should not be afraid to speak out. Then, cheeks aflame with Chianti, I gave them most of Clare Luce's speech, which she was supposed to give in Milano two days from then. The words came easily, burned into my mind as I retyped the speech.

They reacted like kids just let out of school—laughing, jumping up and down, shouting "Viva La Luce!" "Viva l'America!" "Viva la Signorina Alta!" The man who was running the meeting was unable to call it to order again, as several of them came over to hug and kiss me, overwhelmed to see an American in their midst, countering what they had been told by Communist Party leaders. I have a feeling that town lost a lot of Communist votes that night. I felt triumphant, even if a massive Chianti headache followed the euphoria.

Someone who has never lived abroad and defended one's country while working for the government could not understand the great high I achieved that night in northern Italy, delivering a speech in a little piazza at a Communist meeting. It made me very proud to be a member of our Foreign Service. It made me proud of Clare Luce's gift of political acumen in her speeches. It made me very glad to have been given after my performance a good dinner of incredibly good Italian food. Free of charge, too.

It was again time to go home. I had been in this magic country for almost four years. My ambassador would be returning to the United States the next year, and I wanted to leave before she did. She tried to turn it around the opposite way—but I won.

I even had an important project, other than finding a job. I had a book to write. Houghton Mifflin asked me to write about working in Rome with the Luces. I thought they were joking, but Mrs. Luce told me to do it. In fact, she said, J-U-S-T DO IT! She followed this command with one of her typical Luce-isms: "Anyone can write a book who knows how to apply the seat of the pants to the seat of the chair."

No, it wasn't a Puccini opera, this emotional "addio" time, but it felt like it—the drama, the tears, the raw emotions. I had to go home. I had become too much of an Italophile. An entire glorious section of my life was over, and it could never be repeated. When I came back, another ambassador and another executive assistant to the ambassador would be running the show. Rome would no longer be my town. I would no longer walk down the Spanish steps, meet several Roman acquaintances on the way down, and pause for the latest little *chiaccherata* (gossip.) I would no longer be able to spend countless evening hours in the old part of Rome, watching the shadows from the streetlights playing across the delicious burnt amber and paprika-colored facades of the old palaces. No more sitting in the piazzas until two in the morning, sharing a liter of wine among four people, singing, whispering, loving the person next to you, and being enveloped by the city you love, too.

No more Masses in spectacular Baroque churches where the stone garments of the saints swirled with religious fervor around their figures, caught in tornado-like winds. I had always wondered about those winds, how they could be captured in stone. How I would miss all the Roman gossip replayed during Mass, where, if you eavesdropped attentively, the really hot scandals of Rome would be revealed in bits and snatches, even during the most sacred parts of the ritual. I would no longer be able to go down the Via Sistina to buy a small Chiaravari painting of seminarians in bright red hassocks and black flying saucer hats, playing volleyball, or a gloomy moment captured in oil by Mario Russo of a fireworks salesman straining to push his cart piled high with the product. No more eighteen-karat-gold charms of my favorite monuments of Rome. No more affordable tokens of Italian fashion, like a sequined scarf from Laura Aponte that obviously surpassed a sequined scarf from any other place in the world.

I was saying good-bye to a country that had no bad design for sale. The Italy that unfolded its renaissance of the 1950s before my eyes led the world in style—how to dress, what kind of chair to sit on, what special little clock to put next to one's special little Olivetti portable typewriter, everything always perfect in design and incredibly chic. I would no longer be able to park my car in the middle of the driveway of the Villa Taverna and leave at the end of the day to find it washed, bright and shining, and full of gas, thanks to the ambassador's chauffeur. No more picnics on the beach at Ostia or Fregene. No more trips outside Rome to Bomarzo on a Sunday, in the throes of a romance, kissing in the shadows of the huge, bizarre statues that were put there hundreds of years ago without reason or logic. No more vacations, when the ambassador was out of the country, at my favorite spots of Ischia, Lago Maggiore, and Elba. No more scaling the glaciers in the moonlight above Champoluc in the Val d'Aosta with Alpini, mountain-climbing friends. No more answering endless questions from American tourists about how to get to the Fontana di Trevi to toss a coin into its waters. (I didn't have the heart to tell them that that coin tossing had been so passé for so long that only the hickiest of the hicks asked to do it.) No more divine, tiny fresh peas laced with bits of prosciutto, figs that tasted as though they were sent by the gods from Mount Olympus, and slender pieces of veal *al limone* that melted before they hit your mouth. No more passionate screaming for Lazio at the *futbol* games, no more dinners in palazzi under frescoes painted by the great artists of the late Renaissance. No more sitting with a group of Roman pals on the stone wall up on the Gianicolo hill by the American Academy, overlooking the city at one in the morning, six or eight of us drinking wine, at least two guitars going all the time, and all of us singing those wonderful *stornelle Romane* songs. Matters concerning my heart in Italy will remain unchronicled. I would be saying good-bye to a man I loved madly, but knew I could never marry.

One has to have lived there in that particular time to be able to understand what happened to the emotions there.

Saying good-bye to Clare Luce was one of the hardest parts of all. I had been under her influence for almost four years. She had opened my eyes to the worlds of politics, theater, wealth, and diplomatic dexterity as no one else could have. A reporter asked me why I felt working for her was so important, and without having to reflect, I said that to be around her was to learn, to learn, learn, and learn until it hurt, trying to file it away in the brain. I think one of the reasons she gave so much time to me was that my enthusiasm buoyed her own spirit, and I think—at least, I like to think—that gave her happiness. Her intelligence and wit made a powerful impact. To me, she was the most exciting woman in the world, and when our paths separated, it was as if a sky full of balloons had suddenly been punctured.

She sent me a letter that arrived right after I had reached Washington to begin a new life.

> *Dearest Tish,*
>
> *Just one more last farewell word to my favorite aide in the great and glittering battle of the Villa Taverna. In the eyes of their aides Generals are often dreadful ogres—and not very bright. They just will not fight at the tempo, or with the disposition of forces or materiel that any good aide knows makes sense. But there it is. And in the end, the good General gets the job done, and the good aide carries out the screwiest orders with cheerfulness and loyalty. And so it has been. I would I had at my disposal "Il Gran' Ordine della Bella Figura" to pin on you, with a great kiss for either dear cheek, and accompanied by 48 flourishes of a Neapolitan guitar.*
>
> *You will leave behind you many fond friends and lasting memories. And I will be one of the fondest, who will remember you longest. When the dust settles over your files, when the last SMAT is burned, when every folder, paper-clip, photograph, bill, package, box, ribbon, basket, picture is gone—when all that recedes into the distance for you, you will remember—as I will—only the fun and glamour and comradeship—and that it all, in the end, "came off" a victory.*
>
> *I will never think of the Villa without thinking with love and admiration of you, and of the dear contribution you made to my happiness, comfort, and success in Rome. Bless you, dear girl. I needn't tell you to have fun. You do that as effortlessly as you breathe. Thank you for everything.*
>
> *Love, The Boss.*

Breakfast, Lunch, and Dinner at Tiffany's

$\mathscr{I}$ had a delightful weekend on the Isle of Capri the summer before going back to the United States for good. I had a tremendous urge to experience that enchanted place once more, since I thought I might never be back. Being part of the scene on Capri in 1955 was like attending a mixture of a Roman orgy and the Philadelphia Flower Show. It's a fairytale island plopped into the Mediterranean, south of the city of Naples, like a bowl of glittering Jell-O—all shiny color and jazz, no substance but tremendous fun. I would sit at a table in the central piazza, nursing one *caffè filtre* after another, wearing my bright red linen pants, a navy silk shirt, and the latest espadrilles, feeling very *ragazza Italiana*. I loved watching the endless parade of flamboyantly dressed homosexuals and transsexuals who gathered there every afternoon as though they were about to appear on TV for the Mardi Gras parade in New Orleans.

Clare Luce had left Rome for a few days' visit with some U.S. generals in Germany (her favorite ambassadorial occupation), so I seized the precious free time and took a boat to Capri. The morning after I arrived, I went to my favorite rock at the top of the island, Anacapri, to enjoy the sun and admire the unbelievable sapphire and aquamarine sea. Suddenly another person stepped onto my rock. It was an American woman with a lovely soft voice, who introduced herself as Dorothy di Santillana, a managing editor from the publishing house of Houghton Mifflin. "I hope I'm not bothering you by joining you," she said.

I laughed. "Not at all. This rock belongs to you as much as it does to me."

We struck up a conversation, and she interrogated me in an utterly charming way about my job with the Luces and my plans to return to the United States. When she proposed I write a book about my life in Rome with the Luces, I was flattered, but didn't take take her offer too seriously. After all, I wasn't a writer.

I returned to Rome and told Clare Luce about the conversations on the rock at Capri, laughing at myself for having the guts—and the gall—to contemplate writing about life with them. But the ambassador's reaction stunned me. It was immediate, crisp, even commanding. "Do it," she said.

I then recounted the story that I'd been ashamed to tell her before, of having been unceremoniously dumped from my English major at Vassar by the department head. She responded with one of her famous Luce-isms, those little sentences that would roll effortlessly off her tongue: "Anyone can get a book published, no matter how bad it is, just by applying the seat of the pants to the seat of the chair long enough." Then, more advice. "Never say anything nasty about anyone in your writing. You'll always regret it."

I countered with, "But you have always taken nasty cracks at people in your articles and books."

"And I have always regretted it. Why do you think I'm telling you this?"

She knew I would not tell tales out of school about her and Henry Luce if I wrote this book. She knew how much I admired them, and in those days, staff members who said unfavorable things about their employers in print or in conversation were considered the scum of the earth. No one would ever trust them again.

While I was packing up the contents of my apartment on the Viale Bruno Buozzi, the publishing deal with Houghton Mifflin was accomplished by airmail. I was offered something like a $5,000 advance, in my eyes a monstrously large sum, particularly since I had not realized I'd be getting one at all. This was to be one of the highest points of my life, I concluded. To be asked to write a book! Oh, Miss Lockwood, are you listening? Even if the book was going to be awful, which I was certain would be the case, my ego was going *pop, pop, pop!*

Suddenly life was getting exciting again. I had what was probably a sure job offer in New York, at Tiffany & Co., the New York jeweler and gift store. I would be working right in the middle of the most prestigious aspect of America's retail world. It would not be a comedown from my diplomatic life. It would be a sharp turn in another direction, but a glamorous addition to my résumé: the business of diamonds, gold, platinum, and silver—not bad.

Of course, it was totally thanks to Mrs. Luce. A month before I left Italy, when she was in New York, attending a white-tie dinner in the grand ballroom of the Waldorf-Astoria, Walter Hoving was one of her dinner partners. A Swedish-born retail executive, well known to the readers of New York's social, fashion, and financial pages, he had been president of Lord & Taylor and had taken over Bonwit Teller, another leading Manhattan fashion emporium. He had recently purchased a dying, aristocratic old lady of an American icon—Tiffany & Co.

Walter Hoving had held Clare Luce's attention during the entire dinner as he recounted the story of buying the company. He was a formidable man. Mrs. Luce had worn one of her fully matched sets of diamond and pearl jewels that night to impress him. Hoving surveyed her jewelry up close rather rudely, as though he had a built-in jeweler's loupe in one eye. He had said, Clare added, with as much approval in his voice as he could muster about the work of a competing jeweler, "All this seems of good quality and design, Clare, but I could tell it did not come from Tiffany. It's not up to our standards or the new collection of jewelry being made right now. You must come and see us when our, may I say 'superior,' stock is ready." (Of course she did, in spite of his almost insulting remarks about her jewels.) I was shocked that Mr. Hoving would openly criticize her Harry Winston jewelry, and at a public dinner. Mrs. Luce was merely amused by his undiplomatic remarks.

Hoving announced to Mrs. Luce that he needed a director of publicity and public relations, immediately. Tiffany's had been famous for not allowing any press; the family had always considered publicity cheap and dangerous, so it had paid publicity experts to keep the Tiffany name *out* of the social columns, the fashion magazines, and the financial pages. Now Hoving wanted the Tiffany's name *in* them.

Mrs. Luce saw her opening and proceeded to tell him about me, saying that I would soon be on my way home from Rome, that I needed a job, that I knew personally all of the customers he cared about in society, and that I also knew the PR business intimately and could handle any job in the store. Wow! What an overblown recommendation. Hoving's last comment to Clare Luce at the dinner was that he wanted me right then and there, with no delays. He was taking a risk in hiring someone without even an interview, but of course, he knew Mrs. Luce. For my part, I was thrilled by the thought of being connected with such a prestigious American company.

The historic jeweler at Fifty-seventh and Fifth in New York was the oldest and finest jewelry store in America, but Walter Hoving's friends thought him crazy for making such a bad business gamble; only the very old, decrepit denizens of society ever shopped at Tiffany's anymore. With the exception of the St. Patrick's Cathedral site farther down Fifth Avenue, the corner occupied by Tiffany's was the most prized bit of commercial real estate in America. Millions of people through the years had set their watches to the huge clock borne aloft by the bronze figure of Atlas over the front door.

Tiffany's had been in its founder's family's hands since Charles L. opened the business in 1837, running it himself for decades. The store was largely responsible for the term "carriage trade," which evoked the rich members of society brought by fine horses and carriages on their shopping forays. If great social figures did not alight from the carriages in front of Tiffany's, their ladies' maids and butlers did, carrying out errands for the gentleman and lady of the house. These domestics also enjoyed an enormous cachet among the elite of their peers at the time. Their names were well known in society. The butlers used to have an annual "Butler's Ball," to which invitations were harder to acquire than almost any other leading social event.

The Tiffany family had found they could no longer manage the business profitably in this brash new world. Times and tastes had changed, and society in the 1950s was witnessing the change from the old guard to yet another garish new-money group, a repetition of the nouveaux riches colony of the Astors, Whitneys, Goulds, Binghams, and Vanderbilts at the turn of the nineteenth century. The post–World War II affluent had become bored by traditional merchandise—grandmother's exquisite lace or heavy white damask tablecloths, elaborately cut crystal goblets, fine English bone china, towering silver candelabra, and the inevitable centerpiece bowl, tureen, epergne, or mirrored tray (*plateau*) holding antique bronzes or vermeil objects. The hostesses of the late 1950s wanted new, interesting shapes for the dining room table—witty plates with smiling suns or winking moons on them, cavorting monkey candlesticks, colorful linens, and porcelain vegetables so lifelike, you desperately wanted to take a bite. This society wanted diamonds set more often in gold, not platinum, because they wanted to wear them not just at night but in daytime, too, with their sporty tweed designer suits, and even those "shocking pantsuits."

The store no longer needed a staff of Tiffany clock experts whose sole purpose in life was to visit the great homes in New York on a regular basis and wind all the household's grandfather and mantelpiece clocks, keeping them and their lovely chimes accurate to a second. They could no longer support a flying squad of silver polishers who spent their days going to the great homes to polish table accoutrements and other silver pieces every two weeks, even if the household was comprised of butlers and maids who could perfectly well keep Madam's silver beautifully polished. The subtle refinements of life, for which Tiffany's stood, and which most people, including the owners of the grand houses, had taken for granted all these years, were disappearing. It took a Walter Hoving to seize control of the store and turn it 180 degrees. Determined to keep the store more elite than any other in America, he emptied it of handbags, leather goods, anything Lucite or ersatz—anything not related to his focus group of luxury products. He disclaimed silver plate; it had to be sterling or nothing. He threw men's diamond rings out of the store as being in "poor taste," permitting only custom-designed, heavy gold family crest signet rings. If anyone came in to have a signet ring made with a fake crest on it, out that customer went, mission unaccomplished.

Back in Rome, Clare Luce had informed me she knew all the scuttlebutt on Hoving, a newcomer to society thanks to his marriage to a wealthy woman, the former Pauline Rogers, of Standard Oil money. He assumed the manners and conversation of New York's real society. Not born into "class," he nevertheless grew into a natural sense of it. In fact, he figuratively wrapped himself in it. Marrying well cinched his place, and his wife Pauline's old-guard friends became his, too.

Mrs. Luce told me that he was an amazing man, totally focused on his job eighteen hours a day, and working through its problems in his sleep the other six. He had studied New York society as a young man, absorbed its lifestyle in minute detail, and quickly moved to its upper echelons. (This was, after all, an activity with which Mrs. Luce was very familiar.) Elsa Maxwell, the fabled party giver, had once said, "If a man looks good, talks well, has money, and maintains a certain aloofness, he'll make it in society, no matter from where he comes." Elsa had added, "It also helps if he knows how to waltz." Walter Hoving was all of that, and he knew how to waltz.

Mrs. Luce pointed out that Walter Hoving had made history out of a simple box—the distinctive, shiny Tiffany turquoise-colored box, to be specific. It was, and still is, one of the world's most successful, recognizable logos. The turquoise box had been around for a while, but Hoving took it and marketed it in itself. People tried to buy the boxes all the time, to save, to brag about, or perhaps to deceive with by putting another store's merchandise inside for a gift presentation.

"Walter Hoving had an 'eye,'" she continued, "something present in every person of taste I have ever known. Perhaps it's a genetic gift."

I could now hardly wait to work for this man. But what was "public relations," anyway? I wanted to ask. No one really used the term back then, except for the great pioneers like Ben Sonnenberg and Ed Bernays. I couldn't even give a definition of it, and I don't think Mrs. Luce could either, but she had proclaimed me an expert anyway. When I hurriedly called my father in the United States to ask for advice, he said, "There's only one thing to do. If being a PR expert is imperative to landing this job, then become one. Become an expert at bluffing."

My father was right. I had had far worse moments over my head in foreign countries, but "rapidspeak" and distractions had always saved me. When I returned from Rome, I spent one night in New York on my way to Washington, for a five-minute interview granted with "the man" in his office. We stood up for the whole five minutes; there was no time to ask me to sit down. Hoving told me only that I was being given the job, and that I must begin work at once. I was not asked whether or not I wanted it, but was simply told I was taking it. When I said I had a book to write first, thinking he could not help but be impressed, he only scowled and said, "How long does it take *you* to write a book?"

"Three months," I replied, not having a clue how long it takes to write a book. In my heart I knew it would probably be much longer than that, but with Walter Hoving, you don't dilly-dally with an answer.

"Then you have exactly three months, not one day more," he said, obviously displeased at having to wait that long. "Report here three months to this day." I was dismissed.

"But, Mr. Hoving," I protested weakly, "what will my salary be?"

"Oh, that," he said absentmindedly, as though I had mentioned something beneath his notice. Young people were not programmed in those days to go for the jugular in their salary demands. It was considered unclassy for a woman to work, much less talk about what her salary would be. Here I had been working in high-level government positions abroad for eight years, but as far as Mr. Hoving was concerned, they were nonretail jobs, and therefore unimportant.

"I'll give you $10,000 annually," he said unapologetically. "You're not in a sales job. You're not in a profit center. You don't deserve any more."

I was not to receive any commission for sales for which I might be responsible (and there were to be hundreds of thousands of dollars' worth of those during my Tiffany years); I was to work six days a week, but that was nothing new. I had worked six days a week on my embassy jobs. He also made it clear that I should look upon being fortunate enough to work for him as a blessing from heaven. The salary was beside the point.

Of course I agreed, wimp that I was. Hoving gripped my hand in a farewell handshake and said good-bye as he yanked my arm and shoved me out the door. I felt as though I had just been taken out by the left tackle in a football game—truly a bum's rush, but done with finesse.

I knew I had to write the book fast for Houghton Mifflin, so the day after my short appointment with Hoving in New York, I raced back to Washington and started writing as if I were entered in the Mille Miglia car race in Italy. I moved back into my old room in the family apartment at 2101 Connecticut Avenue. My mother unpacked my luggage, and I felt like I never left. I took my writing tools and scrapbooks (for reference) over to the Wisconsin Avenue apartment of a bachelor friend, Francis ("Fig") Coleman, a Philadelphian who was working for the CIA. Handsome, redheaded Fig left every morning around eight for his office, and I would arrive in his apartment, using my own set of keys, at about nine. I made certain to be gone again before he returned at night, so as not to inconvenience him or, far worse, cause gossip. Nice young ladies in those days did not spend time in bachelors' apartments. But away from the telephone and my dear mother's constant interruptions at home, I was able to concentrate in absolute silence and, I might add, luxurious comfort, and I rapidly turned out page after page on the jazzy little Olivetti portable I brought from Italy.

It took me exactly the three agreed-upon months to write that book. I called it *Roman Candle* (a well-known type of fireworks). The stuff just poured out. Writer's block? Never heard of it. If I had had today's Microsoft Word and a PC and laser printer, I could have done the job in one month. I had a story to tell that I absolutely loved, and that helped me relive the happiness of those Italian days. I felt I was back there, munching on fresh figs and prosciutto in a sun-warmed piazza at lunchtime, sipping cold white Frescati *vino* instead of downing my own dry peanut butter sandwiches and ginger ale at Fig Coleman's desk.

After writing all day every day, and at night in a semiconscious state, I sent off the finished manuscript, packed my bags, and moved to New York in a stupor of fatigue and doubts about what I was doing with my life. When I later saw the first copy of *Roman Candle* and held it in my hands, like a mother gazing at her first precious newborn, I felt enormous pride, but also sadness that I would not even have time to read it. I had other things to do. In fact, I have still not read *Roman Candle* all the way through. Maybe in the next life.

To publicize the book, I was to be interviewed by a man I'd never heard of named Mike Wallace, who in 1956 had just started a new talk show. No one had said a word of warning to me about Mike Wallace. I was the first to be interviewed that afternoon and was to be followed by the real estate mogul William Zeckendorf, who could perhaps have been referred to as the Donald Trump of his day. Mike gave me no time for pleasant reminiscences of Italy, no opportunity to express my admiration for the Luces or discuss the chapters in *Roman Candle* where I wrote about how romantic Italian men were and how great it was to be serving one's country abroad. I was even prepared to sing, with my guitar, a couple of verses of "Anim'e Cuore" that would have touched the heart of anyone in the TV audience with a drop of Italian blood in his veins. Instead, Mike spent the whole time quizzing me on how Clare Luce could be such a red-hot Catholic convert when, in the eyes of the church, she was living in sin with Henry Luce (What? What?) because he was divorced and his wife was still alive.

He went on to wonder how Mrs. Luce could receive the sacraments when she was "living in sin," according to the interpretation he had heard.

He wondered how Bishop Fulton Sheen had managed her conversion. The TV audience probably heard the audible choking noises coming from my direction. He added that she and her husband could not, in the eyes of the church, have sexual relations, but must live together as brother and sister.

Here was I, on my first big TV show, making my debut as a star author, a product of eight years of the Sacred Heart Convent, being asked about the Luces' challenged sex life. I had written *Roman Candle* as a tribute to the Luces. No one had ever even mentioned the possibility of an attack on their marriage and on Clare's famous conversion. I decided there was only one course of action—walk out on this mess. Muttering something like, "This is not what I came here for," I unmiked myself (no pun intended), left my chair, and walked away from the lights, cameras, and set. I could hear Mike Wallace protesting, "But— but—" One of the cameramen applauded me as I brushed past him, seeking the exit. Tears were coming down my cheeks now—tears of rage. Evidently the show had to go black for a while, as they tried to locate Bill Zeckendorf, who wasn't supposed to be on for another half hour, and get him back on the set fast. I may have been naive, but at least I maintained my dignity.

On the promised day—April Fools' Day, in fact—I arrived at Tiffany's before I was supposed to, signing in at the trade entrance with the other employees. No one met me; I had no orders. Just be there, I had been told. I shyly sought out the trade elevators and went to the fifth floor, following the one instruction I had been given. The big steel doors on Fifth Avenue would not open to the public for another forty-five minutes. A nice, smiling man named Jim showed me to my desk. He was the executive assistant to the store's president, William Lusk, a survivor from the original Tiffany family, as was young Harry Platt, a vice president who had graduated from Yale in my brother Bob's class, and who came over and shook my hand. It made me feel just a little better in this strange environment. I found myself plunked down in the middle of the executive circle of men, who were sitting at their desks, wondering who the hell this woman was, and what she was supposed to be doing. It was a sea of brown—brown furniture, brown carpeting, brown blotters, brown clocks. Walter Hoving, of course, was not there when I arrived, nor was his secretary, who was to become a great friend. I sat there for fifteen minutes, waiting for The Man, wondering whether I had the right day, whether I should leave, cry, go get a doughnut, or buy a brown suit to match the office. Then the customers' elevators at the front of the floor opened, and Hoving dramatically appeared, striding forth at his usual sixty-mile-an-hour pace. It was as if the maestro had tapped the music stand with his baton. The orchestra was now at attention. Everyone was aware. Life on the executive floor was about to begin.

Hoving was late because he had been at a meeting at Rockefeller Center—with the Rockefellers, of course. He went right past me, smiling a very rapid, casual hello, as though I were one of the regular staff—which I guess I now was. The men in the circle looked at me sympathetically, almost as though they knew what I was going through. They did not. I was humiliated. However, I was not the daughter of Mac Baldrige, celebrated Yale left tackle and decorated hero of two world wars, for nothing. I raised myself to my full height and took a deep breath. *Mademoiselle* magazine had taught me that all people in their twenties should do this stretching and deep breathing automatically in any kind of stressful situation.

If my boss wasn't going to ask for me, I would ask for him. I walked into Hoving's inner sanctum, stopping in the doorway to say, "May I come in?"

"Yes, of course." He smiled broadly, arose from his seat, and stepped forward to shake my hand and usher me into the royal seat by his desk. I kept reminding myself that I was now in big business, no longer an exalted member of the diplomatic corps. In the retail business, I was a big nothing.

"Welcome, Miss Baldrige," he said, as though he had not even really noticed me earlier when he swept by the circle. He waited for me to say something.

"I'm here on the exact day, according to plan," I said, proud of being so much a woman of my word.

"I can see that," he said flatly. I thought he might mention my newly completed book, rather a human thing to do, but he did not. "And?" he asked as though we had been talking for two hours and our conversation could finish right now; did I have any more questions?

"I thought we could discuss my job." At that moment in walked his secretary, who announced that the mayor was on the telephone. I sat waiting while Walter Hoving in his role as president of the Fifth Avenue Association proceeded to tell His Honor the mayor that he could only describe last year's Christmas decorations on some of the Park Avenue buildings as "tawdry, cheap, and unworthy of our city." As he talked, his enthusiasm deepened. "Those inferior colored lights on the Christmas trees strung in front of the Seagram's Building make Mies van der Rohe's masterpiece look like a liquor store." So of course the mayor asked Hoving right then on the telephone to head a new commission to bring taste to the mid-city holiday decorations on both Park and Fifth Avenues, and keep it there.

Walter Hoving was relentless in his criticisms. He was on television, on the front pages of the *New York Times* and the *Wall Street Journal*. His cry for good taste in New York was the subject of a long feature article in *Time* and

Vogue magazines. He was the news anchors' delight on the evening TV news. Here was a man who knew how to make publicity and remain quotable forever, always getting in a quick remark, of course, about how if the Tiffany windows were so tasteful, why couldn't others be as well?

As I listened to Walter Hoving talking to the mayor and raising a tempest in a teapot about Christmas lights on Park Avenue, I felt more inferior by the second. How could I possibly be as brilliant as he in getting the new Tiffany's name into the press? He would always do the job better.

It was obvious I had to get hold of my job at once. I had no idea what I was supposed to do, and there were no files to look through, no memos on previous events from which to learn. No one had been there before me. I would have to start from scratch. Then, and I remember this so well, a warm feeling enveloped me. I began to purr with pleasure. It was true. No one had held the job before. No one had left behind a successful legacy, or made a name for him- or herself. There was no one to whom I would be compared unfavorably. Anything I accomplished would be a plus. I could not go down, only up. What a lovely predicament.

"Mr. Hoving, just what exactly are my duties?"

He answer was a short, simple statement. "Miss Baldrige," he said, looking at me with those cold blue Nordic eyes, "I'm paying you to know what to do." There was my answer. End of meeting and end of conversations with Walter Hoving for almost two months.

Like Clare Luce, Hoving would become one of the most important teachers in my life. He would philosophize to his executives about the law of supply and demand. He could logically compare fashion design in clothing and cut crystal salad bowls. It was exhilarating to be around a mind like that.

None of the executive staff will ever forget when he called us together one night after the store had closed and accused us of being less knowledgeable about fine arts than our customers. He would pick up one object after another from the tables on the china and glass floor, asking, "Do you know the origin of this piece of Herend china? This crystal 'toasting glass'? If you don't, you won't know how to sell it or present it. You need to know everything about this merchandise if you're going to be an executive in this store. And I mean everything, not just the big-ticket items, like jewelry. You must know the styles and design schemes from the past, and pronounce them properly—chinoiserie, passementerie, ormolu, *bouillotte, argento* or *argent, brode, velluto, bronze doré*—all of it! You must be able to distinguish among the different periods of furniture that influence all design, from Jacobean and Queen Anne through Chippendale, Adam, Sheraton, Hepplewhite, the French Louis, Empire, and Directoire periods, and also Frank Lloyd Wright, Mission furniture, and the Art Deco styles of this century. You must learn the different Chinese dynastic periods and recognize a Tang horse as an object of incredible beauty, not just a figurine. You must be able to talk the language of pseudo-curators, and train your salespeople with the knowledge you have. Tiffany must become a place where information on why something is well designed and precious is part of our daily vocabulary." He then accused us of being unsophisticated, even uneducated, a negative he wanted corrected at once. I protested to him in private, reminding him proudly that I had lived in the leading embassies of western Europe, and lived among nothing but museum pieces for all those years. I also had an extensive educational background in fine arts. It was useless to try to protest on any level to Walter Hoving or even suggest that he could be inaccurate or even exaggerating. He interrupted me in a cold voice, "Miss Baldrige, you need night school along with everyone else, maybe even more." Ouch! He would pay for our courses, he explained, and since he was so notoriously tight with his budgets, we all realized he meant business. We took various courses, listened, and learned. I went to the Metropolitan Museum of Art for a night course in eighteenth-century French decoration with Columbia University's renowned professor Carl Dauterman. Hoving was right. It was precious stuff to file away in our minds. Also, in my future dealings with the press and with the customers, it didn't hurt to be able to say, "One day the Metropolitan Museum curator reminded me that—"

It was time for me to stop feeling helpless and get going. Mr. Hoving commanded me "to get our jewelry out there fast in the press!" But how? No one in the store was in a position to help me; they were as confused about the meaning of public relations as I was. There were the sterling silver, fine china, and crystal to promote. That meant calling on the editors of the shelter publications (the house and interior design magazines). There were the jewels to promote, so that meant calling on the editors of the top fashion magazines. I needed guidance, and I decided to appeal to the best.

The most influential women newspaper editors at the time were Elizabeth Penrose Howkins of the *New York Times* and Eugenia Sheppard of the *New York Herald Tribune,* and I made appointments to see both of them. I had been warned that Elizabeth was brusque and no-nonsense busy, but she ended up giving me the keys to the kingdom. When she asked me why I wanted to see her, she said, "I'm curious, but busy. Tell me quickly."

"I'm new in the public relations and publicity business, Mrs. Howkins, and since you are the most respected women's-page editor of all, I was hoping you would give me some tips."

"In other words," she said brusquely, "you're here so I can teach you your job, is that it?"

She was so astonished to see someone from Tiffany's trying to get the store's merchandise into the papers instead of keep it out of them, she looked at me in amusement. Compassion, too. It helped that she respected my former employer, Clare Boothe Luce, and that she truly loved my other former employer, Evangeline Bruce. There were two letter boxes of mail on Mrs. Howkins's desk, one with a printed YES sign and the other with a NO. The one marked NO was packed with stuff—perhaps close to a hundred sets of releases and photos in their envelopes. The one marked YES contained about twelve envelopes.

"This is this morning's mail from people hoping we'll follow up and do a story. Read and analyze them, and that should be enough to help you. Just don't bother me."

"But how do I analyze them?" I asked, sounding pathetic without having to act. I couldn't analyze the label on a can of tomato soup at this point, but clearly I had to get over these feelings of inadequacy. I knew everything about dealing with heads of state of other countries, but I couldn't decipher a press release.

"Look," she said in a tired voice, betraying her feeling that this new first head of public relations for Tiffany's was not all that swift. "Read both boxes carefully, and then you'll see why they are in two separate boxes, one for possible action, one for the wastebasket."

After two hours of study at an empty desk in a dreary corner of the women's-news department, it was apparent why the material was in separate boxes. The YES box contained releases on everything from new styles of panty girdles to chocolate mousse recipes—all short, succinct, tightly written, with a clear photograph or drawing to illustrate the new product, and with all of the proper information neatly listed in the first paragraph: who sent it, telephone numbers and addresses, and reasons why it was news. The NO box contained releases full of misspellings, bad grammar, punctuation errors (like the majority of today's e-mail messages), and inferior illustrations, with rambling, messy texts that said nothing and had no real reason for existence. I learned enough that afternoon in the *New York Times* offices to last me a whole career in preparing press materials. I have been grateful my entire life to her kindness in assigning me that exercise.

Eugenia Sheppard, the women's editor of the *New York Herald Tribune,* on the other hand, was famous for having persuaded *Tribune* owner Jock Whitney into letting her have a glorious amount of space for her women's section. With her encouragement, I began creating editorial concepts, in conjunction with fashion photographs I would supervise, starring our jewelry, table settings, and anything sold in the store. If she liked the idea and the pictures, she would use them.

Eugenia taught me the power of the press in shaping women's attitudes toward fashion, including the kind of clip a woman should wear and how to position it on the shoulder of her suit jacket, as well as the length of her skirts. The editor fell in love with the design genius of the French jeweler Jean Schlumberger (nicknamed "Johnny"), whom Walter Hoving decided to bring over to New York and install in his own little world on the store's mezzanine. (I would later lecture on his jewelry designs at a black-tie lecture benefit at Chicago's Drake Hotel, another one at the de Young Museum in San Francisco, and even in New York's Metropolitan Museum of Art.) His salon soon became the place for women married to men of great wealth to congregate around the lunch hour and view "Johnny's latest trinkets." Of course that trinket could be anything from a $500,000 necklace of diamond-and-turquoise flowers to a $200 jeweled eighteen-karat-gold flower pistil with tiny buds on it, that one could stick in the middle of a fresh carnation, pinned to a woman's suit jacket lapel, and create a still life of great beauty. If a photograph of a Tiffany item was reasonably good, Eugenia would publish a big fashion story around it. The amount of space given over to our jewels and table-setting designs would have cost hundreds of thousands of dollars of advertising revenue. God bless publicity! I now understood the game.

Jessica Daves, head of *Vogue* magazine, Babe Paley (married to Bill Paley, the head of CBS), Kitty (Mrs. Gilbert) Miller, Carmel Snow of *Harper's Bazaar,* Marella (Mrs. Gianni) Agnelli and Bunny (Mrs. Paul) Mellon were, for starters, Schlumberger fans and customers. In Paris it was the de Rothschilds, Paul Louis Weiller, the vicomtesse Jacqueline de Ribes, the countess Louise de Vilmorin, the duchesse de Grammont, and the like. Schlumberger himself let me try on all of his wonderful designs. At times I could even borrow one of his big and bold jeweled pineapples, set in gold, or the diamond-and-ruby brooch of a knight's armor. Estimating what I would have to earn to be able to afford one of these jewels was a humbling thought. This plainly was a precious perk!

For fashion publicity photos, the most important thing, next to the photographer, was the model. The top ones demanded $100 an hour, which we all thought indecently high. (Today it can be $10,000 a shoot.) We also rented live animals (and even dead stuffed ones). I will never forget the rage against me in the Schlumberger and regular jewelry departments when, after four months of begging, Hoving acceded to *Vogue* magazine's request to let the Tiffany Diamond, the world's most famous canary diamond, be taken out of the store to be photographed. Until this moment the stone had been suspended in a black velvet shadow box, brilliantly lit, set into the wall in a burglarproof case. Tourists reverentially made a pilgrimage to stand transfixed before it, as though it were a holy shrine. For this August *Vogue* shoot, Jean Schlumberger designed a special setting for the stone, so it could hang suspended from a diamond necklace. What a dazzler it was! The *Vogue* art department wouldn't let me come to the shoot, because I might make the photographer nervous. Only the two armed guards could be present. I should have realized that they were going to do something naughty, but I was as surprised as Walter Hoving and William Lusk to see the final results in the magazine—the necklace haphazardly placed around the neck of a deer, as though it were slipping off. It was a sacrilege. In those days, there were no photographs of that nature. Management blamed me, of course, for downgrading the dignity of the store and blemishing its reputation. Later Schlumberger's sumptuous necklace of flexible flowers was similarly demeaned, shot close up around the ankle of a model's bare leg.

By the time all this avant-garde jewelry photography had been published in the magazines, I had become accustomed to being read out by Walter Hoving. I labored on, using the philosophy that if I were cautious and unimaginative, I would never move forward, but I would be lying if I didn't say it stung. After my first year with Tiffany's, I decided that what I needed to do to keep from becoming totally depressed was to make a written list of my sizable accomplishments—the reams of international publicity—and go over it repeatedly in my mind while everyone in the store was yelling at me. My own philosophy kept me afloat.

With Hoving at the helm, Tiffany's had become a leader, and what we predicted as "the fashion look in fine jewelry" was now eagerly picked up by the press. My publicity was selling a lot of merchandise. One of my first photographs was a close-up of a languid, beautifully manicured hand wearing an enormous emerald ring. The hand was using a five-dollar Tiffany sterling silver "dialer" to make a call on the telephone. The emerald ring, worth many thousands of dollars, was sold to a person who lived out in the far west and who called the store the day the newspaper publicity appeared. Thanks to the photograph, the store also sold two thousand little silver telephone dialers during the first two weeks after the photograph appeared. The inexpensive dialer was the kind of "loss leader" for which Hoving became famous. People loved having a reason to come into Tiffany's, and never before had they been able to come in and spend only five dollars. Not only that, it was wrapped in a Tiffany blue box. A loyal future customer was born because of it. Jacqueline Bouvier received a Tiffany dialer as a bridesmaid present before she married John F. Kennedy (I received five of them as gifts). Hers was engraved with her initials, and was subsequently sold at that dreadful auction of her possessions at Sotheby's after her death. It went for many thousands of dollars.

When Tiffany placed a beautiful diamond necklace in a *New York Times* ad in the best space, the top right hand corner of the second page, it did not sell; but my publicity photograph of the same necklace on a black-haired model dressed in white silk pajamas, hugging two aristocratic white Russian wolfhounds, Lord and Lady Woffschmidt by name, and a white Persian cat named Nicodemus, sold the necklace a week later.

I really enjoyed working with top photographers like Richard Avedon and Irving Penn, and with the top models in those days, including Suzy Parker, Betsy Pickering, Anne St. Marie, and Carmen, to name a few. (Carmen is still modeling in the new millennium, still perfectly beautiful, after half a century of looking great in the camera's eye, while most of the rest of us from that era look, well, better left unsaid.)

Our Tiffany publicity photos in those days set trends, I'm proud to say. In going over some of the store's design books of the 1920s, I had found detailed drawings of jeweled headbands—"headache bands," as some people called them—worn by famous ladies of society at *grands soirées.* We sewed diamond brooches and earrings on black velvet ribbons and photographed them close up on beautiful girls. Eugenia Sheppard ran an entire page of our makeshift headband pictures, and within a month women all over America were buying jeweled headbands for evening in the costume jewelry department of stores. We were copied. We did the same with jeweled garters, something Lillian Russell, one of Diamond Jim Brady's girlfriends, made famous. We photographed garters ablaze with diamonds, rubies, and sapphires on famous leg models, and sold all the jewelry as a result of men ogling our publicity photos, which went out over the Associated Press wire service across the country. Members of the Tiffany family and the board of directors tut-tutted all over the place. Garters? Male sexual fantasies? I found the only way to survive their criticism was to keep moving fast with other projects, so their disapproval couldn't catch up with me.

We had fun getting publicity on children's gifts from Tiffany's, too. One day I had booked a darling professional baby model. The photographer Kal Weyner set up in his studio a snow-white sea of no-seam paper on which to place the baby and watch him interact with Tiffany sterling silver gifts—mugs, rattles, bowls, spoons and forks, gold angel pins, and the like. We had the small pieces suspended like a mobile over the crib. The shoot was scheduled for 10 A.M. Eugenia Sheppard needed the proofs by 3:00 P.M. to get the story in as the front page lead in the Sunday section, which she had saved just for us. At nine o'clock my assistant Chandra Donnell and I were walking about on the no-seam paper in our stocking feet, to keep it clean and unmarked, when a call came from the baby's very upset mother. Her child had just broken out with measles. There was no time for hand-wringing, but it *was* time for true friends to spring into action. I called Mrs. Charles Rees, a very close friend, who at that point had given birth to only two of her four daughters. Within one hour she arrived at the studio with the perfect six-month-old baby, Camilla, whom we placed in our rented lacy bassinet and who seemed delighted to be there, and with a perfect older daughter, Liberty, aged two and a half, clad in a Heidi dirndl outfit but with a costume change—her own pink silk negligee with pink ostrich-feather trim, right out of a Carole Lombard film! Not only was the photography set now in perfect shape, but the Rees girls, with Mother Nancy close by, immediately took to the most expensive of the baby things and played with them to perfection before the camera. Liberty proceeded to bat the mobile around for Camilla's wide-eyed amusement. If we had spent a year trying to get the perfect picture, we never could have done better. It just happened, and I think it was God's way of comforting me after all the bad luck I had experienced in recent previous shoots.

Whether you're selling baby silver or jewels, human beings make a photograph spring to life. A bunch of pearl necklaces and long drop earrings are nice, but when you put them on lovely, ladylike models dressed in designer ball gowns for opening night at the opera and photograph them in the "Diamond Circle" boxes of the old Metropolitan Opera House (pre–Lincoln Center), you have a killer photograph. And sales. And women attending opening night who have copied the look of those models' dresses and jewels. And Walter Hoving loves you for having gotten all those newspaper pages and the buzz around town, and radio and TV features on the jewelry. And the opera loves you for all the publicity you have gotten for opening night. And the mayor loves you for having added grandeur and beauty to the reputation of his city. There's excitement in the air; people are all dressed up for opening night; the big jewels have all emerged temporarily from bank vaults. The hairdressers have been reserved for months. Everyone who is anyone has his or her own limo with chauffeur, or has rented a splendid car and driver for the opera. As one chauffeur commented, "On opening night at the Metropolitan, you can smell the overly perfumed ladies from three blocks away. What do they do about the air inside the opera house? Give people oxygen masks to breathe through?"

I have passionately loved and coveted jewelry all my life, but never owned any—that is, except for the opera-length oriental pearl necklace (given to my father in lieu of a legal fee) that financed my trip to Yugoslavia. One of the great perks at Tiffany's was that I could borrow the store's jewelry, to show off in all the right places, for publicity purposes. I never left the store to have lunch in an "in" place without eighteen-karat-gold ear clips and an incredible brooch on my suit lapel, or a big, bold gold bracelet. I always had the leather gloves, handbag, and good shoes to go with the suit so the pin would not feel "dressed down."

Black-tie events were common in New York in those days, and I got invited everywhere. Hoving would not pay for a car to take me, and my men friends were too young to make the Society A-list. I was added to the guest lists of much older, richer, and more social people because I was a conversational "giver." With my enthusiasm for Tiffany's and my stories of the amazing, amusing things that went on there, I sold a lot of jewelry indirectly. Other guests would always ogle my borrowed jewels. If I had blemish on my face or a reminder of a love bite on my neck, everyone would fixate on the sparkly stuff and detour around the blemish. Jewels, real or not, are the perfect subterfuge.

I went to private dinners in grand homes and apartments, often via the Madison Avenue or Fifth Avenue bus. I would always get a ride home with some gentleman or a couple, so the jewelry was safe in the darkness of night. I even felt secure popping down on the Madison Avenue bus at seven-thirty for an eight o'clock dinner on the Upper East Side because I was so conspicuous, standing tall in the crowded aisles in my evening clothes, usually next to someone like the delivery boy from the deli, the odor of his hot pastrami sandwiches and kosher pickles deliciously mingling with the scent of my Moment Supreme perfume. I usually borrowed for these black-tie occasions long, dramatic, dangly earrings. Under my evening coat would be a fortune in jewels—around my neck, on my ears, wrists, or fingers. In those days a woman cherished owning a long satin, brocade, or velvet evening coat. The velvets were always in deep jewel colors, and the satin coats in surprising pastels, like lavender or turquoise. I couldn't afford a fur coat, but anyway, a fur in a low price range would never have had the effect of these sweeping evening coats. (They were particularly effective in the crowded aisle in rush hour on the bus!) I loved it when some kid would look up at me and utter an awed "Gee!" It was music to my ears.

To have evening dresses made, I would supply the fabric to a little dressmaker for a pittance (how does $80 sound?). With a matching evening bag, white kid gloves, and a flash of diamonds at the wrist, which I'm sure my fellow bus passengers thought were rhinestones, the effect was quite dramatic. I know those tired fellow passengers, going home after a tough day's work, liked seeing this tall apparition with her dangling earrings and long evening coat, strap-hanging along with the best of them.

I desperately wanted to borrow one piece of jewelry, an ambitious dream, as it was a star of the Schlumberger collection. Walter Hoving had tried on three separate occasions to get Bill Paley to buy it for Babe, his wife.

It was a heavy, intricate eighteen-karat-gold vine necklace, very realistic, from which were suspended magnificent, flexible morning glories, made of sapphires with diamonds set in gold and platinum. Johnny Schlumberger lent it to me one hot July evening when I was on my way home to dress for a dinner at Kitty and Gilbert Miller's. My feelings of joy were indescribable. It was such a work of art, I felt I had plucked some of the famous flowers from Claude Monet's garden at Giverny. I was wearing the greatest necklace in the world. It was *mine* for this evening.

That evening I was the focus of the dinner party of twenty-four people, celebrities from the worlds of theater and music. Then I made a ghastly mistake. As we were finishing dessert at the table, I asked my dinner partner on the right if he could remove the safety clasp on the the back of the necklace, so I could take it off. It had begun to hurt me. It was tight, it was a terribly hot night, and the prickly vines had begun to dig into my flesh. I felt my neck swell from the heat and constriction. The clasp was a delicate, complicated one, and I should have known better. During dinner I had noticed my dinner partner's big burly hands, like a football player's, but when he heard me mention my neck dilemma, he announced proudly that of course he could remove my necklace with ease. He was an old hand at such things. Well, disaster was the result. He pulled, he yanked, he jammed the clasp and broke it.

It was now really trapped on me.

I tried again to remove it in front of the bathroom mirror at home. Two women who lived next door to me answered their doorbell, and both, in their bathrobes, tried to help me out. I was desperately fearful that one of the people trying to yank it off me would send it spinning across the floor, breaking it into a thousand pieces, a masterpiece destroyed. I became more desperate and fearful as the hours wore on. I went to bed with a couple of aspirins and tried to insert white handkerchiefs under the necklace, for two reasons—to save the necklace, and to stanch the tiny rivulets of blood that now trickled down all over my neck. My neck was now traumatized from the stabbing of the little gold twigs. The next morning, on a humid, 99-degree day, I dressed in my favorite fire-engine-red silk dress to improve my morale, in pretty bad shape by then. I made my usual eight-block walk to the store, startling everyone I passed in that busy eight-thirty rush hour. The sun was glinting on the diamonds and sapphires of the spectacular necklace, and drops of blood were also in evidence. New York is full of blasé people accustomed to seeing weird things. My appearance interested them, but not for more than a quick glance. Screwier things were happening than a woman in a red dress walking around with heavy jewelry and a bleeding neck. Once in the store, I went immediately to the off-limits Diamond Office, where the jewelers took a mini-blowtorch, used often in jewelry making, and sawed the necklace off my poor neck. They constructed a new clasp, and never said a word to management about it, knowing I would get into deep trouble if they told on me. Those gentlemen in the Diamond Office, most of whom had been there thirty years or more, were my true friends and supporters. As one of them told me, "You make us laugh all the time."

It was only a question of time before Truman Capote's best-selling novel, *Breakfast at Tiffany's*, would be made into a film. The book was the talk of the sophisticated set all over America. The publicity of its title alone brought enormous financial benefits to the store. A movie producer came to my office in 1958 to discuss shooting a scene or two on location, following the story line. Nothing in the world was guaranteed to bring Tiffany's a bigger publicity bonanza, but it took me at least six months of working on a suspicious Walter Hoving to allow it. I had expected Hoving to do a victory war dance around his office with me when the offer was made. Instead he said, "No, none of that cheap, tawdry Hollywood stuff in this store." It was a hard sell. Harry Platt, the enthusiastic young head of gold jewelry, and a member of the Tiffany family worked hard on Mr. Hoving to say yes.

Audrey Hepburn and George Peppard were the leads, and fortuitous choices. Even Walter Hoving finally had to conclude it was a heaven-sent promotion for the store, but he laid rules and regulations on the producers that would have deterred anyone from proceeding if the production company hadn't been so eager to do this film. Capote's novel was hot, so they wanted to act fast. Hoving decreed that the main floor scene, with the army of salesmen and women behind the jewelry counters, had to be filmed exactly as it was, in reality. No actors were to substitute for salespeople, except for the main salesman who was to show Holly Golightly and her man the diamond rings (unaffordable, so that the couple would decide on a cigar ring). When the union informed Hoving that since he wouldn't allow actors to take the place of the salespeople, every single Tiffany employee on the first floor—about fifty people—would have to be inducted into the actors' union, with a year's dues paid for each, Walter Hoving said, "So be it." Then he turned to the producer and said, "You, of course, will pay for all that." (Another multi-thousand-dollar charge against the producer's budget.)

Audrey Hepburn and George Peppard were charming, patient about signing autographs for the employees, and never showed any displeasure at the inevitable delays. I had several good chats with Audrey when she was taking a break, about boar hunting in the moonlight in Holland and the best places to ski (and break a leg) in Switzerland.

Of course, the film was a huge success. As for its publicity value to Tiffany's, scores of people came to the store when they visited New York because of that movie. Sometimes they would come in and ask, "On what floor are you serving breakfast?" They were greatly disappointed to discover that they could be served diamonds and rubies, but no bacon and eggs.

This thing called television, which I knew very little about, was certainly something to be taken seriously for Tiffany's sake. I had lived a TV-screenless life all those years in Italy, but it was certainly taking center stage in American entertainment.

I was scarcely back home from Rome when actress Grace Kelly and Prince Rainier of Monaco had a wedding that dazzled the world. We watched it on the little TV sets, enthralled. The picture and audio quality were terrible, but we could see what we wanted to through the graininess and the shadows.

I asked my TV-watching friends and contacts to explain which shows booked people who were selling something. I went to the offices of the various networks begging, with hat in hand, for stories to be developed on jewels, with which Tiffany's would fully cooperate. What I had to sell—the romance and intrigue of jewels—was something the TV producers wanted, and certainly Mrs. Housewife would, too, while watching TV and tending to her children and the housekeeping. Anything to escape the humdrum of her life.

I prepared myself to run through, for the producers' benefit, the list of things we could bring into the studios and talk about, from the point of view of fashion, design, history, weddings, entertaining, oriental pearls, and gifts. I had stories on the origin of the famous sports trophies the store designed, the history of the great jewel robberies, and the famous weddings that were Tiffany-managed, including persuading the bride to accept a proposal with the perfect engagement ring.

One of my first television coups was the nightly *Jack Paar Show* on NBC, forerunner to all the nightly network shows, including Johnny Carson's, David Letterman's, and later, Jay Leno's and Conan O'Brien's. The producers asked me to bring a "sackful" of unset diamonds of different cuts and sizes for Paar to show the audience, which I did, accompanied by a nervous armed Pinkerton guard hired by Tiffany's for the occasion. A special insurance policy had been taken out to cover the stones going out of the store. Management was uneasy; this had never been asked for, or allowed, before, and my previous antics evidently had not made our careful old-time executives feel any better about it.

On camera, Jack Paar sat at his desk holding the Tiffany black velvet drawstring sackful of stones. I sat next to him in my little black dress, ready and waiting to discuss carat weight, color, quality, cut, clarity, and the difference between platinum and gold mountings. Instead, he did not address me at all. "You know," he said, looking straight at the audience, "I've always wondered all my life how it would feel to do this." He took the bag of diamonds and threw out the contents on the floor by his desk, as if it were all one big dice toss. The stones flew in every direction. I was gripped with cold terror. This was a great way for Jack Paar to get ratings, but I saw myself in the women's ward at Sing Sing for the rest of my life. Before I left for prison, I saw myself being poisoned in my teacup by Walter Hoving. The Pinkerton guard was almost in worse shape than I was. His eyes bulged out of his head, his gun was drawn, and he was pointing it everywhere in widespread motions. In the meantime, his gun hand was shaking uncontrollably. The audience was laughing loudly, thinking it was part of the act, and Jack Paar was in convulsions over his own humor. Ha, ha. The segment was quickly over, a strainer, whisk broom, and dustpan were brought onto the set, and we canvassed every centimeter of the floor for lost diamonds until—we hoped—we had them all back in the velvet bag. The previous morning I had proudly told everyone at Tiffany's, including the board of directors, to be glued to their TV sets that night. Most important, my mother and father were watching with a gaggle of their friends. What a great way for the new PR executive to make her debut in the TV world. My God!

Everyone got over it. And it did make news all over the world—for Jack Paar, that is.

This was not to be the last television adventure. Mr. Hoving had asked me to publicize the works of the porcelain sculptor Edward Marshall Boehm, whose magical, lifelike birds and animals, executed in bisque porcelain, had just been placed in an exhibit on the china floor. Ed Boehm, a true farmer as well as an artist, was intensely shy, the opposite of his young wife, Helen. He refused to meet the press—or people in general, for that matter. When the young Queen Elizabeth and Prince Philip were about to come over on a state visit in 1957, Helen had a great idea. She conned her husband into making a replica of *The Polo Player,* a large porcelain sculpture of Prince Philip astride his horse, playing polo, a very difficult piece to execute. Helen planned to present it personally to His Royal Highness when he arrived with the queen in New York. We booked an appearance for Helen and *The Polo Player* on

Dave Garroway's morning TV show, the first *Today* show in the NBC studios. Helen was elated and very nervous when we arrived at NBC at 6:00 A.M. I helped her unpack the sculpture, which was in a giant wooden crate, cushioned on all sides by bags of popped popcorn.

The studio people were in a big rush to unpack and light the statue. In my haste, I tore open a couple of the giant plastic bags of popcorn. The stuff went wildly all over the floor, in every nook and cranny of the large studio. Wherever anyone walked, large crunching noises were heard. The sound engineer went berserk trying to get the sound out of his ears. Everyone was sweeping, picking up kernels, searching the floor, cussing, and crunching all through the telecast. The segment went off without a hitch, and the Garroway crew tried to watch their language while Helen and I were in the studio, but I can well imagine what it was like when we finally left.

Helen Boehm and I paired up again when Tiffany's had a big show of Boehm porcelain birds. Helen decided to bring in some of Ed's exotic South American and Far Eastern birds from their aviary in New Jersey. I rented a six-foot-tall antique Spanish wire birdcage, very beautiful and distinguished, and placed it in the special room where the Boehm collection was grandly displayed on shelves. We thought it was a great touch that live and porcelain birds could reside in peace and harmony in that exhibition room. The first disaster occurred when Helen was unloading the small cages of Ed's live birds from her station wagon, parked at the Fifty-seventh Street trade entrance. Two of the cages were not fastened properly, and eight little birds escaped into Fifth Avenue's cold morning air. When news of the colorful, rare, and exotic missing birds went out on the radio and TV, it set off a frenzied bird hunt all over Manhattan. Doormen kept a lookout, and children began scouring the parks and bushes. It was the buzz of all the boroughs.

Longshoremen from Brooklyn brought dead pigeons into the store, wondering if they might be the missing birds. Children came to the store after school bearing every type of deceased bird they could find, including mangy specimen that had been dead for days. Each bird bearer was given one of Tiffany's turquoise gift boxes to use for a suitable burial near the children's homes. Gabe Pressman of NBC News called me to ask if he could bring his crew to the china floor to cover the story for the evening news. I was, of course, thrilled. To give extra atmosphere to the birds in their exhibition space during the TV coverage, I turned on a special record of bird calls I had just purchased, silently congratulating myself for such a creative move. Unfortunately, I had not listened to it in advance, and in the midst of lovely chirps and sweet birdsongs there was suddenly a loud, harsh sound—an owl call. When the sound of this particular bird of prey was heard by the little birds in the cage, as one, they began frantically fluttering around, crying for help. Two colorful African whydahs managed to press their little bodies through the wires of the cage to freedom. They began flying around like the crazed birds they were—all over the ceiling, running into the lights and mirrored pillars, swooping down onto delicate crystal glasses, and landing briefly on the incredibly expensive best Minton china on the floor. It was a madhouse. Women customers were flailing their handbags and handkerchiefs in the air, trying to catch a bird as it passed by, to no avail. Eventually, the Bronx Zoo's chief birdkeeper and some bird experts caught them by waiting until dark, turning off all the lights on the floor, and luring the birds with handheld flashlights. Even though we got a large piece of prime-time NBC national news and made the front pages all over the world, Hoving was furious. He came up to the third floor, grim-lipped and white-faced.

"I'm paying you to make profits for this store," he said to me, gruffly. "Instead, there has not been one sale made on any floor for three hours while you've been hunting escaped birds—that we don't even sell! And all these children, bringing in every dead bird they find, wanting to know if they're our dead birds, it's terrible!"

"Mr. Hoving," I wanted to say, "you have just proven once again that you have absolutely no sense of humor, none!" What I really wanted to add was, "If we had rigged this three months in advance, and practiced it, it never would have worked. We never could have gotten the publicity we have just received—all over this country." Instead I told Mr. Hoving how sorry I was that sales had ceased during the melee. Mea culpa, mea culpa.

We had about three hundred more people than usual in the store that afternoon, and all those children with the Tiffany burial boxes we gave them for their dead birds were our customers. The NBC News coverage of the birds had also drawn into the store every member of the press—wire services, dailies, and even the local stringer for *National Geographic*. And I was apologizing to my boss!

The publicity department steadily grew, becoming a whirlwind of activity. The more people who came to see me for background on stories on Tiffany's, special projects, or tie-ins, the more mail and stuff arrived by the hour, with messengers and mailmen crowding the executive oval circle on the fifth floor. We had outgrown our space, and Walter Hoving himself scouted out the publicity department's new quarters—at the back of the fourth floor, an airless closet space in front of the trade elevator doors. When the doors opened, anyone on the elevator would be startled, as though intruding on someone's intimate space. The three desks—mine, my assistant Chandra Donnell's, and my secretary and jane-of-all-trades Georgia Palmer's—were stuck together like Velcro-covered children's blocks. To have a personal conversation, we had to walk down the employee staircase to the third floor. (When Georgia left to get married, Duane Garrison, a young Vassar graduate, became my chief assistant.)

We had two file cabinets, which served as our lamp tables. The painter asked us what color we wanted the walls. After the lugubrious brown palette of the executive floor, I thought pink would be a welcome, feminine touch. It turned out to be a horrible chalky pink, which closed in on us in that tiny space—the color of the leading medicine against diarrhea. What a horrible symbol of our profession!

Then one morning Diana Vreeland came to see me about a project for *Harper's Bazaar.* She stepped from the elevator cab into our pink closet and appeared stunned. My assistants could hardly believe the famous, slim, deliciously perfumed Vreeland was in our presence. She wore black turtleneck leotards long before anyone knew what they were, and she swirled herself in capes and leopard skins before the World Wildlife Fund pronounced the cats endangered. As head of a leading fashion magazine, she was renowned on the international fashion scene. Later she was to become head of the Metropolitan Museum Costume Institute.

Talk about sisterhood—Diana left my office and went straight to Hoving to register a protest on my behalf. She and Hoving had a mutual admiration society.

"It's despicable, Walter," she said, throwing her fringed cape angrily over one shoulder. "You finally have your first woman executive, a woman of substance with a great background, and you've locked her and her valiant staff in a broom closet! You should be ashamed. It's chauvism carried to an extreme."

Two days later we were released from our pink prison and moved back to the executive floor, into very posh quarters, with thick carpeting, mahogany furniture, and wood-paneled walls.

At times I felt persecuted, overworked, hounded. I was a disposal. At our weekly Monday-morning staff meeting, Walter Hoving addressed his executives: "We must do something about the stationery department. Sales are dead. It's worrying. People don't realize we have the most beautiful writing paper in the world manufactured here, in our own factory in New Jersey. There is a lot at stake, including a number of jobs held by employees who have been with us for at least two decades. Our hand engraving is undisputedly the best in the world. What are we going to do about it?" Not a hand was raised. No one looked at the chairman, for fear that establishing eye contact with him would be a sign of agreement to take on the project.

The Baldrige kids. Tish, Mac, and freckle-faced, redheaded Bob in a rare moment of sibling peace. OMAHA, 1929.

Age seven, with my add-a-pearl gold necklace, then a "must" fashion accessory for every young girl.

At my desk in the American Embassy residence. This was before the era when women put rollers in their hair. Flat hair was "it." PARIS, 1949.

In a Jacques Fath coat, next to my "Titine," a Peugeot 203.

With my beautiful boss, American Ambassador Clare Boothe Luce, at Ciampino Airport, on our way to Paris. Pearls and kid gloves, of course, for air travel.

Writing my first book, *Roman Candle*, in 1955; it was published the following year.

Nancy Rees and I (left) crouch down while Kal Weyner directs the lighting for the publicity pictures he took of Tiffany's baby silver. Baby Camilla Rees (in the bassinet) and sister Liberty Rees are the models. Georgie Palmer and Chandra Donnell help out. NEW YORK, 1957.

At the Tiffany Ball, piling about a million dollars' worth of diamonds on an exquisite model. That's an armed guard standing behind her. NEWPORT, 1957.

At my desk in the White House wearing gold earrings and a jeweled clip borrowed from Tiffany's. My engagement book says 1961, our first year in the White House.

John's first birthday party. His parents and I are smiling as the baby is put into his seat. The first thing John did when confronting the large cake chef René Verdon sent up from the kitchen was to plop his face right down in the middle of the frosting. He loved sweets.

President Kennedy and a military aide walk out the South Door to greet an arriving head of state on one of the president's helicopters. I head out to do a ceremonial something or other.

Jackie and I in the White House. 1963.

One of my favorite PR clients was Miss Elizabeth Arden, shown here cutting the ribbon on her new Red Door Salon in Chicago, with a friend and her niece, Pat Young (right). 1965.

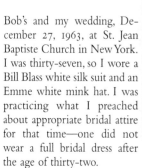

Bob's and my wedding, December 27, 1963, at St. Jean Baptiste Church in New York. I was thirty-seven, so I wore a Bill Blass white silk suit and an Emme white mink hat. I was practicing what I preached about appropriate bridal attire for that time—one did not wear a full bridal dress after the age of thirty-two.

Sitting in one of our Chicago apartments, 1969. A mid-nineteenth-century portrait of my great-great-great-grandmother hangs over part of my fabulous collection of antique porcelains, all wedding presents, and all broken to pieces by various children playing in the living room.

Of Diamonds and Diplomats was an instant bestseller. Here I am at a book-signing at Chicago's Barbara's Books on Wells Street. 1968.

Chicago produced a lot of great things in my life, including Clare and Malcolm. 1969.

I rewrote Amy Vanderbilt's etiquette book, which added another new facet to my career. Our Jack Russell terrier, Dustin Hoffman, always sat by me when I worked. He loved the hum of the electric typewriter on the makeshift plywood bed desk. NEW YORK, 1978. *Photo by Harry Benson*

It's pretty heady stuff, to be on the cover of *Time* as the arbiter of America's manners.
NEW YORK, 1978.

Jackie came by my office and did some promotion for a game, Counterstrike, which Nancy Tuckerman's brother Roger had helped invent.
NEW YORK, 1980.

When my PR firm launched a nightclub in the Hilton Hotel in 1973, old pals like Diana Vreeland came by to help out.

The Tai Missonis put on a superb fashion show in the Metropolitan Museum of Art. Diana Vreeland came around to congratulate them, but I had to do the commentary at the mike. NEW YORK, 1985.

One of my favorite boards was the Institute for International Education. I was bonded to it, because I had been one of the first foreign exchange students allowed in Europe after World War II. Shown here at a box lunch meeting: Senator Pat Moynihan from New York and the president of the institute, Dick Krasno. NEW YORK, 1987.

President Reagan in his loud plaid suit, and I in my loud knit suit. WASHINGTON, 1984.

Nancy Reagan invited me to
the Reagans' last State Dinner.
THE WHITE HOUSE, DECEMBER 1988.

Barbara Bush and I at the White House. It was—and is—always old-home week to go back to
the White House. Even today, I still know people who have worked there for decades and
quarter centuries.

"All right, Miss Baldrige," Chairman Hoving said with resignation. "You take it on, under the head of the department [Farnham Lefferts]. I want immediate publicity." The assignment was not so much handed to me as thrown at me like a diseased bone. Every man around that conference table threw me a glance that said half "Terribly sorry, Tish, you got the booby prize," and half "Thank God I'm not the sucker who has to deal with this."

Hoving ended the meeting by addressing me again. "You will have to use your own creativity. And don't keep bothering me with your plans for this campaign. Just go ahead and do it. Get traffic into that department, but make sure you don't upset Farnham while you're doing it."

It was the eve of the birth of the computer industry, and people were already losing the art of personal letter writing, which had been the hallmark of quality communication in past decades. "Ladies and gentlemen" still wrote graceful letters, but their daughters were marrying young men who had never taken a stylish pen to a quality piece of paper. Who knows? Perhaps this was the start of the decline of manners in our country. To Walter Hoving, it meant only a decline in sales in the stationery department.

What in heck does one do about showcasing a box of ecru stationery? Then the idea struck. Valentine's Day was coming. We would mount an exhibit of great love letters from the past, to be handwritten in period penmanship and on Tiffany stationery that looked appropriate for that famous person. I researched historic letters published in collections in the New York Public Library. Then I had the store calligraphers copy twenty of the most interesting ones by hand on the proper style and color of Tiffany letter paper, and in an appropriate handwriting. Queen Elizabeth's love letter to Sir Francis Drake was written in Elizabethan script, for example, on pale blue paper. His letter to her was written on tan letter paper, with dark brown engraving. There were fascinating letters from Robert to Elizabeth Barrett Browning, from George Washington to Martha, from Napoleon to Josephine, from Abraham Lincoln to his wife Mary Todd, all composed in romantic language— and some full of sexual fire. They were mounted on red-felt-covered standing bulletin boards all through the store's main jewelry floor.

Hoving came tearing into my office the morning the exhibit was supposed to open. He was furious. I hadn't told him what I was doing, and he thought the entire idea was disastrous. If he was angry, I was too. I had worked hard on it. "Just because you may never have written a love letter, Mr. Hoving," I said, "doesn't mean that our customers won't be fascinated to see these historic ones."

"Miss Baldrige," he said, now letting his emotions show, "come down with me right now, and together we will remove this travesty of a promotion idea from the jewelry floor, where it certainly does not belong."

When we arrived on the first floor, a crowd filled all of the aisles. People had come in to read the letters. The morning ad in the papers had brought some, but more were drawn by word of mouth. Two popular morning radio show hosts were talking about it, having seen it at a sneak preview the night before, which Hoving had not bothered to attend. Customers and tourists in the store were reading each letter, lingering over it, savoring its historic and romantic content. One of the men reading a letter closely turned to me as I walked by and said, "How I wish I knew how to write a love letter like that!" Then he added, "But what I really wish is that someone would send me a love letter like that." (I almost went back to my office and wrote him one, he looked so sad.)

By noon the line of people waiting to read the letters snaked out of the store, around the Fifth Avenue corner, and all the way to Madison Avenue. The *New York Times* wrote an editorial on the show, saying that we have truly forgotten how to express our emotions in letters, and that everyone should go read them. One of the women who read every letter was heard to say to her friend on the way out of the store, "Who would have thought that Napoleon could have been such a sexy old thing?"

Engraved stationery orders took off, of course. Walter Hoving apologized to me, and said, "This is one time I was wrong and you were right"— enormous praise, from him.

I had to visualize all of the contents of the store as "my children," which meant not playing favorites with my publicity efforts. I would have liked to do nothing but work on jewelry, but, like the stationary department, there were silver, china, glass, clocks, and watch departments to worry about. Some of this array of merchandise was difficult to publicize. Editors simply were not interested, no matter how much romance you tried to attach to it. A plate is a plate is a plate, as Gertrude Stein would have said. Just how much can you do with a soup spoon, salad bowl, and hors d'oeuvres platter? A certain amount, but it won't unleash torrents of creative inspiration. Tabletop elements are much harder than jewels to sell as the inspiration for a newspaper article; you can't wear what goes on the table. Walter Hoving had given the command: Get publicity on our tabletop merchandise. When I queried, "What do you have in mind?" his answer was the same it had been on my first day with the company when I asked him what I was supposed to do. "I'm paying you to know what to do."

I drew up plans for a romantic launch of the new sterling silver pattern Cordis, which means "of the heart." Logically the pattern is tied to romance and the wedding industry. In those days new silver patterns were rarely brought out, and usually by Tiffany, and they were then copied and adapted by all of the jewelry companies. A new design, the first in many years, was therefore big news. Many of the magazines showed a place setting either up close or in one of their own table settings.

After consulting my muse, I decided to go again with birds—in fact, two live, white, rented lovebirds ("Don't call them pigeons, please"). We opened the show of romantic table settings on Valentine's Day. The two small white doves glowed a pale pink under the lights of the silver floor. Their wire cage was also pink, and I tucked pale pink flowers into the corners. The china on the table had a rosebud pattern. Pink napkins were used on a white organdy cloth. I was so successful in creating a romantic mood that even the birds got into the swing of things. One night when I was working late, the night watchman called up to me in a state of great excitement. "Come down here at once!" he pleaded. The lovebirds had produced two pale pink eggs. I am not joking. Sex had finally come to Tiffany's!

I called the Bronx Zoo birdkeeper, who knew me after my exploits with the Boehm birds on the china floor, and he said, "Get a box, stuff it with some excelsior from the shipping department, and then leave the birds alone. They'll take care of things themselves." The next morning I arrived at 8:00 A.M. and rushed to see what was happening in the Cordis silver pattern table setting, with its very unusual centerpiece. I found Mama Bird sitting on the two eggs in her nest. She and her husband had shredded the excelsior to a much finer degree. They had prepared a proper nursery for the eggs, in a very suitable place—a blue Tiffany box.

The word got out, the public poured in, and once again Walter Hoving remarked how he had hired me to make money for the company, not fill the store with children, old ladies, and bird watchers. A day later Mama Bird and her eggs were returned to the bird renter's, but Tiffany's had already received a spate of national and international publicity on this blessed event. Sales of the Cordis flatware were brisk. "Mr. Hoving," I remarked to my sympathetic staff, "is incapable of appreciating the birds and the bees."

Walter Hoving was indisputedly a brilliant merchant. He knew that we would have to get the customers into the store before we could sell them anything, yet a lot of people were afraid to come inside. He knew people had to be wooed from the outside in, and he found just the man to do it—an artist of immeasurable talent, a window designer named Gene Moore, who was to become probably the most celebrated window designer in history. Traffic on the busy Fifty-seventh and Fifth Avenue corner regularly came to a halt as gawkers in passing cars as well as pedestrians stopped to peer into the small windows, dramatically lit and always surprising. The city traffic division made official complaints to Mr. Hoving—who, naturally, did absolutely nothing about them. No one had ever seen anything like Gene's windows before. (Today, many are still trying unsuccessfully to copy him.) He would build a stage set of a miniature eighteenth-century English library with wing chairs, oriental carpets, books filling the walls of shelves—and an incredible emerald-cut diamond ring sitting on one shelf. He would make a miniature boxwood garden, with Schlumberger jeweled butterfly brooches flitting among the hedges. He had little enamel creatures sitting chatting in a row, like gossiping frogs, dangling their legs from the top of a row of gold bracelets. He ran a cool waterfall over diamonds in one of the hottest Augusts New Yorkers had ever suffered through. (There was a serious water shortage at the time, so Gene patriotically used gin instead for his waterfall.) When the weather turned cold, he would put a miniature black iron potbellied stove in a window, spewing forth hot coals of unset rubies. Tiny black pearls were spread on toast rounds like caviar next to the store's champagne flutes, filled with champagne that an aerator kept fizzing. Going into the display department, hidden on a high floor in the store, was like visiting a magician's workshop—full of beautiful as well as fantastic objects. The interesting thing to me was that Walter Hoving repeated again and again to Gene, "We don't have to sell anything in your windows. Just follow your creative instincts."

It was innevitable that we would become involved in the charity ball business. The Tiffany Ball loomed large on our horizon. Mr. Hoving had been asked by the Newport Preservation Society to sponsor the first ball ever allowed to be held in the great mansion called Marble House, in Newport, Rhode Island. One of the best known of the "summer cottages" on Belmont Avenue, the Marble House was designed by Stanford White late in the nineteenth century for the William Vanderbilts and their robber baron friends. Mr. Hoving said, "Yes, we'll sponsor it, provided you do not call it 'The Preservation Society Ball,' but rather 'The Tiffany Ball.' " I was shocked at his audacity in making such a request. They were too, but, of course, they acquiesced. It was a brilliant idea.

The beneficiary was the tiny organization that supervised, as best it could, the preservation of not only the great mansions by the sea but also a great number of eighteenth-century houses that needed saving from the wrecking ball. I found myself studying American colonial architecture in Newport, as well as the historic mansions of the turn of the century, so that I could write intelligent press releases to whet the appetite of the press. We used the Tiffany Diamond, worn as a necklace for the first time outside the store on the neck of Grand Dame Mrs. Sheldon Whitehouse, in order to attract publicity not only in the American media but all around the world. This spectacular attraction to ticket sales almost exploded in our faces on the night of the ball when Mrs. Whitehouse was followed into the ladies' room by a burly armed Pinkerton guard. He would not let the diamond go unprotected *anywhere.* She announced that no man was to be present with her in the bathroom. *She* won.

Another disaster was barely averted when *Life* photographers and journalists showed up to do their big cover story for the "*Life* Goes to a Party" section of the magazine. The ball committee decreed that they could not stay at the ball, dressed as they were in blue jeans and sweat shirts—their work clothes. After an hour of almost missing the *Life* coverage because the journalists were as outraged as the ladies, we succeeded in opening up after hours a naval uniform shop in Newport. Soon the photographers appeared, dressed as enlisted men in the U.S. Navy, and all was well.

It was such a prestigious social event that even Senator and Mrs. John Kennedy, who were going to spend the weekend with her family at the Auchincloss home in Newport, came up for it. I shared a small chartered plane ride with them from New York to Newport, and their presence at the ball further assured its intenational success. The senator obviously already had his eye on bigger things. He came over to me and said, "The *Life* photographers want to take pictures of Jackie and me, but I don't want them to take any of me holding a drink. See to that, will you?"

"Jack, I cannot promise any such thing," was my answer. "This is a public place. If you want to leave a lily-white impression of yourself in the public's mind, you are simply going to have to get through the evening without a drink in your hand. Or else hide it under the table."

"Don't you have better control of the press than that?"

"No, and no one else should, either." It was my first argument with the future president of the United States.

I held fast, he hid his drink, and the spectacular pictures of the Kennedys and the Tiffany Ball in general were seen around the world. Everyone had a terrific time. I felt euphoric over the success of our efforts and the beauty of this history-making party, and at the same time I felt ready to return to a hospital. I was totally, inexorably exhausted, having just emerged three days earlier from a nasty emergency appendectomy in the New York Hospital. When you think you're going to die, as I did several times standing and feeling faint and dizzy in the rosy splendor of Marble House, you just don't do it. I had achieved super-publicity of the most glamorous kind for the ball, and I did not want it overshadowed by a story on my untimely death in Newport. Walter Hoving would not have liked it one bit.

Summer balls were to become a common fund-raiser for the Newport Preservation Society, but our Tiffany Ball was the first and probably the best. We were copied time and time again—but always look to the original!

Part of Walter Hoving's genius as a merchant is that if there was a deficit somewhere in his knowledge, he corrected it at once. Hoving had known nothing about the jewelry business until he made plans to buy Tiffany's, except for some fairly extravagant rocks his wife Pauline owned before she married him. When he bought the company, he became an overnight enthusiast in the field—expert enough to talk the talk with the smartest of jewelers. He became an expert on fine porcelain, crystal, and objets d'art. He had obviously worked hard at educating himself; his knowledge was much too profound to be only on the surface. He also knew the value of being around people who epitomized class, a knowledge of the arts, and a genuine love of beautiful things. Such a man was Van Day Truex, the former head of the Parsons School of Design and the "companion" (or "walker," as *Women's Wear Daily* would describe it) of the really rich and social ladies of New York. Hoving retained Van as head of design for the store, and as the galvanizer of his grand plan for Tiffany's. He was brilliant, certain of his taste, and able to do things no one else could—like go, on a hunch, to a little island in Italy's lake country, to uncover a hermit artisan there who could design tabletop accessories that would enchant anyone who saw them. During the Hoving regime, Van was destined to leave no tureen, silver pepper shaker, or crystal candlestick unexamined for quality and integrity of design. Hoving had decreed that the store's merchandise was to change to a better design format at once. Van would then airily point to an entire line of successful china that he thought was passé and say, "This goes. It simply goes," and the salesperson standing nearby would feel like choking from despair, because it had been her best selling china line for years. His certainty about his own taste bordered on pure arrogance, but he was usually right, and he was also a kind man. I loved Van, with his gray hair, his natty gray suits, and his in-depth knowledge of who was who even before who knew it!

Before Tiffany's table setting shows, stores usually stacked china, glass, and samples of flatware on little tables around the selling floors. There was no artistry in the way merchandise for the table was displayed—or, consequently, in peoples' homes.

Tiffany's changed all that. We showed stores, specifically their customers, all over the world how to display china, silver, glassware, linens, and accessories in graceful and imaginative ways. It gave a new dimension to entertaining. Van Day Truex set all kinds of tables, brought in beautiful antique furniture and priceless rugs and screens to create dining rooms, and then invited America's top interior designers of that era—William Pahlmann, Jimmy Amster, Billy Baldwin, Sister Parish, Ellen McCluskey and the like—to come into Tiffany's. They would design imaginary tables in honor of their best clients, using Tiffany merchandise but also borrowing something unique from their client's collection of treasures to put into that setting. The public came, ogled everything, loved it, and bought, bought, bought. Other American stores begin to follow suit and did their own dining room displays. Unfortunately for them, they did not all have a Van Day Truex, but they were all influenced by and profited from Tiffany's new art form of table settings.

Every kind of party imaginable was honored by its own setting in these exhibitions, from "Dinner in a Tree House" to a "Children's Birthday Party on a Carousel," and from "Dinner in a Sheik's Tent in the Sahara" to "A Wild and Woolly Bachelor's Dinner Party." Sometimes the hostess would even send in her own chandelier to be suspended from the ceiling over her table. The public would read her menu for her party, lying on the table. They knew who her guests were from the place card set at each place. She might have brought in her little dog's bed to put down next to her chair. (The dog lying on the bed in the table setting would be a stuffed toy dog borrowed from F. A. O. Schwarz for the occasion.)

The hostesses competed against one another the entire time, first to be invited by Van Truex to set a table, and then to make it the most spectacular of their group. The maid or butler or a hostess would come in each day to make sure the table was fresh and sparkling, with the silver polished and the floral decorations fresh. The personal staff would thus spy for "Madam," and report on her rivals' new additions to their settings. A telephone call would be made. "Madam, Mrs. So-and-so has added an original oil of a horse by George Stubbs, and she has changed her oriental rug to a finer one. I think we need to add something to our setting."

The day before one of the table-setting shows, Mrs. William Paley, dressed in a beautiful Balenciaga sheath that matched her blue chaise longue, came in with pillows from her bedroom. She also brought in her pretty Portuguese rug, and a breakfast tray balanced on a small Billy Baldwin table next to the chaise. Her breakfast setting, in her role as best friend of author Truman Capote, was titled "Breakfast at Tiffany's." Truman's book of the same title was left lying open on the chaise. Many people rushed to see what page she had opened it to, wondering if there was some deep psychological meaning to it. The beautiful Babe and Truman had a giggling, wonderful time setting up this display, ignoring the autograph seekers and fans that followed him wherever he went in those days.

With these great hostesses and designers involved in setting tables in the store for the public to enjoy, the press people fought one another to have first rights to publish photographs of their favorite tables. A journalist would come rushing off the elevator.

"Where's Mrs. Astor's table?"

"Don't you want to see any of the others? The governor's wife's table? Sir Laurence Olivier's?"

"My editor told me to get Brooke Astor's table, even if it looks like a junkyard." So the journalist would stake out Brooke Astor's table for her magazine, make arrangements to photograph it, and never even look at it. (It was, in fact, beautiful and classic, with English antique china set on an intricately carved mahogany table.)

Tiffany's exerted a strong influence nationwide upon entertaining in the 1950s and '60s, and our table setting shows had caused a great stir after a year, so I suggested to a publisher, Thomas Y. Crowell, that he consider a book on the subject, which we published. I wrote the text from my press releases and photograph captions for a beautiful coffee-table book entitled *Tiffany Table Settings*.

I was proud of my role in this project. I had helped Walter Hoving talk the show participants into doing it for us. I had worked every inch of the way with the ladies and the designers, and had worked fourteen hours a day every day a new show was being organized. I had overseen the photography and worked with the newspapers and magazines on the coverage. It was my baby. Of course I didn't get credit for it, because Mr. Hoving did not believe that a book on the store should have an author's name on it. I guess I was used to things like this by now.

The book sold many thousands of copies, and it became the first in a beautiful series of books on the store's tabletop design and on entertaining— the later ones authored by and credited to talented John Loring, a vice president, who was to become an important part of Tiffany's by the 1970s and beyond.

But I got there first.

I realized from the minute I landed that job at Tiffany's how much I had lucked out. My previous work experience had been entirely in the diplomatic world, and abroad. I really did not know my own country from a business point of view. Working at Tiffany's was the perfect bridge between life at

American embassies and the new life I would begin in the White House. One was always on an excellent learning curve just being in Walter Hoving's presence. He was intelligent, strong in his beliefs, and impatient with anything less than perfection. The more I think back on those Tiffany days, the more I realize how much he taught me. He kept me immersed in the worlds of luxury, society, show biz—all tempered by the constant reminder: "Remember the customah!" He was a disciplinarian like a master sergeant of a boot camp. I'm sure he epitomized "the person who doesn't suffer fools gladly": a tremendously tough taskmaster. Thank you, Walter Hoving.

Welcome to the White House

In July 1960 I took six weeks' vacation from Tiffany's—the longest one I have had in my adult life. I had been invited to stay with artist Louisa Jenkins in her house atop Partington Ridge on the fabled Big Sur coast of California. After three days, Louisa went off to visit friends and left me her delightful house, where I began a novel about Rome. I was writing in the most romantic of landscapes. Below lay the indigo blue of the Pacific Ocean, above rose the hills of Big Sur, and every hour the texture of light and shadows changed as the sun moved around me. Flowering vines covered the houses, and great stone planters full of exotic plants graced the terraces up on the ridge. I felt my muse not only with me but pushing me as I set out to write a love story about Rome in the 1950s. I was not alone; Louisa's dog Maxl' (short for Maximillian), a dachshund, had been left in my care. Maxl' was not only company but a lifesaver. When we were walking up in the hills, he would freeze to a point when a rattlesnake made its presence known, which was my cue to start singing loudly (rattlesnakes don't like singing, particularly my kind). The rattler would slither away in disgust, and we would continue on. I had been instructed never to venture forth without a snakebite kit on my belt, but the mere thought of having to cut with a knife around the bite and suck the poison from it would have finished me off anyway. I loved to walk through the magnificent, oft photographed scenery of Big Sur, with its fabled seals honking down on the rocks below us.

Part of what made Big Sur so special was the community of artists it contained. As I typed away on my great novel, I was in good company. All around the ridge flowed a sea of strong creative waves emanating from the homes of my neighbors, including eminent sculptor David Smith and writer Henry "Ulysses" Miller and his most recent young, attractive wife. They invited me twice to join them for a short cocktail hour (really more like forty-five minutes), and I felt honored to be in the presence of greatness. Beyond the artists, there was a wider community of home owners in this small neighborhood who were united in their goal: keep the developers and their little Cessnas and Piper Cubs, which would fly over to survey real estate possibilities, away from Partington Ridge, in fact, away from all of the Big Sur region. The community was intent on protecting their lovely piece of the country, and rightly so: this summer was also particularly dry, with forest fires raging nearby, and there was a real fear that a small plane flying too low could crash into the mountainside and start a massive conflagration.

A small plane did crash late one afternoon, after infuriating the ridge inhabitants for two hours by swooping low, right over the rooftops. Everyone came out of their houses, shaking their fists angrily into the air, but then there was the sickening sound of a sputtering engine, smoke, and a small plane spiraling downward deep into the canyon below us. The emergency bell on top of the ridge began to clang, its alarm resonating through the hills around us. Male volunteers came running, fastening knives, first aid kits, and snake bite kits to their belts. They wore workboots and heavy gloves to protect their hands in the forest. Two of them carried axes; others carried canisters of firefighting chemicals. It was an emotional scene. The wives and children stood silently by as the men set off down into the forest, which was dangerously steep to navigate even without a fire.

Four hours later they looked like a group of combat soldiers returning from the front, exhausted and bloody after their ordeal, but no one was critically injured. They had easily found the plane because of the smoke, and due to a lull in the winds, the woods had not caught on fire. They covered the crashed plane with chemicals and carried its two injured occupants up to the top of the ridge on stretchers. The rescuers had saved the lives of the developer and the pilot, but more important to them, they had saved their homes from destruction in a quick-spreading forest fire. When the ambulance arrived on top of the ridge to take the men to a hospital in Carmel, the head of the Big Sur volunteers gave them a solemn lecture on what a terrible thing they had done, breaking the law and putting all of the residents' homes at risk.

A few days later, Clare Luce called me on the eve of the Democratic Convention to see how I was doing in my Edith Wharton reincarnation. Her Republicanism was waxing strong. She let loose a blast at Joe Kennedy, John Kennedy, Bobby Kennedy, and the whole party, which I knew she would do, and then she said, "I have found the perfect man for you. He's a thirty-two-year-old bachelor, tall, attractive, smart, and he will be really rich one day when he inherits his parents' estate. He's never married. He'll be there at Louisa's house for dinner tonight. Are you going to be ready for this?"

I went down the mountain to the food and liquor stores and back up again so fast that I must have made an impressionist blur on the ridge. I turned up the radio volume high on the convention doings as John Kennedy's candidacy was being lauded by the political analysts, and I prepared a fantastic gourmet dinner for this man who was coming to the ridge tonight. I placed baskets of flowers in tasteful arrangements around the terrace and then shut off the radio to get in the mood, with Frank Sinatra records crooning Cole Porter and Jerome Kern songs. I sprayed cologne everywhere, including up into the air, so that the birds flying around could enjoy a little Moment Supreme, too. I changed from my cooking pants and shirt into an exotic black cotton Moroccan caftan, large black hoop earrings, and gold sandals. I was looking forward to this man's visit with great enthusiasm. I needed a relationship that could lead to the altar.

He was charming, as predicted, and after enjoying my rather fine gourmet meal, we relaxed on the terrace on adjoining chaises, speaking quietly, lulled by the excellent wine and Pacific Ocean breezes. I felt close to the brilliant stars in the midnight sky that seemed easily pluckable from our chaises. Sounds of Sinatra from my record player drifted across the canyon.

I felt that romance was definitely in the air, and finally he spoke. He had been silent for a very long time, but I knew he knew it was time to make a move, and he must have been planning just how to do it perfectly. He took my hand. "You know," he said in that attractive, low-pitched voice of his, "if you would have your nose operated on, you'd be a really good-looking girl."

Instant shrapnel hit Partington Ridge. There were smoke and debris everywhere. "You know," I said in as cold a tone as I could summon, and that is very cold, "we've had this Baldrige nose in our family for generations. We're very proud of it. In Rome, the Romans praise my nose all the time. They know something about noses, too, in case you've ever looked at their sculpture. I'm sorry if you prefer a Schenectady nose, or a Philadelphia nose, or a Hollywood nose, or whatever. Good night."

I went into the house without looking at him, turned up the record to an ear-splitting volume, and began scrubbing the pots and pans. I heard his jolly "Good night" as he started his car and began to descend the mountain. So this was the fantastic bachelor Clare Luce had chosen to be my husband? I went to bed thinking about all the men I had adored in France and Italy. Thank God for my memories. At the time I was convinced I would die an old maid, and for once, the thought did not depress me. I had many other things to do than identify marriage as the only goal in life.

The next day I heard news on the radio that made my head fairly burst from excitement. John F. Kennedy won the nomination at the Democratic Convention in Los Angeles, and then, over Bobby Kennedy's objections, Lyndon Johnson was nominated vice president. My nose became better looking in my estimation by the second as I listened to the Los Angeles convention proceedings on the radio. What a fantastic coup for the Kennedys! I knew Jackie was sitting in Hyannis Port, very pregnant, unable to travel with her husband, and missing all this excitement in Los Angeles. What must she be thinking and feeling right now? Would this put her into early labor? Good Lord!

The next telephone call was a male voice, a signal corpsman, announcing that Mrs. Kennedy was calling from Hyannis Port. There was a background hubbub of people talking, but the familiar breathless voice came through loud and clear, as though bells were ringing through it.

"Tish, can you believe it? He made it! He made it!"

I could mentally visualize her jumping up and down for joy on the other end of the wire, incredibly pregnant, but ever the graceful athlete.

"Will you come to help us out?" I heard her saying. "Will you head up my staff? I'm really going to need you."

I had planned to leave Tiffany's at Christmas and follow my star to Milano. Once again, I had been plotting and planning for the exotic in my life. I would go to Milano, the fashion capital of Italy, and set up a much-needed service, a public relations agency. This plan now, of course, disintegrated on the spot. I liked to think that my country needed me more than Valentino and Armani.

Life on Partington Ridge came to an abrupt halt. I cut my vacation short, packed up my typewriter and manuscript, arranged to leave Maxl' in loving, caring hands, and gave away my snakebite kit to a neighbor on the ridge. All the way back on the plane I rehearsed my resignation speech to Walter Hoving. I put away my great unfinished love story of Rome, *The Iron Lily*, in a file folder, probably to remain unpublished forever. Edith Wharton would not have to worry about the competition after all.

I resigned from Tiffany's, effective as of November 1, 1960, rented my apartment on Seventy-third Street to someone else, and moved my furniture back to Washington. Walter Hoving was in disbelief that I would leave a store like Tiffany's to go to a place like Washington with a Democratic presidential hopeful. I said good-bye to every single employee of the store, from the diamond cutters to the china packers, shaking each hand and fighting wet eyes as nice things were said in wishing me well on this next great adventure.

The election was touch and go, but Kennedy triumphed. The president-elect named me to the presidential transitional team so I could be of personal assistance to his wife in the midst of the expected turmoil—with all of the hard-driving politicos working around the clock at full speed to establish their own bases before anyone else stole them away. I had a desk and a phone in a grungy cubicle, part of the transition team's space, across from the side entrance of the Mayflower Hotel. Jackie had a businesslike discussion with me about the pay I received on the transition team ($100 a week, but I would have done it gladly for nothing) and did the same with my White House salary. She asked what Walter Hoving was paying me at Tiffany's. I was ashamed to answer.

"Fifteen thousand a year," I whispered, hoping no one around would hear me. What was more humiliating was that I had started at ten thousand. I was just about to add dramatically, "which is a pathetic, shamefully low salary, and Walter Hoving knew it," but Jackie interrupted.

"Oh, dear," she said, sounding worried. "I guess we'll have to match that, but it does sound frightfully high."

I couldn't believe my ears—but then again, she was naive and unused to the ways of business. She had received a low salary for her one paid job—just a few hours a week as an inquiring photographer for a local newspaper—and she couldn't imagine how a woman would be paid any more than she was. I swallowed my indignation, rationalizing that this job was worth the low pay. (The indignation would return later in life when Liz Carpenter, chief of staff for Lady Bird Johnson, started in my job at a salary of $60,000 annually, and subsequent First Lady staffers were paid well over $100,000.)

Jackie was suddenly on fire with plans for making her mark as an exceptional first lady. She wrote memos by hand and researched information throughout the process of bringing John F. Kennedy Jr. into the world prematurely in the Georgetown Hospital. She fired off memos to me from the hospital, later from her Georgetown house, and then from the Kennedy house in Palm Beach over Christmas and New Year's, where she was supposed to be quietly recovering from a difficult cesarean birth.

Those memos were intelligent, showing her gift for organization, as well as the wonderful creativity with which she was born. That asset was always present, whether she was writing letters from Europe illustrated with whimsical drawings or enumerating steps the Fine Arts Committee for the White House would have to undertake to be in compliance with government rules on donations to the White House. She understood with clarity what her mission was going to be as first lady, because she had designed it herself. She had given it a lot of thought, and I have never known anyone to be as firm as she was about what she wanted to do. She planned on such a broad idealistic scale that long before the assassination and the end of the Kennedy dream, she had realized every component of it—preservation of her family, entertaining with style and grace in the number one house in the world, the makeover of the White House itself as a focus of American history and accomplishment, and the raising of the cultural stature of this country. She was to achieve every single aspiration in her tenure at the White House. She was also to make a remarkable journey through the history books of this country. But back then, when we were all groping around with plans for the inauguration and the move into 1600 Pennsylvania Avenue, the best we could hope for was to survive all that had fallen down on top of our very diverse heads.

Prior to the inauguration, my job was to serve as Jackie's liaison with the whole world, it seemed, while ensuring her privacy and the chance to recuperate. I was to keep everyone away from her, mail and phone calls included, and family as well. Her "best friends" were now crawling out of the woodwork. She probably knew fewer than half the people who called, wanting to speak to her and claiming to be "intimate friends." ("You realize, don't you, Miss Baldrige, that I'm *very* close to her?")

Everyone wanted at her, from Buckingham Palace to an order of cloistered nuns, and from the American Lung Society to the Daughters of the American Revolution. By the first of January she had received at least three hundred personal appearance and speech requests, and over a thousand requests for her name as "honorary patron" of this and that benefit. We decided that the best way to keep her name effective in the mishmash of all these charity events was to limit her sponsorship to a very few organizations that were effective in helping the community or the nation at large. The result of this decision: anger from all quarters and pressure from every person who had ever known her or any of her thousand relatives!

In early January, I began working with J. B. West, the chief usher, on moving all of the Kennedy effects into the White House, including certain pieces of their own furniture that would be needed in their private quarters on the second floor. This had to be done gradually over a month, and secretly, so that that the moving vans and crates of furnishings could be hidden by J. B., and their presence would not upset the present occupants of the house, the Eisenhowers. It is ever thus when the house changes hands at election time. Mary Jane McCaffree, Mamie Eisenhower's crackerjack social secretary, invited me over to her part of the world and gave me some excellent advice, including, "Watch out for the men in the West Wing, the president's men. They'll try to walk all over you." I told her I had brothers, so I was well prepared.

During this time it was my good luck to be able to live with my parents in their Connecticut Avenue apartment, close to the transition team head-quarters office and the White House, too. During those frantic weeks, I couldn't have found time to heat up a can of soup, much less buy it in a store. My mother joyfully returned to her former role as the mother who did everything for her child, which was the way it had always been through my school days. If I got home at midnight, she would reheat my dinner on the stove and sit down with me at the kitchen table to listen to an account of my day. She reveled in it. She took care of my laundry and dry cleaning and kept her friends from calling her because I needed the telephone line open for my calls from transition headquarters. My father, newly retired, spent half his time relishing my reports of what was going on at Democratic headquarters and the other half feeding the tropical fish in his newly acquired tank with all the trappings. I listened in on some heated marital arguments when Mother repeatedly found in the fridge—where my father insisted on keeping the food for his aquarium fish fresh—cartons of creepy, crawly things, like worms and tiny shrimp.

Former congressman Baldrige made only one remark about my leaving the Republican Party, which had been his lifelong dedication.

"You're not expecting your mother and me to change our party registra-tion, are you?"

"No, Dad, no," I laughed. "You'd make lousy Democrats." I gave him a big hug. End of discussion. If the Baldrige family Republicanism were to cause me the slightest embarrassment down at the White House, he and Mother would have changed their party affiliation at once. As it was, the whole family became loyal Republican advocates of the Kennedys. They were hardly the only ones in the country. No one could say a word against the Kennedy administration to my parents. If Tish loved them and admired them, then they loved them, too. Clare Luce, on the other hand, could not believe I would work for a Democratic administration. "I always thought you had a modicum of brains in you," she wrote; "now I see you do not."

Two months before the inauguration I fulfilled what had been a big dream for a long time, becoming the star of a major national press conference held in mid-November. Pierre Salinger, the president-elect's press secretary, arranged it because of the immense pressure on him "to get news of Jackie out to the public."

"Mrs. Kennedy will accept no interviews" had become the new administration's mantra, and the press had at first grumbled, then rebelled. Every time we appealed for a change of her policy, she stood firm. There was a good excuse for her lack of cooperation—she was weak from the cesarean operation during John's birth, and exhausted from having to make several hundred decisions a week. The press would now have to rely on me for information on her; Pierre had his hands full with the president-elect, the new cabinet appointments, and leadership changes in the Congress.

My press conference began well. I felt properly chic, as Mrs. Kennedy's representative should be. I wore a copy of a brown Christian Dior suit and a leopard-skin hat. (There wasn't an anti-fur campaign in those days.) I had a big Schlumberger sapphire-and-diamond-striped brooch on my lapel (borrowed, of course). I was used to the press, having handled journalists in all of my previous jobs. I was relaxed, with all sixty of them in that crowded room—far too relaxed. I knew so many of them personally, from Washington and also from my Tiffany years in New York, and even from my Clare and Henry Luce days, when I knew all of the Time Inc. people from around the world. But the White House press is different from any other in the world.

The conference started, and I quickly had them chortling. Every TV and radio station, newspaper, magazine, and news agency was represented, plus correspondents from tiny towns who had successfully lobbied to wangle invitations. I thought everything was going really well until CBS News anchorwoman Nancy Hanschman (later to become Nancy Dickerson, and later still, Nancy Whitehead) pushed her way close during the proceedings and whispered in my ear, "I'm telling this to you as a friend, Tish. Watch it! Cut the jokes." A cold shower suddenly soaked me. I now knew that I was in trouble. She had given me a much-needed warning. Too bad I hadn't received it a half hour earlier.

I immediately ceased being trying to be a wit. I was not there to entertain. I was there to represent the new first lady of the land. The last mistake I made was to say, in answer to the question of what made Mrs. Kennedy qualified to step into this important role, "Of course, Mrs. Kennedy has everything, beauty and brains. She also has the president of the United States!"

It sounds like such an innocent statement today. Back then, it was being fresh; such familiarity was considered totally unacceptable. The press office had wanted me to be reticent, standoffish, and above all dignified. Pierre Salinger was furious, giving me a justifiable tongue-lashing. The very next day Pierre brought over to me a very inexperienced, beautiful young woman named Pamela Turnure (later to become Mrs. Robert Timmins) to handle the press under me. She had been instructed by Mrs. Kennedy to tell them nothing ever, except for occasional spoon-fed bits of information when she was given the signal. No jovial repartee with journalists from now on.

Pam would grow into a cool professional and a press secretary of enormous talent. Even when she had absolutely nothing to report on a sensitive subject, she was so pretty and graceful, and so sincerely sorry not to be able to help, that reporters simply couldn't get mad at her. Her appointment was a momentary slap in my face, in that I was no longer in charge of the press, but I was used to slaps, for heaven's sakes, and running the whole office and staff was more than enough on my plate. I could not have handled both jobs. We became great friends in the White House, where we had no one in whom to confide our moments of real anguish except one another. The White House was a fishbowl containing certain cruising sharks in its glistening waters, people coveting someone else's job. There was also great jealousy over the personal access Pam and I had to the president and first lady.

One of my most time-consuming and delicate chores, as I discovered during the transition stage before January 20, was to be the liaison among the Kennedy, Auchincloss, Fitzgerald, Davis, and Bouvier families—answering their many questions, getting them cars, solving their problems, feeding them gossip so they could sound to their friends as though they were in the know on everything, and making sure they were invited to the "right events" as the inaugural steam began hissing around us. With the exception of her mother and sister Lee, no one in the family could get through to Jackie on the telephone at this time.

The president-elect's father, Ambassador Joseph Kennedy (aka "Papa Joe"), realized that some kind of luncheon party on inaugural morning was necessary, to have the families all in one place and to afford the president-elect and Jackie some peace to prepare for this momentous day. The family needed something to do, but also transportation to the Capitol for the swearing in. A bus was arranged, since otherwise they might get lost in the snow or be very late in all the traffic and confusion at the swearing-in site.

"I want you to arrange this lunch for me, Tish," said Ambassador Kennedy. "I want it to be nice, and what I don't want are a lot of crashers or hangers-on. No press. Family members only."

With great difficulty I got them all assembled in a large private room at the Mayflower Hotel. The central buffet table practically filled the room, with large platters of cold meats, smoked salmon, baked ham, pasta dishes kept warm over burners, baskets of different breads, and platters of salad, fruits, and cookies. The bar in this mini-ballroom was doing major business. The floral and fruit arrangement in the center of the table was exquisite, like a Luca Della Robbia Renaissance wreath. When Ambassador Kennedy arrived, I fully expected to be patted on the head and praised for my successful planning. Instead, he was a study in fury, and a furious Irishman is furious indeed.

"Who are all these people?" he barked. "You have plainly gone against my explicit orders. I wanted a small, intimate, family-only luncheon."

"I have carried out your orders, Ambassador Kennedy. These are all relatives of one kind or another. They're all part of the family list. You have a lot of divorced and remarried people on both sides, you know, and cousins on all sides, and they've all had a lot of children."

Refusing to believe me, he went charging off to interrogate anyone in his path, bluntly asking, "Who are you? Why are you here?"

He returned within ten minutes, very apologetic. "You're right. I never wanted to admit, even to myself, I guess, how big this family really is."

Before everyone left for the Capitol, he told me "it had been one great party," and he was glad he had hosted it. We became fast friends that day. Until his stroke, eleven months later, he would bring a ten-gallon carton of very special Louis Sherry ice cream down to Washington on his plane, the *Caroline,* on his visits to his son. He was a director of the company, and the ice cream was meant for the president, yes, but also for my office. He would appear in the office with the ice cream and a quantity of little plates, plastic spoons, and napkins, and instruct all of the first lady's office staff to "dive in." While we were doing just that, we would fill him in on what was happening in the East Wing, which was the first lady's wing. We must have looked like a bunch of barnyard cats, all licking and purring with pleasure over the ice cream.

I loved that man. He always took my side in every dispute, and we had many talks on the telephone. I learned much about judging decisions wisely from him, and I would grieve deeply, along with his children, when a stroke took him away from us.

I have heard the president's inaugural address many times on tape, but I wasn't there to see it on Capitol Hill. I was aleady at work—in the White House. At exactly noon, as is traditional, the house changes hands from the old administration to the new, so on the hour, a White House station wagon, jammed full of suitcases and footlockers, and a limousine bearing Provie Paredes, Mrs. Kennedy's maid; George Thomas, the president's valet; and me drove up to the southern entrance. George had the president's white tie and tails on his lap, and Provie held the first lady's white inaugural ball gown on hers. This dress was destined to receive a thousand camera flashes that night and then to be seen the next time on a mannequin in the permanent exhibit of the first ladies' inaugural ball gowns at the Smithsonian Institution. J. B. West, the chief usher, greeted us, and we raced through the mansion, busy at our tasks. I went into the East Wing and quickly commandeered four excellent electric typewriters for my office from the president's military aides' suite of offices down the hall from me. They could easily find replacements. The new administration had officially begun, The Kennedys' open limousine would come up a snow-packed Pennsylvania Avenue and discharge the presidential team in front of their new home. Mr. and Mrs. Kennedy would watch the giant inaugural parade that afternoon from the stands built in front of the North Portico, they would change into their formal apparel for an exuberant night of cheers and screams of adulation at the two balls, and they would go to sleep for the first time in a very special place. I, of course, would get no sleep at all that night. There was too much to do. That was the nature of the job.

Right from Inauguration Day I began referring to Jackie as "Mrs. Kennedy," and so did my staff. Even in private, I now called her "Jackie" infrequently. It just didn't sound right anymore, and she also liked the formality of address in her new position. Notes to her were addressed to "JBK," to get around the awkwardness of using a formal title in informal communications. When other people were present, she was always "Mrs. Kennedy." I was in awe of her position in the world, having served too many years in embassy life, where strict protocol had to be followed. President and Mrs. Kennedy may have been young, and personal friends from earlier times, but a new aura of great dignity surrounded them now. From November 1960 on, I never referred to John Kennedy as "Jack" anymore. He was "Mr. President" when spoken to, and "the president" when spoken of.

My skills were tested immediately, and like most people new to a job, I made some honest but glaring mistakes. I got the president into trouble right away with the first large party I organized, two days after the administration had begun. It was held on a Sunday night, for all the heads of government, Congress, the Joint Chiefs of Staff, the Supreme Court, the major government agencies, and their spouses. The press was there, and I organized it exactly as I used to organize embassy cocktail receptions, with an easy disposition of bars and food tables in strategic spots all over the first floor. There were ashtrays everywhere, for the convenience of the guests.

The press adored all my mistakes. There had never been ashtrays before to encourage smoking at big receptions. There had never been liquor served when the press was present to cover the party. It was given on a Sunday night, the Sabbath, which in the eyes of those in the Baptist Bible Belt was a grievous sin. There had never been a bar in evidence before in the White House—drinks had always been passed on trays—and we had ten bars at this first public party. I had broken so many rules at once, quite innocently, that the president was in hot water with all the temperance leaders and the entire religious right. The president showed me the morning headlines about our "debauched" Sunday party (which was not debauched at all, but a lovely, successful event) and told me he didn't need to get in trouble, because of me, on his third day in the White House. I did not sleep for four nights, I was so worried about the trouble I had caused.

A year later he would stop me in the hall to remind me it was the first anniversary of that tradition-breaking party. I shuddered at the thought of it, but he laughed and said that the fact we continued to serve liquor at our parties (without any bars, though) had made a world of difference—for the good—to White House entertaining. "People have a good time in this house today," he remarked, "so I hope you have forgotten my giving you such a hard time a year ago!"

As Mrs. Kennedy's chief of staff, I was to keep the East Wing running smoothly. My diplomatic training came in handy as I contended with the often conflicting needs of the West Wing. At times my staff and I were at war with the president's men in the West Wing, who would try to control the first lady's schedule to benefit their purposes, and to exercise control over guest lists, filling them with their pals and the people who had helped most in the campaign. The guest lists were my responsibility; the Kennedys' preferences came first, of course, but there was a lot of juggling with the rest of it. One time I removed the name of a big contributor and his wife, placed there by one of the president's men in place of a renowned figure in the arts, from a proposed state dinner guest list. He had pulled the switch secretly, thinking I would not notice it. I immediately replaced the fat cat on the list with the champion of the arts, after calling the president's assistant and telling him that our guest was more important for Mrs. Kennedy's purposes than the political contributor was to the president's, and that therefore the East Wing was holding fast. He knew he had lost the battle.

I found my best ally was always the president of the United States. He would not let his assistants walk over us, bully us, or control our activities. He once said to me, "You fight like a Kennedy." I have been wondering ever since whether to take that as a compliment.

One of the most fascinating things about working in the White House was the window it provided into the hearts of everyday Americans, their dreams, and their concerns, as expressed in the letters they sent to Mrs. Kennedy and the children. There was an avalanche of press queries on the Kennedys during this period, as America began to saturate itself with every possible personal detail about its young incoming president, its first truly glamorous first lady since Dolley Madison, and the new brace of presidential children—a beguiling daughter, Caroline, and a newborn son, John. The children's photographs in November 1960, taken by master photographer Richard Avedon, absolutely captivated the world. In one Avedon photo, a newborn premature baby is nestled in his mother's arms; in another, a just-turned-four girl in a frilly sleeveless dress sits with her hands clasped in delight in her father's arms, her eyes an exact replica of those of the man holding her. Later, photos taken over the years in the personal family quarters by Mark Shaw and Jacques Lowe were spoon-fed to an adoring public, who only kept shouting, "More, more!" For official happenings, Cecil Stoughten of the Signal Corps and Chief Bob Knudsen of the navy brilliantly recorded every White House event. You could see their love of any assignment involving the family with one glance at their pictures. The three previous occupants of the White House—the Roosevelts, Trumans, and Eisenhowers—had been much older. Now there was an incredibly photogenic young family and a bevy of other White House occupants, including ponies, cats, dogs, birds, even hamsters. The mail addressed to these creatures or to Caroline and John about their pets was answered by my correspondence pool.

I was assigned two secretaries, in addition to the fifteen people working day and night in our correspondence pool, to handle the mail load. I brought Anne Lincoln down from New York and borrowed Barbara Keehn from another government agency, and Betty Hogue from yet another agency. (This is why the public will never get an accurate answer to the press question "How many people work in the White House?") Pam Turnure's secretary, Pierrette Spiegler, was of French origin and helped us with all the French mail that was pouring in. We responded with form letters whenever we could; problem letters or those emanating from important sources were brought to my attention. It was a monumental task then, in comparison to today, with no word processors or computers with memory to help us out. Every letter was answered. Mistakes were made, too, such as the time a form letter was sent out over my forged signature to a Catholic priest who had invited President and Mrs. Kennedy very proudly to his one-man art show. The letter that went out in answer said nothing about his art show but congratulated him on the birth of his son, and wished the baby a long, happy life. The celibate priest was not amused. A few apologies later, he finally forgave me.

The majority of our incoming mail fell into the categories of fan mail ("I think you're wonderful, Mrs. Kennedy."), requests for information ("How many rollers do you put in your hair at night, and does the president object?"), or mail addressed to the children ("Do you have to eat your vegetables? I bet you don't."). Thousands of letters, cards, drawings, and gifts were to flow into the White House. Hortense Burton, my chief of that section, would bring me the really amusing letters, to bathe our somber office in a little sunshine. Mail from children helped cut the pressure when we were really being hammered by an overly active schedule. One child wrote that he hoped Macaroni, Caroline's pony, was not made too cold from the snowstorm, "because I can spare an extra blanket from my bed for him." Another wrote, "If the puppy married the kitten, what would their babies look like?" There would be a lot of child-generated smiles around the world in those three Kennedy White House years, whenever a journalistic peek was allowed into its nursery world. The personal Christmas card the Kennedys sent the first year to friends was a photograph of Jackie driving her antique sleigh around the White House South Lawn in fresh, deep snow, with Macaroni pulling the sleigh and Caroline and John aboard. That photograph caused thousands of additional letters to flood the White House. Children, animals, snow, and a beautiful first lady—it was what America wanted!

Women poured out their marital woes to the young first lady, too; the letter prepared in answer for my signature "regretted that time does not permit fulfilling your request, but Mrs. Kennedy sends you her very best wishes." Women sent her pictures of themselves ("because everyone, just everyone says I look exactly like you") and asked her advice on everything from toilet training of children to the treating of acne. When Jane Q. Public disapproved of Mrs. Kennedy's short skirts, her answer was to shorten them even more. (She knew how to dress, and they didn't, but we couldn't say that in a letter!) When the mail grew heavier and heavier in disapproval of little John's Little Lord Fauntleroy haircut, the president's office made Jackie have his hair cut. Most of the letters claimed he looked like a sissy, and that cut through to the president's heart. (Jackie didn't speak to me for three days after that one; I had been the one to report to the president on the number of disapproving letters received.)

What was really heartening were all the letters praising the first lady's beautiful manners, posture, and grace of carriage. Mothers wrote that this influence was the first thing that made an impression on their slumped-over teenage daughters, who wanted desperately "to be like Mrs. Kennedy." "Straighten up!" became a message to young America. Jackie never knew how strong her influence was. When I would write her a note, pleading with her to help a cause, saying, "You have the potential to change this situation," she would send a note back, saying, "I don't care about that particular situation." End of discussion. She had her priorities and was to keep fiercely to them throughout JFK's presidency. Again, she was right. It worked.

The distaff side of the press—namely, Frances Lewine of the Associated Press and Helen Thomas of the United Press—lived with us, it seemed, rather than in their own homes. Helen was later to become dean of the White House press correspondents and a national treasure in her own right, considering all she had seen and reported on in what was to add up to almost fifty years.

The ladies' assignment was to dig up all the personal trivia about the first family that they possibly could. Nothing was too unimportant. The world was starved for news of Jacqueline Kennedy, but she felt one of her main jobs was to thwart these journalists. She tried to escape them, particularly when she wanted to do something with her children. She called them by the code name "The Harpies," but Pam and I respected and admired both of them. So, eventually, did the first lady.

In March of our first year in the White House, I was embroiled in yet another White House crisis and was innocently taking the rap for it. The Kennedys had asked me as a priority to find a good French chef, in place of the naval service-staffed kitchen, which had been a tradition in the White House since the war days. These were talented Filipino cooks, but Jackie wanted French cuisine of the highest caliber. (This was before an interest in fusion cuisine had developed in America.) I followed through on a tip from Jackie's mother, Mrs. Auchincloss, who had heard from her Vietnamese manicurist at Elizabeth Arden's salon in Washington that her Vietnamese boyfriend, who was chef to the French ambassador to the Court of St. James in London, wanted to come to America. According to the manicurist, he was considered to be the "best chef in the entire international diplomatic service," and he wanted to come to the United States to be with his lady love. The manicurist told Mrs. Auchincloss that the French ambassador already knew that his chef planned to leave his prestigious culinary post in London to come to this country. This was not the case, as I was to find out in the ensuing flap; the French ambassador knew nothing. I had called the Vietnamese chef, Bui Van Han, from the White House, at eight P.M. London time, when he would have finished the main part of the advance preparation of the ambassador's dinner and would be free to talk. I told him I heard he wanted to come to America, and asked if he'd be interested in the White House job. He said yes, and I told him I would call him again the next day. Meanwhile, the French ambassador heard of my call through one of the staff at his residence. He became incensed; as someone from Agence France-Presse, the French news agency, told me, I had almost started a war. The ambassador called the top French journalists to protest President Kennedy's trying to steal his chef in this underhanded manner. "What a lack of courtesy and international sensitivity," he grumbled; *"ça ne se fait pas."* The press in France, England, and the United States had a fiesta. It was because of this that I received my one personal telephone call during the administration from the secretary of state, Dean Rusk, who was chuckling: "Tish, trying to create an important international incident, are you?" One headline in the London press the next day read, "JFK Ends Up in International Soup." *Le Figaro's* headlines read, "Take My Wife, but Never My Chef," which the American comedian Henny Youngman would have enjoyed. I was totally innocent in this matter, but the American papers blamed me without reserve, repeating what the frightened Vietnamese had said to the press to save his hide with his ambassador: "Miss Baldrige called me at one o'clock in the morning, got me out of bed, bribing me with an enormous fortune in wages, offering me anything I might want, anything, but of course, I cannot leave my ambassador and his wife here in London. I cannot possibly leave them. Miss Baldrige was being *très mechánte.*"

Mrs. Auchincloss was furious with her manicurist; the manicurist lost her chance to have her lover shipped over to the United States; and the Kennedy staff teased me ad infinitum and made jokes about my cook-napping. Not one member of the press chose to believe my side of the story. I complained that night at the White House press correspondents' dinner, sitting next to Hugh Sidey at the *Time* table, and he had no sympathy: "Look, Tish, this is just the beginning. It's only March. You've got to toughen up. Fight the important battles, but let ones like this just lapse. They're not worth the fight."

He was so right. I learned to do just that, relax when an unjust charge was brought against me. Besides, we managed to land a top-notch chef named René Verdon from La Caravelle restaurant in New York, who, thanks to his White House exposure, would later become a celebrated chef internationally, but would always remain my very good friend.

It is a daunting task, writing about someone whom one used to know well personally and who became probably the most photographed woman celebrity in the twentieth century. It is not easy to write about a friend who later became "the boss," which casts everything in a totally different perspective. It's complicated, too; this woman would slip in and out of the pages of American history during the last half of the twentieth century, never stopping to grieve too long over unspeakable events of the past, always going forward, looking above and beyond everyone. A good part of the world was locked into a pattern of watching and admiring her—at the distance she firmly set for herself. Her aloofness would make her public want her more, more, and more. Everyone was always rubbernecking in her direction. There were thousands of different ways of looking at her, angling this way and that, each person searching for "the real Jackie." She was a chameleon, changing so often that no one could ever find the real Jackie for more than a few hours at a time, because suddenly, she would become someone else. Astride a horse, with perfect posture and looking better in jodhpurs than anyone else, she was the perfect equestrienne. Sweeping into the East Room of the White House in a spectacular strapless ball gown, she looked and acted the part of the perfect chatelaine of the castle. In a pair of tight jeans and an old sweater, on a mission to uncover in dusty government storerooms furniture of sufficient quality to put into the White House, her spectacles atop a head of messy soot-covered hair, she looked like the Queen of Rummage Sales. Her public persona was undeniably fascinating and mysterious, but the persona she cared about the most was that of an extraordinarily good mother to two children. She loved playing games with the public all through her life, because it was a way of getting back at those who invaded her privacy. She knew exactly when to imply that the press might photograph and interview her all they want—that is, "for the next ten minutes." Then she would seem to say with her manner and her facial expression, "Your time is up, you know. Maybe we can do this again six months from now." Of course, that made the public and the press wild with desire for more, more, more. The more Garboesque she became, the more they liked it.

Jacqueline Kennedy was the exemplary manager of life with children in an impossible official goldfish bowl. She laid down strict laws, and woe unto anyone who disobeyed them. No one could have handled small children living in an official tourist attraction with thousands tramping through it every week better than Jackie. It was like trying to give one's children a normal life in the middle of Disney World. Granted, she had that precious asset called "help." Help *really* helps. There was the warm, kind British nannie, Miss Shaw, and Provie, Mrs. Kennedy's talented personal maid from the Dominican Republic. Even George, the president's accomplished valet, lent a hand when needed. There was a squad of Secret Service men assigned to the children, as well as Mugsy, a much-loved Irish leftover from the Kennedy campaign days in Massachusetts, who was always around to drive the children, animals, and agents. The children's Secret Service agents were young and athletic, and one had small children of his own. Caroline and John were not only comfortable around them but considered them much-loved playmates. Jackie taught them to be respectful and polite to their agents. (One of John's schoolmates in the White House School asked his mother, "Where are my age-aunts? Why don't I have them, too?")

The school, in the top-floor solarium of the White House, was in session five mornings a week. Two well-trained young women ran the program, and the student body consisted of children of Jack and Jackie's friends from before White House days. All the proper little desks and chairs, workstations, colorful pictures, blackboards and bulletin boards, wall pegs to hold coats, and cleaning devices were appropriately in place, but nothing could have duplicated the view from the top floor of this historic house, overlooking the city's great monuments, down to and beyond the Potomac River. For an American, it has to be the world's most breathtaking view.

When visitors of note—such as important Native American tribal chiefs in full ceremonial regalia—came to the president's office in the West Wing, we would take them over to the school after they had seen the president. When the chiefs suddenly appeared in the solarium one day, their presence frightened the children, who greeted them with tears of fear instead of smiles. Unprepared for their visit, they had seen only bad-guy Indians, depicted on television as savages with tomahawks in hand, setting fire to the white settlers' houses. The two teachers ushered the Native Americans back out of the solarium into my care, while they gave the children a little briefing on their true nature. Then the chiefs were invited back in with smiles of welcome, and soon everyone was doing war dances together, beating tom toms, and joining in on ceremonial chants.

Caroline and John, of course, were hidden from the public as much as possible. Only on rare occasions, and unintentionally, would they be seen on their way in or out of the mansion by the hordes of tourists or invited visitors passing through. Usually the ushers and police would keep outsiders at bay until the children had left the house. When the accidental face-to-face encounter did occur, there would be a groundswell of surprised "Oohs!" and "Aren't they cute? Isn't John adorable? Doesn't Caroline look like her father? Have you ever seen such lovely clothes?" and on and on. They would call over to the children to get their attention, hoping to entice them, but it did not work. When one woman stuck an autograph book in baby John's face with a pen for him to sign a scribble, one could feel only sympathy for Jackie's feelings about the public getting at her children. It was hard to keep the tourists unaware of the children when the whole school descended from the top floor to play out on the South Lawn, particularly when Caroline's ballet class would practice outdoors, fluttering like little pink birds in their pink leotards, tulle tutus, and ballet slippers. The public delighted in finding, while waiting in the ground-floor corridors for their White House tour, vestiges of little people—an occasional tricycle erratically parked, or a forgotten roller skate.

I have wonderful memories of those children in their early childhood. They were beautiful to look at and always exquisitely dressed, but amazingly unself-conscious. They received many hugs and kisses from their parents, but Jackie would not allow the people around them to gush over them or permit effusive accolades to be directed their way. It was as if she wanted them to do something first that would merit verbal praise, not just be born, be attractive, and bask in the bright golden glow of the world's spotlight. She protected them from the ravenous public by having their play dates and parties in the White House, where privacy and protection could be maintained. (A party in a restaurant would have courted a mob situation.) There were sports to be played, in and out of the White House, jungle gyms, a trampoline, a pool, movies in the White House theater, and birthday cakes to be baked by chef René Verdon (who also taught Caroline how to bake little pink cupcakes on her toy kitchen equipment in the nursery).

When the Kennedy children became tired and petulant, they were disciplined like every other child. Their mother refused to allow them to feel they were privileged, even though they were certainly that, by virtue of where they lived and who their parents were. Jackie said over and over that she didn't want her daughter and son to consider themselves rich or elite. It would have been so easy to have that happen. She wisely saw to it that it did not.

Occasionally there would be a great escape through the prison gates of the mansion. Devoid of makeup, wearing a scarf, and dressed in an old raincoat, jeans, and a black sweater, but of course accompanied inconspicuously by Secret Service agents, Jackie managed to take the children to the circus, theater, and puppet shows without being recognized. Sometimes they would wait in the back of the theater until the houselights went down before sneaking in to their seats. That these photogenic children had been declared off-limits to the press threw the president's West Wing into a constant state of frustration. The children helped influence the public's perception of the president, even the Congress's attitude toward the Kennedys. It was pretty difficult for a legislator to rise in the House or Senate and blast the man who had just been in the morning papers, captured in a telephoto lens playing with his children and their toys. When the average person needed to be cheered up, it helped for him or her to hear the latest on those two children at 1600 Pennsylvania Avenue. When things were going badly in the media for the president or the Democratic Party, the powers that be in the West Wing would decide it was time to stage a photo op with the children, with probable touchy-feely results. Since the boys in the West Wing knew that Mrs. Kennedy would never agree to this, they would wait until she was out of town, perhaps even riding out in Virginia, and then take Caroline and John down from the family quarters (a sneaky kidnapping operation, one might say) to play in the president's office. The photographers were then allowed into the office, like a swarm of agitated bees, with much pushing and shoving, which the children did not even seem to notice. Evelyn Lincoln, the president's secretary, would look on approvingly, beaming. She loved it when the children came over, pictures or no pictures. The photo results were inevitably adorable and made the front page of every newspaper in the world. The president's office, I might add, always heard back from the first lady when this happened, in no uncertain terms. The moratorium on press coverage of the children would be back in place—for several months at least.

The East Wing rather enjoyed the battle of the sexes with the West Wing, savoring the victory when we thwarted attempts to take over Mrs. Kennedy's schedule and plan her program. The West Wing always failed in this; Jackie would be furious; I always went to the president and complained; and the president always immediately called in whoever was responsible and gave that person proper hell. We had a champion for all our causes, and his initials were JFK.

It was remarkable the way that Jackie taught her children manners. One of her priorities was to make them aware of their own movements. She may have had many arguments in her life with her mother, but she obviously admired the way Janet Auchincloss had made manners important to all her children and stepchildren. No, to the Kennedy children, meant just that, and John learned it by age two, even in the throes of the terrible twos. There would be no bratty, noisy, objectionable children in the Kennedy household. When people spoke, they listened; they did not interrupt their elders. When people gave them presents, they said thank you with grace and a minimum of prompting. Endless thank-you notes went out from the White House, thanking other children for their birthday presents and party invitations. Until they were old enough to write, Jackie would write the letters for the children, and they would make scratches at the end to show their authorship. They always watched their mother and her notes. They learned. They watched her writing their thank-yous on their behalf, and watched her writing her own. The sealed handwritten notes, ready to mail, were always piled up on a silver salver by the elevator on the second floor.

The children must have concluded that this was the way you lived your life. When people gave you things and did favors for you, you wrote them about how nice it was, how much it pleased you. After a party for Caroline or John, Jackie would take them down to chef René Verdon in the kitchen to say thank you, much to the delight of the kitchen staff.

Maude Shaw, the children's nannie, may have successfully worked on their table manners every day, but their mother worked on their relationships with visitors and with the great numbers of adults who flowed around them in their house. There were the men who came up to see Daddy for conferences in the family quarters, the men and women who conferred with Mommy on the White House decoration, the meetings with Mommy and her staff, and her conferences about the school program on the top floor. It was "How do you do" day and night, not only to Mommy and Daddy's friends but also to the ushers, butlers, maids, policemen, Secret Service, and gardeners, and the people in the kitchen and in the butler's pantry—whomever they happened to pass. They were taught to be aware of others around them, not just concentrate on their own thoughts, ignoring others in their path. What I first noticed about the children's manners was how they would greet adults while repeating their name and looking them squarely in the eye at the same time ("How do you do, Mrs. McNamara"—or a reasonable facsimile thereof; "Mrs. Nama" would do).

Heads of state would come up to the family quarters to have a cocktail with President and Mrs. Kennedy before going down to receive the guests for state dinners in their honor. Caroline and John, usually in their pajamas and robes, were always brought in to meet the guests of honor on these occasions. They were taught how to shake hands, as part of the meeting ritual. John would give a slight bow, Caroline a slight curtsy. Jackie coached them on conversation when there were to be illustrious visitors.

"You'll see the shah of Iran tonight, who lives far, far away in Persia. He has two little children your ages. They live in a palace. His wife, called an 'empress,' like in the storybooks, is very beautiful, and they have asked particularly to meet the two of you, so they can return home and tell their own children about you." Caroline was old enough always to have something to say. Her little brother could get by with a finger in his mouth when the repartee began, but at least he was always good for the handshake. There was an exchange of gifts between the heads of state during this upstairs cocktail hour, before the state dinner with all its pomp and formality began on the lower floor, but more importantly, if the visitors had children, the Kennedy children would give beautifully wrapped presents to the visitors, with the names of their children on the gift enclosure cards. Then the Kennedy children would be able to unwrap the gifts from the children of the visiting heads of state. It was gift-giving on a senior and junior diplomatic scale at the same time.

When heads of state arrived, Jackie would take the children down to the South Lawn to watch the impressive military salute given to them, or else they would watch it from the second-floor balcony. There was much pomp and ceremonial color—marching bands, booming cannons, a review of the troops by the two heads of state, the flash and dash of all those military uniforms and polished guns, flags flying from tall masts—everything set against the rich green rolling landscape of the grounds, with the stately White House behind.

The Kennedy children, at least Caroline, were to have amazing and wonderful memories of this era, from their own perspective. And they contributed greatly to the memories of those of us who served under their parents.

Jackie was a very intelligent first lady, and she showed this intelligence in many ways. She dazzled heads of state with her knowledge of foreign languages. When she led the world through the White House on the first televised tour on CBS, information flowed from her about the history of the house and the styles of the furniture and decorative objects of the period with the ease of a museum curator. (Unfortunately, if you asked the average American woman what she remembered of the telecast, she would probably talk about the beautiful two-piece costume the first lady wore.)

She knew how to receive guests, and how to make conversation with princes, ambassadors, and potentates of all kinds when they came to call on her family. Her eye told her where flowers were needed in a room, and her color and pattern sense in fabrics was infallible. She knew who was doing the best room designs in any given period style. However, no one expected this determined fireball of creative spirit to turn with such focus on her first lady preset agenda—including a complete makeover of a tired, undistinguished, frumpy White House, as well as a radical change in the traditional entertaining that until now had been stuffy, starchy, and awe-inspiring, but devoid of fun and real taste. She even managed to maintain enough privacy for her husband and children to allow him to do his job and their children to grow up in as happy and as normal an environment as possible. She set herself almost impossible goals, but she attained them, and who knows how many more she would have attained had it not been for the tragic conclusion of the Kennedy administration.

She was a completely disciplined creature. If she put on two pounds in a week of endless official meals during an international state visit, she would eat nothing the next day, and drink water and eat fruit the day after that. Off went the weight. She watched that scale with the rigor of a diamond merchant counting his carats. If she needed to lose a couple of pounds, she would add an extra hour of working out on the trampoline the next day, or ride three hours longer, or play another couple of hours of tennis. It helped that she had a great staff and that there were escape hatches to the outside world for herself and her family—the Kennedy compound on Cape Cod in

Hyannis Port, Massachusetts, in the summer; the Kennedy House on Ocean Boulevard in Palm Beach in winter; Camp David in the Catoctin Mountains (the perfect presidential perk); and the house in Virginia for weekends all year round. They could remove themselves from the frenetic goldfish bowl of life in the White House when they had to—and they did. All I could do during those years was remove myself from the White House late at night in the backseat of a White House car, be driven home to my apartment, fall into bed, and get up at six o'clock the next day to get back to work. Seven days a week. To rest on the Seventh Day, the Lord's Day, was wishful thinking—but I did manage to make it to Mass every Sunday. I always had many prayers, requesting the Lord to get me through this White House experience without my landing America in a war with another country, and to find me a wonderful man who would take me away from all of this pressure and put me in the paradise of regular hours, lots of legitimate sex, and babies born to me with wonderful nannies attached.

I would be a wealthy women if I had a quarter for every person who asked me in those days, "Just what do you do?" This was my least favorite question, along with the one asked of me most often, even today, forty years later: "What was Jackie Kennedy really like?"

It would have taken me an entire box of bond to answer these two questions. She cared about her children most of all, then her husband, then the task of becoming the most effective, graceful first lady in the history of the White House. She got there, too. If she had one failing—not actually a failing, but let's call it a lack of enthusiasm—it was a reluctance to spend a lot of time with women's groups. Women, of course, were fascinated by her, and every female organization in America, and other countries in addition, did everything possible to jockey themselves into the position of being entertained, or at least received, by Jackie in the White House. She would finally acquiesce to receiving a large group, as I had begged her to do, and sometimes at the last minute she canceled "because of sudden ill health." I had a roster of last minute fill-ins who would sub as hostess for her. Pam and I lived in fear that the press would catch her playing hooky, riding her horse out in Virginia, when she should be at one of these women's receptions. They never did. Number one sub was Lady Bird Johnson, who changed all her plans at the last minute every time to help us out. (We called her "Saint Bird" around the office.) Number two was mother-in-law Rose Kennedy, who loved subbing for Jackie and felt she wasn't asked often enough to do it. Rose was always trying to reinvent the White House social agenda, which pleased her daughter-in-law not at all, so I became the ultimate coordinator between

Mama Rose and her White House visits. Actually, I admired her tremendously, particularly that unshakable, firmly implanted religious faith of hers, the wonderfully trim figure she kept, and the fashionable way she dressed. I'm sure that when she finally died in her house in Hyannis Port, at the age of more than one hundred, her family members found her dressed in the world's prettiest dress. (She would have insisted on making that final trip appropriately dressed.) Pat Kennedy Lawford was out on the West Coast, Jean Kennedy Smith was a busy young wife, but we had another very effective family substitute, Eunice Shriver, Sarge's wife, a fireball of energy and commitment to the cause of mental retardation. She was always a tremendous help to us. I understood perfectly the first lady's aversion to women's groups— she deserved some time off to go riding, for health purposes, but also to save her sanity and prevent her from feeling like a prisoner in her own house.

Jackie had stepbrothers, like Yusha Auchincloss, and half sisters, like Janet Auchincloss, whom she adored. There simply was no time in her schedule to be with them—it was hard enough for her to see her own children—but I also understood why the relatives were so clearly upset. Two beloved aunts on Jackie's father's side, for example, were constantly being questioned by their friends in New York at the Colony Club where they often lunched: "Aren't you close to Jackie anymore? When did you last see her? What state dinners are you invited to? Why weren't you invited to the dinner for the Nobel Prize winners?" They perceived it as a rejection by Jackie, and it was tough for the Bouvier, Auchincloss, and Davis relatives to handle on the distaff side of the family. It really was not a rejection. If the first lady had done everything important for her children, the president, her country, and her relatives, she would have had to have forty-eight-hour days. I worked out little "compensatories," gestures to appease the hurt feelings of the relatives. I would get one of her relatives on the line for an occasional telephone call, or type up warm little notes on White House notepaper with bits of news, which she would then sign, always adding a sentence or two by hand. The relatives would come for an occasional "Tea in the Green Room," along with some famous guests. If Jackie was not present, at least being in the White House, and at a tea hosted by a couple of cabinet wives, made up for it—almost, that is.

One of the notable aspects of the Kennedy presidency was that the president and first lady really cared about the gifts they presented to other heads of state. Traditionally, this would be taken care of by the Protocol Office of the State Department, who would usually give the same each time. The importance of state gifts has been documented down through history since the Dark Ages, not forgetting, of course, the gifts of the oriental kings, the Magi, when they went to Bethlehem to see the newborn child. America's state gifts are paid for out of the State Department's state visit budget. The Kennedys' gifts usually came from Tiffany's, which was easy for me to arrange, since I had just been there on staff. The Kennedys would make careful decisions on gifts like frames, boxes, and the like, but there would be a special twist. A large vermeil box ordered from Tiffany's for the mayor of Paris on JFK's state visit to France was engraved on the lid with a historic map of the city of Washington, originally drawn by the master planner for the city of Paris, L'Enfant. Their state gift to President Charles de Gaulle was not the usual large incised crystal bowl but a letter written by George Washington, thanking the Marquis de Lafayette for his help during the Revolutionary War. Mrs. Kennedy came up with a very creative idea that was used for a series of important visitors—a paperweight of a large, beautiful, uncut semiprecious stone (rose quartz, malachite, anthracite, turquoise, and so on) taken from the U.S. soil, then wrapped like a parcel by the jeweler David Webb in slender eighteen-karat-gold rope and put on a small base with an engraved message.

I enjoyed going back to my old office in Tiffany's to research those gifts. One time we would decide on a vermeil table dressing set for the wife of an important foreign leader; another time it might be a long-stemmed vermeil rose in a vermeil bud vase for the teenage daughter of a famous international prime minister. For the Kennedys to present to the Holy Father at the Vatican, Mark Cross made a leather in-box, its lid gold embossed with the papal seal and the U.S. presidential seal as well. For his state visit to Ireland, the president gave me and Tiffany's enormous troubles with a huge engraving order on objects made of sterling silver for members of the Irish government. Everything had to be engraved in the Celtic language, which the Irish prime minister was promoting at the time. Its alphabet was confusing to the German and Dutch engravers in the store, but they finally managed to cope with it. (The only trouble was that many of the Irish government officials were unable to read Celtic themselves.)

We gave gifts like small framed etchings of the White House to all the secretaries abroad who worked tirelessly to make these foreign visits a success, and to the maids who took care of the Kennedys' suite. Even the motorcycle escort cops received JFK presidential tie bars, engraved with his PT boat number from his South Pacific battles.

Jackie and her first lady's office met sporadically, but the telephone was in constant use between floors. I worked out a system of file folders, in which decisions were grouped into priorities. The straw baskets containing these folders and correpondence were carried up to the the private quarters and back down again by footmen. She would always return the work involved in the "Must Do" folder by the end of the day, but as the months passed and we grew busier and busier, I knew she was chafing under the workload. She never realized that I sent her only a fifth of the decisions to be made: I coped with the rest, and she never had to see it. Since I made a great number of decisions myself, without bothering her, even though it was at her request, I naturally had to take the rap when they were the wrong ones. I had been doing that since I began working on my first job in Paris. It was second nature to me.

But the first lady's and my strong, easygoing relationship had changed by the end of the first year. That was no surprise; I had realized its inevitability before even starting the job in the White House. Jackie and I had been girlhood friends, and now she was my employer (although one could argue that the U.S. government was really our employer). I thrived on pressure; she hated it. I knew the world would never tire of seeing her, and her presence would make every occasion a success. But I also knew how she dreaded the urgent files put on her desk. I tried to make my notes amusing and to present the serious, difficult stuff in a humorous way. Her own sense of humor was so well tuned, she would pick up on me and add her own asides. She knew I was trying to talk her into doing more than she wanted to do. We played a game with one another. "Let's make the medicine taste better, so that it will go down faster." She was articulate with her yeses, nos, and maybes. She was a good communicator. I saw in her the great vision of an intelligent woman leader, with her own special place in history. The women's movement was stirring. What better proponent than Jacqueline Kennedy, so utterly feminine and graceful, to be out in front of the awakening of women's rights?

That was my mistake. She had no desire to be a great woman leader. A great hostess, yes; an accomplished connoisseur of the fine arts, also. As Senator Kennedy's wife, and as one of the leading celebrities in Washington, she had received an invitation to every important party in town, including White House state dinners. Jackie had used her penchant for detail during these evenings, filing away in her mind what was wrong with White House entertaining. The food was mediocre, not outstanding, as it should have been. The chandeliers were overly bright throughout the house, putting men and women of a certain age in a pitiless light. "Wrinkles take on wrinkles under this cruel light," she once remarked.

The State Dining Room in those days was painted a dark, lugubrious green, making it impossible to appreciate the beautiful moldings and details of the ceilings. The drab color pulled everything down in the room, including people's spirits. The U- or E-shaped table or the long white rectangle was cold and anticonversational, and when towering urns of flowers had been lined up down the center of the table, it became impossible to see anyone in the room other than one's dinner partners.

Pre-Kennedy guests had to stand in the East Room, drinking punch. There were no cocktails to lift their spirits. No music could be played until the presidential party appeared, right before dinner started. The president and first lady would come down the stairs with the guests of honor after an agonizingly long time (thirty to forty-five minutes) spent in their private quarters, during which time the regular guests had to stand around, waiting for the "Ruffles and Flourishes," the president's ceremonial entrance music. Once the march was heard, the military guard of honor would precede the hosts into the East Room and post the flags of both nations. The principals would follow behind them, signaling the start of the receiving line. Guests would pass through the receiving line (those with official rank going first), then immediately enter the dining room, social aides and protocol officers hurrying them along. Tired guests, having suffered through this interminable process, without an evening cocktail, were not in a great mood.

In the Kennedy style of entertaining, guests were served upon their arrival a glass of champagne, fruit juice, or a cocktail of choice. The marine orchestra would play wonderful Broadway show tunes from the minute the first guest walked in the door. The White House atmosphere had changed from formal, rigid protocol to a bright, attractive party.

Pre-Kennedy-era food had been pedestrian, unexciting; under the Kennedys, it grew lighter and more interesting. With chef René Verdon in residence, it was destined to change, and the American public was so excited to have culinary news issuing from 1600 Pennsylvania Avenue that they flooded the mailbox with requests for recipes. We sent out menus with Chef Verdon's recipes, as requested, which meant thousands of mailings, and thousands of hostesses immediately served the same food to their guests—even if it did not taste exactly the same! Perhaps the reason for this was the total inability of the chef to write a detailed, accurate recipe. He always cooked by intuition, not by instruction.

The first lady caused a flurry of criticism when she abandoned the huge refectory table in the State Dining Room and used round tables for eight or ten guests each (the best kind for conversation), with charming circular cloths in yellow or pale blue hanging to the floor. For large dinner parties, she obtained the chairs she had seen so often in Paris—little gold faux-bamboo chairs—instead of the big cut-velvet ones formerly used, which seemed to weigh a ton. She reduced the number of courses and wines so that evenings would be shorter and the guests less sleepy and sluggish. She used low vermeil baskets of spring flowers as centerpieces, so that everyone could see everyone else in the cavernous room. After dinner and demitasses, the guests walked through the Green, Red, and Blue reception rooms off the red-carpeted hall-ways of the first floor—to the delightful, sprightly violin music of the "Strolling Strings." Then the guests were ushered back into the East Room, which by now had been set up with chairs, auditorium style, for the performance.

White House entertaining had not merely undergone a change with the Kennedys; you might call it a revolution.

"There's no business like show business." The Kennedy Center had not been built. Washington had no theater in which to show off the American per-forming artists that the Kennedys wanted to showcase, proving to the world that our country had some of the greatest of the great. I found myself sud-denly in show biz, thanks to having had a portable stage put in the East Room. We had the National Park Service build it for us—no union trouble, either. It was bulky, hard to store and set up, but at least it made a handsome impression with its slanted panels between two walls, all encased in crimson velvet. The stage was about eighteen inches off the floor; ballet dancers, in the process of being hoisted on high, on one occasion almost crashed into the low-hung massive Waterford crystal chandelier. (To avoid having the dancers beheaded, we gave all future dance groups plans of the elevation of the stage and chandeliers in the room, so that they could choreograph around them.) The entire overloaded electrical system blew one night in the middle of a performance of the Broadway musical *Brigadoon*, plunging everything into si-lence and darkness. The Secret Service men quickly took over the doors of the East Room, fearing an assassination plot. I feared for my job until the fuse was fixed some five minutes later, and we had light again. The guest of honor, King Hassan of Morocco, was totally bewildered. The president put him at ease by whispering, "Your Majesty, it's all part of the show."

In our first stage production, *Hamlet*, the performers had trouble finding the one stage exit amidst all those look-alike velvet panels. One actor almost broke his nose when he rushed offstage in a dramatic moment, his sword un-sheathed, and ran into the wall, not an exit. (I solved that one by having someone stand in the exit with a flashlight signaling up and down!) The good thing about the White House is that there is simply no unsolvable problem. An answer can be found for everything, and the ushers' office and the Na-tional Park Service allowed the Kennedys to accomplish a fantastic coup with the design of our first stage. (Before the Kennedys, if there was entertain-ment, it had usually been something pleasant and relaxing like Fred Waring and his Pennsylvanians.)

There were even evenings of unparalleled distinction and excellence in the East Room. Pablo Casals returned from self-exile for the first time since the 1930s for a White House performance honoring his friend, Governor Muñoz Marin of Puerto Rico. When the magic sounds of his cello filled the East Room on this historic occasion, sighs of delight were heard around America that evening, not just in the East Room. The maestro was back. People would be able to hear him again.

I remember seeing Caroline sit on her mother's lap in the East Room as they watched the Jerome Robbins Ballets: USA dancers rehearsing onstage for the after-dinner entertainment. Anything to do with ballet intrigued Caroline, but she was heard to comment to her mother with disappointment that the dancers should have been in their costumes. "Why aren't they, Mommy?" Of course, this was the dawn of modern dance, with its sometimes down-to-earth, gritty side. The dancers had just begun to wear leotards and sweatshirts for their performances, instead of just for rehearsal. The children appreciated much more the exotic Turkish costumes worn by the Metropolitan singers, who did a performance of Mozart's *Così fan tutte* in the East Room, complete with turbans, colorful tunics, and pointed slippers.

Of course, I have additional memories of such delightful, cultural performances. At *Così fan tutte*, one of the tall male singers, dressed like a Middle Eastern potentate in a satin tunic and a towering satin turban with feathers, came into the dining room to have tea with the children of diplomats who had just seen the performance. He stood too close to one of the burning candles in a wall sconce, and his turban ignited into a flaming torch. Fortunately, a nearby Secret Service agent grabbed a huge pitcher of milk that was to be served to the children. He extinguished the blaze quickly, the singer was unhurt, and all was well, except for the smell of singed feathers and burned satin and milk, which permeated the whole mansion.

The Kennedys gave the first dinner in honor of the living Nobel laureates, honoring the liberal arts, science, economics, literature, and peace efforts. It was the ultimate salute to excellence. Poet Robert Frost and novelist Pearl Buck, both "way up there in years," reminisced about other historic events in which they had taken part. The widows of General George Marshall and Ernest Hemingway sat in the front row with the Kennedys on this Nobel Prize winners' evening, mindful that their husbands were being honored in memoriam. Renowned actor Fredric March read General Marshall's speech made in 1948, when he proposed the Marshall Plan (and won the Peace Prize), the intent of which was to save Western Europe from economic ruin after the war. March, with his beautiful voice, also read excerpts from an unpublished novel by Hemingway. I took Mr. March up to the family quarters on the second floor so he could have a half hour's rest between dinner and his performance in the East Room. "This is the Lincoln Bedroom," I announced dramatically. He pointed to the bed; "And you mean, Miss Baldrige, that I'm supposed to take a rest on that bed? That historic bed?" He was overcome with emotion. He inspected every detail of that room, with its Lincoln family personal possessions, and the framed signed copy of the Declaration of Independence. As he left the White House that night, he took my hand in both of his and said that he had never been so moved or honored in his life—to be asked to lie down in the Lincoln Bedroom! "None of the honors I have received in my life equaled this, tonight," he said, deeply moved by his whole White House experience. (This made it doubly hard for me to accept, decades later in another administration, the "selling of the Lincoln Bedroom" for overnight stays to the biggest party contributors.)

Isaac Stern enraptured the guests with his violin after a dinner for André Malraux, the French minister of culture. Malraux, on whom I think Jackie had a crush, and vice versa, at least in an intellectual sense, brought Leonardo da Vinci's *Mona Lisa* to the National Gallery in Washington at this time, in what was probably its only visit away from its home in the Louvre. It was a gift to America for two weeks, and Jackie was responsible. The first lady made more than cultural international news at this dinner, for she wore a fantastic strawberry pink silk strapless dress that prudish Americans complained was "much too décolleté."

Jackie told me to respond to those who wrote objecting to her décolletage by saying she was having all of her strapless gowns cut much lower, but I instructed the correspondence section to answer these letters in the usual way: "Mrs. Kennedy was interested to hear your opinion, and she has asked me to send you her very best wishes."

It was amazing how important a role in the affairs of this nation Jacqueline Kennedy's physical appearance and wardrobe played. Before the Kennedy years, most Americans were not all that interested in the international doings of their leaders. But when the Kennedys went politicking on behalf of the United States to foreign lands, everyone, it seems, knew about the trips and kept abreast of the details—particularly of her clothes.

The first state visit was to Canada, and the ambassador from Canada to the United States paid a call on me to express his worry that the Kennedys might misunderstand his countrymen's lack of emotion on the occasion of the presidential visit. "We Canadians don't show our emotions," he said apologetically. "Even the queen of England was very upset when she came, because she was used to an enthusiastic reception everywhere she visited in the British Empire. So please tell your president and first lady that the unemotional reception they will receive does not at all represent the Canadians' true feelings about their visit."

I warned the Kennedys, but what we saw from the minute Air Force One set down at the airport in Ottawa was the exact opposite. Enthusiastic, cheering crowds lined the roads into the city, and the shouts of "Jack-ie, Jack-ie" were heard above all the other cheers. She was a smash hit, and, of course, it did not hurt that she wore a bright red suit (her Canadian Mounties' suit) on the day she reviewed the troops. The president saw clearly on this first visit that his wife was the biggest asset he now possessed. We all noticed that he had a new appreciation of and respect for her.

Every state dinner was written about in detail on the front pages of every newspaper in America, there was so much glamour, excitement, and distinction in the guest lists. The fashion industry went gaga when the shah and empress of Iran paid an official visit to Washington. Forget the official business of their husbands—the entire story was a comparison of the beauty and fashion know-how of the two young, beautiful spouses of heads of state, both mothers, both well educated and sophisticated, and both wildly pursued by every fashion designer in Paris. What the women would wear on the night of the state dinner was the lead story in the media time after time in advance in their arrival. Christian Dior let slip that his house had made a ball gown for the empress woven of a special gold cloth, which she would wear with all the famed emeralds in the treasury of Iran. News items of serious importance were shoved off the pages by conjectures as to who would be the most beautiful, Farah Diba or Jackie. American jewelers offered to lend our first lady a shipload of diamonds to compete with the riches of Iran. After several weeks of reflecting, Jackie decided to be a *jeune fille* on this night. She wore a simple pink-and-white silk dress, her hair piled high in the brioche hairdo that Alexandre de Paris had originally designed for her, but that New Yorker Kenneth Battelle now did for her, with one diamond clip at the top center, and simple diamond earrings. The exotic Farah Dibah looked spectacular that night, like a tall, flashing, jewel-studded Renaissance goblet, but the war was won by Mrs. John F. Kennedy, in a borrowed clip and earrings and a simple pink-and-white dress.

Certain of the celebrities who came to be entertained at the White House grabbed the attention of my staff more than others. Princess Grace and Prince Rainier of Monaco, for example, were heavy hitters, whose arrival was greatly anticipated. A short romance had been long rumored between Grace and Jack Kennedy before either of them was married; that, in my opinion, is why Jackie changed the White House meal in their honor from a four-hour black-tie dinner dance to a small eighty-minute-long seated luncheon—a bit of jealousy, perhaps. Princess Grace, we all noted, stood close to the president and gazed at him with adoring eyes. The photographs of this reunion made us shriek with laughter in the East Wing. She looked like a teenybopper up close to her favorite rock star. The lovely Grace, who was always known for her beautiful clothes, had really failed on this one occasion. She wore what I would term a surprisingly dowdy suit by Yves Saint Laurent and a white turban with little white flowers that covered all of her hair. The East Wing, acting as fashion observers, concluded that her turban looked exactly like an Esther Williams Aquacade flowered rubber bathing cap, lifted straight from one of the swimming star's movies.

In late June of our first year in the White House, we had a double-whammy travel plan. First a state visit to Paris was scheduled, momentous enough; then there would be a summit meeting immediately following in Vienna between the heads of the Soviet Union and the free world.

The preparations for Paris were unbelievably complex, on both the American and the French side. The French were out to be the superior organizers; we were out to prove them wrong. To start with, the first lady's French blood, the close ties between the two countries, the memories of World War II, and the discrepancy in ages between the two leaders—Charles de Gaulle and John F. Kennedy—made it an emotional encounter.

The three days when the Kennedys visited France were the most emotional visits in French history, with the possible exception of the time the young Archduchess Marie-Louise of Austria came to court to be introduced to her betrothed, Emperor Napoleon, and his subjects.

I flew to Paris with some of the president's aides to "advance" the trip a week before their arrival. I had two large, heavy notebooks already filled with notes, a small amount in comparison to what I had at the end of the trip. When I stepped off the plane in Paris, after that long flight from New York, an embassy car took me to the Hôtel Crillon, next door to the embassy on the place de la Concorde. I was handed the key to my room and told I had exactly thirty minutes to get to a meeting in the embassy. Having been up all night flying, and having not been to bed thirty-six hours before that, I was in no shape for this meeting—but that does not matter when you're on a presidential advance trip. I picked up the telephone to reach the *valet de chambre*. If nothing else was going to be right, at least I would have a pressed dress from my suitcase to wear that night.

A familiar woman's voice answered. It was one of our White House telephone operators. I knew all of their voices well. "What are *you* doing here?" I asked.

"I'm not there where you are. I'm here where I am," she answered, laughing. I had a direct line to the White House in my hotel room. This was my first experience with the saying, "Where the president goes, so goes the White House."

It felt good to be back home in the embassy again. Many of the faithful French employees from the David Bruce days were still there. Once the preparatory meetings began, they never ended. We lived without sleep. I was unable to call even one of my friends. We had to spell out every single minuscule detail of the Kennedys' joint and separate movements: transportation, apparel, precedence, diet, who gets introduced to whom, what kind of mattresses are needed, what gifts Mrs. Kennedy will give to whom and on what occasion, which members of the American colony should be presented to her and who says what, what she will be served for breakfast, lunch, tea, and dinner, who will be sitting on her left and right at each meal, when she should walk ahead of the president, alongside him, or behind him, who will be making the presentations, what gifts children will be making to her and what gifts she should be making to them, what museums she will visit and which sections, which curators will be allowed to give a spiel in front of a painting, which doctors she will be presented to at the children's hospital she will visit, when will she go to the bathroom, and for how long? It was a morass of endless details, complicated by the security details of which car she should get into at each place and which side of the car she should sit on, which changed each time, possibly to foil an assassin's evil plan.

On the day of the Kennedys' arrival at Orly Airport, I moved into the Quai d'Orsay state apartments on the Seine, where the Kennedys and a handful of their staff were to stay. From the balcony I watched as the motorcade progressed from the place Vendôme across the river to the quais, with the de Gaulles and Kennedys in open cars in front, preceded by the Garde Républicaine, blowing trumpets, wearing shiny helmets with long red plumes, and mounted on beautifully groomed black horses. French and American flags fluttered from every lamppost, and the streets were lined with people shouting, "Vive la France!" "Vive l'Amérique!" "Vive le Président Kennedy!" "Vive Jac-kie!"

The president and first lady were like little kids, running all through the presidential apartments and relishing details like the bathrooms that looked like a meeting place for the Roman Imperial Senate. Flowers arrived by the many dozens, which we had carded and delivered to hospitals. Expensive presents arrived by the hour from the best houses in Paris—gifts of handbags, costume jewelry, silk scarves, gloves, perfume, and even exquisite French lace lingerie. It all had to be sent back—almost all, that is—with a little note signed by me: "Unfortunately, Mrs. Kennedy does not accept gifts of value, but she appreciates your kind gesture so much."

We smuggled into the apartments the leading hairdresser in the world (at least that was what he told us), Alexandre de Paris, with his two assistants, and a quantity of hairpieces *pour Madame la Présidente*. They started to work on her that night, and it seems they never left for the entire three days. Her hairdo the final night, to accompany her magnificent Givenchy white satin dress with a sequined, flowered top, was a new brioche design. The top of the brioche was ringed with diamond-leaf bracelets. France talked of nothing other than her clothes the whole time. When the president appeared, dressed as usual, in his white tie and tails, he teasingly asked, "Isn't anyone interested in what I'm wearing tonight? Does anybody care?"

The days were filled with appearances, speeches, lunches, tours, and presentations. Jackie spoke to reporters in French. The president was more than a little aware of what an asset his wife was: at the large Chamber of Commerce luncheon, he announced he needed no introduction, since "I am the man who accompanied Jacqueline Kennedy to Paris." President de Gaulle appeared smitten by her, and there was not a doubt in anyone's mind that the visit was a success in cementing Franco-American relations.

In the meantime Alexandre continued his frenetic efforts on Jackie's hair, Rose Kennedy's hair, and Eunice's hair—he even tried to get at mine ("Mlle Baldrige, you *really have need of my services!*").

The nights were filled with entertainments grand and magical, including the Opéra. The most dramatic, of course, was the final night, when the de Gaulles gave a good-bye fete for the Kennedys at Versailles, in the Hall of Mirrors. The frescoes on the ceiling had just been restored and were illuminated for the first time. The immensely long white table was centered with peach-colored blossoms in vermeil containers. All of the plates and flatware were of vermeil. (I felt at home, having done the big vermeil promotion for Tiffany's just two years before.) The candelabra and the ceiling provided the only light for a fantastic dinner of six courses. There were no kitchens at Versailles in this period, no electricity, yet the food was perfectly prepared behind magical eighteenth-century tall screens in the corner. After dinner the guests followed the two presidents and their wives through the entire chateau, led by footmen bearing large heavy candelabra to light the way and accompanied by musicians dressed in Louis XV period costumes, playing instruments of the period. They led us into the newly restored Louis XV theater, a confection of powder blue, white, and gold. We sat on tiny, uncomfortable seats (made to fit small eighteenth-century derrieres) and watched a ballet commissioned by the king.

On our way back into Paris, the motorcade stopped in the garden where a tall, illuminated fountain was sending geysers of water into the air to the accompaniment of the "Marseillaise" and "The Star-Spangled Banner." The young president and his wife got out of the lead car, walked over to the fountain, and just stood there for ten minutes, enjoying a moment of history that was for them and no one else.

From France we proceeded to Vienna, where a summit meeting was to be held in neutral territory, Austria. President Kennedy and Premier Nikita Khrushchev were to have their first face-to-face meeting. It was a serious, historic moment. The eyes of the world were watching. The president arranged to have the sofa the two leaders were to sit upon shipped back to America for his library.

Olivier, the assistant to the most celebrated hair stylist "in the world," had been taught by *le gran maître* how to do his new brioche hair creation, so Jackie wanted him along on the trip to Vienna. What was good enough for General de Gaulle's pleasure would be good enough for Nikita Khrushchev's. Olivier was nineteen years old and Mediterranean-handsome, and Jackie gave me the job of smuggling him with me on the press plane from France to Austria, without anyone discovering who he was. It would not have gone over well if the American public knew that Mrs. Kennedy was flying a French hairdresser with her on such a strategically important mission. When I asked Jackie just what was I to give as the reason I had this young man with me, she replied with a grin, "Oh, just tell 'em he's one of your boyfriends." The press on that plane, now convinced I was having an affair with a nineteen-year-old kid, teased me unmercifully for the rest of the trip. TV journalist and correspondent Sandy Vanocur at one point told me to stop complaining about the bad rap I was getting for being a cradle robber: "Think of how jealous the women are on this trip. Every one of them wishes she were you."

The great leaders meeting here were enemies. The Soviets had been unwelcome occupiers of the city. Anti-Soviet feeling was running so strong, the Viennese would give the Russian motorcades flying their flags on the front fenders the cold, silent treatment as they passed by. The Austrians would make no noise, show no emotion, only look away. By contrast, the American motorcades received jump-for-joy, scream-and-yell reactions from people in the street whenever they passed. On our first night at the Palais Schönbrun we watched the dumpy Soviet leader, in his ill-fitting black business suit, siz-ing up John Kennedy's beautifully tailored tuxedo. It was impossible not to notice how the Russian premier kept sneaking furtive glances at the first lady of the United States, who looked like Cinderella at the ball in a dazzling white sequined ball gown and, let us not forget, her Alexandre de Paris up-swept brioche hairdo. Poor Nina looked as though she had bought a shapeless dress from a thrift shop—but to her husband, that was entirely appropriate.

The next day was unforgettable. At a small luncheon given for Mesdames Kennedy and Khrushchev by the daughter of the president of Austria, Frau Schaerf, Jackie noticed how embarrassed Nina Khrushchev was, and how up-set Frau Schaerf was, when the Austrians filled the big square outside the window and began shouting "Jac-kie, Jac-kie!" They never once mentioned Mrs. Khrushchev's name. Jackie caught my eye and winced. Frau Schaerf, who was hosting both countries, did not know how to make this situation less painful for her Soviet guest.

Jackie knew what to do—what her good breeding, education, and yes, intuition, had prepared her for. She moved suddenly over to the window across the room, opening the big casement window onto the square and giv-ing a royal wave to the thousands gathered there. The crowd, when they saw her, increased their cheering. Then she went back to Nina Khrushchev, liter-ally pulled her from the sofa, and forced her to come to the window with her. She pulled Nina's arm up high, alongside her own, and made her wave at the crowd below in the square. The Austrian public showed their own good manners by wild clapping and shifting their chant to "Jac-kie—Ni-na, Jac-kie—Ni-na." It was sheer genius on Jackie's part from a diplomatic point of view, but also it was an act of kindness. Historians will note that Kennedy and Khrushchev failed to agree on anything at the Vienna summit. My memories of the distaff side are much brighter and happier.

The Kennedys, always interested in the pursuit of history, wanted to leave a legacy of highlighting our great historic shrines. That's one thing about living in Washington; you don't have to be the president to appreciate the ghosts of America's leaders, warriors, and statesmen. The inhabitants can naturally grow very close to the history of our country, since every part of the city is a reminder of it.

President de Gaulle had just feted us at Versailles on the state visit to France, so the Kennedys wished to capture some of that feeling for history in their party honoring their newest and very important military ally, General Ayub Khan of Pakistan. Jackie, with her great sense of history, asked me to see if we couldn't have this state dinner at Mount Vernon, George Washing-

ton's home. Both President Kennedy and General Ayub Khan felt a kin-
dred spirit to George Washington, a man who was president and a former
general.

Mount Vernon was, however, sacred territory. No entertaining had ever
been allowed there. It was not equipped logistically to give anything more
than a small, simple cocktail party. A state dinner was pronounced an impossible feat.

We pulled it off. Jackie asked Cecil Wall, the resident director, in her best
little-girl voice, if it was possible. He got on the telephone and worked on
the women vice regents from all around the United States who govern
Mount Vernon, "the Ladies' Association." After a great deal of lobbying, we
received the okay, and the evening came off. It wasn't Versailles, but it was a
night of unbelievable beauty and history. For our dinner party, refrigerators,
warming ovens, and electrical generators were trucked out to Virginia as
though a military operation was being mounted. (Eight-holers, too, to use as
"bathrooms.") The dinner tent, constructed on the grounds overlooking the
Potomac, was a dream in greens, yellows, and blues, decorated by Gene
Moore, Tiffany's famous window designer, who came down from New York
to "make it right" for our party.

The guests were carried up the Potomac on PT boats (the president had
his say on that idea); there was a landing ceremony on the dock at Mount
Vernon with a Marine military salute as each boat docked, and then, once all
the guests were assembled, there came another military salute up on the "piazza" at the back of the house. Arriving guests were handed mint juleps made
from George Washington's own recipe, served in the same kind of cups he
used. The army's Colonial Color Guard and Fife and Drum Corps, in their
tricornered hats, powdered wigs, and Continental Army uniforms, performed a Revolutionary military drill that Washington had ordered to be carried out many times at Mount Vernon.

Getting this event organized was a journey through hell for my staff. The
army mosquito sprayers came to cover the grounds in the morning, because
this was one of the worst years in history. By 4:00 P.M. the mosquitoes had
returned, fighting mad, so the army was called again. They covered the
grounds, even inside the kitchen tents, and sprayed with a vengeance. This
time Chef Verdon was convinced all of the guests were going to die of DDT
poisoning. I dispatched two Secret Service agents to offer up their lives for
their country, so they tasted all the food with great glee and lived to tell the
tale, unscathed. René was momentarily placated. At four, we discovered we
had to have the outdoor concert stage rebuilt for the after-dinner concert of
Washington's National Symphony Orchestra: the sounds made by the musicians were completely sucked down into a ravine behind the stage, never

making it up the hill to the natural theater where the guests were to sit. It was now six hours before performance time. The symphony conductor solemnly announced to me, "There will be no concert tonight," but within four hours the Park Service managed to build an acoustical shell behind the orchestra and on the stage that delivered the sound up the hill the way it should sound. The show would go on.

The press corps survived being accidentally positioned by Pierre Salinger right in front of the Revolutionary soldiers' drill for the guests out on the piazza as they sipped mint juleps before dinner. At the conclusion of the drill and at the command of the senior officer, the soldiers lunged forward in perfect formation and fired fake ammunition from their eighteenth-century muskets—right into the surprised, and frightened, faces of the press corps! They were stunned. The noise was thunderous. Smoke was rising everywhere. The *New York Times* correspondent covering the event had the sense of humor to raise a white handerchief in surrender. The entire participants of this scene of guests, waiters, and performers broke out into raucous laughter that General Washington himself must have heard down in his burial vault.

It was a night to remember in more ways than one, and sitting there, looking out over the serene Potomac on a perfect summer evening, enjoying the same scene the father of our country and his wife Martha enjoyed night after night, I think everyone there realized that we were savoring history in an incredible way. As for me personally, after the whole event was over, after every crisis had been averted, and after the last guest had left Mount Vernon for the district—carried back in cars, this time, not PT boats—I thought I had died and gone to heaven.

In Mexico Jackie wowed them, dressed in a watermelon-pink silk dress and matching hat, speaking to the luncheon audience in Spanish. *Olés* filled the air. In the meantime, I was coping with literally hundreds of floral offerings sent to Jackie by starstruck Mexicans. I organized a brigade of embassy wives and stenographers to make a list of who sent what, with addresses, so we could send the flower donors a thank-you note later, and commandeered a group of trucks, driven by American and Mexican security agents, to dispatch the flowers far and wide to orphanages, old people's homes, and hospital wards. That night at a ball in Mexico City, the Mexican president asked Mrs. Kennedy if she had seen his flowers. Jackie, trained to say yes, of course, said that they were "just so beautiful." He let drop the fact that they were orchids, so Jackie went into a symphony of praise of orchids. Then he asked her, "And what did you think of the vase holding the orchids?'

"Oh, beautiful," she gushed, "simply lovely," envisioning a crystal one.

"Well, I'm so glad," he said, "because it is a twenty-two-karat-gold Incan vase, very rare, and comes from one of our museums. I knew, with your love of art, it would be meaningful to you."

Jackie shot across that ballroom floor so fast, she looked as though she were running in an Olympic event. She wanted that vase, and fast. I told her all the flowers had gone to charities. She repeated: she wanted that vase, and fast. I alerted the senior Secret Service agent, and the trucks set off again, at one-thirty in the morning, to all the places they had gone that afternoon, knocking on doors, waking people up, to search for the precious gold work of art. By four a.m. they had found it. I fell to my knees to send Saint Anthony, finder of lost articles, a prayer of thanks; once again he had saved me.

Jackie's trip to Greece as an official guest of Prime Minister Caramanlis in August 1961 was one of the first totally open signs that the first lady had begun to resent my management of her office. Her sister, Lee, accompanied us, bringing along her amusing, quite dashing husband, the Polish prince Stas Radziwill. All of a sudden I was put in the unbearable position of having to defend the program the prime minister had laid out for Mrs. Kennedy "in the best interests of Greek-American relations." The two sisters put their heads together and started to plan some fun—on shipowner Nomikos's yacht. Challenging plans that had been weeks in the making, they rejected the official schedule laid out for them by their host, Caramanlis, and went off at sea to be guests of a man who had been purposely omitted from the prime minister's guest lists. I sensed a change in Jackie's attitude toward me, her senior staff person, and I could only describe it as a mean-spiritedness I had not seen before. There was whispering behind my back, and conspiratorial giggling when they made yet another appointment with the playboy Nomikos. Every change they made in the schedule set the Greek desk of the State Department into a disaster mode. I had to take the State Department's side; the first lady's security was involved, and this was not supposed to be a fun-and-games vacation only. The sisters began playing tricks to avoid me, which hurt, and at the same time made me think, Why am I doing this? I don't have to be doing this. I started telling Jackie in no uncertain terms, "You can't do that!" and she started telling me that she could. (She could.) I called the president because our Secret Service agents were extremely upset over the changes in schedule and travel the Bouvier girls were foisting on them. Security is tough enough to deal with in the United States, but in Greece, Jackie was the official guest of the head of state, who had laid on a magnficent program of history, ancient art, Greek drama performances in outdoor theaters, island hopping, and beautiful parties. Lee again said she found the entire agenda boring. When I got a message through to the president about the yacht expedition, he was furious, and I, of course, was now in the position of having become Chief Tattler. At the president's suggestion, Jackie invited on the Nomikos cruise old friends of mine, John and Letitia Mowinckel. John was a U.S. Information Service official stationed abroad, whose presence calmed down the president and the people back at the White House. I remained in Athens, but John and I developed a kind of code with which to communicate daily and secretly, ship to shore. No one must know the first lady was cruising on that boat, and no one must hear what John and I were saying to one another. We spoke to one another on the radio in Italian, as if it were a code, a completely naive, ridiculous thing to do—of course, Italy and its yachts were close by, and the Italian radio operators understood every word of our "coded" messages. The Nomikos yacht was followed by a fleet of small boats, like guppies swimming around a fast, lovely zebra fish in the family aquarium.

I managed to have a wonderful time in Greece, problems notwithstanding, because of the great guides we had in historic places, the special performances in Greek outdoor theaters, and the reception at the Parthenon with only top Greek officials, the first lady's party, Chargé d'Affaires Tap Bennett and his wife, Margaret, and limited press. The press portrayed the trip as an enormous success all over the world. Caramanlis covered up Jackie's absence from Athens on the yacht with amazing aplomb. A shot of Jackie, in a beautiful white dress and gloriously tanned, sitting next to the prime minister of Greece on the ancient stone steps of the giant outdoor theater at Epidaurus, watching a Greek tragedy, was the leading international photograph of the summer.

I naturally confided my discomfort after the trip to my two biggest supporters, my parents. My father said immediately, "When the bloom is off the rose, you get out of the garden. You don't even stop to pick the rose."

My mother protested. "Mac, this is the greatest experience in the world for her—don't talk like that. Stay on, Tish, be strong."

My father was adamant. "Go see the president. Tell him you simply want to leave. You don't have to give any reasons. Just do it."

I did just that. I called Evelyn Lincoln, his secretary, and asked to see the president. She immediately gave me an appointment, knowing I never asked for one unless it was of some urgency. All of our other interactions were on the fly, informally, just a need for a call back, an explanation, a quick request. This request to see her boss was not in the normal flow of business.

The president rose at his desk when I came in and motioned me over to one of the white linen sofas flanking the fireplace.

"You know how much I have loved this job," I began. He sat and put his hands to his eyes in a very tired gesture. He knew what was coming. "This has been unbelievably wonderful for me, and I know you know that. I have felt like I was in on making a part of history. It's been like fulfilling a dream, but I also have to know when it's time to move on."

I was hoping he would say something, but instead he just looked at me sadly. "I need to get out of government and into the business world," I continued. "Your father told me that, you know, before his stroke. He said I needed a business background. I really want to succeed in life. I have a lot to learn about the world that is nongovernment."

I felt I was babbling, trying to find reasons for my wanting to leave, and loath to say it was because of my now failed relationship with his wife. He finally spoke. "You can't go now, Tish, please." He knew why I was asking to get out now. He told me he understood, that I did not have to elaborate, but he asked me, please, to stay on.

"I know it hasn't been easy, but you're an important part of this team. I have felt this was one part of the White House I didn't have to worry about. I thought everything was in place."

I countered with, "I'm sure Jackie is saying the same thing about me, right now, that it hasn't been easy for her either."

The president laughed again. "I thought your brothers had raised you to be tough, to take things on the chin."

"I'm worn out," I said. "I have no life—except this."

"But I need you there, in the East Wing, in that very spot. I want Jackie to feel protected and not persecuted by the demands of her job. I want you to keep doing the terrific things you do. Just lighten up on the workload, and it'll make things easier on both of you. She gets pressured very easily. Come to me when there are problems. You don't have to suffer in silence. But don't leave now—"

He was being typically JFK, not believing that any of his loyal crew could desert his ship. And, of course, I couldn't. I adored this man, not in an amorous way but as our president, a man of principle and strength. I was unaware at the time of his dalliances. If I had known about them, I would have adored him less, but since those stories were to be revealed after his death, they did not color his staff's exalted opinion of him.

We quite simply loved this man.

He rose from behind his desk. The appointment was over. There was a final handshake, a tacit agreement on my part to stay, and a look of understanding between us that needed no words. I went to a public phone and talked to my parents, who were waiting for news of what had happened. My mother was elated I had agreed to stay on, but my father tempered his elation with cynicism. "If it gets bad again, don't think you have to stay. Don't be anyone's patsy. The next time, just leave, don't explain, just get out."

The president obviously gave Jackie a big talking to that night—for a while, she was particularly kind and cordial, but I knew it wouldn't last. My staff knew I was hurting, but they were relieved I had at least rebelled against the status quo. I had not discussed my feelings with them, but they saw it all in my depressed demeanor. We all wanted this disagreement to disappear, so we could do our work without even thinking about it. The only problems we were supposed to address in our offices were those of making President and Mrs. Kennedy's lives more comfortable and successful. That was our mandate. This was the White House. There was no time for anything else.

The president realized the effectiveness of Jackie's diplomacy abroad, and the experience in Greece convinced him she could do wonders on trips to other countries, even without him along. He did not have time to make those official journeys, which were public relations gestures anyway, meant to prove friendship between the two countries involved. Jackie could handle it by herself, with me there serving as his eyes and ears, and with Lee along for companionship.

The Bouvier sisters had made such a hit when the first lady received an official invitation to Greece, that the president decided it would be good for international relations to have Jackie and Lee do the same thing in India. Prime Minister Jawaharlal Nehru had invited Mrs. Kennedy with a charming letter. What a glorious trip it would be, what an educational experience, and what an effective way to bring India closer to the United States! Ambassador Ken Galbraith was one of the most popular envoys India had ever had. And so the planning began for a precedent-shattering state visit without the president. Photographs of Jackie and Lee riding an elephant, Jackie gazing at the magical Taj Mahal in the moonlight, Jackie being feted by the Maharanee of Jaipur in her white lace palace, Jackie buying Indian Moghul miniature paintings—it was all beautiful, colorful, and exotic. At times, activities were added to the program for which none of us was prepared—like the time Prime Minister Nehru and his sister Indira Gandhi invited Mrs. Kennedy, Lee Radziwill, Ambassador Galbraith and his wife, Kitty, and myself to tea in the garden of his home. There was to be entertainment at this event, while we balanced our teacups. It turned out to be a fight unto death between a mongoose and a giant cobra, which were brought into our presence in large, decorative baskets by men wearing white turbans and white loincloths. The creatures were ceremoniously ushered forth from their baskets so we could watch them battle one another. No nausea pills are sufficiently effective for such an occasion, but instead we had to put diplomatic smiles, not grimaces of horror, on our faces.

The India and Pakistan visits were a real lesson in sleep deprivation. I had not slept for weeks, not only preparing for the trip but undergoing it. I made a mistake that came a real cropper at the time. I had prepared some sixty-five double-autographed photographs of the Kennedys, in different sizes, and had handsome navy leather frames custom-made to fit, with the gold presidential seal at the top, destined for the top Hindu members of government. We could not give one of these stunning gifts to their recipients. The frames were made of cowhide. Since the cow is sacred in India, it would have been a serious insult to have the president and first lady of the United States presenting themselves encased in the loathed cowhide. Fortunately, I was able to have sterling silver frames made in Italy within two days, and a cross-cultural disaster was averted.

All night long in Delhi, Hindus and Muslims alike managed to bribe the *chowkador* (the guard at the gate) of the guest house where I stayed. Every fifteen minutes another group came into the bedroom, addressing me most respectfully to plead for this and that. I sat in my nightgown in bed, feeling a bit like Louis XIV receiving his subjects in his boudoir, as these people silently slipped into the room and bowed low to the floor before me. By my bed were thousands of unanswered letters begging an audience with Mrs. Kennedy, asking for money, asking for a signed photograph, asking for a one-way air ticket to Washington. The letter that particularly got to me was one from a man who wrote in a vivid color of red ink, on pink stationery. Very attractive, was my reaction, until I read on and realized that, to prove his sincerity, he had written the letter with a pen dipped into his own blood.

Another wrinkle on the India and Pakistan trip was the competition between the Indians and the Pakistani to have Mrs. Kennedy spend more of her time in their particular country. The schedule kept changing, and as it did, I was on the receiving end of a barrage of complaints from the embassies in New Delhi and Karachi, the Indian and Pakistani desks at the State Department, and the representatives of Prime Minister Nehru and President Ayub Khan. "Please persuade Mrs. Kennedy not to change her program," pleaded one source. "Please right the wrongs in this schedule," pleaded the other. The two countries hated one another, and I, on my conspicious yet low level, was right in the middle of it.

My memories of the White House days are interrelated in ways that seem curious at first, but are quite logical if examined closely. For example, the Cuban missile crisis is firmly lodged in an imaginary file marked "History/Cuban Crisis/Mayor Daley."

On a Monday in October 1962 I had been very busy putting the finishing touches on the state visit of Grand Duchess Charlotte of Luxembourg and her son, the grand duke, as well as the personal visit of Mayor and Mrs. Daley of Chicago. The Luxembourg retinue was to stay in Blair House, the official guest house of the U.S. government, but the Daleys were to stay in the private quarters of the White House, called the Mansion, on the family floor, an honor accorded only to a minuscule group of people. When I asked just why this official was being treated so grandly, the president replied, "Because I wouldn't be president if it weren't for him." That was a good enough reason. The mayor's actions during the presidential campaign had brought success to Jack Kennedy. Illinois was delivered to the Democrats in a package tied up with a pretty bow.

The following morning, the red phone rang in my bedroom at four a.m. It was Jackie, informing me in a very grave voice that all social events were to be canceled for the next couple of weeks, and I should get myself to the White House right away. I made it there in thirty minutes, and then began a thirteen-day odyssey into drama, fear, prayer, and eventually success. The "Cuban missile crisis" unfolded like a nightmare. The president and his senior staff literally moved into the basement Situation Room. Press briefings were given with almost no details. The tension in the house was unbelievable, as Russia and the United States locked heads, the military of both nations prepared for war, and we sat waiting in breathless suspense for our president's demands to be met: that the Russians remove their ships—their nuclear warheads and guns pointed at our shores—from Cuba.

Our victory brought overwhelming relief and jubilation. The president ordered me to arrange for calendars to be made of sterling silver, with the thirteen days of the crisis to be specially engraved on the October calendar. When I called Tiffany's, Walter Hoving, true to his character, refused to give the president even the smallest discount on these expensive items. In a rage, JFK told me to tell Hoving he could "go to," and that he would have the calendars made in lucite instead. Hoving retorted that the store would have nothing to do with anything as cheap as lucite. The president was furious at Hoving, and also at me, because I had worked for the store for so long and had fallen down on the job of arranging a simple commemorative object of great importance in history. The president had to pay for these out of his own pocket, a fact of life he hardly relished. He had his friend Lem Billings arrange for the making of a lucite calendar prototype. A few days later he called me on the red phone after midnight, ordering me to tell Hoving that he had won, that the lucite calendars did look "cheesy," and that he would pay for sterling silver calendars on wood bases, to be given to all of the thiry-odd people who had stayed down in the "dungeon" of the White House during the missile crisis. The engraved calendars became the most precious mementos in the lives of the men who were part of this team.

Almost a year later, the grand duchess's state visit was rescheduled. We had an entirely new guest list. I didn't even consult the old one, because the cast of characters had changed so much; we started anew. Two days before the dinner, I encountered the president in the Mansion. "Let me know when the Daleys reach here tomorrow," he said, "because I want to be sure to be in the Mansion when they arrive from the airport."

Of course, I had completely forgotten the Daley visit. But the president had just now made a request—and I had to answer.

"I'll let you know the time of their arrival, Mr. President," I said in a normal tone. I returned to my office and summoned my staff; we discussed what new positions we might find after we were fired from our jobs, thanks ultimately to me, their boss. Then, on impulse, I decided to try the impossible. I called the mayor's office in Chicago, talked to his executive secretary, who reported that he was "in a meeting," of course, and then I said that if I couldn't speak to him, I was going to jump out of the tallest window in the White House so that my suicide would be effective. She became my heroine. She interrupted her boss—who really was in a meeting. I told him what had happened, that the Kennedys expected him and his wife for the Luxembourg state dinner, and that if they were not there, it would be the official end of my entire Social Office.

Talk about heroes. The Daleys changed all their plans, boarded a plane for Washington the next day, and, as I had begged them, did not mention my terrible mistake to the Kennedys. I wrote the Daleys afterward that "a life was saved that day at the White House, mine."

During our second year in the White House, I sensed the first lady's resentment of my constant nudging. She wanted to do less, and only those things that she wanted to do. I wanted her to do more, knowing that her power to help her husband and the country was unlimited. She had a real opportunity to change history in her interpretation of her role in the White House. She flashed angry eyes at me once and said, "Not everyone has your energy, you know. I certainly don't. I don't want to do all those things. Keep it away!" She knew my heart was in the right place, and that I had been responsible for many of the projects that brought her the best press and the greatest acclamation, but it had come at the price of our previous, easygoing friendship. She was tired, too, of hearing everyone say, "Oh, how lucky you are to have

Tish!" She began to resent press clips that mentioned my influence on the entertaining after dinner, on the youth concerts on the White House lawn to inspire children into taking music lessons again. Early in the administration, she had admitted that this was an important service for her, to keep her relatives happy and feeling that they were in the loop. She did not want to cope with it.

Enough was now really enough. I had had it. I called my staff together in March 1963 and told them I was going to resign in June. There was an explosion of emotion in the room, and our beloved Fred Jefferson, an African American who solved everyone's problems and healed all wounds, said with an endearing sadness, "But, Miss Baldrige, no one leaves this job. They stay on to the end. You can't do this. We need you. Mrs. Kennedy, what will she do without you?"

"Jeff, there comes a time when there are other things in life. There's my health, for example," I said. My trips to the office of the president's doctor, Janet Travell, had become more frequent—for tension, dizzy spells, novocain injected into my neck to relieve neck spasms. I had been working without time off, without weekends, without one day of vacation. When everyone else was away from the White House on holidays, I was the sucker left behind to give any heads of state passing through town a personal tour through the White House, serve them tea, and try to substitute for the people they had really come to see, the Kennedys. I had been standing in my medium-heeled pumps, night after night, attending every embassy reception the White House staff refused to attend. I would go on behalf of my bosses, filling the air with a shower of effusively warm greetings from the president and Mrs. Kennedy, all of which was dutifully quoted in dispatches sent back to the diplomatic hosts' home base. I made up each Kennedy "personal" message as the White House driver took me to the embassy. I also had worked out a plan that allowed me to walk in the door, greet the ambassador and his wife in the receiving line, go into the dining room, where the buffet was inevitably placed, and walk out through the kitchen, which had a back door into the driveway. My driver, in the meantime, would be waiting for me at the trade entrance in back. No one saw me except the kitchen personnel, whom I shushed, and they giggled and didn't know who I was anyway. It worked well. I would be driven home to get out of my black velvet dress and into bed. The entire operation, from arrival at the embassy to departure, took ten minutes per embasssy, the end of a fourteen-hour workday.

There were other reasons I wanted to leave. I missed being alone with real, red-blooded, heterosexual, nonalcoholic single men. I had forgotten what it was like to be out with one of those. I had not had one date in Washington with a man who wanted to take me out for myself: a favor would inevitably be asked before the main course was served. Washington was full of climbers and strivers who loved to flatter women in high positions in order to push their agendas. It was time to pack my bags and leave. Mother said that everyone would say I was fired. I replied that anyone of any importance would know I was not, but of course a Washington scribe immediately conjectured in print that I had been.

Jackie was thunderstruck when I went up to see her in the family quarters and told her that this time I was really leaving. I was giving four months' notice, enough time, I assured her, to get everything in order for a smooth transition. She looked upset at the news; I am sure she had not thought I would have the courage to do it. Things had reached a point in our relationship where it would have taken much more courage for me to stay.

I have written many articles about Jacqueline Bouvier Kennedy Onassis during the last forty years, but they have been general descriptions of her life in the public domain. I have always avoided becoming more personal. Yet much time has passed, and in telling my own story I feel compelled to speak honestly about our relationship. I loved and admired her. I defended her, lied for her, and never felt it was too big a burden. She was an extraordinary first lady. She was an old friend. I was also awestruck to be close to our country's seat of power, and to be living in an incredible era. Although there are stories of what happened during those years that I will never repeat, she was responsible for affording me my White House position. I will never forget that. When she rode roughshod over me on occasion, I learned how to take it, because that is the role of a staff member. But almost three years of taking it is a long time.

The good-byes were emotional and tough. I cried all the time the last two weeks. Everyone gave me parties, from the chief of protocol, Angier Biddle Duke and his wife, Robin, to Liz Carpenter, Lady Bird Johnson's right arm, who was, sooner than any of us realized, to become Lady Bird's chief of staff after the assassination. I loved every person in that White House. I felt part of it. Right before Memorial Day weekend, Jackie gave me a champagne party, with the Marine Band serenading me with the Italian love songs that I used to sing all around the place. Jackie gave me a large sterling silver frame with the presidential seal engraved at the top, and a nostalgic photo of the Kennedys and André Malraux at the dinner given in his honor. Above their signatures on the photo Jackie had written "For dear Tish—with so many happy memories—and our appreciation and love and good luck to you always." The White House staff gave me a round black table, obviously an idea of J. B. West's, that had been crafted in the White House carpenter's shop.

What this table lacks in beauty it more than makes up for in historic importance. The piece of white parchment at its center, addressed to me, was signed by the Kennedys and all the presidential assistants, the senior staff, my staff, and old friends like chef René Verdon, head butler Charles Ficklen, and the ushers. That table is sitting in the corner of one of our bedrooms today, very unprepossessing-looking but worth a zillion dollars in history and sentiment to me. There is even Caroline's signature, and some rough pen marks, under which Jackie signed "John" on the toddler's behalf. On my very last day in June, I sat with the president for fifteen minutes while he thanked me several times for being a strong support system. He knew I would have walked into fire for him, and he knew that I would have for Jackie, too, in spite of the last tense months. He laughed when I told him that his special assistant Kenny O'Donnell had told me that my idea of going out to Chicago to work but also to run for public office on the Democratic ticket was nothing short of asinine, that I'd be "fired in ten minutes by the machine out there before I even got started." Kenny nipped my political aspirations in the bud rather early that way, but of course he was right. I wasn't tough enough.

Nancy Tuckerman, one of Jackie's roommates at Farmington, took over my job, not as chief of staff but as social secretary. She was the opposite of me—quiet, soft-spoken, not a zealot, and a person with no international diplomatic experience. Obviously, Jackie welcomed a change from the overly strong dose of managing I had given her. The avalanche of folders going up to Mrs. Kennedy's bedroom ceased. The pushings and pleadings by me, the overzealous staffer, ceased. Jackie was happy, and Nancy was happy to be there. She was to spend the rest of Jackie's life as her assistant, an invaluable part of her life and her happiness.

My family was happy to have me calling them again without my being in a crisis mode every time.

Jackie left almost immediately after my departure to spend the summer on the Cape, as I flew to Chicago to begin a new life in the business world, learning the home furnishings business, with an office in the Merchandise Mart. Jackie called me several months later in Chicago for a personal chat. She sounded so utterly happy and proud, so like the old Jackie. "You won't believe it, but I'm going campaigning to Texas with Jack next week, and I'm doing it because I want to. I'm even glad I'm going! I know this is hard to believe, but believe it. I'm anxious to hit the campaign trail again. Did you ever expect to hear me say that, Tish?"

I was delighted to hear the note of genuine happiness in her voice. The last time I had talked to her had been a couple of months earlier, right after she had suffered a miscarriage, and there is no way to describe the gloom that had enshrouded her voice then. Now she was so exuberant, I suddenly knew that her marriage was going well. In a way, this was why she was calling me. Things must be good in their relationship, I could tell.

It was cruel fate that the next time I would speak to Jackie and return to the White House, just one week later, would be to help with the state funeral plans for President Kennedy.

I had just sat down to lunch with *Town & Country* magazine editor in chief Henry Sell at the Mid-America Club atop the Prudential Building skyscraper. In the middle of our chicken crepes, a waiter brought us some more wine and said, "I can't believe it. Someone has shot the president."

Within five hours I was back at the White House, to spend the next two weeks assisting with the funeral arrangements and then helping Lady Bird's staff settle into the first lady's offices. It was all part of a dream sequence. Hundreds of people were walking around those corridors silently, numbly. They used to be such happy, bustling, noisy corridors. Now people moved slowly, bowed, and when they spoke, they whispered, as if afraid their emotions would burst forth. It was eerie. I got the Black Watch Highlander Regiment to come back to Washington for the funeral, answered telephones, and even selected the president's coffin from the undertaker's brochure of selections, because Bobby Kennedy informed me that no one in the family had the time to make that decision, and I should "just go ahead and make it." The undertaker was miffed because I selected a modest, mid-priced casket, but no one would ever see it; it would always be covered with the American flag. I knelt in prayer in the East Room, where we had given so many wonderful parties, but where today the body of John Kennedy lay in state in a flag-enshrouded coffin, with an honor guard standing at attention at the four corners. Jackie moved quietly in and out of the White House rooms for short periods, greeting people, telling them to be strong, standing straight herself, her face ashen white, and with those big dark eyes never having looked so vacant. She planned that funeral, every second of it, following the plan for Abraham Lincoln's, and the result was the most solemn, majestic two days this country has ever seen. Every head of state who could get on a plane came. Somehow they were all met by the State Department, taken care of, and set off to march in the funeral procession. Jackie received them in the Red Room after the funeral, with Teddy Kennedy in his morning coat and striped pants standing to her right, and chief of protocol Angier Biddle Duke, dressed the same way, standing on her left to handle the introductions.

No one needs to be reminded of the poignancy of the pictures of the children standing on the steps of St. Matthews Cathedral, while little John stood saluting his father's coffin as it went by. He had seen many military salutes in the White House. He knew what it meant, even if he had to be prompted to use his right hand instead of his left to make it. It became the picture of the century, as far as many people were concerned. And through it all, on that day of burial at Arlington Cemetery, there was the haunting symbol of the widow Jackie, slim, beautiful, and with a heavy black veil dramatizing the sadness that lay beneath it. She taught the nation how to mourn that day: not one pause, not one slip, not one departure from dignity and grace.

Chicago

When my White House career ended, my friends asked, "Where next, Letitia?" I had lived in Geneva, Paris, Rome, New York, and Washington— not to mention Omaha, Nebraska. At a good-bye party given for me in Washington, friends took bets on my next destination. "It will be London," one of them said, "I have no doubt about it." Another guessed Madrid. Another said, "No, it's time for the New World. I'll wager it will be either be Buenos Aires or Rio."

I outfoxed them all. I went to Chicago.

You don't need Frank Sinatra singing that song about Chicago to remind you that it's a wonderful town. It just is. I went there to learn the business world at Ambassador Kennedy's suggestion, made to me before he was incapacitated by a stroke at the end of 1961. "You don't know a damn thing about business," he had lectured me one day in my White House office. "You've led a life like an overdecorated cake, with layers of whipped cream and sugar roses."

He was right. I had spent most of my life in the unreal world of international diplomacy, walking on only the finest of Aubusson and Persian carpets, sitting beneath eighteenth-century Venetian or Waterford crystal chandeliers, and working at desks previously owned by eighteenth-century French or Italian nobles. Great chefs had prepared my meals, my clothes often came from European designers, and I was whisked around during my European years in ambassadorial limousines or in my own car with diplomatic license plates, which allowed me to park anywhere. I would often wonder later in my life why my standard of living was so much higher in my twenties and thirties. Is it not supposed to improve as you age and rise in rank?

So now I was to learn the business world. As far back as I can remember, everyone kept advising me to learn this and that, when I thought I had learned a lot already. At this rate I'd be going to my grave in the process of learning, or maybe I would someday become "the most learned person in the world." My new office was in the Merchandise Mart, a Kennedy-owned giant of a building, a labyrinth of four million square feet of office space and showrooms of the home furnishings world. I was going to work for the management of this gigantic enterprise. As a member of the Mart's executive staff, it was my job to promote the wholesale markets held there every month, with thousands of buyers, architects, interior designers, manufacturers, retailers, and press coming to Chicago to see what was being offered for sale, to buy and resell to the public.

After leaving the White House in June 1963, I had flown straight to Chicago, without taking any time off. I had to start my new job at the Merchandise Mart at once, and I had only a three-day weekend to settle into a small rented apartment that I had not even seen on the Near North Side, overlooking Lincoln Park and the monumental redstone mansion that was the cardinal's residence. Of course, Regina Connell Baldrige materialized at once from "back East," donned a housedress, and in one day scrubbed everything in my small North State Parkway apartment to a shining whiteness, as well as unpacked all my luggage and boxes. When any of her children made a household move, Mother always appeared to do the dirty work, even putting shelf paper in all the drawers and cabinets. Then she returned to Washington, Connecticut, where she and my father were now living. But before she left, she always gave me a big hug and a kiss, and the same refrain: "You know, darling, some day you're going to have to stop all this jumping around and get married. A glamorous job doesn't keep you warm on bitterly cold nights."

The Mart in that era was an intriguing mecca for home furnishings retailers, manufacturers, the contract market, architects, designers, carpet mill reps, upholstery fabrics companies, lighting fixture designers, and lamp and accessory manufacturers for the home—and everything else imaginable, from tiny porcelain ashtrays to giant armoires and from area rugs to chandeliers. Every week there seemed to be another national market to prepare for—one week it was furniture, the next it was floor coverings, the next it was accessories, another fabric, and another Contract Market, where the best of contemporary design and good taste in office furnishings were presented to wholesale buyers and interior designers. The home furnishings press covered these doings with enthusiasm. I fed them news and photographs, and even wrote articles for reporters at the smaller publications to print under their own names. (I didn't mind the extra work; at least the news of the market would be accurate.) I made sure that the people who had "come to market" were wined, dined, and happy as they learned what the public would be seeing and buying a year hence.

I had to cover so much acreage in any given day around the Mart corridors, and it was the easiest building in America in which to become lost. I longed for a bicycle or a pair of skates during those twelve-hour days. Joe Kennedy had purchased the giant warehouse from Marshall Field for a song in the depression of the 1930s, and the space rentals had been paying all the family bills ever since. Wally Ollman was the big boss of the Mart. Tom King was second in command; he impressed me greatly for several reasons, including being married to the glamorous blond Olympic Gold Medal figure skater Barbara Ann Scott. Harry Finkel was my number three professor of this new world of the home furnishings industry. Sarge Shriver worked there for several years, and other Kennedys from several generations spent time there, too, learning how the markets worked and enjoying their profits.

There was no bigger culture shock for me than to come directly from the nation's capital to the Mart, where I was an oddity and the subject of much gossip among the people running the showrooms. I decided to make friends with all of them. They were curious. It was a kind of "What in hell is she doing here?" atmosphere, but when they saw that I knew what hard work was, they changed their opinion. I made new friends everywhere, from the doormen to the waitresses in the restaurants to the managers and assistants in the showrooms on all floors. I was determined to become likeable in their eyes, and admired professionally, not just as a product of the Kennedy era.

I really loved it. The town was as male as you can get, full of energy, vigor, strength, and vitality. One Mart official explained it to me: "No pantywaist officials here, none of that striped-pants, cookie-cutter diplomatic stuff, no b.s. here." When I went out there at the end of 1963, Chicagoans in general welcomed me; there were thousands of Kennedy fans around, and the president had just been assassinated. But they also thought I was a bit strange. Who would want to come to Chicago after the White House, New York, Paris, and Rome? In the 1960s this city had a pronounced but totally unnecessary inferiority complex. Probably thanks to television and jet travel, midwesterners no longer dressed differently from easterners. The midwestern accent had become less pronounced in a world unified by television. Chicago had awakened to its own charms, its booming business, incredible museums and concert halls, magnificent architectural history, and the unchallenged beauty of its lakefront.

Yes, the winters were cruel, but they lasted only four months, and if others could survive the gusts of icy snow blown by sixty-mile-an-hour winds into one's face, then so could I. Everyone had his or her own way of surviving. Besides, after living through the heatless, hot-waterless European winter of 1946–47, I believed I could take anything.

Joe Kennedy would have been proud of me. Right away I became an enthusiastic promoter of the Mart and the whole city, too. I made a diverse group of new friends, became a weekly columnist for the *Chicago Daily News*, and was proud of my friendship with people like Irv Kupcinet, the legendary *Sun-Times* columnist and TV host, and the marvelous, indefatigable Eppie Lederer (aka "Ann Landers") as well as her sister, Pauline Phillips ("Dear Abby").

I began working on the Mart's big markets and then opened my own public relations company, so that I could do the work the Mart wanted me to do, but much more besides. I could take on other accounts. Bursting with energy and ambition, I christened my new company "Letitia Baldrige Enterprises, Inc." My first clients were all from the American home furnishings industry, but gradually I took on international companies in the field, then clients from any business that wanted me. I wanted to put up a sign on my door saying: "Enthusiastic, eager, good press release writer, and know how to seat a dinner by rank for a thousand."

My office on the nineteenth floor of the Mart, overlooking the Chicago River and Lilliputian in scale, was a point of immense pride. No ormolu-trimmed eighteenth-century antiques this time. Instead, it was furnished with Knoll Associates black metal and oak-veneer modern office furniture. I felt like a little girl who had suddenly grown up. I decorated it in charcoal gray, bright red, and chrome, with hot red accessories, file cabinets, and telephones. Even the IBM electric typewriters were specially ordered in red. I used a big Scandinavian rug symbolizing "fire" on the floor. Today, my bright red and charcoal gray office in the Mart would seem pedestrian and unexciting to people in the business world, but then it was very *avant-garde* in a field dominated by industrial green and gray. People came from all over the Mart to peer inside at my unusual little space, and to chuckle over the modern graphics on the wall. Clients sat in my fiery red wool womb-shaped Kroll chair or Herman Miller black chrome swivel chairs and selected their reading material from a new Warren Platner coffee table—a large round glass disk on a base that looked like aluminum sheaves of wheat. Back then, part of being young and full of ideas was to be out front in everything. I had a Danish sculpture on my Platner table—a tall wooden totem pole of red and black disks, and other objects to catch and hold the eye. I had become familiar with contemporary design and fallen in love with it, such a change from my previous obsessiveness with the eighteenth century. Wally Ollman gave me an excellent rental deal and allowed me free full use of all his support machines, such as copiers, calculators, and mimeograph and Xerox machines.

Mine was the only office on the accessories showroom floor. No neighbor on our floor was like any other. Holiday candles were carried in a showroom next door, bathroom accessories down the way, decorative dogs next to that, and lines of stemware and flatware across the hall. Getting to know all of the showroom managers was educational, and pleasant, too. I learned what moved each market, how a product progresses from the design stage to the manufacturing one, then into the wholesale marketplace, and finally to the consumer. Everything was designed many months ahead, and sold from six months to a year and a half in advance to designers and retailers.

I successfully lassoed a crackerjack secretary, Angela Gillespie, a tall, slim, devout Catholic, whose patience and tact were to be put to the test every day of her life. I think she must have prayed a lot to keep our clients paying us and to keep her fast-moving boss from ending up in real fiscal trouble. No one used the term "executive assistant" in those days. Secretaries were well trained; everyone had enormous respect for them; unlike the electronic world to come, they had hearts. As my accounts and responsibilities grew, I talked Quaker Oats, a new client with their headquarters in the Mart, into hiring a secretary to work just for me on my work for them. Her name was Sue Tobin (this time a peppy blonde). I wrote romantic copy on everything from Quaker's dog food to their famous oatmeal ("Ladies, do you realize you can use your leftover breakfast oatmeal to make a complexion mask with remarkable results for your skin?"). I put attractive young models into ski suits and photographed them around a roaring fire, having an après-ski pancake party, made with Quaker Oats pancake mix and maple syrup. Then I sent out a "Pancake Party for Après-Ski" press kit, with photographs and recipes, and got enormous pickup on it all over the country.

My door into the corridor at the Mart was lettered "Letitia Baldrige Enterprises, Inc." It made me euphoric every time I looked at it. It meant much more to me than if the door had been lettered "Jacqueline Kennedy's Office." This was mine! And it was such an ego inflater to hear someone else answer the red telephones with the name of my company, and to listen to a secretary protecting *me* when my schedule imploded, apologizing on my behalf with little white lies, just as I had apologized with great big white lies on behalf of my bosses for twenty years.

I managed to publish another book, an autobiography, *Of Diamonds and Diplomats*, and stole some time to promote it all over the country. I was astonished when it hopped onto the best-seller list right away. I kept running into

Jacqueline Susann, the best-selling woman novelist of the time, who traveled with her promoter husband to most of the same cities as me. We became good friends after sitting for hours in the reception areas of radio stations and newspapers, as well as the never-green "green rooms" of TV studios, waiting to go on camera for interviews. She was extremely nice and sweet, but her husband, Irving, kept prompting her to say sexy, brash, even shocking things. He fed her lines, which she dutifully memorized, but she didn't look happy doing it. It was plain to see she was his puppet. When she wasn't "on" with the press, she was delightful, but when she went into the studio and the little red light came on the TV camera, she instantly metamorphosed into a sexy, hard, wisecracking, vulgar woman—just like the heroines in her books. I will never forget how vulnerable and nice she really was, and how sad I felt when she died an early death from cancer.

As my public relations business grew, so did my freelance writing assignments for major magazines, and my lectures for women's clubs and town halls all over America. My articles and appearances inevitably centered on my embassy experiences, the White House, Jackie-Jackie-Jackie, and my role as one of the earliest women business owners to make it on her own. I was paid grandiose fees from $250 to $500 for these lectures, plus expenses. I didn't charge anything to the nonprofits, and word got around, so of course my annual income from lecturing was small, but my crown in heaven grew more sparkling.

I enjoyed making these public appearances. There was an adrenaline rush when first facing the audience, a time to size up their faces, and a window of opportunity to win them over to my side before losing them. Once I had three-quarters of the audience half-smiling, I knew I had won them.

I frankly never envisaged falling in "marriage-type" love in Chicago. I had had relationships abroad of an unbelievably romantic nature, but somehow I knew that walking along hand in hand by the Seine in Paris, or lying listening to the whispering pines at Ostia, or to the waves lapping at our boat on the island of Elba, was not what marriage was all about. My getting married was always foremost in my mother's mind, but it certainly was not in mine. I was doing fine without it. I was thirty-seven, and I was not resigned to being single—I was *happy* being single. I was invited out all the time, but had grown tired of divorced men who gave me a sob story about their sad state of affairs every minute they spent with me, never realizing that the woman they were with might have stories of her own she would have enjoyed sharing. I had also grown tired of bleary-eyed men whose breath smelled of alcohol when they picked me up on a date, and who became unbelievably boring within an hour and a half. The passes at the end of the evening were inevitable. A man was never too drunk not to believe that a single woman in her mid-thirties had to be hungering for a little sex—particularly with him. I was tired, too, of being seated at dinner parties between two husbands because of the shortage of eligible bachelors. I was weary of going out with my gay male friends as dates. I really preferred seeing them as friends at lunchtime, not in the evening, which only made me realize I had no serious dating possibilities.

One night, however, would change all that. Jean and John Greene invited me to dinner at their home in Lake Forest, a beautiful Chicago suburb. I would have probably ended up in Wisconsin if I had tried to drive myself, so the Greenes asked a Chicago bachelor, Bob Hollensteiner, to give me a lift in his car. He was actually invited that night just to provide wheels. He was in real estate development, had no money, was five years younger than I, and did not at all fit the profile of someone the Greenes considered to be a romantic interest. He was described to me as tall, fair-haired, broad-shouldered, very good looking, and quiet, as well as an ardent fan of the Chicago Cubs, the Bears, and the Black Hawks. He was not interested in politics, I was told. There would be no conversational topics to share concerning concerts or opera performances with this guy, I decided—not that I could have discussed the Cubs, the Bears, or the Black Hawks with him either. He was simply my transportation to Lake Forest for the party.

I discovered he was a great deal more than that, and it happened not when we were walking down a moonlit path in Giverny or watching the fading sunset over the Taj Mahal. It happened on the Edens' Expressway driving back to Chicago at the end of the party. We had not even spoken to one another at the Greenes' house because we were talking to people at opposite ends of the room. But something mysterious happened. I guess it might be characterized as chemistry, but in any case, three weeks from that very night we were engaged. Pretty speedy, but we knew it was right. Three months to the day from that dinner party, we were married in St. Jean Baptiste Church in New York, where I had gone to Mass all of the years I lived there. When you're in your thirties, you don't horse around; you've already done enough of that. Bob was a breath of fresh air, a real person, with the gift I prize most: a perfect sense of humor.

My parents couldn't believe that the daughter they had worried about all these years was getting married to a man from Chicago they had never met, never heard about, and would not meet until the day before the wedding in New York. Bob and I decided the only way to pull it off was to do it quickly, give my mother the task of organizing it on a split-second schedule, and not allow her or my father the time to think about what was happening. My two brothers, Mac and Bob, moved in on my parents like a flying commando squad to calm them down and keep them from trying to stop me; my parents had fantasized about my large "state" wedding to an ambassador, senator, or governor, at the least.

My magical mother did it again, pulling off the impossible, the perfect small wedding, in ten weeks' time. She made all the decisions herself while I remained hard at work in Chicago. To her endless questions about what to do about this and that, I said, "Mom, do it! Just do it!" And, of course, no one could have done it better.

In our eyes, St. Jean Baptiste was as magnificent as St. Peter's that day for our noon wedding. Because it was December 27, all of the Christmas decorations were splendidly fresh. Wide banks of scarlet poinsettia plants soared up from the altar steps toward the domed ceiling. Two giant, stately, fragrant fir trees flanked the altar. Our florist bill came to nothing, except for the nosegays of red flowers, ribbon, and pine cones that decorated the pew posts. (If you want to save on your florist bill, get married at Christmas, although that was not our reason for choosing a late December date.)

Since Bob had a reputation for being late, my brothers formed an escort battalion to pick up the groom and get him to the church on time. He was even ready and waiting for them. This made everyone relieved, particularly since a day and a half before he had missed his plane from O'Hare Airport to meet the parents of his fiancée for the first time. The Baldrige family, dying of curiosity and anticipation, had come to the airport to greet Letitia's intended, but the embarrassed intended was having a tough time paging us at the airport to inform us that he'd arrive on a later flight—he was still in Chicago. It was not a great way to make an impression on your future in-laws.

Bob's parents and sister Louise flew from Chicago to New York the day before the wedding, too, to be there for the rehearsal dinner. Norman and Lucille Hollensteiner were in an equal state of shock over the quick decision of their only son to marry me. Fortunately, everyone got along with everyone else. Bob turned on his considerable quiet charm with my parents and entranced them, as I knew he would. Missed airplanes were forgotten in the glow of events. The rehearsal dinner, the night before the wedding, was an immensely cheery one at Giovanni's restaurant. There's nothing like a perfect plate of pasta and a glass of *plus-que-parfait* Italian wine to turn potentially nervous people into comrades.

In those days brides over thirty years of age, even first-time ones like me, usually did not wear long white bridal gowns. It was considered slightly in poor taste; satin, lace, and chapel veils were for brides in their twenties. I wore a white silk "Costume" suit made for me by couturier Bill Blass, an old friend from my Tiffany days, along with white satin pumps and a small white mink hat with a little white veil made for me by the famous hat designer Emme. I wore white kid gloves and carried a white prayer book with white satin streamers intertwined with white orchids.

The marble church was very baroque in its splendor, and the choir sang Christmas carols as well as Bach. Bob and I knelt on two white satin-covered prie-dieux at the altar, numb from the realization that this was really happening. There was much crying at that wedding, the bride included. My fourteen-year-old niece Alice sobbed openly through the entire nuptial Mass. Mother's tears flowed freely in the front-row pew, while my father swallowed hard and noisily, trying to keep his composure. When he blew his nose from inner emotional turmoil, the sound of it reached all the way out the church to Lexington Avenue. My brothers and their wives just wanted the whole thing to be over with. I was overcome by the beauty and meaning of the religious ceremony in this incredible church, with this incredible man by my side. My special white lace wedding handkerchief finally was no longer sufficient, and Alice went to fetch me some paper tissues. I now knew why bridesmaids were so important. A *New York Times* photographer recorded us coming out of the church, and we saw the story of our wedding in the celebrity news section the next day. (Mother, of course, was incensed that the photograph and story weren't in the regular society section.) In the falling snow, we were limousine-ferried over to the Colony Club at Sixty-second and Park Avenue, where we had lunch at round tables with champagne flowing, and serenades by strolling red-coated Hungarian gypsy violinists. The toasts were monumentally good, funny, and just the right length, except for my father's, which had everyone crying again because his emotions won out over his usual wit.

For our honeymoon we flew to Phoenix to stay with the Henry Luces in their house on the grounds of the Biltmore Estates. Bob and I played tennis opposite one another, a memorable match, because we were never to play opponent singles again. The same thing happened to our bridge game with the Luces. We were intelligent enough to know our marriage could never withstand it. That week was more than a honeymoon; it was also the last time I would see HRL in a relaxed, personal way. He would die not too many months later.

Reality and work awaited us back in our undersized apartment on the Near North Side. My friends and Bob's friends, later to become "our friends," could not believe this match had ever been made, we had surprised them so completely. We were opposites in almost everything, but when the chemistry between two people is composed of dynamite mixed with dynamite, it can be very compelling. And we certainly were.

The day we came home from our honeymoon, I asked my secretary to refer to me as "Letitia Hollensteiner" in numerous calls to New York and the West Coast, but no one could cope with my new married name. Even the Mart operator, a great friend, pleaded with me to keep my maiden name. No one could understand "Hollensteiner," remember it, or spell it, so I decided to retain my maiden name for daytime and become "Mrs. Hollensteiner" for weekends and social events. Society was shocked. Nice girls didn't do this. Bob steadied the boat and managed to keep his ego intact, until some unfortunate would refer to him as "Mr. Baldrige." Then there was thunder and lightning. It was a mistake he would have to bear throughout our marriage.

Now that I was finally married, I wanted to be the perfect wife. I knew what the manual said. I had to be at my office more than an hour ahead of Bob, so I would make him breakfast and serve it to him on a tray every morning before I departed, even with a flower in a wedding-present bud vase on the tray. After ten days, he said he had only one favor in the world to ask of me. I replied, "Anything," and then he said, "Don't be offended, but would you mind stopping the breakfasts? I really don't like eating breakfast in bed, and I like to make my own anyway." Romantic behavior was not to be Bob Hollensteiner's strong suit.

We couldn't have been more different. He was a night person, I a morning one. He liked spectator sports, I liked cultural events. I adored museums and concerts. He wouldn't go to the movies of my choice. His idea of courting me was to take me to a Black Hawks ice hockey match, where my good clothes (I didn't have any other kind in those days) were regularly squirted with mustard and catsup from the people behind who couldn't control their enthusiasm—or their burgers and hot dogs. We never read the same books. Our ability to sit at the same bridge table was identical to our ability to play tennis with one another—in other words, zero possibility. I liked the mountains; he liked the beach and the sea. I insisted on promptness; he was infuriatingly late, but he would sweet-talk me, and I would forgive him at once. It is amazing, but perhaps the reason we were attracted to one another was just because we were such opposites. We appreciated one another's sense of humor, which was the basis of our happiness. When we got into a dispute, I would give a dramatic Sarah Bernhardt stage presentation. He never heard it; he would leave the apartment just as I started my angry tirade. We had to learn the blessed art of compromise, and of being able to weigh what we had on the plus side against the negative on the other side. The plus side always won out, and still does.

I thought I was too old to have children. It never occurred to me that we would have them. Lo and behold, along they came, when I was thirty-nine and again at forty-one. In those days such an advanced age for childbirth was considered scandalous (but how the pendulum was to swing in the other direction later!). I worked through the entire day both times and went into labor in the evening. It was considered scandalous, too, to work up to the moment of labor, but when you own your own company, you can do things like that. In fact, you have to.

Bob was not only absent from the labor room of the hospital, he was absent from the hospital. With the first baby, he dutifully took me to Wesley Memorial Hospital, but once across the threshold, he heard a group of women screaming at the top of their lungs. Bob showed signs of starting to pass out, so the doctor sent him home in a taxi. He went right to bed, the whole thing had been so traumatic for him, and woke up seven hours later when the doctor called to relay the good news that we had a daughter, Clare, born on March 12, 1965. Had he been forced to play the role of the new fathers of the twenty-first century in the labor room, he would have quickly been transferred to intensive care. Fortunately, his talents nevertheless displayed themselves very quickly as our babies grew. Bob was the best father they could have possibly had, always there for them, doing the things I could not because of my work. He was a great father, but even more important, their great friend.

That March, I recalled how I'd held all my friends' babies for years, admiring them, kitchy-cooing them, and predicting they would grow up to rule the world. And now I was holding a beautiful big baby that was mine. Mine! Oh, yes, and Bob's, too, of course, but every time I looked at little Clare, I could see a different member of my family in her features. I was writing my column for the *Chicago Daily News* in those days, and the topics were baby-slanted for an entire year, by which time I discovered that other people had babies, too, not just me.

I needed help from the minute baby Clare was born. Letitia Baldrige Enterprises needed my presence to survive, and as a family we needed the income my business provided. We needed someone knowledgeable and mature to take care of our newborn, Clare, and of Malcolm-to-come. We were the luckiest couple in America to be able to receive the last of the nannies allowed to enter the United States legally. Nannie Mary Eileen Pakenham, as Irish as they come, and as professional and talented a child nurse as ever existed, arrived to take over baby Clare's life, and ours as well. She walked into our apartment wearing her English gray nannie's trench coat, her gray felt nannie's hat with the enamel emblem pin of her school on the front of it, white gloves, and solid black oxfords, which were to take her over miles of Lake Michigan Drive and Lincoln Park paths in the next few years.

Baby "Malcolm to come" eventually came, two years later.

I was working long hours, getting my business going, paying for office help, but Nannie was more important than anyone on my payroll. She allowed me to work, to travel, and to feel, completely sure that the children were in safe, secure hands. Our apartment always seemed to be filled with the sounds of laughter, children playing games, and children's records being played. Bob and I managed to look the other way when our handsome new custom-made Empire striped silk draperies were embellished with traces of chocolate sauce and vanilla ice cream, thanks to a children's party.

Nannie announced she would not stay in Chicago if we did not buy her an English Sol Whitby pram, the kind used by all of the queen's children. Marshall Field's store's best top-of-the-line baby buggy was judged too inferior to be used. "I shall not be seen with one of those," she pronounced grandly. So we had to buy a Sol Whitby from London and have it shipped by boat, even traveling at its last stage through the Great Lakes to the Port of Chicago. It took the combined efforts of Sears' international customs division and the British Consulate in Chicago to get it into the country. It really was a princely vehicle, made of a dark blue waterproof wool fabric, sitting high on giant, shiny steel wheels. The inside of the hood was lined in pale green. "White in a carriage top is terrible for a baby's eyes," Nannie explained, "because it reflects the sunlight back into its face."

On Sunday night, after a weekend of my taking care of Clare and Malcolm, I couldn't tell who was happier to see Nannie walk in the door—the children or me. All of the young parents knew about her and would seek her out in Lincoln Park to ask her questions about everything from potty training to delayed speech. What they got was instant wisdom.

There was no way, having been out in the work world for seventeen years, that I would have been able to stop work when I got pregnant. That was not me. If I had been a stay-at-home mom, our children would have been warped souls, living in a household run like a public relations agency.

We had begun our married life in a small, elegant apartment at 1550 North State Parkway, but with Nannie and a baby added to the floor plan, we were bursting at the seams. Then came another great stroke of luck on the eve of the birth of our second child. We purchased from the bank estate of Marion Deering McCormick (International Harvester) her more-than-grand cooperative apartment overlooking Lincoln Park and Lake Michigan. The Lakeview Avenue apartment had been vacant since Mrs. McCormick's death several years earlier, and the heirs were anxious to close the estate. It was an immense white elephant, and with a recession dawning, no one was buying big places. They sold it to us at a ridiculously low price, just to get rid of it. Unlike the McCormick family before us, we were prepared to make do with a meager staff—a cleaning woman in the morning, Nannie, a cook called Letitia, and a butler called Bob. The black-and-white domino-patterned marble floor of the entrance hall, measuring thirty by eleven feet, made one think of roller skates or bowling alleys. There was an enormous dining room, living room, a carved-oak-paneled library, a linen room large enough to hold a seated tea party, five bedrooms with baths, and for our large "staff," a butler's pantry, servants' dining room, and four maids' rooms. It was sumptuous—palatial, in fact, with faux marbled walls, boiseries, high ceilings, lovely chandeliers, and carved wood and marble fireplaces. What Bob liked best of all was the walk-in silver vault, with a steel door and combination lock just like a large bank's. It was supposed to house the sterling silver hollowware and flatware used for entertaining. He used it for his shotguns and hunting paraphernalia, and for our liquor reserve, which had been built up during spectacular wine sales. There had probably been a staff of six in and around the apartment when the Cyrus McCormicks held sway over Chicago society. Downstairs there was a wine cellar and housing quarters for the nonexistent chauffeur.

If you used your imagination, the Lakeview Avenue apartment was fully and efficiently staffed. I would make my breakfast every day, put it on a tray, and get back into bed, pretending my imaginary French maid, Yvette, had just brought my *petit déjeuner,* along with the morning papers. I remember we moved in the day the astronauts were to walk on the moon, right in front of us, on our television sets. National euphoria set in. Even though the economy was down, the nation was very definitely up. And so was the Hollensteiner family. Those astronauts made us feel we could conquer the world.

Early on, I had so much to learn, managing a business by myself, that I spent as much time learning from my mistakes as I did serving the clients. It was hard to make a budget and stick to it. In getting my office organized and equipped, the debit side exceeded the profit side on the ledger for over two years. This unduly upset my brother Mac, a future secretary of commerce and the consummate businessman. He would come to visit us in Chicago, immediately go over my books, and give me a blistering lecture on not sufficiently controlling costs in my business.

"Jeez, Tish, do you know what you are doing?"

I felt I was studying for an MBA without being at graduate school every time Mac came to check up on me. I did not resent his critique of my business style, though; I needed it, and I was so grateful to be able to interrupt him during the day when I needed an answer to something puzzling. He was always there, on the other end of the telephone—perhaps wiping his brow with his hand in frustration, but always there. That's what brothers are for.

I didn't have to worry about how to proceed in handling the PR accounts once I landed them, thanks, I suppose, to my experience at Tiffany's, as well as the White House and the embassies. I simply had to turn on the same creative juices I had used then, and the formula would always work just fine. As the years passed, I had a growing sense of security and accomplishment. Once you make the client think he or she is the most important part of the universe, much more so than other clients, once you master the art of writing the perfect press release, once you learn to juggle all the clients, keep in constant touch with them, feed them information, ideas, and encouragement, you have found a formula for success.

I had a mixed bag of products to promote. There were the home furnishings markets in the Mart, of course, and I began another aspect of my career, training the First National Bank's and the Northern Trust's main-floor personnel in customer relations. Now I had another career aspect to add to my résumé. Then there were new clients in the French fashion industry as well as pots and pans. I was ready for *anything*.

I was thrilled to receive a telephone call from Paris saying Madame Grès, one of the greatest of all the French dress designers, was coming to Chicago for the first showing of her collection in America, bringing her models from Paris with her, at incredible expense. It was to be a black-tie evening benefit, held in the Drake Hotel, and would I arrange the whole project?

Would I! I had not thought of Madame Grès since White House days when Jackie Kennedy wore one of her dresses, copied by Oleg Cassini, to the White House dinner for Nobel Prize laureates.

We all worked fiercely on this show. Madame Grès had invested so much money, and it was such a big event in the fashion industry, it had to be a success. I have never seen such magnificent, haughty, skinny models. We rehearsed them over and over, to give them a feeling for the narrow runway in the darkened ballroom. I wrote the commentary, practiced it along with the show, and everything seemed to work. Madame Grès saw me working my head off all day.

"My dear," she said in a concerned voice, "you look tired. And are you slightly pregnant?" I hardly showed at all with our second child, having put on only fourteen pounds, and on a big frame the weight gain was not really visible. I assured her I was indeed pregnant.

"How lovely, how wonderful," she continued, smiling like a grandmotherly Madonna. "And when is it due? You're so small, it must be months away."

"It was actually due last month, Madame Grès." Malcolm truly was a whole month late as of the show time. If he had been born when he was supposed to, I would have been raring to go a month after his birth, and perfectly able to do her fashion show.

The designer looked as though she were going to faint without delay. Two aides rushed to steady her. She told them in rapid French I would obviously produce my baby in the middle of the show. It would all be ruined. And the danger! The danger of something happening, with the birth in the middle of the show! *Oh, Mère de Dieu!* Then she instructed one of her staff to call her lawyer in Paris immediately to see what lawsuits were possible when a baby was born in the middle of the show, with a resulting injury to mother or child.

I sailed through the commentator's role with ease, before a thousand people. I wore a rather ravishing dress myself that night—a pale pink caftan, richly embroidered with pearls, crystals, and silver embroidery at the neck, sleeves, and hem of the skirt. The baby did not come until a week later. By now he was so late, he was big enough to get up and go play football. Madame Grès sent him a beautiful present from Paris, and wrote me she had said many prayers for me and for the baby—and I think, probably, for her show, as well.

I orchestrated the openings of several of the city's luxury stores on Michigan Avenue's "Golden Mile." Tiffany opened a boutique on this choice avenue of the city, and it was old-home week when I began to do promotional launches for them. It felt good to be back in the world of gold, diamonds, rubies, emeralds, and sapphires. Elizabeth Arden opened its Chicago salon a year ahead of Tiffany, bringing out to Chicago the imperial duchess of the beauty business, the company's founder and president, Miss Arden. She was an octogenarian contemporary and competitor of Helena Rubenstein's (but a million miles ahead of her in social graces and clout). It was several years before Estée Lauder gained enough success and prestige in her field to be mentioned in the same breath.

I started working on Arden's Chicago "Red Door" opening a year in advance. We needed to build some excitement, make people anticipate the opening. It took what seemed like an eternity to finish construction on the lovely little building with its famous trademark red door. When the sidewalk was torn up and the hard hats were out front working with cranes, jackhammers, and cement trucks, I lured the press into covering the opening of the Arden windows. We drew back the curtains at a signal from two trumpeteers, and there were stunning live mannequins standing in the windows amid all the dust and plaster, clad in Oscar de la Renta ball gowns and luscious décolleté nightgowns and peignoirs. That may sound old hat today, but back in 1965 it was considered a news story, and the photographs of the glamorous girls waving at the burly guys in hard hats made the press all over the world. The models stayed put all day, to the delight of the crowds passing by on Michigan Avenue. Suddenly everyone knew that Elizabeth Arden, with its designer clothes, hundreds of beauty products in the famous pink jars, and its spa and beauty treatments, was coming to Chicago.

The grand opening of the store was the social-fashion-retail big news of the day. I learned many things from Miss Arden. One of them was how to use kindness to disguise a really tough move against someone. I had invited "le tout Chicago" society for the open house. The Andy Frain Ushers, the main security agency in town, furnished us with a large number of its crowd control people, all in bright blue uniforms. The head of the Andy Frain organization stationed one of the ushers (probably his son) in the very front and central space, just inside the door, in the most definitely conspicuous spot. The young man had a serious acne problem, and Miss Arden took me aside. "We can't have that young man with his skin problems upsetting all of our guests. Our business is about skin, you know."

"What do you want me to do?" I asked, dreading the answer.

"I know exactly what to do," she announced with confidence. "Just watch what I do." With that, she took the young man by the hand and led him into a back room, where the guests' furs were hung on racks. I followed. She got out a jar of her famous "8-Hour Beauty Cream" and put it all over his face and neck, rubbing it in carefully with deft finger movements. He was stunned. He didn't know what was happening to him.

"Now you put this on every morning and every night," she said kindly, "and you will notice a quick change in your skin condition. This jar of cream is for you and you alone. You are a fine, capable young man, so I want to give you a job today with real responsibility. You seem to have more maturity than the others, so stay back here, guarding the furs of our guests." He was now totally out of sight, and he had not been humiliated. On the contrary, he felt honored. Smart Miss Arden!

Then she located an unblemished, handsome usher and dragged him into the prime spot at the front door. After hearing him say a few words—poorly—Miss Arden ordered him not to talk to the guests as they arrived, other than to say "Good afternoon," but to smile broadly. She called the Andy Frain Ushers organization a couple of days later and asked to speak with the young man who had the serious acne problem. She got him on the phone and said she wanted to know how he was after using her skin treatment, and was he keeping it up? She cared, she really did. He reported that his skin was much better. She then confided to me that her 8-Hour Cream was truly magical. She used it on her own racehorses' sore legs and hooves, and it always cured the problem. She did not promote this fact with her skin product clients; women buying expensive face creams do not exactly wish to identify with a horse's problems. Elizabeth Arden was one of the greatest characters I ever knew.

What a coup it was to land Sears as a client! I had grown up in the Midwest, thinking of Sears as a store for automobile tires, washing machines, and cheap clothing. In the 1960s and '70s, it grew into a retail giant, opening first-class stores ("A" stores) all over America. I was asked to be their consultant on women's activities and organizations. With over 800 stores, their power in the markets was formidable. When a new superstore would open, I would address women's groups on the subject of everything from writing books to organizing clubs that serve the community, and from career choices for young women to the flavors of baby food Jackie Kennedy fed her son John in the White House. The audience questions were predictable. Other "celebrities" would appear at the same store openings. Movie star Vincent Price (of horror-movie or Shakespeare fame—take your pick) and gorgeous redheaded Arlene Dahl were often part of the group, and we became very close friends. Vincent set up an original art program, Arlene promoted her wig collection, and we all promoted Sears' fine diamond jewelry inventory—the largest of any store in America, including Tiffany's. Arlene would tell me about her husbands, and Vincent would fill us in on the latest art scene, as well as Hollywood antics. Those were the very best of days for Sears, and I enjoyed being part of the "traveling road show" the three of us put on. The power of Sears's buying system guaranteed success for whatever item they were stocking in their stores. The momentum was there—in the mere act of buying something for all 800 stores—but Sears was also the perfect case study of a store "trading up." Watching their management strategy and planning operations in stocking the stores with appropriate merchandise, whether it was tires, overalls, cosmetics, or diamond rings, was another year of graduate business school. I was still learning. I always would be.

The Mart sent me to Europe on a large project under its sponsorship, promoting a forthcoming international home furnishings fair, called INTER-CON (the International Contract Market in Home Furnishings), to be held in Chicago. It was my job to woo foreign home furnishings manufacturers who should logically be interested in expanding their markets to come to Chicago, rent space at the giant convention hall, McCormick Place, and show and sell their wares, which had never before been seen in America. The time was ripe, even if we were about to enter a recession. Interest in international design was at its height, a natural outcome of the product-starved war years. Prize-winning furniture designers were just beginning to achieve the fame couture designers already enjoyed, but the western European manufacturers, except for Italian and Scandinavian designers, still had a long way to go in the global interior design picture. INTERCON was a most ambitious global economy effort on the Mart's part. Because of my languages and European experience, I was the lucky one chosen to make the selling trip. There was a large territory to cover—England, France, Spain, Germany, Austria, Italy, Sweden, and Scandinavia. My mission—not impossible—was to address groups of home furnishings manufacturers and designers (always men) who were invited to listen to my pitch and have a few cocktails, learn about IN-TERCON, and hopefully sign up to exhibit their designs in Chicago.

I was elated to be able to use my foreign languages for an important seven-week trip like this one. When I couldn't speak the language of the country where I was making a speech, I made sure that a very competent interpreter was there, translating every major point in my address. My female presence was not only strange and innovative, but also intimidating to the audience, or as the interpreter reported in Austria, "a little scary." One very frank and undiplomatic question that a Finnish designer and manufacturer put to me, one to which I had become accustomed, was, "What kind of authority gave you the authority to deal on this level with men?" I always answered such questions with a laugh, even if I felt ready to don boxing gloves. I would usually say, "You know, I've had a lot of experience [wanting to add, 'a lot more than you'll ever have, buster!'']," and then I would say, "Don't forget, I was raised by tough older brothers" (translation: It's advisable not to mess with me). They thought that was very funny, but I could tell they liked my sense of humor. The wives of these chauvinist protestors were at home, perhaps seeing to their children and doing their nails, but with no idea of ever crossing an ocean to speak to men on a serious business matter like international trade. In Germany, the men were so uncomfortable that they hid behind the pillars of the Munich hotel salon where I spoke. I broke out laughing at their intense shyness. Many of them came from small German towns where furniture factories were situated. I finally flushed them out from behind the pillars by having the interpreter explain the "Don't shoot until you see the whites of their eyes" story in American history. In Madrid in the beautiful Chamber of Commerce Palace, some sixty-plus men, all very formally dressed, refused to sit down unless I sat down first. Their code of manners prohibited them from remaining seated in the presence of a standing lady. I told them that I could not successfully address such an endlessly long table seated, because I would only be able to see a few of the faces. Finally, I won that battle. I stood, and the sixty-plus sat, all very uncomfortable. I ran into one of those courtly Spaniards on Fifth Avenue seven years later. He recognized me, which I told him flattered me immensely. "Things are much better for businesswomen today in our country than they were when you were there," he said, smiling, "but in spite of the strides they have made in business, there are still some things women cannot do. It is not totally an equal world." With that, he took my right hand and kissed it with a grand flourish. I had forgotten what a hand kiss felt like. He was correct: hand-kissing is strictly for the male sex to execute, thank heavens. That's something women don't want to have to learn how to do.

In Paris I really put my foot in it. Returning to the scene of my extreme youth and my Kennedy state visit triumphs, I gave a press conference in a glittering Louis XVI salon in the Hôtel Crillon on the place de la Concorde. I recognized several members of the writing press from the Kennedy days who were still on the job. How nice to be remembered! It was a slow news day when I made my appearance, and the reporters knew the food and drinks would be first class, so more than a hundred members of the press attended. The name "Jacqueline Kennedy" was still a magic draw. I was back in my beloved Paris and delighting in the flow and rhythm of speaking French. I said they must all come to INTERCON in Chicago. I pronounced it "Ehn-tear-kon," giving the English word a clear French pronunciation. The only trouble was that the French pronounced INTERCON the same way we do—and to give it a French pronunciation was to turn it into a word of an entirely different meaning. It was to describe the sex act between two men. Here I was, urging the home furnishings industry to come to Chicago for gay sex. Direct from the mouth of the very dignified, former social secretary to the first lady of America! Howls of laughter erupted in the room. They knew I didn't realize what I had just done, and when one of the reporters from *Le*

Figaro explained it to me, I burst out laughing, too. The press conference obviously could not proceed. The room was shaking from merriment. There was no way of getting the subject, or the audience, back on track. I thanked them for coming, told them to have another drink, and said, "You must take the INTERCON brochures on the table in the back of the salon. At least you must do that for me." It was not one of my finer moments, but I remembered Clare Luce's wise advice: "Forget the horrible thing that has just happened. Put it out of your mind, because the next one will be a lot worse." Comforting.

I had learned many things in Chicago about what kind of press party really succeeds—easy parking, smiling faces at the door, flattering introductions of guests to the party hosts, good music (not too loud), pamphlets, books or press kits with the host company's latest news, five minutes maximum of speech making, lots of booze, good, simple food, and more waiters than usual to clean up cigarette butts, damp paper cocktail napkins, spilled drinks, and hors d'oeuvres toothpicks scattered in snowstorm fashion over the industrial carpet.

By now I was used to organizing and speaking at every press party we had, and lecturing on the side to women's groups and for charities. I delivered well over a hundred slide lectures in six years in Chicago on interior design and the Burlington House Awards. I had been through every kind of slide projector disaster, from cords not long enough to projector bulbs that blew up after five minutes. My brother Bob wisely said, "They would probably pay you more to hear you talk less, and that goes for any speaker on any subject. What people really want to do is talk to one another, so don't deprive them of that opportunity."

I had learned to conquer any shyness in front of an audience by chuckling all the way through my presentation at my own witticisms. It was not ego-related, but a plan to avoid dead silences if the audience wasn't laughing along with me. I also learned an absolute fundamental: if you are unknown to your audience, and so is your project, make sure everyone has a drink in hand when you give your speech, except, of course, in the morning. It's amazing how friendly, even curious, an audience becomes after a glass of wine or beer.

At rare times in a career a dream of a project lands in your lap, and it's yours alone, and it lasts for eight years. Ray Kassar, the bright young head of all the home furnishings divisions of Burlington Industries (at that time the largest textile company in the world) gave me The Burlington House Awards program—and he should have anyway, since it was my idea. It became my job to design and implement every aspect of it, a responsibility I joyfully accepted.

The program was a salute to the good taste of Americans, in the way they designed the interiors of those homes and the way they lived in their homes. It was permissible for homeowners to use interior designers to assist, but the main role in decorating the home had to have been that of the owner himself or herself. Although this program was essentially pure public relations, with no Burlington products mentioned, the fact that Burlington was the number-one company in the world in textiles, with retail floor coverings, draperies, upholstery fabrics, and furniture, made it logical to tie the company's name to awards for good taste in the home.

I invited a prominent group of women to serve on a jury panel for two years at a time, to select the winning homes, and was surprised when there was not one turndown. They were unpaid, but they looked upon the judging in New York as one of the most enjoyable moments in their whole annual schedule. There is a natural curiosity to see inside people's homes, particularly when they are located in every part of America, and decorated on every kind of budget.

The entrants would submit photos, everything from candids to layouts in fancy magazines. The photographs of each home were mounted on a large board, with the explanatory text on the back. We had from two hundred to three hundred entries per year. Each board required several minutes of study, so judging was a tedious, lengthy task. The members of the Burlington House advisory board loved their jobs, and bragged about it to all their friends. Judging took two whole days of their time, and we entertained them lavishly in the evening, at places like the "21" Club and Le Cirque. The women were a veritable who's who of society. The first chairman of the group was Mrs. Albert Lasker, philanthropist and widow of one of the founders of the advertising industry. She was succeeded by Lady Bird Johnson, a gracious lady who needs no introduction. The board members were well known—names like Nancy Reagan, Betsy Bloomingdale, Robin Duke, Dina Merrill, Ann Slater, Mrs. Philip Wrigley, Mrs. Claiborne Pell, Ann Taylor, Bonnie Swearingen, Martha Ingram—from all over the United States. I did a book for Viking called *Home*, showing the 1969 and 1970 winners. As I look at those pictures thirty years later, the homes have held up well in their design and human interest, from the humble tract house in Fargo to the rehabilitated eighteenth-century plantation on the James River, and from an authentic log cabin in Cody, Wyoming, to a raft house in Portage Bay, Washington. I will never forget the Nelson Peltz apartment, for example, with the window walls of the living room overlooking New York at its sparkling best. A huge abstract painting of bright red, yellow, and white was just meant for this room. Since there was no wall space, only windows, the Peltz solution was to hang it in the exact center of the ceiling, where it would be admired by anyone sitting down on the comfortable sofas and chairs. What a great idea! Even if there's a clutter of paintings on your walls and you have one more to show, why not put it on the ceiling? After all, Michelangelo used ceilings.

The correspondence on the BH Awards was formidable. Young people with space problems asked where they could get a special kind of room divider that would transform the dining room into a nursery after the luncheon guests had left. People would send in Polaroids of their homes, hoping they would be judged winners. Some of them were in such bad taste, we would wince, then laugh, and apologize mentally to the people who had sent in the entries for having laughed. Taste is a very personal thing. Who's to say our trained taste in the interior design field was any better than the woman's who proudly papered her dining room walls with old White Tower Hamburger newspaper ads? One woman sent in her lover's home (he was married at the time), because she was certain that by the time the awards were announced, her man would have divorced his wife, and she, the paramour, would now be the proud mistress of his house. I got right into the middle of a spat between the husband, his wife, and his girlfriend on that one. It concluded with the husband forcing me to tell his girlfriend that there was no way he was planning on divorcing his wife, and therefore, would I please withdraw the house from the Burlington House Awards at once? The poor girlfriend dissolved into hysterics on the phone. I tried to comfort her, not an easy thing to do under these circumstances. I gave her a thirty-minute therapeutic "cheer-up" of ways in which she could meet nice new men who were eligible, meaning not married to anyone else at the time. She had stopped crying and was thinking creatively by the time I hung up. I frankly could not continue taking on the personal problems of every person I met or who wrote to me, but I could not help doing it anyway. Instead of moving away from the involvement, I would plunge into it, wanting to know all the details so I could offer advice and solace, whether it was desired or not. Perhaps I was trying to be an unpaid combination of Ann Landers and Laura Schlessinger.

One of the biggest nightmares in my professional career occurred with the Burlington House Awards. For the annual judging, I would compose two letters each year, one telling the losers how sorry we were that they lost, but "thank you anyway for entering the competition, and you do have a lovely home," and the other saying "You're one of the winners, (hallelujah), and you must plan to come to Chicago for the big announcement in January." I would give the two letters to our mailing house, plus the list of names and addresses of the two groups of recipients. One year the mailing house confused the two lists, sending out a couple hundred letters of congratulations to the losers, not the winners, and the losers' announcement letters to the twenty-five winners. I had to get all of those losers who had received winners' letters personally on the telephone to explain, apologize, and pull a Sarah Bernhardt drama of remorse. I organized a squad of my friends with lovely voices and with acting ability, and had them come to my office, where we manned the phones for twelve hours, working from coast to coast, apologizing for having sent the wrong letter. I made them act out that we, the program heads, had practically died from the humiliation we put everyone through. My friends did a terrific job. We narrowly missed a major public relations disaster, but since people are much nicer than we give them credit for, I received a tongue-lashing and a threat or two from only one homeowner, who insisted I make her a winner anyway, since she had already told all her friends and given a newspaper interview about her award.

Every year there was excellent coverage of the Burlington House Awards program in every newspaper and interior design publication in the United States. It was featured on numerous TV programs and was a constant topic of conversation in design circles. People recognized the Burlington Industries logo in department stores and bought the products that bore it because of the snob reputation of the program. It was indirectly very financially rewarding for the company.

Ely Callaway, at that time president of the company (later the CEO of Callaway Wines, and subsequently the president and founder of the Big Bertha Golf Club business) was impressed. He persuaded Bob and me to move to New York, a major decision. We worked it out. Bob was to go to a new job at James Landauer, a star company in real estate consulting, and my new job was to be director of consumer affairs for Burlington Industries, a job title that was very much à la mode at that time. (Nowadays, the only "consumer" job seems to be "consumer relations," which means that after being kept on hold on the telephone for forty minutes, you are finally able to reach a human being to complain about your order.) Ely Callaway told me very frankly that he was under pressure to appoint a woman to top management because of the increasingly loud voice of the women's movement. The consumer mail was heavy with questions about where the women were in BI executive management and on the board of directors. (The women's movement had a vigorous letter campaign going against every major corporation, threatening real trouble if the companies didn't immediately hire women at all levels.) I decided I wouldn't mind being the solitary member of my sex at this big corporation. The pay was far better than in any previous job. The perks and benefits were glorious, with stock options and so forth, and I felt this was going to be it. Instead of fretting about paying salaries and bills in my own company when it was a bad month, the corporation would be paying the salaries. It was a tough decision—and mine to make, because Bob did not care one way or another. Moving back to New York meant leaving the first friends we had made together. That was the big minus.

It was tough saying good-bye to Chicago. We had packed so much into six short years. Favorite restaurants were to disappear forever. We treasured every "last time"—like eating hamburgers in the Wells Street restaurant carpeted with peanut shells, and playing tennis on the ridiculously named Wapsi Valley Tennis Club courts, surrounded by the biggest skyscrapers on Michigan Avenue. Three years after we had left, the tennis club was no more, replaced by the giant John Hancock skyscraper. There would be no more dances on an occasional Friday night at the Casino Club, no more weekends with the P. K. Wrigleys at Lake Geneva, Wisconsin, wallowing in luxury, which has always been my favorite extracurricular activity. We would miss the wonderful, loyal friends we had made in Chicago, and never again would we have such a grandiose space as our white-elephant apartment on Lakeview Avenue.

When you leave a city where you've been happy, you give up a lot. And hopefully you've left behind a lot, too. I had left New York as a party of one. I was now returning to it as a party of four, plus a nannie. A lot can happen in five years. You can get married, have two kids, and open your own business without even wondering what hit you.

Manhattan

On a Saturday morning in September 1969, we made a flying jump from Chicago's O'Hare Airport to New York's La Guardia, "we" being Bob, Letitia, Clare, Malcolm, Nannie, and the pram, which by now had taken on a life of its own. We had moved to New York at just the right time. Real estate values were depressed, and thanks to my husband following the scent of a good deal with his real estate nose, we were able to buy another grand apartment at an incredibly low price.

The move happened so fast, it was almost painless. Forty-eight hours after our arrival, it was Monday morning, and a new start for the entire family. On this momentous day, Bob started a new real estate consulting job at Landauer Associates, I began my new job at Burlington Industries, Clare began her first day of school—kindergarten at the Convent of the Sacred Heart at Ninety-first and Fifth Avenue—and Nannie took twenty-two-month-old baby Malcolm to the Diller Quaile School of Music to experience his first day in a class of his peers. Each member of the family felt he or she had the hardest adjustment, and that he or she had been most impacted by the move. It was probably a draw.

In my previous move from Washington to Chicago, I had been single, and concerned only with me, myself, and I. Now, just six years later, I had an important job in New York and was responsible for yanking my new family out of a comfortable situation into a strange new city. Female tongues in Chicago clucked disapprovingly. "But your husband," they would sputter in my direction, "you are forcing him to move. It's just not right!" Well, it was right. If you don't make decisions to move forward in life, you can become quickly covered in mildew. This move was a question of possibly making some money and having a future. Bob and I were a team, not two separate individuals, and we both agreed that moving to New York City and my job with Burlington was a great boon for the family. It was no longer "I" but "we." It was no longer "my" but "our."

It wasn't easy at first. I felt like a juggler, with very precious balls up in the air, none of which I dared drop. One ball marked "Family" got the first toss, swiftly followed by a ball marked "Career, i.e., Pay Your Bills," another one was marked "Friends," another marked "Continuing Education and Enrichment," and I added one more to the set of juggling balls—"Volunteer Service"—out of an inherent sense of guilt for having so many good things happening to me.

Changing cities, lifestyles, jobs, friends, and dry cleaners is an act of disruption and chaos until quite suddenly, everything begins to work. When the right directories and files are opened, the programs start to function. As a group, I knew that our family had the energy and the motivation to take New York for all it was worth. It was exhilarating to go that fast. I even rode my bicycle around the Upper East Side for shopping and church. We feasted on the offerings of New York. If there was a giant Macy's parade on Thanksgiving Day, we were there. Fireworks over the Hudson on the Fourth of July? We were there. Life was filled with weekend visits to the giant whale, the great elephants, and other wild animal trophies in the American Museum of Natural History. We took the children ice-skating in Central Park in the winter, and picnicking in Central Park in the summer. We went regularly to the famous shows—the Christmas Show at Radio City Music Hall, the circus at Madison Square Garden, and Greenwich Village to see Bil Baird's great puppet shows. I dragged the children to museums almost every weekend until they formed a kids' rebellion against cultural indoctrination, saying they absolutely refused to look at one more painting or sculpture.

"Mom, did it ever occur to you that we'll never be interested in the same things you are? Would it matter so much?"

The answer was, No, it would not. If they resisted my attempts at inculcating them with history, I could always go to the New-York Historical Society by myself—and I did. I knew one surefire way to hold their interest on a Saturday—their stomachs. I took them to Serendipity, a popular gift-and-ice-cream place close to Bloomingdale's, to feast on giant chocolate sodas and hot fudge sundaes, but also to feast on that which New York is most famous for: people. They learned not to ask in a loud voice, "Why is that funny man dressed that way?"

Although New York was a homecoming for me, it had changed perceptibly in the decade I had been away. There were new stores, the personalities of the taxi drivers had grown surlier, matched by the increase in traffic and prices. The restaurants had all changed, and so had urban manners. I basked once again in the warm, effusive energy that fills the New York air. It's a perfume mixed with pollution, pollen, and various gases—a kind of New York potpourri, one might say. There is nothing like this city. I knew it, but it was my job to make everyone else in our group know it, too. I had to remain upbeat, enthusiastic, and optimistic for the others. If you're young, impatient, and resilient, you settle into a new life quickly. If the parents feel confident and secure, the children do, too. Bob kept reminding me of this fact.

Actually, you could plant Bob Hollensteiner anywhere from here to the steppes of Russia and he would adapt in his easygoing, amiable way. He became "a New Yorker" the minute he stepped off the plane. He was so determined to have his own life, his own friends, and his own agenda, I had nothing to worry about. Nor about Clare's adjustment; she found the nuns and her lay teachers at the convent challenging and warm, and she would come home in the afternoon smiling. On her first day at school, I was prepared for an emotional scene that would be devastating to both of us. My first child was attending the first day of school in a new city. She would be terrified. Of course, I was completely wrong. She could hardly wait for me to depart when the reluctant parents began to leave behind their teary-eyed children at kindergarten that first day. She wanted to get on with the fascinating projects that lay before the little girls in their red-and-white-checked aprons over their gray convent uniforms. As for Malcolm, nearing his second birthday, he was *born* happy and adjusted. Any changes were just fine with him. The only thing he insisted upon was that we feed him on schedule, and feed him as though he had just climbed an alp instead of the children's slide in the park.

Nannie finally stopped complaining about the move from Chicago. It would have been intolerable otherwise. When she was in one of her Black Irish moods, the darkness permeated the whole house and spread out for blocks around, as if the moon had suddenly gone into a full eclipse. But within two months she had found her bearings and become friends with every "real nannie" on the East Side. Wherever Nannie went, along went Malcolm, sitting in the pram, and Clare tagging along behind, holding the pram railing.

Our children were by far the best-dressed members of our family. Nannie was always hand washing and ironing for them. In comparison to today's kids, they were all walking fashion plates. Hand-smocked dresses from England and France were the rage, and little boys would play in the park in gray flannel shorts, sweaters, knee socks, and oxfords. Denim? It was considered vulgar on little children in those days. The same for overalls.

It was nothing like today, when the Madison Avenue boutiques are full of chic imports from Italy and France, offering a "total look," from specially designed diapers to dresses, suits, and coordinating shoes, socks, hair ribbons, coats, and hats with every outfit. A child today whose mother shops on the Upper East Side can dress her daughter with a "coordinated look" retailing for a thousand bucks or more per outfit. An aside: this kind of new-old economy zillionaire family sometimes considers their children as "fashion accessories," meant to coordinate with and complete their mommies' fashion statement. (I wonder how future sociologists will handle reporting this trend of haute couture designs for the little ones in the new millennium in the history books.)

Mothers and nurses spent the day in Central Park with the children. They were a great support to one another. Nannie saved a child's life one day when he fell on his head from a swing. He sat there on the ground, dazed, but his mother had not even noticed the accident. Nannie, the closest thing to an expert lifeguard, except that now she considered herself a "parkguard," immediately rushed over to him and returned with the boy in her arms to a benchful of mothers, none of whom seemed particularly interested in allowing their conversation to be interrupted. "Whose child is this?" Nannie demanded in a voice an onlooker recounted was icy enough to have sunk the *Titanic* without need of an iceberg.

"Oh, he'll be all right," his mother replied, taking him in her arms. "He's just had a bump, that's all." She was making light of it, showing what a big brave boy he was. Of course, he was also unconscious.

"He's not going to be all right," Nannie responded angrily. "He has the possible signs of a concussion. Take him to the hospital emergency room right away!"

The now frightened mother, who was visiting friends in New York and did not know where anything was located, stammered, "But—but where?"

"The closest hospital is Lenox Hill. Go over there to the exit to Fifth Avenue at Ninety-sixth Street, and get one of your friends to hail a cab right away."

Almost a year later the little boy's mother, having returned to New York for another quick visit, found Nannie again in the park, and told her she had been looking for her to thank her from the bottom of her heart. Evidently the boy had suffered a bad concussion in the fall, and his mother had made it to the ER with no time to lose. She offered Nannie a monetary reward, which was quickly refused. Nannie's reputation was made. The word got around. Mothers, strangers all, came up to her from then on, asking her about things that were wrong with their children: "Should I take Pamela to the hospital, or is it all right to wait for an appointment with our pediatrician?" Another one asked, "Should we continue with the pacifier for Michael, or deprive him of it?" Nannie sharply told her that you do not deprive your child of anything, but you do not let him have a pacifier in the first place. To

Nannie, this was an instrument of the devil that made a baby's jaw mal-formed. She was tough, that Mary Eileen Pakenham.

Nannie was the best organizer of social activities for children I have ever witnessed. We had a constant flow of our own guests coming for drinks or a meal, but the children's social schedule far surpassed ours. She knew that a child's exposure to guests at home meant that he or she would grow up to be a confident host one day. Our two were always beautifully dressed when guests came, even when they would only be with the adults for about ten minutes. Nannie taught them to look each guest in the eye and say, "Hello, Mr. So-and-so," while shaking that person's hand. There were many re-hearsals in the nursery for this little social act; but knowing how to introduce and be introduced was one of the greatest assets they were to carry through their lives. Nannie used our apartment as her laboratory in teaching all of Clare's and Malcolm's friends their manners. Every so often she would hold a "nursery tea" late in the afternoon after school had been let out. Nurses and their charges were sent "kiddie invitations" with clowns and teddy bears on them. The festivities, such as they were, would all be over no later than six o'clock. I have concluded that these parties were much more for the nannies than they were for the children—it was the crux of their social lives. I never knew in advance when Nannie was holding one of her parties, because frankly, being at work, I was considered unimportant in the social scheme. None of the other mothers was invited, of course, only the exclusive clique of children and nurses. The bill of fare was simple and without surprises— peanut butter and jelly sandwiches, milk, lemonade, and cookies, served on my mother's antique Dresden china and in my Waterford crystal glasses. Nannie was not about to receive her guests on anything less than the best. The stainless steel would be left in the kitchen; only my good engraved sterling silver would do for the nursery teas. The only touch of reality was in the paper napkins used, and even these were special children's party ones. (Thank God she wasn't into Beluga caviar and foie gras at this point.)

Even Nannie's best efforts didn't safeguard me from a very embarrassing, but human, incident when Malcolm was three and a half. In 1970 I had not been in the White House since I helped Mrs. Johnson and her able staff settle in at the time of the assassination. Then I received an invitation from Mrs. Nixon, via her social secretary Lucy Winchester, to "come with your two children to see the changes in the House since the Kennedy years." When we met, she said, "It's never too early to teach children history and the impor-tance their mother played in it." I will love her forever for that statement.

So off we went, Clare, Malcolm, and I, on the train to our nation's capi-tal. Mrs. Nixon gave us the tour of the Mansion, and we had just sat down for a private talk in the Red Room when Malcolm proceeded to lie down on the red Aubusson rug at Mrs. Nixon's feet and throw a tantrum. He yelled, his face as scarlet as the walls of the room, until Mrs. Nixon, in a far kinder, quieter voice than I would have used, coaxed the reason for his great unhappiness out of him. I had told the children—more than once—the story of how my brothers had a competition when we were all guests of President and Mrs. Hoover to see who could down the most orange juice and the greatest number of cookies without stopping. Malcolm was now very hungry, and the fact that the Nixon White House had produced no cookies or orange juice so far had set him off on this embarrassing tirade. Clare was prissiness personified during this incident, sitting convent-style, with her hands folded in her lap, the perfect lady, completely embarrassed at this horror of a brother screaming on the floor. I was picturing my reputation as a writer on manners and entertaining evaporating quickly. Mrs. Nixon rose to the occasion with her usual grace, and a butler magically produced the chocolate chips and o.j. on a silver tray. Malcolm's appreciation of great historic moments was definitely related to his hunger pangs, but certainly so were many other children's—I kept telling myself.

Bob and I never missed a child's school performance during those years. One of us was always there. I believe that if you cheat a little on your work at the office to see a child perform, you can always make up for it by working harder or taking on another project to compensate for time lost. (I spend a lot of time persuading CEOs even today that this is the way to go with their employees who have young children.) I couldn't miss seeing Clare, the tallest in her class, play Saint Joseph in the Nativity play every year at the convent, just as I had done before her. Bob attended Malcolm's major soccer games at St. David's, but I wasn't invited. It was a man's thing. Back then, no mothers needed apply.

Clare's plain gray uniforms, gray wool knee socks, and brown oxfords were similar to mine from years earlier at Duchesne Academy in Omaha. These uniform-wearing schools must have been the despair of the fashion industry, they cut so heavily into sales. Malcolm's uniform was gray pants, white shirt and tie, and a navy blazer with the red St. David's crest on the pocket.

I was proud of the way Letitia Baldrige Enterprises grew. As we grew in numbers of clients, we grew in rented space in mid-Manhattan. When times got tough, as they did, for example, in the late '70s and early '80s, I reduced our square footage. One summer my staff took no wages but stayed on anyway. I told them if they would stay on, and business got better in September, as it was supposed to, I would pay them back their salaries plus interest. Divine Providence intervened; on September 15 I got an increase in fees of several hundred thousand per month in new business, the employees were paid back, and we were back in business again. My brother Mac remained in the background, shaking his head with disbelief. But we made it.

Alongside my business, my number of directorships grew. I was the only woman director of all but one of them. They did not take on any other women directors, which I wanted to think of as a compliment, but perhaps the thought of another one just like me was too much for them. Brother Mac told me, "Don't open your mouth for one year at board meetings," but of course I opened it often, for better or for worse. I telephoned him at the Commerce Department in Washington whenever I was about to do something really drastic and needed some experienced advice. I always got through to his office. Mac would listen to my dilemma for exactly five minutes, then he would say either "Go for it!" or "You're out of your mind!" which was our code. I realized I was probably the only woman director in history seeking high-level advice from the secretary of commerce, who happened to be her brother. I took these directorships very seriously, did all my homework diligently, and derived great joy from them, except in one instance when an incredibly chauvinist director played up the bad chemistry between us and succeeded in causing me to resign from that one board. Mac was no longer alive to advise me how to get back at him, but he would have said, "Just forget it," so I just forgot my myriad plans of revenge—almost.

Clare's and Malcolm's experiences as parents, without the benefit of trained nannies, are far removed from Bob's and mine. If I had to raise my children in today's society, I would sail off into the sunset on a boat without a bailing can, unable to cope with the noise, confusion, and unrelenting stress. My children tell me thank heavens I was not a young parent of their generation, because *they* would have been the ones sailing off into the sunset without a bailing can, to escape from me. I guess each of us is grateful we were born when we were.

The great perk of working in the home furnishings industry is that you get to know the major furniture and fabric manufacturers personally, which means that you can have a rather splendid-looking apartment at a reasonable price (40 percent off, because you've bought everything wholesale). I had become an interior designer by osmosis through these years, and was able to bluff our apartment into looking well because of the few things I had brought back from Italy years earlier, and the deals made at market time in Chicago. If you were in the right place at the right time, you could purchase a prized piece of furniture as a floor sample for 60 percent off, provided that particular showroom manager loved you. (To earn that "love" in those days was to be nice, cheerful, funny, and full of amusing, sharable White House stories.)

My collection of antique porcelains, a visual highlight of our apartment, had been my pride and joy since the days of collecting them in the Paris flea market on Sundays. The collection was now greatly enhanced by the wedding presents sent to us by members of President Kennedy's cabinet. Their wives, knowing how much I coveted Chinese export porcelain, had banded together, and sent us wonderful pieces. We displayed them on tabletops, bookshelves, and the mantelpiece in our living room. By the time the children were ready for college and had played enough forbidden football and baseball with their friends in our living room and hallway, not one single piece of my collection was unbroken. The cost of having them repaired was astronomical, so we glued them back together with Elmer's Glue, making them worthless, but special to us anyway. One day I felt ready to inflict capital punishment on one of Malcolm's friends, who had swung a bat in the living room, against explicit orders, and broken an exquisite Chinese export porcelain coffeepot, a wedding gift from Secretary of Commerce Douglas Dillon and his wife, Phyllis. I was giving an agitated sermon to the boys when Charlie, the assistant doorman, came up to our apartment, shaking with emotion, to inform us of a terrible tragedy that had just befallen the young couple on the third floor. A half a block away, one of their toddler twins had pulled away from his mother's hand and suddenly darted out into Ninety-fourth Street. He was killed by a car that was turning the corner.

Chinese export porcelains suddenly didn't matter anymore that day, and frankly, they haven't since. Our children and their friends could break every bloody thing in our apartment. After all, possessions are things, and children and life are quite a different story.

Even if you're living high up in a New York apartment, animals can play a big role in your lives—if you let them. My brother Mac and his wife, Midge, had given us the Jack Russell terrier Dustin Hoffman because he didn't fit in with the group of huge dogs on their farm in Woodbury, Connecticut. When you put a massive bull terrier and a couple of mastiffs together with a little brown-and-white terrier, it is not aesthetically pleasing. Dustin held his own at all times with these dogs, but they tended to obscure him when they ran in a pack around the farm. They didn't exactly run with Dustin, they ran over him. Thinking he looked like an attractive runt when he was born, Mac and Midge christened him with the actor's name. There were no other Jack Russells around at the time, so he became a well-known neighborhood character. Everyone knew his name, including strangers to us. I took our Dustin over to meet his namesake when he was shooting a scene from *Marathon Man*, an action film with Sir Laurence Olivier. The producer was using the exterior of Clare's convent school a block away on Ninety-first Street as a background for a violent scene in the film. With Dustin in my arms, I approached the actor when he was on a break: "Mr. Hoffman, may I present your namesake?" I was expecting him to be wreathed in smiles of pride. Instead, the actor gave me a look of utter disdain and turned away, not realizing, of course, that he should have been flattered that such a remarkable dog had been named for him. I might add that Paul Newman, who knew the canine Dustin from our mutual apartment house, commented that he would be very flattered if a dog of Dustin's outstanding intelligence, popularity, and élan were to be named for him. In any case, my real disappointment that day was that Sir Laurence Olivier was not filming. I had longed to go up, grab his hand in adulation, and explain, "Sir Laurence, do you possibly remember March of 1947 taking a group of four American and Swedish girls—University of Geneva students—to dinner at Osso Bucco in Florence when we ran into you and your wife, Vivien Leigh, at the Pitti Palace in Florence? And do you remember when we visited you at the Arthur Rank Studios in London that summer?" He probably would have grinned and said enthusiastically, "Of course I remember you. We ate *bistecca alla Fiorentina*, didn't we?"

Our junkyard cat, Pierre, whom we had acquired from a Waterbury, Connecticut, dump, did not take to city apartment living when we took him to New York from my father's house in Washington, Connecticut. I have to hand it to Pierre, a very handsome cat; he always let us know exactly how he felt about everything. He proceeded to spray over the upholstery only on our best designer furniture, and scratch and tear only the carpeting and comforters on the beds that were in the best condition. He also fell out of an open window from the twelfth floor one day, making a perfect landing on his feet in the grass below. Was it a suicide attempt or just a boastful act to gain attention? We quickly returned him to the trees, lawns, and birds around my father's house in Connecticut. It was his kind of country, his kind of life, and he enjoyed Grandpa Baldrige's company when he wasn't killing and toying in a disgusting manner with some little rodent captured in the nearby woods.

Henrietta the Hamster was also a member of the family, although Clare was the only one who truly appreciated her. Her home was in Clare's room, and one day she escaped from her cage and was discovered late in the afternoon on her back on the living room rug, feet up, thoroughly deceased. Dustin had not been involved (we hoped). Clare went into a proper mourning period; Bob took one of his empty cigar boxes, painted it a rich lacquered black, and lined it with one of his white handkerchiefs. It made a most respectable coffin. The following weekend, we buried Henrietta in the backyard at Grandpa's house in Connecticut in a respectful ceremony. These were memorable moments from the family's scrapbook

One of the things I witnessed during my years of being in and out of New York was the demise of entertaining at home and the increased use of restaurants. My mother would have decried this, complaining that they're cold, impersonal, and noisy. I would have rebutted with the fact that restaurants make life easy, and are good for people-watching and excellent for buffing one's self-image. If restaurant food is lamentable, it's not the hostess's fault. And, of course, restaurant food, excellent or terrible, is cooked by someone else!

The sociological importance of the victory of restaurant over home was that the family glue had melted. You didn't need a psychiatrist to tell your troubles to when you had access to a family dinner table. Your problems were pulled out of you in this place, teased out of you—but you got it out. And you were given advice, not only the unsolicited, unwelcome kind from siblings, but the good kind from your elders. No dinner in a first-class restaurant recommended by the *New York Times* food critic could replace that. Guests at family dinners at home are now missing out on that family glue, too. They used to absorb some of that warmth and conviviality when they sat around the family table, even if only the hosts were present. It was in the atmosphere. To receive an invitation to lunch or dinner in someone's home today comes as a shock.

As an elderly retired CEO remarked to me with no small amount of cynicism about the young executives of today, "These kids don't know how to express themselves or make conversation. In the restaurants, they don't have to. They can just sit there, eating excellent food and looking around at other people. They don't have to speak to anyone at the table, because it's too noisy to hear what anyone says anyway." But I disagree with the CEO to some extent. The young today do have to talk when they're in a restaurant of high visibility; it's a vital part of the impression they give as working professionals. Young people who show themselves to be "givers" in conversation will find themselves ascending that success ladder with speed.

As a company president in the last three decades of the twentieth century, I learned how to take a man to lunch. At the beginning, everyone was confused, and the male guest would usually fight with the waiter over who got the bill, even if the woman said it was hers. Today it's commonplace. If your male client feels more comfortable in his favorite restaurant, that's where you take him. If he doesn't want to be seen there having a woman pick up his check, that's where you don't take him. If he likes a restaurant reeking of hot pastrami sandwiches, onions, and french fries, that's where you take him (along with some breath mints) without making any sarcastic comments. At some new restaurants in vogue in those days—places like the Brussels and the Four Seasons—you were recognized as a professional and given a "good seat" (where everyone could see you, and vice versa). In others—Le Cirque, La Côte Basque, and Mortimer's—you got delicious food served with more-than-delicious gossip. The parade of people trying to be noticed was a good show in itself. If you worked really hard at it, you might get mentioned in *Women's Wear Daily* or in Suzy's, Eugenia Sheppard's, Joey Adams's, or Earl Wilson's columns. That was considered a mighty achievement. And it was all blessedly affordable in those days. Today, this fashionable lifestyle requires you to be a star in the entertainment or sports world, or in technology or finance, or you simply have to be a BOH ("billionaire or higher"). That gets you attention. When legendary *New York Times* fashion photographer Bill Cunningham takes your picture on the street in New York, you know you have arrived. You know that your friends will all be jealous, and that you will have to buy a hundred copies of the *Times* when the story appears. Friends won't want a photocopy; they'll want an original. You've told everyone to watch for it. Then the story finally appears in print—but your name is not under your picture; nor is anyone else's under theirs. It's a page of anonymous feet. Bill has done a fashion trend story, highlighting with candid shots the new shoe styles making the scene. Thanks to the *Times*, your feet will be socially famous, but you will not. Then, suddenly, something wonderful occurs. You realize it doesn't matter!

It has always fascinated me how men in particular live and die to gain entrance into the club of their choice. Certainly, membership in a good club in any major American city, as well as in Paris, London, Rome, and Madrid, makes a person feel accepted, part of a special clan, in the right circle. It might furnish a new member with an opportunity to become friends with influential people who, in some circumstances, might help his or her business.

Bob thrived in real estate consulting, and was constantly teased about his proud membership in the Brook Club, a famous old men's club. If you were to compare an entire room of overstuffed furniture to that club, you would still find the Brook stuffier (an opinion not shared by its loyal members, of course). In the meantime I had resumed my membership in the Colony Club, the first American women's club of its kind, founded just after the turn of the twentieth century. The Colony had only women members, as did its rival, the Cosmopolitan Club, while until the last few years men's clubs—the Knickerbocker, Union, Racquet, Century (predominately for writers), University, Union League, and Harmonie (predominantly prominent members of the Jewish community) Clubs, and various university clubs like the Harvard, Yale, Princeton, Cornell, and Williams Clubs—admitted only men. When the political correctness and antidiscrimination chant picked up with a vengeance in the 1970s and '80s, begrudgingly the men began to invite women to become members of their male bastions, nudged along by Supreme Court rulings. Frankly, I could never see why women wanted to join them anyway. They reeked of tobacco and dark brown leather chairs in need of repair. The male members obviously resented the presence of women, except at mealtime, when women proved to be necessary for financial reasons. When it was announced women were going to be admitted to full membership, few women applied, so the clubs, to maintain their legal status, would reach out to "safe" members like Mrs. Vincent Astor, who could be relied upon not to flirt inside the club, get drunk, talk to the press, or break into the men's locker rooms.

Before membership in the men's clubs was thrown open to women, women guests in the dining room, or even attendees at board meetings, would have to use a special entrance, elevator, or private stairway so as not to invade the men's privacy. My feminism always boiled up inside me on these occasions, particularly when the only reason I was in the club was to attend a corporate director's meeting. At business lunches, at both the Knickerbocker and Century Clubs, which were very strict about women not being permitted except at special times, I would run up the front staircase from the lobby to the third- and fourth-floor meeting rooms, exalting in the shocked, momentarily frozen-in-horror faces of club members and staff. Behind me floated soft protests: "Oh, Miss Baldrige, you can't do that! Please, oh, Miss Baldrige ... ." I loved it, but my mother, had she been alive, would have expired from shock at my behavior.

When the women's movement was in full bloom in the 1970s, I was no Gloria Steinem or Betty Friedan, but I was very conscious of my role as someone out front who should actively support the cause of women in the workplace. Conservative feminism, one might call it. My temper really exploded the night when my fellow directors of the investment banking house Dean Witter Reynolds and I had gathered in San Francisco for an important meeting at the Pacific Union Club, a historic men's club. Only a couple of months earlier had women been allowed into the dining room, and for dinner only. Historic! The women of America were supposed to bow down and touch their heads to the floor in gratitude for this new privilege. When I reached my hotel room from the airport, three messages were waiting for me from the Dean Witter group, all saying the same thing. I was not to go to the club at six o'clock for the working cocktail-dinner; I was to use a special entrance, arrive promptly at seven o'clock, and proceed immediately to the dining room. When I found out that the other directors were to arrive at six for their male rite of cocktailing, but I was not allowed on the premises before seven, I lost it. I got into my black velvet dress and black satin pumps, put on my jewels and pearls, and, smothered in perfume, arrived in the dining room anteroom exactly at 7:00 P.M. I announced to my twenty-five fellow directors and DWR executives gathered there, "Hello, one and all. I hope you had a good cocktail hour. I hope you will have a good dinner meeting, too, because I won't be joining you. I'm going to a fabulous restaurant with some friends who could not believe that grown-up men would behave in this fashion."

When my chagrined fellow directors stumbled forth with questions about why I did what I did, and what should they have done, I told them they should have immediately changed the place of the dinner, or at the very least changed the cocktail hour from six to seven so that everyone could gather at the same hour. At the end of my oration, my cheeks flaming hot, I left, leaving a room full of men in shock. We were to meet the next morning, but I had walked out on the first half of the working meeting, the dinner part. The looks of astonishment on the men's faces were quite remarkable. Even the bartender looked as though he had just swallowed a mouthful of cocktail onions. Each director mumbled a separate apology to me the next morning. One of them said, "I am afraid to tell my lawyer daughter about this." I'm happy to say my directors' fee was not docked, for my having missed half of the meeting.

This Pacific Union Club incident occurred in the mid-1970s. It would not happen today. The women's movement has succeeded in teaching a lot of people about the equality of the sexes in the workplace. Nowadays most clubs cherish the presence of the opposite sex at lunch and dinner. How else could they survive financially? They don't make women walk up a special staircase or use a special entrance anymore either.

I joined the Colony Club in 1956, enjoying the solidarity of female friendships, just as strong as any old boys' network. I love the stories of how scandalized New Yorkers were when the Colony Club opened in 1903 as the first woman's club of its kind. Ministers took to their pulpits to decry the moral decline of women in the city, and predicted that these women with their own club would now be drinking, smoking, and using bad language in each other's company, rather than staying home and cooking for their husbands and children. I'm proud that my photograph hangs on a special member's wall, along with those of the club's founder, J. P. Morgan's daughter Anne, Eleanor Roosevelt, actress Katharine Cornell, writers Cornelia Otis Skinner and Edna St. Vincent Millay, Secretary of Labor Frances Perkins,

Kitty Carlisle Hart, and my pal Eleanor Elliott. My claim to fame on this wall was probably that I was one of the first full-time working mothers in the membership. "Ladies" were not really supposed to work when I first joined the Colony Club. I, on the other hand, was still cooking dinner for my husband and volunteering regularly in the nonprofit sector, but I was also working for corporations and participating with other women's husbands in the world of commerce—not all that proper, you understand.

If only I had been clairvoyant enough to look far ahead at that time, into the new century and millennium, it would have been fantastic to see women working full steam ahead, pleading cases before the bar, running their husbands' construction companies and architectural firms after their deaths, operating as surgeons in the best hospitals, flying commercial aircraft, and starting up successful new businesses. They would be bringing home the much-needed bacon. Whether widowed or divorced, they would probably have to work harder than most hardworking men, because of their children and their role in the home. Supervaliant, too, would be the women who chose to stay at home raising their children—and did a darned good job of it. Gutsy ladies of the present, past, and future. Bravissima! I smile with a glow of satisfaction to see women change their roles from subservient housewife and soccer mom into today's partner in marriage, or single provider, as well as executive leader—and still be a soccer mom.

"Home" means as much to me today as it did when I was growing up, sliding down the banister in Omaha, hoping to miss being skewered by the statue of Mercury at the bottom. The apartment we eventually purchased, at Ninety-third Street and Fifth Avenue, had the best perspective of the city, or at least it seemed so to us, with a twelfth-floor view overlooking Central Park and the city reservoir. We now even had our own lake. Once again, Bob had accomplished a miracle—finding a luxury apartment for an incredibly low price at the worst point of the recession. We weren't a national monument, but we had our own *son et lumière* show every evening at sunset: a changing light and color show played against the trees of Central Park and the apartment buildings of the West Side that any French Impressionist painter would have killed for. Jackie Onassis lived a few blocks down from us on Fifth, right across the street from the Metropolitan Museum of Art. Her view could not compare with ours. She had the museum interfering with her perspective of the park; we had nothing but light and air.

Entertaining is a skill, and an art, but at this moment in our society, it might even be called a sociological necessity. We need the comfort, support, and infusion of courage brought to us by just sitting around someone's table. The skills required in entertaining have changed drastically over the past few years. There were no delicatessens and caterers in my childhood years. You cooked everything yourselves or, if you were "a formerly rich person" in the depression, hired someone to come to your house to cook, and a butler or bartender as well, or maybe the teenager next door. My parents used to discuss who was entertaining well in town, and who was not, with the same joy with which we dish today the celebrity dirt from *People* magazine. Those who had the means to entertain did it for the morale of the community. I remember how delighted my parents were to receive dinner-party invitations, and how quickly the members of their set would don evening clothes, even out-of-style or in need of alterations, for the occasion. It cheered them up to get all dressed up. If it was a "Dinner at Eight" kind of invitation, they didn't need to be reminded on the invitation to come dressed in evening clothes. They just knew.

My parents would return from such a social event and usually find all three of us awake. They would sit down on our beds, in each child's room, and give us an account of the evening, Mother always wafting a cloud of perfume around her, like a filmy stole. "Tell me *everything* about the party," I would command, and then she would give a journalist's report: the music, flowers, linens, menu, burning tapers on tall candlesticks with little red lampshades on them, casting a lovely glow in the room, the gowns, and after dessert, the little Venetian glass blossom floating in each guest's crystal finger bowl. Mothers would bring home from these black-tie evenings the customary "party favor," given to each woman at the dinner, and usually passed on to their daughters the next day. I remember vividly some of the favors—a small brocaded notepad with a tiny gold pencil attached, miniature flower-decorated soaps, decks of really tiny playing cards, a miniature bottle of a sickly sweet orange blossom perfume, and delicate white linen handkerchiefs from Switzerland, embroidered with colored flowers in one corner. There were favors like postcards painted with ballet dancers on them, their costumes actually made of fabric and sewn onto the card. Even their toe shoes seemed like real white kid. There were paper cigarette holders, decorated in gold and black. Mother would describe the party favors Consuelo Vanderbilt used to give her guests at the family mansion dinners ("Marble House") in the late 1880s, things like jewel-studded gold *minaudières* (small evening bags) from Cartier's in Paris.

Enjoying entertaining is in the genes. My passion for it originated in my childhood, with birthday luncheons for girls and a menu of creamed chicken, potato chips, and peas, always, and pink ice cream for dessert in molds like rabbits, hearts, or ducks. In my embassy days in Paris and Rome, the hors d'oeuvres made by the residence chef as a favor to me guaranteed the success of my cocktail parties. Many other times, the hors d'oeuvres were just cheese and Ritz crackers from the American commissary, the only kind of hors d'oeuvre I knew how to make. It didn't matter. The liquor came from the commissary, inexpensively, and never-ending. People came together. That was what mattered.

Luckily, Bob enjoyed entertaining as much as I. In Chicago and New York, we would have guests for drinks, Sunday lunch, or dinner any night of the week. We'd mix up our guest lists with young, attractive friends and celebrities, like movie actress Joan Fontaine and actor Vincent Price, who crisscrossed our professional lives. We usually had a hodgepodge of nationalities. Each group loved being exposed to the other.

We could manage a meal for eight or under without help. Bob was the coat taker, bartender, and master cleaner-upper after the party was over. I prepared all the food myself for most of our parties, sometimes with enormous success and sometimes with horrible results—but I would roar with laughter at myself when that happened, and the guests would soon be laughing, too.

Every once in a while, I felt the urge to do everything right, as in my embassy and White House days. Once during the planning of a black-tie dinner for twelve (two United Nations ambassadors and their wives and three other high-ranking couples as well as ourselves), I realized I couldn't do it properly alone. For the first time in my life I hired a butler—a famous highbrow, freelance British butler, who had worked in Buckingham Palace. An acknowledged snob, he charged an eye and a tooth for his services. There was an even bigger problem: on the night of the dinner, he never showed. He had a drinking problem and had passed out on his bed before our dinner. (My only consolation was that it was his bed, and not ours.)

There we were the night of our "diplomatic dinner," with a houseful of guests, the hostess in the kitchen, with an enormous apron now covering her billowing Bergdorf Goodman taffeta evening skirt, heating up the food that had been left by the caterer earlier. There was Bob, taking care of the coats, passing the hors d'oeuvres, serving the drinks, and wondering aloud, "Where the hell is the butler?" I did my best to carry on a brilliant international conversation at dinner, seated as I was between two ambassadors but dashing in and out of the kitchen, hands full of plates, donning the apron again out in the kitchen with no time to fasten the strings. I would tend to culinary matters out there and then rush back into my seat in the dining room, apronless, nose shiny and face flushed red from the heat of the stove, wondering if my next book would be *I Know Who Murdered the Butler*. My excuses to our distinguished guests flowed forth in rapid succession. The two ambassadors had an empty space between them, and they were not particularly friendly, so conversation between them flowed like heavy mud. Finally Bob and I wised up and began to laugh at the situation, it was so terrible, and the tension in the dining room evaporated. The guests began to chuckle, too, and then the laughter never stopped.

Then it was time for dessert. I took the dinner plates out into the kitchen, happy that everyone had eaten everything on them, but forgetting that my hands were now greasy from remnants of the veal sauce. When I grabbed the large soufflé dish containing our dessert from the fridge, the unthinkable occurred. The cold strawberry soufflé I had made the day before from a Julia Child recipe slid from my hands, crashing down onto the kitchen floor. The entire soufflé mixture poured out like a pink River Styx, losing its stiff texture as it went. It was now a mass of gelatinous pink globs. There was no time to call anyone for help; I had to get through this myself. To protect my huge taffeta skirt, which was not meant for kitchen work, I hiked it up and pushed it, now disastrously crumpled, into the legs of my panty girdle. I now waddled like a nine-months-pregnant woman. I got out from the cupboards some stunning large crystal brandy snifters from Sweden, a wedding gift from one of my Swedish roommates at the University of Geneva. I took a serving spoon, scooped up the pink glop from the floor, and filled the glasses with it. Then I topped each snifter with a dollop of vanilla ice cream I happened to have in the freezer, put a strawberry on top, and poured cognac all over it. It was an enormous success of a dessert, but I prayed all night long that the dog hairs from Dustin, who had been dozing on the kitchen floor all day, had not mixed into the guests' strawberry mousse.

My life has always been crammed with careless emergencies of my own doing. Another example was when I ran into a rather famous young couple on Madison Avenue whom Bob and I had met but wanted to get to know better. Chatting on the street, I was inspired to invite them to come very informally for an early dinner "next Sunday at home." They accepted readily—no one in New York ever has anything to do on Sunday night. I neglected to mention it to my husband or even think about it again, because I had stupidly not written it down that very moment. When "next Sunday night" came, Bob was in his jeans, sweater, and moccasins, smoking a cigar and doing the Sunday *New York Times* crossword puzzle. I was in a bathrobe, which could pass for a peignoir, if you used your imagination and had a sense of charity. When the doorbell rang, I was in the kitchen, cleaning up from our late lunch. "For God's sake, who can that be?" a grumpy voice called out from the library. My heart started beating hard, a panic sign. I knew I had committed the biggest social faux pas of them all: I had forgotten I had invited people to a meal, and now those people were there, at our door. What a personal insult! I had to somehow cover up my mistake. Bathrobe, dressing gown—it was all in the way you viewed it.

"Oh, but you're so beautifully dressed," I chided them at the door, "we're so informal on a Sunday night. Look at me in a dressing gown!"

I took the couple's coats, rushed into the library, threw them into my startled husband's lap, and whispered, "If you have ever gone fast in your life, please make it this time a lot faster." In ten seconds I explained to Bob what had happened, and he shot out of his chair. He took over their coats and the drink orders as though he had been expecting them.

I rushed into the kitchen, started warming up a meat stew from the freezer, and then threw into the pot a package of frozen peas, to enlarge it. I poured enough red wine into this humble mixture to turn the sauce from brown to a burgundy color. I set the table in the dining room in exactly four minutes, plopping down in the center a covered silver jar that should have been polished first. I turned down the dining room lights very low, so that the guests would not be able to see the tarnished silver or the terrible food they were about to be served. I took the remaining limp bits of our lunch salad, floating in remnants of dressing, and added about five fresh, unused pieces of Boston lettuce left over in the fridge. That pumped up the old salad considerably. There were some stale rolls in a plastic bag in the fridge, which I reheated in the oven. Who would know? There was a bit of ice cream in the freezer. We could have that for dessert, even if it was about two months old. It was coffee ice cream. I put it in a pretty *famille rose* bowl, threw some pancake maple syrup over it, and shook some powdered cocoa on top. Subterfuge, social face-saving subterfuge.

Bob in the meantime was doing his best to entertain ("I made the drinks a little stiff," he said ruefully). We think our guests never realized that we weren't expecting them—at least, we hope they weren't acting. It would have been too embarrassing for us all if we had admitted our faux pas. After all, these were people we really didn't know. When I remember emergencies like that, I conclude that you can handle just about anything that comes along. You just have to know how to move fast and be an excellent bluffer, and a bit of a liar, too, I suppose.

Today, less and less entertaining is done at home, more and more in restaurants. When I talk to young couples or single people about entertaining guests in their homes, they give excuses, usually having something to do with dissatisfaction over the state of their abodes.

"I need to re-cover the sofa in the living room before we have anyone over."

"Have to get new bathroom fixtures installed first."

"The carpet is frayed. I just haven't had the time to get new stuff installed."

"Oh, no, I can't entertain with the floors looking this way."

"We're going to redo our hallway. I'll wait for that."

Those people, by the way, are still waiting.

The children were growing. After graduating from St. David's eighth-grade class, Malcolm went on to the Deerfield Academy (a fine boys' boarding school in the Berkshires of western Massachusetts) for his high school years, still wearing the obligatory jacket and tie. You could see him growing if you looked hard at him. It was incredible. He was on his way to becoming six-foot-ten. Some of the kids called him the Jolly Green Giant, but he didn't mind. Keeping him in clothes and shoes that fit was a fiscal Herculean labor. At eighteen he would take a year off between high school and college to hone his basketball skills, taking the subway to and from Harlem at night to play with an outstanding team of African American eighteen-year-olds that was organized by the fabled basketball supporter Ernie Lorch at Riverside Church. Malcolm never told his teammates that when he disappeared down the stairway into the subway at night, his destination was a Fifth Avenue apartment. His wardrobe now consisted mainly of sweats, T-shirts, and forever odiferous sweat socks and basketball sneakers. I was afraid even to air that footwear outside on our window sills, for fear that other tenants would be downwind of them. Besides, if one of his size 16½ basketball shoes were to fall off the narrow ledge, anyone passing below would have been killed.

After her graduation from eighth grade, Clare went on from the convent to Miss Porter's School (MPS), which I had also attended. The dress code had changed in the 1960s from skirts to pants and jeans, and from brown loafers to sneakers and running shoes. The only remnant of my days at MPS was that my daughter's crowd had to wear skirts in the dining hall for dinner. She and her contemporaries listened to music constantly, harkening back wistfully to the music of Woodstock, a cultural event they had missed but yearned to have been part of. To them, Woodstock was heroic. In 1982, the year of her graduation, MTV was in, radio was out, and music videos were "it." I rejoiced in the fact that our daughter had become a musical expert, if not of Chopin and Wagner, at least of Led Zeppelin, Duran Duran, the Grateful Dead, and all the techno-pop and British bands that swept the world. Clare may not have known who Joan Sutherland was, but she certainly could tell you all about Joni Mitchell and Joan Baez. Trying to raise my self-esteem, since I had totally ignored the rock scene to this point, in the seventies I became a fan of the British rock singer Sting, and then alternated the compact discs of Wagnerian opera with Sting's latest albums as background music in my office. It made me feel less divorced from my daughter's culture, and I am still an avid Sting fan.

My life was marching forward as well, always in tempo with the White House. Rosalynn Carter called me to Blair House two days before her husband's inauguration to help her with some briefing. Then, when Ronald Reagan went to Washington from California in 1981 to begin his administration, his wife called me to ask for my help. We had become friends years earlier when she was a Burlington House Interior Design Awards judge, representing California. I spent the first six weeks of the Reagan administration, back in my old office in the East Wing, helping her organize her files, staff, and programs. The first night, when Nancy and I proceeded to the third floor to look at some decorating projects, we surprisingly ran into the president. He gave her a big smooch, and I made a mental reminder to tell Bob that President Reagan gives his wife a little kiss just because he hasn't seen her for a couple of hours. He had been exploring the third floor of his new home for the first time and, delighted with the discovery of a pool table, had immediately started to play. He talked with us right through his game, concentrating on both effortlessly. A comfortable president, a comfortable man. Nancy Reagan was determined to make her mark as first lady, as a great hostess, and as a protector of her husband. She did them all, and among her proud moments was being compared to her predecessor Jacqueline Kennedy as a hostess. In the days I worked with her at the White House, our talk was of great parties, and of making the White House sparkle again, as well as of her own effective program aimed at protecting children from drugs. Like Jackie, fortunately she had no idea of what lay ahead of her. The press was unmercifully unjust to her in the White House, criticizing her designer clothes and the gifts of china and crystal she accepted from her old friends for the White House entertaining needs. I'll never understand that. Here she was, helping to save the taxpayers money in providing for the house. It was a perfect example of "No good deed goes unpunished." Her husband would survive being shot, but would later succumb to an almost worse fate—Alzheimer's disease. I will always remember Ronald Reagan cracking jokes at the newly discovered pool table on one of his first nights in the White House. He is alive, but Nancy has lost him, the worst of cruel destinies for them both.

If you do the same thing day in and day out in your work through the years, tedium can attack your mind as viciously as osteoporosis. I've had osteoporosis—but tedium, never. When you're running a perpetual race as I did to acquire new accounts, massage the old ones, finish deadlines for publishers, make lecture trips and participate fully in the nonprofit sector, you might start to feel like a robot, as well as act like one. Over the years, when people would ask us at LBE (Letitia Baldrige Enterprises) what our specialty was, every member of the staff would give a different answer, usually according to the type of project on which that staff member was currently working. I gave each account executive the title of vice president; it looked awfully good on her business card and made the client working with her feel important. It was a small recompense to my staff for doing first-class work and not being paid what they should have been. With a few exceptions, I think they all loved to come to work every morning. When anyone became testy with anyone else, even openly antagonistic, I would put them in an empty room and keep them there until they resolved their differences. Sometimes it took an hour, sometimes a couple of days, but they always worked things out themselves. The staff of my company remained proudly female, with the exception of Steve Lamb, a former travel writer who joined us to deal with our demanding Philippines account. Steve made news in the *New York Times*, all by himself, a few years after he left LBE, in a lengthy article with his photograph. It was the first detailed profile the *Times* had ever done, the first of many to come, on a gay man dying of a terrible new disease called AIDS.

Clients like Phil and Rowena Kelley of Baker Furniture became great personal friends. We handled Baker's launch of expensive, beautiful reproductions of important furniture from the stately homes of England. The lords and ladies—i.e., the peers and their spouses who lived in these stately homes on great estates, and who earned a hefty royalty on every reproduction sold—would come to America at Baker's (great) expense, to appear at press parties and major department store promotions. They were shepherded around by the engaging Sir Humphrey Wakefield. They even went to High Point, North Carolina, for the home furnishings market, to mingle with the press and the awed furniture buyers. The Viscount and Viscountess Astor, Lord Elliott, the Duke and Duchess of Argyll, Lord Thin, Viscount William de L'Isle, and other lordly creatures all stood by their furniture reproductions and promoted them in the most engaging high-class fashion ever seen. They thought it was all "frightfully amusing." One of the lords, a dark-haired, romantic-looking one, made an enormous impression when he appeared in black leather and raced around the North Carolina highways on his Harley. One night one of the "stately" spouses drank a bit too much at the High Point furniture market. She disrobed from the waist up while sitting at the bar of the Bur-mil Country Club. The best view, of course, was had by the bartender, who frankly will never get over the display of the "titled bosoms winking at him," as someone described it, from across his bar in this sleepy town of North Carolina. The peers sold a lot of their furniture reproductions by making an occasional personal appearance for Baker in major department stores before the royalty-hungry American public, fully dressed or not.

I found myself training the tellers in comportment at major banks around the country, and then executives in financial firms like Dean Witter, Donaldson & Lufkin, the Boston Company, Deloitte Touche, and Equitable. The moms and dads of America had not been doing their job in passing on manners and people skills to their children, so the corporate heads of most companies began to be concerned. By 1980 many decided to introduce training on some level, lest the public accuse their executives of being less than suave and polished. This meant a healthy chunk of business for me. I was amused to see CEOs who had once told me firmly, "We only hire polite, polished executives. We don't need that kind of training. It would be an insult to our people." They reversed themselves completely, saying, "We need a little help on people skills around here."

There was always a fresh bunch of surprises, like an unusual bouquet of flowers with every account. I was asked to produce important, problematic weddings for famous people, to give lessons on being "a class act instead of an uncouth jerk," as one of my clients described it. We handled PR campaigns that lasted six weeks, for a press launch, or several years, to rebuild a company's image or launch new concepts in products. We learned patience and survival even when well-merited praise was not dispensed—such as working with the *Wall Street Journal* and getting a major positive feature story on a client, only to have the client ask testily, "But when is the next feature coming, and why aren't we in the *New York Times*?" If we got a client on the *Today* show for a five-minute TV spot, he would be angry that it wasn't a twelve-minute spot. I spent a lot of time urging the staff to keep their cool. One of them told me later that because I had trained her well in this respect, she had held her marriage intact. "When we fought," she explained, "I would pretend my husband was one of our impossible clients, and he was therefore always right, even though I knew he was *never* right. It has worked."

Nauseating requests were made of me to get social publicity for some very rich people. I would turn those down at once. "But you've got connections" they would insist in a singsong. To them, being mentioned in Suzy's or Liz Smith's social columns meant everything. It would prove to their friends that they had finally made it. I poured soothing salve on my spirit by writing about these would-be social climbers in my novel *Public Affairs, Private Relations*, published by Doubleday. (All fictional characters, of course.) We handled a momentous project for Mary Welles and Harding Laurence of Braniff Airlines and the Mexican government by flying planeloads of photogenic celebrities from the United States to Acapulco for four days of playing. Designer Halston, "the hot one of the decade," flew his clothes and his models down, too, and I discovered something new—that people can be absolutely blotto with drugs for days on end and still manage to look good for the photographers. Our celebrity guests, many of them rounded up by nice Earl Blackwell, the social "arranger" of that era, were very demanding. One famous CEO blew up and said I had ruined his reputation by putting him and his girlfriend in the same villa (I was only following his secretary's orders). So I changed them to two different cottages, which was difficult, because the resort was full. They then proceeded to spend the entire time openly in one of the two villas. So much for one's reputation! Another executive's wife complained that the photographers accompanying this expedition had not taken her picture once, and she might as well not have come to Acapulco. I wanted to tell her she looked like a fat seal in the bikini she insisted on wearing everywhere, but I demurred.

My seeming attraction for hotel business took me all over the place and often back into history. For example, 1904 was a really big year in U.S. history. First, the New York subway was inaugurated, revolutionizing the movement of people from place to place, no longer dependent on horses and buggies. Second, that same year saw a fabled bastion of American society opened for business, the St. Regis Hotel at Fifty-fifth and Fifth Avenue, a veritable grande dame replica of Parisian Beaux Arts architecture. It was built by the socialite-financier John Jacob Astor, who was to continue his newsworthiness to the very end, when he had the bad luck to book a suite on the maiden voyage of the *Titanic*. In 1904 his New York hotel landmark loomed large in what seemed then like a horizon of empty, muddy fields. We were given the job of publicizing the hotel, and its seventy-fifth anniversary in particular. Many people were still around who had been part of the hotel's history—like Prince Serge Obolensky, formerly of the White Russian nobility, who at age eighty could outwaltz any man in the world and still dance the demanding, rigorous sword dance at the annual Russian New Year's Eve party. The Barbara Huttons, Doris Dukes, and Jimmy Donohues had walked in and out of the hotel and the gossip columns for decades. I glimpsed the last years of Salvador Dali's

American experience from the lobby of the St. Regis. He lived at the hotel with his pet cheetah, whom he walked on a jewel-studded leash. People said he did it only for publicity, but he did not need the cheetah for that. His brilliant surrealist paintings, his bizarre, waxed mustache, and his eccentric clothing matched his rhetoric to perfection. Of course, he was a figure of great allure to the press, and of course, the name of the St. Regis figured prominently in each story.

Delving into histories of turn-of-the-century New York, I read about how the St. Regis Hotel opening dazzled New York society, including the Astors, Whitneys, Ogdens, Vanderbilts, Morgans, and Goelets on the guest list. Even "Diamond Lil" (Lillian Russell) made the scene that night with her rich lover, Diamond Jim Brady. Lillian Russell had been a special figure in history for me ever since I read in my early childhood that one of her lovers had presented her with a jewel-studded bicycle. (That's the kind of creative gift any woman would like to receive, whether she knew how to pedal or not.) On opening night in 1904, specially groomed horses and shiny black carriages drove up to the hotel's Art Nouveau entrance, bringing their formally dressed and lavishly bejeweled passengers to the Astors' party. In a very few years these handsome conveyances would be replaced by shiny black Daimlers, Packards, Pierce-Arrows, and green Locomobiles.

I read about how all the architects and engineers in the United States were enticed to go to New York just to inspect the revolutionary air-conditioning system that Astor had proudly installed—as well as the first centralized vacuum cleaner system. The St. Regis was the first hotel with a telephone in every room, and it kept its reputation for many decades, remaining a leading focus of social activity in America, from christenings to postfuneral receptions. (A celebration is a celebration, whether it's for a life or for a death.) When I had mounted a large photographic reportage of the hotel's history, New Yorkers and tourists crowded the lobby to see the photographs of the rich and the famous, smiling, waving their cigarette holders, and trying to vamp the cameramen.

The legendary debutante balls on the St. Regis roof continued for as long as the large private dances did, up through the 1960s, but the craze for the "Debutante of the Year" began at the St. Regis in the late 1930s. As a publicity happening, it far surpassed national interest in Miss America or Hollywood stars. A typical late-1930s debutante did not have to be challenged in the brains department. She wasn't required to make any kind of contribution other than to look pretty, be the center of party attention, and have a multitude of beaux with good names or phony European titles attached. The Debutante of the Year appellation was for the golden girl who most loved to be photographed, the one in whose honor the most parties were given, and the one who looked best in a strapless evening dress. (Brenda Frazier Duff was one of the early recipients. Jackie Bouvier earned the title in the mid-1940s.)

In the old days, if a debutante who had been properly launched with a private dance and the obligatory tour of European cities was not married within four years of her debut, the gloom and doom of desperation would settle over her family's mansion like a tent of stagnant smoke. A forced marriage to a rotter of a man would not be a joyous occasion for her family, but spinsterhood would be worse—absolutely unacceptable.

Growing up, I had devoured all of this debutante mania when photographs and descriptions of the girls' parties appeared in *Life* or the fashion magazines. I dreamed of being just like them some day, but how quickly that awe would disappear as the years passed by. I remember hearing my mother ranting all over the house when the daughter of one of their good friends announced her engagement to a "suitable" young man. After subsequently discovering he was not so suitable, the young woman "disannounced" her engagement. He immediately sent a whopping, completely itemized bill to her parents. He was charging them, in essence, the cost of a year's courtship of their daughter—everything from orchid corsages and dinner bills at El Morocco to rented sports cars for weekends at the houses of his friends and the price of tickets that ranged from movies to polo matches. He had invested in this young woman. He had laid out all that money because he fully expected to take her off the marriage market and share in her millions for the rest of their lives. Very romantic.

We made the reopening of the St. Regis's largest restaurant, the Old King Cole Room, major news in the press. It had been closed for years. The large, colorful Maxfield Parrish murals of Old King Cole (who was "a merry old soul, and a merry old soul was he," if you remember your nursery rhymes) had been holding court over the St. Regis bar for decades. The artist was one of the world's foremost illustrators at the time, so it was decided to move the painting onto the walls of the newly redecorated big dining room, and to rename the room in honor of this merry old soul of a monarch. I overheard a stylishly dressed woman with her young daughter discussing the delightfully colored figures in the Parrish murals at lunch one Saturday.

"But what are they doing?" the child asked, pointing to all the smirking courtiers flanking the king on his throne.

"I don't know," replied the mother, obviously bored by the question.

"But why are all the courtiers laughing?" The child insisted on knowing what was going on in that mural.

"They're just amused because the king is farting," replied the mother matter-of-factly. She obviously wanted her daughter's interrogation to end, but she was also being historically correct in her answer. The painting had been Maxfield Parrish's inside joke.

Generations have been attached to the St. Regis. Eve Symington, the wife of Missouri Senator Stuart Symington, sang the blues in the Maisonette Room in the 1930s, wowing the audiences, including my parents and many of their Washington friends. Now here was I, a generation down, doing public relations for the hotel and arranging for their son Jimmy, of my generation and an astonishingly good tenor, to perform as a balladeer in the Old King Cole Room. He sang with Peter Duchin's orchestra at a benefit dinner for Boys' Harbor. And Peter Duchin's father, the famous Eddie Duchin, had played at the St. Regis when Eve Symington used to sing there. How everything that is past is never past, when subsequent generations continue to connect!

Infuriating though the public relations profession may have been in my life at times, there were many more moments of success and enjoyment than of frustration. I had landed for LBE the PR account for Max Factor's major new fall makeup promotion. Linda Wachner was president of the company (and destined later to become the first woman CEO of a major corporation, WARNACO). It was big bucks and big business; the hottest ad agency in the country handled the account. Their million-dollar promotion for Max Factor's fall makeup line was the question, "Don't you love being a woman?" They billed hundreds of thousands of dollars, while we billed a maximum of $2,500 per month. I had the idea of going out on the streets of New York with a TV cameraman, a sound man, and three of my pretty young interns. We stopped women of all sizes, shapes, ages, and nationalities on the street, and asked if we could film them answering a simple question, not "Don't you?" but "*Why* do you love being a woman?" We had no police permit to do this on the street, which was very risky, but it would have taken weeks to obtain, and we would have been hassled by the police; but we moved so fast, from corner to corner, the police never caught up with us. When we asked women of all ages, skin colors, nationalities, and income levels why they loved being born female (we took it for granted they did love it, and received only two negatives in the whole group), their answers were fresh, spontaneous, and often incredibly funny. "I love being a woman because I want to be made love to all the time. I was born for that"; "I love being born a woman because I get to pick the color of our car and the living room carpet"; "I love being a woman because I have so many years of education left to accomplish, and no one is going to stop me." I found that if I stopped strangers on the street, they were frightened by this very tall, daunting figure suddenly facing them with a microphone and a camera, so I used my young interns, who were not at all intimidating, to do the stopping and asking. The women on the street could not resist them. No one refused to talk to them.

The film that resulted from this on-the-street interrogation was a great success, achieving a lot of publicity and being used in national training for Max Factor's new line. One of the ad agency executives informed me that the ad agency was furious with me because I had billed Max Factor such a paltry sum, just my monthly consulting fee of $2,000 plus $500 for expenses. If I had been a graduate of a business school, my billing would have been a lot different—a hundred times higher.

I spent almost two years working for the principality of Liechtenstein. It took me three weeks to learn how to spell it properly without a cheat sheet, and it took my friends three months to find it on the map, between Austria and Switzerland. The princely family was coming to New York with a major exhibition from their jewel-like private museum, mainly an important collection of Peter Paul Rubens paintings seldom seen in public. New York's Metropolitan Museum quickly agreed to exhibit them. It was a coup for them as well as for Liechtenstein, and we took advantage of it with press coverage and high-level luncheons and dinners, mixing diplomats, society, the art world, and Wall Street. The principality is tiny, nestled in the Alps, smaller than Washington, D.C., but with a royal castle on high. It was exactly like the fairy-tale castle towns in all the books I had read. My dealings with Prince Hans Adam and his former financial director, Christian Norgren, and others in Vaduz—the capital and only city of this mountain kingdom—were worth a book in themselves. Vaduz looked like what Oz should have looked like, except that it had a special characteristic Oz never had: it was "the false teeth manufacturing capital of the world."

The women of Vaduz kept looking at me strangely, because I was traveling to their country without my husband. I kept looking at their teeth, wondering if they had special discounts on false ones. The royal family was uniformly good-looking (they did not have false teeth), and they caused a good bit of "s.e." (social excitement) in New York.

We handled the Missoni family's colorful, knitted sportswear show in the Metropolitan as well as the first Valentino haute couture presentation in the museum. Valentino was such a hit in public acceptance that single-designer fashion shows in the museum became almost commonplace. By now I had so much experience with the Metropolitan, I knew exactly which spots would be the coolest in the building, the secret location of some rest rooms, and how to keep the goody bags of gifts for guests who had purchased expensive benefit tickets from being stolen.

Somebody asked my now-teenage daughter just exactly what her mother did in her company, and Clare replied, "Oh, she's always opening this and that." That just about describes it. One minute my company would be opening a tiny lingerie boutique on Madison Avenue, and the next a giant skyscraper of a building, the Elmer Holmes Bobst Library at New York University, one of the largest learning center libraries in the world. It had been donated by the Warner Lambert pharmaceutical king for whom it was named. I loved Elmer's story—he had begun his career as a poor kid delivering prescriptions for a druggist in Philadelphia. We were all fascinated by Dodo, his wife, many years his junior and a lawyer from Lebanon who had worked with the United Nations. She was an outstandingly beautiful Arab woman who wafted around in the evenings in gold caftans, wearing incredible jewels.

There were no set hours at LBE. We worked sometimes around the clock, because of big projects and few hands with which to implement them. I couldn't resist taking on new clients, they were so much fun, and the variety kept us going. We did not mind the crushing workload. Every problem became a challenge that creativity could solve. The work for Edward and George Wasserberger, two attractive brothers and gentlemen from the old school, originally from Czechoslovakia, who owned Mark Cross, was what is known as a "labor of love." The store was probably the leading purveyor of luxury leather goods at that time. They posed their problem simply: "How can we get publicity on this store? How do we get people to come in who have never had the courage to pass through these expensive doors?" Whenever I told my office I had an appointment with "the Gentlemen," they knew who I meant. I didn't have to use names. We launched "The Perfectly Organized Desk," with the windows on Fifth Avenue and the floors filled with different types of desks, and famous people bringing in their clutter, accessories, and desk lamps to re-create their offices. Everyone enthusiastically read the personal correspondence lying casually around in the leather in-boxes on the desks. We organized "The Perfectly Packed Suitcase," an exhibition of Mark Cross luggage for which national celebrities sent us their clothing and accessories to pack into them. Every "different" show we tried caused a traffic jam on the two selling floors. The public always loves a peek into the private lives of famous people.

I would say that the most satisfying development in my business life has been when a client becomes a real friend. It did not happen often through these decades, but it certainly did with a Texas family called Horchow. Roger Horchow walked into my life in the early 1970s when he purchased a luxury mail order catalog he had managed and made successful, called *The Kenton Collection*. It was one-of-a-kind at the time. I met him in the Oak Bar of the Plaza Hotel, and in forty minutes he had explained his project, I knew what I had to do, we had a deal, and we went our separate ways. It was great chemistry at first sight. He had asked me what I thought of his name for the new fancy catalog, *The Horchow Collection*. I gulped and said, "Mr. Horchow, you'll always find me frank. I don't think that name will fly at all." He looked at me and said in his soft drawl, "Well, you know, 'Smuckers' is a pretty ugly name, too, for a jam, but everyone in the world knows what 'Smuckers' is." He was right, as he always was. The *Horchow Collection* catalog was a gigantic success and was finally sold at an enormous profit to Neiman's. Roger went on to serve as a consultant to many businesses, but always did as much non-profit consulting for free as he did for money. He invested in successful Broadway shows, and in the meantime his wife, Carolyn, and daughters Regen, Lizzie, and Sally became part of our family, as we became part of theirs. It can happen—it's rare in the business world, but it can happen.

Every account was different, but fascinating in its own right, including joining Francis Kellogg in handling HRH Prince Philip (don't, for heaven's sake, call him Phil) for the World Wildlife Fund benefit at the Waldorf. Doing the public relations for the Charles Lindbergh Memorial Fund benefit meant a reconnection with Lindbergh, my hero, whom I had last seen at the White House dinner for André Malraux. No one could have accused me of not being diversified. I handled the engagement announcement of the striking Evangeline Gouletas and Governor Hugh Carey. The waves of romance became a bit churned up when the governor, his intended, and I were all at the Horst Photo Studio to make sure their formal engagement photographs for the press were "done right"—a phrase often given as the reason why a client hires me, as if I had the power to summon the Holy Ghost to make everything just properly perfect in a project. During the photography session a reporter, sniffing around for a story, offhandedly mentioned to the governor that Evangeline Gouletas had been married not once, but twice before. The fact that she had previously been married at all was news to the governor. He was stunned, but the Greek goddess kept her composure, saying, "I'll explain later, dear." I have always been fascinated by the type of woman who can confront a smoking gun and, with a look deep into a man's eyes and a low, throaty voice, can say, "I'll explain later, dear," and shrink an entire crisis into the zero column. (Of course, their marriage did not last, but among other things, they each got a Horst photograph out of it.)

We handled the singing Osmond family's announcement, at a high-level business press luncheon at "21," of their new state-of-the-art TV and film studios on the family property in Provo, Utah. We handled Colgate's launch of a new product, Tenaflowers (a new method of drying flowers), for which I walked into the mayor's office in Erie, Pennsylvania, our introductory market launch city ("If it goes over in Erie, it'll go over anywhere"), and interrupted his noon press conference, very rude indeed, to hand him a bouquet of Tenaflowers. He was so surprised, delighted, too, that he gave over the majority of his press conference to me, asking me to explain the process in front of the TV cameras and handing out a flower to everyone in his office. Of course he had to introduce me to his TV audience as "Jackie Kennedy's former aide." I knew that was why we were on TV, not because of Colgate's product.

I executed enough major promotions for French champagnes, California wines, Polish vodka, and Scotch to make a roaring dipsomaniac out of me, but I survived and managed to offset the hard-liquor push by promoting Canada Dry ginger ale and club soda as mixers. We went up against the club soda's major rival, Perrier, by using a board of society women across the country to promote it, and had a marketing victory: greatly increased sales, at Perrier's expense.

During all those decades of marketing, nothing ever got stale, because I crossruffed between public relations, writing for my book publishers and newspaper syndicates, and lecturing to women's groups. The youth of America became my friends because of my several appearances on the *David Letterman Show*, during which I teased him about his manners; he didn't like this at all, but his audience did. That I finally appeared on most major network news and talk shows had everything to do with the increasing number of my published books on behavior and absolutely nothing to do with my public relations activities. TV became a natural medium for me, which displeased several of my clients, who couldn't understand why I did not get *them* on TV instead of myself. This was a difficult one to handle.

Every time there was a royal wedding, divorce, scandal, or some show of celebrity bad manners, the network news would invite me to give a short lesson on the protocol and etiquette dilemmas involved. My time problem had become acute because of the additional bombardment of questions from the public, seeking help for their lifestyle problems. It took a lot of time answering each one, and I was giving a free service that my clients resented.

I found myself burning out. I really worried over whether I had properly answered queries like, "If a woman's face-lift has made her uglier than she was before, do you tell her a big lie, and say that she looks beautiful anyway?" "If you have leftover flowers in your apartment and can't afford to buy new ones, is it all right to use slightly dead ones for the dinner party you're giving?"

I was being harassed to give a speech here, do something special for a group there, serve on a committee here, and organize seminars for people who had lost their jobs there. The unmitigated joy I used to feel in going over to my office at Eighty-first and Lexington just wasn't there anymore.

It was 1988, and obviously time to move on. I know the signs. I had said yes too often, in too many directions. I had book commitments coming out of my ears. I was tired of running an agency with women who needed better maternity leave benefits than I could offer. I had survived a nasty bout with colon cancer, had a colostomy, and was suffering more and more pain from arthritis. I had always thought I was Wonder Woman without the steel bra. I had to face up to the fact that the years were climbing up on me. I had promised myself that I would retire from all of my board directorships when it was time. I closed up Letitia Baldrige Enterprises, a real heartbreaker, and saw to it that my staff all got good jobs. They were well trained, experienced, and highly marketable. I threw out twenty years of LBE files—of my life, really— just because I couldn't bear to organize them properly to leave them to the university that had asked me for my papers "for posterity's sake." It would have taken an entire year to do a proper job, so I simply chucked my entire business life into a trash bin. There was no time to regret it.

It was time to go back to Washington—back home, really. I wanted to write, undisturbed by the millions of minutiae in my life in New York that had been chipping away at my productive time. Bob was amenable, as I knew he would be, after a proper amount of time spent in protest. There were new fields of writing to conquer. I needed a quieter rhythm of city; New York was becoming more of a pounding madhouse on roller skates than ever before.

The children, as children will do, grew up and weren't kids anymore. After Farmington, Clare graduated from the University of London and went to work. Her job between school and motherhood was not with the Metropolitan Museum of Art or the United Nations or the *Foreign Affairs Quarterly* but with the avant-garde *Rolling Stone* magazine. She met a handsome young medical resident from New York Hospital, the son of Irish immigrants, in an Irish bookstore one New Year's Day. During an entire day spent perusing Irish books (that's what they said), the only customers in the store, they fell in love. They married, and my daughter and her doctor husband, Jim Smyth, have subsequently given us an immeasurable amount of joy through three grandchildren, Luke, Lila, and Liam. Malcolm, in the meantime, graduated from Harvard, and after spending the next year playing professional basketball in Australia, not the most traditional career move, finally had his first date. All through college he had gone out with large groups, too shy to ask a girl to go out alone with him. He found the perfect antidote to shyness, called Carey Shoemaker, a petite blonde from Virginia Beach, and they were married soon after. Their production line so far comprises Alice and "little Mac," and much to the chagrin of his basketball-playing friends, he is in the conservative business of mortgage banking. They would rather see him out playing with the Knicks.

Lordy, how I would miss New York, every inch of it. But I had had the city at its very best, and it had had me, too; it was time to go.

Back Home Again

𝒮o we have reached the final stop: Washington, D.C.

To me, home is the most important part of your life, next to the people who share your surroundings with you. This move from New York was to be our final one, and appropriately enough, we were moving to a fantastic 1906 apartment house steeped in history and poorly aging water pipes—perhaps descriptive of me as well.

Washington had changed, I noticed—but then, so had I. Any city that stays the same decade after decade is dead in the water, and that would never describe Washington. I was returning to a place with so many memories, I felt multi-tugs-of-war, pulling me emotionally this way and that. Different decades keep popping up unexpectedly in my consciousness, and my years with Jackie remain forever front and center. As I write this, Hamish Bowles has just organized an outstanding exhibition of her clothes and her imprint on American society for the Metropolitan Museum of Art in New York. Her clothes are as stunning and as tasteful today as they were when worn on official business. How can I help but remember every time Oleg Cassini came to Washington with a new gown for her, and how can I help but remember every time she appeared in that gown before the public, glittering like a precious jewel?

Today when I go by the reflecting pool in front of the Washington Monument, I think of being there with my doll and its wicker doll buggy in the early 1930s. Then I think of coming to work there every day in 1951 in my CIA period—a horrible, air-conditionless, temporary Quonset hut that dated from World War I, and that was supposed to have been torn down in 1919. Now when I go by the reflecting pool in this new century, I see only the beauty of the monument behind it and the reflection of the trees in it. I can't think about the immense statue of the seated Abraham Lincoln inside the memorial without immediately remembering the assassination of

President Kennedy—and how the day after it happened, Herb Block drew one of the most outstanding newspaper cartoons in his life—Abraham Lincoln, rendered in marble, sitting slumped and dejected in his chair in his memorial building, grief stricken and weeping. Many people have their own emotional ties to this monument.

I feel the same way about Mount Vernon, George Washington's home in nearby Virginia. Since our return to Washington, I have had the opportunity to go out there often, as a member of the advisory committee. Every time I approach the house, the memories flood again—of being there with my parents in the early 1930s, and of arranging the state dinner given there by the Kennedys in 1961 for the president of Pakistan, and of restaging that famous dinner, with Mary Ourisman chairing it as a fund-raiser for Mount Vernon, in 1999.

We arrived in town in the latter part of the Reagan administration. My brother Mac had died the previous year, literally "in the saddle." He had not exactly been a run-of-the-mill secretary of commerce for President Reagan; a calf roper at heart, he made it to a rodeo whenever he could on weekends. He died falling from his horse in a freak rodeo accident outside San Francisco. President Reagan spoke at his funeral in the National Cathedral, and Vice President Bush spoke at the memorial services held in Woodbury, Connecticut, where Mac and Midge lived. The tributes paid him were never-ending. He merited them all. His wife, daughters Megan and Molly, and their children have stacks of scrapbooks, tapes of TV interviews, plaques, and citations Mac had received during his life.

I look with fondness at the *demi-lune* in our living room, an enormous piece of furniture that holds all of our important framed photos, including, along with the family's, those of Bob and me or of me alone with the Kennedys, the Johnsons, Mrs. Nixon, the Reagans, the Bushes, the Clintons, and, most recently, with President George W. Bush. The Malcolm Baldrige National Quality Awards program has been the catalyst for many of these photographs. The president, whoever he may be, always shows up at the annual Washington ceremony to give these awards for great strides in business excellence and quality. Each winning company is allowed to have fifty of its employees present in the audience. Their whooping, hollering, whistling, and shouting is a major noise blast that we eagerly await each year. The Baldrige Awards have become a living, continuing memorial to Mac.

Next to a photograph of Clare Luce holding baby Clare Hollensteiner at her christening is one of baby Clare grown up with her husband, Jim Smyth, on their wedding day. Next to that is the portrait of Malcolm and Carey's wedding attendants, standing in a row, with the very tall groom in the center, next to his petite bride. There's a grandchild's photo next to the one of the Henry Luces talking to the John F. Kennedys at the cardinal's dinner in New York, and then another grandchild's photo next to one of Nancy Reagan and me chatting away. The *demi-lune* holds the story of my life, but also of our life as a family, with the promise of the future in the pictures of our five grandchildren.

It was inevitable that my generation of family would start to disappear. First to go was Mac, then my wonderful sister-in-law Nancy, brother Bob's wife, suddenly in 1999. The letters written after her death by the people who loved her would fill a library. She did so much in her life with flowers and gardens, she will be remembered for the thousands of beautiful, growing things for which she was responsible. I hope her daughters, Alice and Jeanie, and their seven children will proudly remember that. Bob is lucky. A wonderful woman named Liz, from Little Compton, Rhode Island, is now his wife and a lovely addition to our family.

The same day that Nancy Baldridge died of cancer, three-year-old Lila Smyth, Clare and Jim's middle child and only daughter, was diagnosed with serious brain cancer. When you hear that kind of news, you either sink down and die on the very spot where you're standing, or you get going, lobbying the Almighty. We had friends and strangers praying for Lila from Jehovah's Witnesses to a Muslim group, from the entire congregation of a Jewish synagogue to every imaginable Catholic order of nuns and priests, as well as friends in every Protestant church. It worked. After undergoing two operations, after having her brain attacked with chemotherapy and radiation, the prayers and the surgeons' efforts all worked. She is still with us. Her parents, Jim and Clare, deserve four Croix de Guerre for their heroic action under fire. How proud we are of them! As for Lila, she was determined to stick around on earth, and God has allowed her to do just that. She's terrific.

Although I rejoice in my family and the present, I don't mind the risk of being accused of living in the past, of too much looking back. I've got a lot of substance to look back upon. What is painful is that I have outlasted the women for whom I worked so hard, and who were responsible for my being with them in those extraordinary places—places that were not only glamorous and exciting but also the centers for important points of history. At times it feels weird that I am left behind with the intense memories of all three.

Clare Luce died in her mid-eighties in September 1987, but I had been with her when she was the U.S. ambassador to Italy—in the best period, the pinnacle of achievement, of her life, as she repeatedly said later. Her main funeral Mass (there was another smaller one in a Washington church the same week) was said, appropriately, by the cardinal, in St. Patrick's Cathedral in New York. But it was just the regular twelve noon Mass. There was no way of singling out the important people of rank in the White House, the State Department, and the military who came to pay her honor. There were no real ushers. The VIP mourners were lost in the crowd. She would have been absolutely furious! I was, too, on her behalf, at the sloppy protocol. I could feel her indignation from beyond her grave. She was buried next to Harry Luce in South Carolina, on their Mepkin Plantation, a beautiful estate that had given them both rest and escape during their lifetimes, and now, forever after.

Evangeline Bruce died in December 1995 of a brain tumor. The funeral service was in St. John's in Georgetown. Former State Department friends of David Bruce's like Henry Kissinger flew down from New York for it. All of social Washington was there, as well as highly placed government officials—anyone who had partaken of the wet bar and Bloody Marys at her famous Sunday noon parties. There was a buffet luncheon served afterward in her house on Thirty-fourth Street, soon to be divested of its French windows' eighteen-foot-tall draperies of heavy chartreuse silk, with gold, green, and apricot woven tiebacks and tassels. The Venetian paintings would soon be gone from the walls, as would the French and English pedigreed antiques, the Savonnerie rugs, the sparkling, merry crystal chandeliers, the rare and fascinating oils, and the amusing objets d'art like monkey candlesticks and a rhinoceros figurine that few could resist picking up from the table and petting, like a dog. The house was sold. I could not bear to think that the chatelaine of that Georgetown house was no longer in residence. I owed her so much, there was no way to measure it on a human scale.

It's been almost forty years since Jacqueline Kennedy's days in the White House, but the legend of the glamour, beauty, and taste of that era continues unabated. So do the classic tragedies that have haunted the Bouvier-Kennedy families through those same years. The latest disaster as of this writing occurred in July 1999, when John Kennedy Jr., his young wife, Carolyn, and her sister Lauren Bessette plummeted to their deaths in the cold waters of the Atlantic. A collective sigh of relief was heard around the world that John's mother, Jacqueline Onassis, was no longer alive to have to bear with her innate dignity yet another horrible series of blows.

When Jackie died of cancer in May 1994, she received a massive state funeral at St. Ignatius Loyola on Park Avenue in New York. It seemed as though all the princes of the Catholic Church were in attendance. Subdued, respectful crowds covered the sidewalks on both sides of the block. Loudspeakers carried the service—the hymns and the remarks that were made on her life. Her children and brother-in-law Ted delivered beautiful and perfectly expressed tributes to her. Her great friend Maurice Tempelsman spoke, too. The church was packed; it was a media event of the highest interest, but it was also a dignified laying to rest of one of America's favorite women. As usual, taste ruled. Her coffin carried only a small, simple white cross of flowers. Jackie is buried in Arlington Cemetery, next to President John F. Kennedy. There are happy, wonderful memories to be evoked up there in the peace of that grassy hill, with its own undying flame—a symbol she herself was responsible for having placed there, "in memory of Jack."

The fact that Bob and I today look first in the obituary section of the newspaper rather than in the wedding section to find our friends' names is merely proof of the passage of time. Soon, there will be such a disproportionate number of our friends up there, instead of down here, we will have a hard time organizing a party list—down here, that is. We will certainly be able to organize a terrific one up there.

Washington is the kind of city where everyone passes through. The phone rings with people who are "here for a few days." We have people over for meals or drinks as often as we can. Nafiz Sisman, an Egyptian cook, is a miracle worker who will come to us to prepare a meal fit for royalty. (He often *has* done it for royalty.) Thanksgiving, Easter, and Fourth of July table decorations are brought out faithfully each year. I still have Christmas table decorations from fifty years ago. They have held up better through the years than some of our guests, but that's life.

We have sunshine all day in our apartment. There is so much light, at times it feels as though we are living alfresco. We peer over the rooftops of the embassies on Massachusetts Avenue, and from the back of our building we have an absolutely splendid garden to gaze upon, belonging to the Woodrow Wilson House (a presidential home protected by the National Trust, and open to the public). We don't have to water the flowers or trim the bushes. We just gaze out the windows, enjoy it, and feel the vibrations from one of our greatest presidents, Woodrow Wilson, who enjoyed the same view during his last years on earth.

Anne Clifton, the widow of General Ted Clifton, military aide to President Kennedy, lives on the first floor. General Clifton's office was down the hall from mine in the White House, and his face appears in many of my photographs from those days. Priscilla Liggett owns the apartment on the floor above her. She is the widow of a distinguished naval officer and the proud possessor of two well-bred Pekingese who engage in a mutual hate relationship with our Jack Russells. Above her is Betty Burton, who lived in Paris when I did, and who represents "old Washington society." She is a walking encyclopedia of information on the city and its inhabitants. I don't ever have to call a research librarian about our town—I just ask Betty.

* * *

At first I went right back into the social side of my old embassy life—with all the receptions and national holiday celebrations. The crowd was the same as forty years ago, but I didn't have to go up to the ambassador anymore to deliver a message of greeting from the Kennedys. Present administration people are still being forced to make a quick appearance, and the majority of the guests, the old-timers in town, are still eating two days' worth of meals from each cocktail buffet. There are fewer hot meatballs on toothpicks, and more raw peppers, but it's still basically the same bill of fare, with smoked salmon, chafing dishes, and hot cheese puffs ready to explode all over your clothes and burn your tongue. Bobby and Mary Haft, our handsome young neighbors across the street, still entertain nonstop. The embassy residences are as beautiful as ever, the ambassadors and their wives as fascinating and attractive, but the days when one could sit down and have an intelligent conversation with them are gone; they are too busy, with too many people trying to get into their milieu, for whatever reason. The ambassadors now give their embassies over to charities to stage benefits. The charities raise a lot of money this way, and the ambassadors and ambassadresses are generous and gracious to do it, but they become victimized by these organizations at the same time.

I found the city full of lobbyists with deep pockets to spend on entertaining, but the list of grande dames with great houses in which to receive notables and would-be's at private parties had evaporated to almost nothing. Octogenarian Ruth Buchanan and her husband, Ed Wheeler, still give grand parties, but except for a small number like them, the "class" in the city is just—well, gone. But since the world has become one new classless society anyway, the parameters of what constitutes class are changing, too. The one constant is that *real class* still means *real kindness* and *consideration*. Nothing will change that.

My working life, no matter how hard and grueling, has been fun. So I simply couldn't stop working completely, just to write day and night. I was part of a group that consulted with Martin Scorsese on his film adaptation of Edith Wharton's great novel *The Age of Innocence*. I rounded up my friend Lily Lodge, daughter of Ambassador John Lodge and niece of Ambassador Henry Cabot Lodge of Massachusetts, to help me with that film about society at the turn of the century in New York and Newport. Because of my time problems, Lily—also an actress who runs a school for professional actors in New York—took over the job full-time as the on-the-set social behavior expert for several weeks. Scorsese wanted the film to reflect the customs and mores of the time with authenticity. We gave the actors little things to remember—

how to meet someone, how to walk into the room, how a man sits holding his top hat, and how a woman sits in those fussy, tight dresses of the period. (If the women of the Age of Innocence were to see young women of today with their low décolletages and bosoms thrust into everyone else's faces and their denim-covered legs spread wide apart, they would probably be shocked as the men would obviously be delighted.) Actress Michelle Pfeiffer was lovely and absorbed everything I said like an enthusiastic sponge. Daniel Day-Lewis, the son of the English poet laureate, did not have to be taught anything. He dropped his English accent, assumed a cultivated American one, and handled his manners, his top hat, and his walking stick like a true "new American aristocrat" of that period. I fed Lily results of research I gleaned after chatting for several hours with Mrs. Oliphant in Washington, who happened to be past a hundred years of age at the time, and who remembered well the life of debutante balls and the behavior of proper young ladies and gentlemen in the early 1900s. She would talk to me, I would report it to Lily, and Lily would report it to the movie's producers: "Young ladies were to stay away from the front door when the bell rang. It was not considered proper for them to be seen by anyone arriving. Only a maid or footman could go see who was at the door.

"On the afternoon of a ball, a young man's valet would bring over several pairs of his employer's white kid gloves to the host's house or wherever the ball was to be held. His card would be attached, and his gloves and card would then be arranged with the others' on a table off the entrance hall. When dancing ensued, and when a young man's gloves became the slightest bit soiled, he would change to a clean pair immediately, in deference to his dancing partner's bare back." (Men's white gloves soiled easily, considering that their white-tie-and-tails outfits never saw a dry cleaner during their entire existence.)

It was exhilarating to see the social nuances of that period in American history come out on the screen in subtle touches in *The Age of Innocence*—the kind of artistry that Scorsese, and few others, are capable of producing.

From representing to the press the lavishly formal St. Regis Hotel in New York, I moved easily to the informal charms of Bermuda. Reggie Cooper, who owned one of the smaller hotels on the island, involved me with a program of marketing his and other small, unique hotels to the American public. Everyone in our family had been in love with Bermuda since many years before—the perfect prototype of a civilized escape, with pink beaches, sailboats and huge yachts, lawn tennis courts, a proper English tea every afternoon, and many courts for that most gentle of all sports: croquet. People in my office would gaze in admiration at a framed photograph showing the good-looking legs of my clients—the hoteliers in our group, called "The Bermuda Collection." Of course they were all wearing Bermuda shorts, navy blazers, and white knee socks. *Really* great legs.

And it was a hop, a skip, and a broad jump to working on a small hotel in Perry, Iowa, in real farm country, owned by Roberta Ahmanson, who had married Howard Ahmanson of a banking fortune in California. She grew up in Perry, resurrected a closed hotel, brought business to the depressed town, collected well-known works of art by Iowa artists, began research on a soon-to-be-built museum dedicated to Iowa's history and artistic heritage, found a fantastic chef, and turned the Hotel Pattee of Perry, Iowa, into a well-known destination not only in the Midwest but across the country. An incredible, supercharged woman, she is one of those treasures—a client who has become a friend.

Of course, the work I had done on the Ritz Hotel in the 1970s in Paris for Mohammed al-Fayed came back to haunt me when I saw the pictures of his son Dodi and Diana, Princess of Wales, leaving the Ritz in a car to have dinner in a Parisian restaurant on a warm summer night in 1997. I felt as though my life has been connected somehow to all the famous events in the world—at least, it seems eerily like that.

If you are passionate about your job, dealing with the Ritz Hotel in Paris, with the St. Regis in New York, with the Bermuda Collection of Hotels, and with the Hotel Pattee in Iowa is the same. There have to be some blasts of enthusiasm and creativity to get the projects launched. How sweet it is when it all works, and the mix is never, never boring!

Now I work for some really wonderful nonprofits in a volunteer capacity. It is a relief to turn to the Washington organizations that truly represent the best of need and purpose, like RIF (Reading Is Fundamental). There are no $5,000-a-seat dinner dance tickets. Instead, it has a loyal, enthusiastic board and group of volunteers working under Bill Trueheart that puts books into poor children's hands and spreads literacy in places desperately in need of it. I have always all my life been one of Lady Bird Johnson's biggest fans, and to see her daughter, Lynda Robb, wife of former senator Chuck Robb, take over the unpaid chairman's role for a several-year tour of duty was an inspiration. She worked on it every day, went all over the country, used her home in Virginia for fund-raising and meetings, and stood on her head to make it work. We do have heroes—female ones, too—all around us.

I realize that a full life happily lived is not the joyful prerogative of everyone, so I can't help but do a little summing up on what is important in that joyful life. Family, past and present, is first, and I have scored a hundred on that. Friends are second, and I have scored a hundred on that, too. There is Mary McLaughlin Wellington, who spent her earliest years also in Omaha, and whose father followed mine into Congress. She joined me on European excursions, flirting with a quantity of men our parents back in Washington would simply not understand. I'm reminded of her this very minute because a noisy little Vespa just went by in the Massachusetts Avenue traffic—the motor scooter that is so Roman and so reminiscent of the 1950s in Italy. And there is Ann Reinicke Peabody, my New York pal, who has helped so many people so lovingly, we call her "Saint Ann" behind her back. She was probably helping the obstetrical nurse during her birth. I have scrambled over snowy crevasses in northern Italy and jiggled champagne swizzle sticks with her in Paris (does anyone ever use swizzle sticks in champagne anymore?). And then there is my former Tiffany secretary, Duane Garrison Elliott, who has amused me with her great gifts of gab and gossip for forty years and continues to do that for me, all of my family, and, of course, her husband, Robert Elliott. What is lovely is that you start out being friends with your contemporary. Then when he or she marries, you become friends with the spouse, and their children to come, like the full complement of Rees family members, who have been part and parcel of our lives since the days when Nancy and I were young girls. She married Charles ("Cat") Rees, they had four girls, and tried desperately to get me married off from 1950 until the day it finally happened, thirteen years later. We know the Rees guest-room beds as well as our own. And there are our great friends Mary Davis Holt and her husband, David, who opened up a new part of the world to us with their superb summer house on the ocean at a place called Duck, on the Outer Banks of North Carolina. It is as delectably the opposite of Long Island and its chichi Hamptons as you can get. I have always used Mary, a Time-Life senior executive, as an example to young career-minded women of how far and how fast you can go—provided you work hard and keep your eyes open.

I'm fascinated with the movement of women up the ladder—fascinated at their progress in the business world, but also because of the increasing numbers today who are leaving the workplace for home when children are born. I think they instinctively sense they are desperately needed by that little bundle lying in the crib, at the mercy of whatever pair of hands is holding him or her. This return to the nest is so against the trend of the last quarter of a century, which was to put women into the executive workplace and keep them there. The only conclusion I can make, in looking hard at the role of women in the last fifty years, is that there is no conclusion. What many women have gained in job satisfaction and accomplishment, some have lost in not having spent that time with their children. What is the answer? Should only women without young children at home work? Who would dare use that as a standard for a woman and a career? Who can afford to do that?

I hear from the public on all these subjects, much of it coming through cyberspace. Probably the fact that I answer everything that comes at me via e-mail is proof that I like it, that I enjoy hearing from the public, that I enjoy giving advice. Thanks to my work with Bill Dugan and Dennis Bass on my monthly newsletter on behavior for business executives, *Executive Advantage*, I hear from people all over the world, including countries I have never heard of. The questions are sometimes daunting:

"What do you do when your chairman has split from his wife, plans on bringing his cutie-pie as his hostess to the big annual dinner, but his wife still plans to attend, and the board is unanimous that the wife should be there and not the cutie-pie?"

"We have an American business associate coming to visit our country. Is it true every American requires a very special pillow to sleep on, and if so, how can we tastefully have it made to order without asking questions in advance that might be considered audacious and unsuitable by our American visitor?"

Certainly the requests for information on protocol and the proper way of doing this and that are very different from those of fifty years ago. Today someone will e-mail me a question in all earnestness, "I don't believe in dressing up. My fiancée says I have to wear a suit to our wedding, but is that really a necessity? I don't think it is." I e-mail him back that, yes, it is a necessity, and "don't forget to wear shoes to your wedding, either."

People keep asking me when I'm going to retire. The answer is never. I now have a godsend, a wonderful friend and fellow etiquette writer, Mary Mitchell from Philadelphia, aka "Ms. Demeanor," helping me with the next voluminous book on manners. We know we're needed out there. As long as someone e-mails me that she is the only disabled employee in her company, but also the only employee not invited to her boss's home for a holiday dinner dance, then we are needed. There is much to be done on teaching civility, but it would help if parents would show their children what civility is by modeling it with their own behavior. Our society may have slipped badly in recent times in civility and decorum, even in matters of the heart, but we can put it back together again, like a magical Humpty-Dumpty. When we really hurt another person's feelings, we can always apologize face-to-face at once, make a couple of telephone calls, write a wonderful letter, or send flowers—or maybe do it all. I've been apologizing all my life, and I've always been forgiven.

At book signings, I often sign above my name: "Have a wonderful life!" I have certainly had one myself.

LIST OF PEOPLE WHO HAVE MADE MINE A GREAT LIFE!

This section will give short shrift to just a few of the people who may not have been already mentioned in the book but who have walked in and out of my life, serving as its fuel, support, education, and joy. When you live as long as I have, many of the great people are gone and more are going every year, unquestionably to a better place. Still remaining are a few thousand friends to whom I'm indebted, including the following, listed in no order or logic:

Family: Midge Baldrige (Mrs. Malcolm), her daughters Megan Murray and Molly Baldrige, Megan's husband, Craig Murray, and their various wonderful children; Bob and Liz Baldridge; Alice and Walker Wainwright, and Bob and Nina; Jean and Jim Yates and their three children, plus two older Bilus sons; my cousin Herb Connell and his family; Carol Collins (Mrs. Bradley) and Carol, Brad, Jim, Lee, and their families; Kathy Sincerbeaux and Carolyn; Louise vanderVort and the Glen Glasells and the Hiram Gutierrezes; the Jack Millses and their children; the Robert Mooneys and their children; the Karl Connells and family; the Michael Shoemakers and the John Waites and their little ones.

Vassar classmates—"our own old girls' network": Kay Evans (Mrs. Rowland), Janet Whitehouse (Mrs. Charles), Nan Ellis (Mrs. Alexander), Lucy Moorhead (Mrs. William), Emily Malino (Mrs. James Scheuer), Mary Wheelwright (Mrs. Jeffords), Nancy Gray Pyne (Mrs. Eben), Nancy Caldwell (Mrs. Andrew), Martha Ford (Mrs. William Clay), Anne Bates (Mrs. Wm. Maffitt), Anne Fredericks (Mrs. Wayne), Colette Douglas, Ellie Harvey (Mrs. Eldon), and more.

Former associates: Page Kjellstrom, Bonnie Block Levison, Ellen Lanicca, Lexie Tanner, Madeline Zuckerman, Tracy Cooper Drippe, Nana Katsiff Greller, and Gray Reisfield Horan.

B. J. Finnerty (Mrs. Peter), the Bob Binghams, David Davis, Eleanor Rawson, Cindy Skaff, Jack Smith, Mary Bolton, Lanny Gardiner, the John Davises, Jack Hilton, Susan Chamberlain, Richard Schubert, M.D., Raymond Murakami, John Irelan, Pamela Keogh and the late Patricia Keogh, the Charlie Bartletts, the Robert Hafts, Jean Wyman, John Flynn, M.D., the John Mowinckels, the Bert Hands, the Arthur Gardners, Carew Lee, Jim Rees, Pat Hass, Bill Truehart, Mary Lindsay, Rosalina de Jesus, the Anders Lofbergs, the Bennet Harveys, the Thatcher Wallers, the Howard Kranes, Betty Pollock, Alice McIlvaine, the Mandy Ourismans, Mohamad and Miriam Baldi, the Dennis Lambs, Reece Howard, the Blair Meyers, the Robert Quinlans, the David Kirks, the Hugh Jacobsens, Emily Nixon, the Bucky Blocks, Ann Hirou, Tom Murray, Osvaldo Flores, the Richard Breckers, Ludwell Gaines, the Charlie Larkinses, the Brad Palmers, the Don Henrys, Peter Dingman, Paul Douglas, Ann Geracimos, Mimi Gilpatric, the Fig Colemans, Clive Watson, the Ludwig Glaesers, the Henry Bloomsteins, the Randolph Guggenheimers, the Stanley Waranches, Sandra McElwaine, the Lloyd Hands, Claude Hankes-Drielsma, Barbara Harrison, Danny Levinas, the George Hubners, the Bill and the John Macombers, the Harry Newmans, the John Noonans, the Michael Walterses, Brainerd Warner, Esq., Brigitte Treumann, Dennis Wholey, Maggie Wimsatt, the Lawson Willards, Susan Mary Alsop, the Paul Florians, Alyne Massey, Jeanne Flynn, Steven Shulman, Yuko Arai, Barry Diamondstone, the George Graebers, Susie Hilfiger, the Henry Bettses, Helen Boehm, Denise Boucher, John Boyd, the James Buckleys, Priscilla Buckley, Reid Buckley, Jay Buckley, the Jack Northrops, the Johnston Northrops, Chris and Kathleen Matthews, Gail Berendzen, Michael Butler, Charles Mulzac, Suzy Carter, Kevin Chaffee, the Ras Klomans, Colette LeGuay, Frank Richardson, Zhang Shukun, Viki Kinsman, Eliska Coolidge, the Reggie Coopers, the William Coopers, the John Paxtons, Stephanie Copeland, Robin Duke, the Bill Dunks, Nancy Dunnan, the Edvard Brandstroms, the Oakley Brookses, the Scrap O'Donnells, Mario Buatto, the Wilson Nolens, Perry Knowlton, the Tom Kahns, the Hans Koehlers, Duane Hampton, Providencia Paredes, Eppie Lederer, the Ben Leamans, Aileen Mehle, the Henry Middletons, Wendy Morgan and Dick Krolick, Diane Paton, the Philip Morrises, J. Carter Brown, Enid Nemy, Sandra Payson, Ann Rauscher, the Edward Neys, the Thomas Nigras, the Miromir Zuzuls, the William Nitzes, Margaret Ward, the Richard O'Connors, Melanie Parker, the Nick Petrys, Roger Zissu, Donald Piper, Felicia Rogan, Joy Sundlun, the William Salomons, Helen Schubert, Mary Thacher, the Pibulsonggrams, the Kent Zimmermans, the Tom Clarkes, Mary Douglas, John Barnes, the Philip Geyelins, Dominick Dunne, Dr. James Eaton, Martin Edelston, Hsiu Lin Lee, Catherine Edwards, M.D., the Donald Rices, Michael Edwards, Joe Esposito, Mary Jane Pool, Tom Fahey, M.D., Tom Farmer, Sheila Tate, the John Postleys, Patsy Preston, Donnie Radcliffe, the Ed Russells, Mari Chihaya, Julia Shivers, the Clyde Smiths, Bruce Sundlun, Lady Surtees, the Charles Tanguys, the Fred Tarkingtons and Ferrin; Landon, David, and Julia Thorne; Fernanda Gilligan, Jim Brosseau, the Jay Treadwells, Frances Fergusson, the Robert Odens, Jane Podesta, the Rinaldo Petrignanis, Norman Rentrop, Nancy Reynolds, Ann Peabody (Mrs. James), Fred and Suzy Maroon, Eric and Mary Weinmann, Rev. Winthrop Brainerd, Mary and Ed Wellington along with Bruce, Tracy, Kathy, and offspring; Diana Tran, Ed and Helene Cummings, Francis and Ann Thorne, Katsy Thomas, the Bill Purtells, Al Cummings, Hugh Brewster, Laurie Coulter, Wanda Nowakowska, the William Cottinghams, the Red Fays, John Culligan, the Walter Curleys, Rev. Alexander Daley, the Daniel Davisons, Mrs. Morton Phillips, the Robert Dilenschneiders, Susan Donnell, Virginia Doran, K Lee Kim, Birch Ford, Lucky Roosevelt, Phyllis Bonanno, Michelle Cox, and Eleanor Atuk.

White House social secretaries (instant lifelong friends by virtue of their jobs): Catherine Felton and Jeanie Figg, Capricia Marshall, Ann Stock, Linda Faulkner, Gahl Burt, Muffie Cabot, Laurie Firestone, Maria Downs, Nancy Ruwe, Nancy Tuckerman, Lucy Winchester, and Mary Jane McCaffree; and Rex Scouten and Gary Walters of the White House Ushers Office.

INDEX